Jewish American Literature

Genreflecting Advisory Series

Diana T. Herald, Series Editor

Jewish American Literature

A Guide to Reading Interests

Rosalind Reisner

Genreflecting Advisory Series
Diana T. Herald, Series Editor

LIBRARIES UNLIMITED

A Member of the Greenwood Publishing Group

Westport, Connecticut • London

British Library Cataloguing in Publication Data is available.

ISBN: 1–56308–984–X

First published in 2004

Libraries Unlimited, 88 Post Road West, Westport, CT 06881
A Member of the Greenwood Publishing Group, Inc.
www.lu.com

Printed in the United States of America

The paper used in this book complies with the
Permanent Paper Standard issued by the National
Information Standards Organization (Z39.48–1984).

10 9 8 7 6 5 4 3 2 1

Contents

Acknowledgments

It has been a terrific experience to spend three years intensively reading, thinking, and talking about Jewish literature, rereading wonderful books and finding new ones. I couldn't have done it without the support of many people. Thanks to Henry Rasof, my first contact at Libraries Unlimited, for his encouragement. The circulation desk staff at the Eastern Branch of Monmouth County Library handled huge numbers of reserve requests and inter-library loans for me, always with smiles. Special thanks to Mary Knapp for her cheerful phone calls. Mary Balk at Middletown Township Library was always helpful in tracking down New Jersey locations of titles for me. The Dorot collection at the New York Public Library was a quiet haven for research, as was the Center for Jewish History in Manhattan.

Many friends and acquaintances have contributed to this book just by their encouragement and belief that it would get done. Thanks to all; you know who you are. Special thanks to Phil Siller for hunting down Canadian sources, Ellen Loughran for young adult advice, and Rabbi Sally Priesand for her encouragement.

Heartfelt thanks to my editor, Barbara Ittner, for her excellent advice, patient answers to my questions, and encouragement all along the way.

There are no words to thank my husband Gerald, spouse extraordinaire, for the time and effort he spent as tech support, literary critic, cheerleader, and housekeeper, all with grace and good humor. While all mistakes and errors of judgment are mine, without his help and noodging, I'm not sure this book would have been finished in this millennium. And special thanks to Alex, David, and Rhoda, who make it all worthwhile just by being there.

Introduction

Purpose

Jewish American Literature: A Guide to Reading Interests is a gateway to contemporary Jewish American fiction, autobiography, and biography. The aim is to serve Jewish and non-Jewish readers in their enjoyment of a literature that explores human experience in ways that touch our hearts and minds regardless of religion or ethnicity. The focus is on works by Jewish American authors whose writing illuminates and reflects the Jewish experience, whether that experience is specifically Jewish American or just Jewish. Titles are not included solely because the author is Jewish, because a character is incidentally Jewish, or because a few words of Yiddish are sprinkled in the text. For the most part, characters' awareness of their Jewishness is made plain to the reader and has an effect on their thoughts and actions. The reader perceives that it is the author's intention to explore Jewish characters, settings, or themes. The range of attitudes, opinions, and religious observance reflects the lively diversity of the Jewish community today.

For a large part of the twentieth century, Jewish American literature reflected the experience of the European and Eastern European Jews who came to the United States between 1880 and 1924 and then as Holocaust survivors in the late 1940s and 1950s. The early novels are filled with the shock of encountering another culture, adjusting expectations, and building a new identity. Biographies and autobiographies recount the success stories, but novels portray the struggles, failures, bitterness, and guilt felt by many. Life in America required accommodation to a secular culture with a different set of values. Novels by the immigrants and their children through the middle of the twentieth century illuminate the conflict between the generations over issues of assimilation and the internal conflicts of the immigrants and their children. It seemed to be an inexhaustible subject.

By the 1950s and 1960s Jewish American fiction was among the most exciting literary fiction being written—everyone was reading and discussing the novels of Roth, Malamud, and Bellow. By the end of the 1970s, as acculturation became more complete and the distance from the Old World greater, Jewish American writers found new subject matter. The immigrant stories became historical fiction. Jews, now more firmly part of mainstream American life, redefined themselves in relation to the dominant culture. Novels, like news bulletins from that process, disclosed the changes. Jewish American fiction began to portray Jews for whom Judaism was a casual, cultural attribute. In this atmosphere, writers explored what it could possibly mean to be Jewish in America in the last half of the twentieth century. The headnote to the section of the *Norton Anthology of Jewish American Literature* covering the last quarter of the twentieth century asks the following:

> What does it mean to be Jewish when ties to ethnic heritage
> have loosened? When anti-Semitism is no longer as overt as
> it once was? When an American can no longer wholly sympa-
> thize with Israeli politics? How does the Holocaust continue to
> shape Jewish American identity? What relationship do Jews
> have with a common past? What makes a Jew Jewish if he or
> she does not practice the rituals of Judaism? Will all Jewish
> Americans eventually assimilate? What is the future of Jew-
> ish Americans as a community in the United States?[1]

In the last quarter century, characters in novels, like many members of the Jewish com-munity, search for the role Judaism might play in their lives. Anne Roiphe's novel *Lovingkindness* explores the issue of what an assimilated mother feels when her daughter finds peace in the Orthodox community. The main character in Cameron Stracher's *The Law of Return* tries to avoid at every turn being identified as Jewish until he can no longer elude his heritage. Catherine da Costa, the grandmother in Naomi Ragen's *The Ghost of Hannah Mendes,* develops an elaborate scheme to teach her very assimilated granddaugh-ters about their Sephardic traditions. Myla Goldberg, in *The Bee Season*, looks at the conse-quences of intense religious experience in one very unusual family. E. L. Doctorow, in *City of God*, looks at the ways in which religion is meaningful at the end of the twentieth century.

From the problem of how immigrants could accommodate traditional Judaism to American culture, these novels explore how American Jews make room for Judaism in their lives in a variety of ways. But in parallel to this trend, there are writers for whom traditions and observance have remained strong and vital. In this context, Chaim Potok's wonderful coming-of-age novels have helped to explain the world of Orthodox Judaism to Jews and non-Jews alike. Sharon Spiegelman, the protagonist in Allegra Goodman's *Paradise Park,* searches modern civilization for spiritual sustenance, coming home at the end to the tradi-tional Judaism of her childhood. Pearl Abraham's novels *The Romance Reader* and *Giving Up America*; Goodman's novel *Kaaterskill Falls*; Ehud Havazelet's linked story collection *Like Never Before*; Risa Miller's *Welcome to Heavenly Heights*; Nathan Englander's col-lection *For the Relief of Unbearable Urges*; and Tova Mirvis' *The Ladies' Auxiliary* are told from the point of view of writers and characters for whom Orthodox Judaism is part of the fabric of their lives. Several of these novels have become staples of book discussion groups. In an article in *Moment Magazine*, novelist Anne Roiphe wrote:

> This new Jewish writing among the younger generation tells
> us that American Jewish life has had its confrontation with as-
> similation. The end of the melting-pot dream has been
> reached. What we are seeing is a returned energy to the par-
> ticular Jewish experience, the religion and the history and the
> intimate knowledge of Jewish life. The subject has changed.[2]

It remains to be seen what the next decade will bring, but it is certain that the younger generation of Jewish American writers has a great deal to say about the varieties of being Jewish in postmodern America.

While it may have been true in the past that Jewish American fiction was primarily lit-erary or mainstream fiction, the last twenty years have brought a Jewish sensibility to all types of genre literature. Observant and assimilated Jewish characters populate the mystery world, thrillers are filled with Mossad operatives fighting Arab terrorists, there's a growing body of historical fiction set in biblical times, and women's fiction is filled with twenty-something Jewish women worrying about their love lives. As of this writing, there is no comprehensive source of information for readers of Jewish American literature that spans the range from literary to genre fiction. Other readers' advisory guides identify only a limited number of titles that could be considered Jewish American literature. The few existing bibliographies and guides to Jewish American literature concentrate on literary fiction or Holocaust fiction and memoir. Online sources that offer author and subject search capability are helpful but limited. The most useful of these sources are listed in each chapter and in chapter 1, "Building and Maintaining a Collection of Jewish American Literature."

This guide is not an effort to define a Jewish canon or "best" list. It is an attempt to help readers find books that they will enjoy, expose readers to the remarkable range of Jewish American literature, and introduce readers to new authors and titles. Although it is not about best books, it is about good books. All books listed have won awards, were listed in bibliographies of recommended titles, or were positively reviewed in the media. *Jewish American Literature* is a descriptive, not a critical guide; the reader must look elsewhere for analytical reviews. Over 700 titles are annotated in these pages, and many additional titles and authors are suggested for further reading. Detailed information about selection criteria is found in the following section, "Scope."

The general reader will find this guide helpful in exploring and expanding his or her reading interests, whether literary fiction, genre fiction, or nonfiction. Librarians will find it a useful readers' advisory tool in public, academic, school, and synagogue libraries. It will also help readers and librarians find answers to reference questions about authors and their works. Since it emphasizes award-winning and well-reviewed titles, it can serve as a collection development tool for assessing collections and making purchasing decisions. Anyone interested in Jewish American literature can use it as a source of titles for reading lists, bibliographies, book discussion groups, and book fairs. It can be used to recommend adult books to young adults. Booksellers can use it as a purchasing guide and to make recommendations to customers. It is hoped that this guide will lead to many hours of pleasurable reading for all who use it; the books described are as varied in styles, plots, and themes as any group of titles could possibly be.

Scope

Selection of authors and titles was determined from award lists and other recommended sources, tempered and expanded by this author's judgment. All winners of the National Jewish Book Award, E. L. Wallant Award, and Koret Foundation Award were considered for inclusion. Titles likely to be available to a public library borrower were given preference, although there is a selection of titles from the smaller, religious publishers. For the most part, the titles that the reader finds here would have been considered for purchase in public libraries because they were reviewed in the standard sources used by librarians for collection development. Many have appeared on the ALA *Notable Books List*, were chosen for *Public Library Catalog*, or received positive reviews in library review sources (such as *Booklist*, *Kirkus Reviews*, *Publishers Weekly*, and *Library Journal*) or mainstream review sources (such as *The New York Times Book Review*). The emphasis is on titles published from 1980 through 2002; earlier titles are included if they are significant or classic titles that have retained their popularity. Some titles published in 2003 are included as well. Icons indicate suitability for young adults (**YA**) and book discussion groups (📖). Large print, recorded books, and videos are not included because of problems with long-term availability of these formats. Internet addresses for the Web sites of individual authors are noted with the date the Web sites were accessed.

No effort has been made to provide an exhaustive bibliography of an author's works. The intent is to provide a useful readers' guide to the American Jewish experience in literature, not an overwhelming one. With this criterion as a guide, not every novel by every author has been included. Most of the novels are set in the United States, Canada, or Latin America and represent a Jewish American "take" on the experience of being Jewish, but setting is not a basis for inclusion. (Much of the historical fiction is set outside the Americas.) Biographies and memoirs are about or by people who have lived their adult lives in the Western Hemisphere.

A few works by non-Jewish authors appear where it seemed appropriate. For example, a novel like Michener's *The Source* is included because it is widely read by Jews for an understanding of the history of the Middle East. Pete Hamill's *Snow in August* is included for its unusually sensitive and perceptive portrayal of the relationship between a Holocaust survivor and a young Catholic boy. Most of the titles by non-Jewish authors are genre novels with well-researched historical settings. Increasingly, the Middle East and the Holocaust are used as settings for mysteries, thrillers, and literary fiction by non-Jewish authors; a few of these novels are included in the "Related Titles" sections because of popularity, for example, *Black Cross*, by Greg Iles and *Schindler's List* by the Australian author Thomas Keneally. In the biography and autobiography chapter, readers are referred to titles like Mary Gordon's *The Shadow Man* and Susan Jacoby's *Half-Jew: A Daughter's Search For Her Family's Buried Past*, because they illuminate an interesting and troubling aspect of the Jewish experience in the United States.

The emphasis is on U.S. authors and titles readily available through libraries in this country. Canadian authors are represented if their books have been published in the United States. For Latin American authors, only titles published in English in the United States are included. The only other translated titles are by writers who have made homes in the United States but write in other languages. Two examples of writers who fall into this category are Isaac Bashevis Singer, whose novels were published in Yiddish first, and Elie Wiesel, who writes in French. As a general rule, only writers living and publishing in the Western Hemisphere have been considered for inclusion. A few authors, like Ze'ev Chafets, who live in Israel but write in English for an American audience, are included. This excludes the rich and diverse literature of Israel, which deserves its own guide.

The coverage of this guide is primarily fiction, both literary and genre. However, there are a few exceptions. The chapter on biography and autobiography helps provide insight into the Jewish American experience from another perspective. In addition, this literature often contains elements that readers seek in fiction—memorable characters, intriguing story lines, evocative settings, and distinctive language. The Holocaust literature chapter covers fiction and memoir because they are so closely related. The authors are survivors who have made their homes in America. Again, the nonfiction selected for the Holocaust chapter has qualities that appeal to all readers.

Organization

Chapter 1 includes suggestions and sources for keeping up with the literature. In chapters 2 through 8, annotated bibliographies provide information about different genres and suggestions for further reading. Chapter 9 is a bibliography of general readers' advisory materials and sources for book discussion groups. This is followed by two indexes, one by author and title and the other by subject.

As much as possible, titles have been assigned to a genre and subgenre on the basis of "best fit," based on classic definitions, but there will certainly be differences of opinion among readers. Genreblending sometimes makes it difficult to say with certainty that a novel belongs in a particular category. Librarians need to be attuned to the way readers describe what they look for in a novel, so they can suggest titles that cross traditional genre lines. Pacing, characterization, setting, or mood may be as important in recommending a novel as its identification as a romance or mystery. The "Related Titles" part of each annotation helps identify fiction and nonfiction in other genres that the reader may enjoy.

As a readers' advisory tool, this guide is arranged to help librarians and readers make connections among authors and types of literature in several ways:

- Books are grouped into genres and subgenres or by appeal characteristics.
- Annotations provide brief plot and style information.
- A "Related Titles" part of the annotations identifies fiction and nonfiction for further reading.
- Themes are assigned to each title and listed in the index so readers can find additional titles in the same subject areas.
- The author/title index includes all titles and authors named in the "Related Titles" listings.
- Information is provided about Jewish publishing and reviewing media to help librarians build and maintain their collections and to help readers pursue their interests.
- Chapter 9: "Readers' Advisory Resources" lists sources for learning about readers' advisory work for anyone unfamiliar with these techniques.

Entries

The purpose of the information in the entries is to provide readers' advisory support and identification of titles. Bibliographic information is provided for the original publication in the United States or Canada. Reprint information is given for many older titles. Wherever possible, the Library of Congress catalog was used for verification. Since books go in and out of print frequently, publishers' catalogs or online databases are suggested as the best sources for ordering information.

Bibliographic Information

Titles are listed under the author's name as it appears in the book. If that name is a pseudonym, the author's real name is given as well. Most of the annotated titles are published by trade publishers whose books are carried by general bookstores and public libraries. Some titles by smaller, religious publishing houses, like Carmi Press, Devora

Publishing, Jewish Publication Society, and Shaar Press, are included for breadth of coverage. Several university presses, like Syracuse University Press, University of Wisconsin Press, and University of New Mexico Press, have outstanding series in Jewish literature; selections from those series are represented. More information about publishers is found in chapter 1.

Annotations

The annotations provide enough information to identify the subject of the work, tell something about the content and the treatment, and make note of anything unusual about the author's style without revealing significant elements of the plot. By using the annotations with the subject index, librarians and readers of this book should be able to find answers to the following types of questions:

In which of Faye Kellerman's books is Peter Decker's daughter a main character?

What is the novel about the Jewish community in Memphis, Tennessee?

Can you suggest books written by or about children of Holocaust survivors?

Are there any books of Jewish sports fiction?

Themes

Themes (subjects) are provided within entries to identify significant topics, geographic locations, time periods, and character names. For series entries, the themes apply to the entire series. There are additional topics for each book that appear only in the subject index. These additional subjects are all mentioned in the annotations. Additional themes for individual series titles will help readers looking for certain types of stories or trying to identify a novel already read.

Related Titles

Since one of the pleasures of reading is finding other, related books, readers can use the "Related Titles" section of the annotations to expand their reading interests. These suggestions may be:

- Other books by the same author, since not every title by an author is annotated.

- Related titles that may or may not be annotated elsewhere in the guide.

- Related titles that cross over from fiction to nonfiction and vice versa that may or may not be annotated.

- Titles that expand the criteria of the guide.

Related titles are based on themes and appeal characteristics: plot, character, setting, language, pacing, etc., or in the case of nonfiction, by subject matter as well.

Young Adult Recommendations

Where appropriate, readers will find the icon **YA** on titles that are suitable for young adults. The basis of these recommendations are awards, recommended lists, and consultation with young adult librarians. There are additional recommendations for young adults in the "Related Titles" part of the annotation. The purpose of recommending these adult books for young adults is to provide an introduction to adult titles for interested teen readers and to expand the books librarians can recommend to high school students for curriculum support. Since these books were not specifically written for young adults, there may be language or scenes that are not appropriate for every teen in every setting.

Book Club Recommendations

Book discussion groups have mushroomed in popularity in the last few years. Libraries, synagogues, and community organizations are frequent sponsors, but many groups are created by interested friends and neighbors. The icon ▭ denotes books that are suitable for discussion. Discussion guides are available on the Internet for many titles, and some publishers have bound discussion guides into the trade paperback editions of their titles. Further information on book discussion groups can be found at the end of chapter 9.

Book Awards

 indicates titles that have won the following awards:

National Jewish Book Award

E. L. Wallant Award

Koret Foundation Award

National Book Award

National Book Critics Circle Award

Pulitzer Prize

Pen/Faulkner Award

A list of the titles that have won the National Jewish Book Award, the E. L. Wallant Award, and the Koret Foundation Award can be found in chapter 1.

Indexes

To help readers identify titles there are two indexes:

- An author/title index, which includes all titles that are annotated, and all authors and titles listed in the "Related Titles" part of the annotations.

- A subject index, which lists each book by theme. Each annotated book has several themes listed in the entry. The subject index includes additional subjects for terms and themes that appear in the annotations. Listing actual titles, rather than just page numbers, in the subject index makes it easier to compile bibliographies and find books across genre lines.

The novels and memoirs in this guide offer something for every reader. They confront timeless issues from a Jewish perspective: maintaining ethnic and religious identity in the larger community, dealing with tragedy, understanding who we are and what we stand for. Literary fiction, genre, and biography readers will find new titles and authors to expand their horizons, new perspectives to contemplate and discuss, and memorable stories to treasure.

A Note on Usage

Where there are variations in the spelling of words, *The JPS Dictionary of Jewish Words* by Joyce Eisenberg and Ellen Scolnic, published by The Jewish Publication Society, has been used as the authority. This accounts for discrepancies in the way names are spelled in book titles and themes. The terms "Bible," "Torah," and "Tanakh" are used to refer to scripture instead of the Christian term "Old Testament." Similarly, B.C.E. and C.E. are used in place of B.C. and A.D.

Notes

1. *Jewish American Literature: A Norton Anthology*, comp. and ed. Jules Chametzky and others (New York: W. W. Norton. 2001), 979.

2. Anne Roiphe, "From Jewish Writing to Writing Jewish," *Moment Magazine* (October 1999): 79.

Chapter 1

Building and Maintaining a Collection of Jewish American Literature

Introduction

Jewish American literature is not confined to one segment of the publishing industry. Every year, large and small trade publishers like Random House, Farrar, Straus & Giroux, and Algonquin Books, to name a very few, publish Jewish American fiction, biography, and autobiography. These books are routinely reviewed in the standard review sources used by librarians: *Publishers Weekly*, *Library Journal*, *Booklist*, and *Kirkus Reviews*. Many titles receive "starred" reviews, win awards, or appear on recommended booklists. The authors speak on radio interview programs and at bookstores around the country. Given the visibility of many Jewish American authors, it would be easy to assume that a Jewish American literature collection is not hard to build and maintain. But these high-visibility titles and authors are the tip of a large, varied, and fascinating iceberg. There's no one place to look for current information. To build a representative collection of Jewish American literature, the librarian needs to dig deeper and become aware of other resources beyond the secular reviewing media. Strategies for keeping up include monitoring a wide range of publishers, journals, and, increasingly, Web sites. This chapter provides a pathfinder through the very active and vibrant world of Jewish American publishing, reviewing, and marketing for ongoing and retrospective collection development. The sources discussed are appropriate for selecting the type of materials covered in this guide: literary and genre fiction, biography and autobiography, and Holocaust fiction and memoir.

Review Sources

Deciding which books to buy for a library requires making difficult choices, since resources are finite and readers voracious. (The new title output of the U.S. publishing industry in 2003 was 175,000 titles; of those, 17,000 were fiction, and over 5,000 biography and autobiography.[1]) The process of making those decisions, part of what is known as collection development, is done with the clientele of the library in mind. As the library is used, the librarian who is attuned to readers' needs will develop judgment about which titles to purchase. This is true no matter what the setting: public library, synagogue or institutional library; or academic library. The review sources described below will help identify titles of interest beyond those reviewed in the general media.

There are many sources of commercial reviews now available to the general public. The major online booksellers, Amazon.com and Barnesandnoble.com, reprint reviews from *Publishers Weekly*, *Booklist,* and other sources, and allow subject and keyword searches. The proprietary online database *NoveList* reprints reviews; has author, title, and subject search capability; and has a feature that provides recommendations for read-alikes. *Novelist* is found at many libraries and schools and is often available for library patrons to access from home. The selected list below identifies some nationally distributed sources of book reviews of Jewish American literature. In addition, many communities have Jewish newspapers that carry book reviews, for example, *Baltimore Jewish Times*, *Cleveland Jewish News*, *Detroit Jewish News*, and *San Diego Jewish Journal*. To find additional online sources, a good search engine and a few keywords will yield other sites.

Print Resources

Association of Jewish Libraries *Newsletter*

www.jewishlibraries.org.

The AJL promotes Jewish libraries and provides continuing education and networking opportunities for Judaica librarians. Its *Newsletter*, published quarterly, is part of membership in the organization. Each issue contains book reviews written by AJL members. Membership information can be obtained online at the organization's Web site, listed above.

Forward

45 East 33rd St.
New York, NY 10016
www.forward.com

This weekly newspaper is the English-language descendant of the Yiddish *Forward*, a popular newspaper in the Jewish American community throughout most of the twentieth century. (The *Forward* is still published in Yiddish and now has a Russian-language edition.) The cultural section usually contains several book reviews, and there are occasional articles about well-known authors or literary trends.

Hadassah Magazine

50 West 58th St.
New York, NY 10019
www.hadassah.org

Published by the organization Hadassah, the women's Zionist organization of America, this monthly journal features articles on topics of current interest and always includes several long book reviews.

Jerusalem Report

401 North Wabash, Suite 732
Chicago, IL 60611
www.jrep.com

Although this biweekly journal is devoted to issues of Israeli politics for the diaspora community, each issue has several reviews of current fiction and nonfiction.

Jewish Book Annual

Published by the Jewish Book Council (see next entry), each volume contains bibliographies of Jewish American fiction and nonfiction published in the previous year as well as scholarly articles on various aspects of Jewish literature in English, Hebrew, and Yiddish.

Jewish Book World

Jewish Book Council
15 East 26th St.
New York, NY 10010
www.jewishbookcouncil.org

Twenty to thirty books are reviewed in depth in each of three issues per year, with shorter reviews of additional titles. The mission of the Council is to promote Jewish books, and it is a good source of information about the American Jewish book market. It sponsors the National Jewish Book Award, maintains a speakers' bureau, supports Jewish book fairs, and publishes a number of useful bibliographies of Jewish literature.

Lilith

250 West 57th St., No.#2432
New York, NY 10107
www.lilithmag.com

A quarterly Jewish women's magazine focusing on issues of identity and feminism. Each issue contains short fiction and several book reviews.

Moment

4710 41st St. N.W.
Washington, DC 20016
www.momentmag.com

A bimonthly magazine that deals with cultural, religious, and political concerns for diaspora Jews. Several reviews are included in each issue.

Online Resources

These sites represent a few of the most useful among many. The Internet has made a major change in the way books are marketed, allowing authors and publishers to reach their audiences directly. Many of the authors listed in this guide have their own Web sites at which they provide information on published and forthcoming books and gather reader feedback. Those individual URLs have been included in each entry. Although every effort has been made to verify these as close to publication time as possible, the Internet is so volatile that it is impossible to guarantee the accuracy of this information for any length of time. Readers are encouraged to search on their own for additional Web sites not listed. If an author has no Web site, the Web site of the author's publisher will often prove helpful. Additional searches on an author's name may lead the curious reader to sites hosted by scholars or fans, citations to articles, press releases, calendars of author appearances, etc.

www.jbooks. com

Subtitled "The Online Jewish Book Community," this site contains reviews of new fiction, nonfiction, and children's books. It also includes author interviews, book excerpts, and occasional essays on Jewish literature.

www.myJewishBooks.com

A useful source for information on new Jewish fiction and nonfiction, updated monthly, with numerous chatty reviews and searchable archives back to 2000. The site is also known as SeferSafari and can be accessed at www.sefersafari.com.

www.nextbook.org

Billing itself as "a gateway to Jewish culture, history, and ideas for Jews and non-Jews alike," the site, which changes daily, contains reading lists, literary news, and links to outside sources. A free daily e-mail newsletter alerts subscribers to cultural news and links back to booklists and book recommendations.

Publishers

Virtually all U.S. trade publishers publish titles by Jewish American authors. Sometimes mainstream publishers will issue separate lists of titles by Jewish authors in marketing brochures or on their Web sites. Sales representatives and publicists at trade shows are a good source of information about forthcoming titles and can supply advance reading copies. The list below is a selection of Jewish publishers, Jewish imprints, Jewish-interest series of secular publishers, and small presses that feature American Jewish literature. Publishers that do not offer a significant number of titles in the areas of fiction and memoir are not listed.

Jewish Lights Publishing

P.O. Box 237
Sunset Farm Offices, Rt. 4
Woodstock, VT 05091
www.jewishlights.com

A publisher of "books that reflect the Jewish wisdom tradition for people of all faiths, all backgrounds," primarily nonfiction for spiritual seekers.

Jewish Publication Society

2100 Arch St., 2nd Floor
Philadelphia, PA 19103
www.jewishpub.org

JPS is the source of standard, classic translations of Tanach and Torah commentary, as well as scholarly and popular fiction and nonfiction.

Jonathan David Publishers, Inc.

68-22 Eliot Ave.
Middle Village, NY 11379
www.jdbooks.com

A publisher of nonfiction in all subject areas, with a specialization in popular Judaica, Jonathan David is both a publisher and a bookseller.

Schocken Books

1745 Broadway
New York, NY 10019
www.randomhouse.com/schocken/home.html

An old and respected Jewish publishing house that was founded in Germany in 1931 and moved to the United States in 1945, Schocken became part of Random House in 1987. Its list is a mix of new and classic titles, both American and European.

Syracuse University Press

621 Skytop Rd., Suite 110
Syracuse, NY 13244
www.syracuseuniversitypress.syr.edu

Through the <u>Library of Modern Jewish Literature</u> series, Syracuse has an active program of publishing new literary fiction and reprints of older works, like Joyce Reiser Kornblatt's *The Reason for Wings* and Arthur Miller's *Focus*.

The Toby Press

P.O. Box 8531
New Milford, CT
www.tobypress.com

A publisher of an eclectic mix of literary and commercial fiction, Jewish and non-Jewish, including reprints of classics and popular titles, first-time authors, and translations.

University of New Mexico Press

1720 Lomas Blvd. NE
Albuquerque, NM 87106
www.unmpress.com/unmpress.html

The <u>Jewish Latin America</u> series from this publisher has made translations of important Latin American Jewish writers available to an English-speaking readership.

University of Wisconsin

1930 Monroe St., 3rd Floor
Madison, WI 53711
www.wisc.edu/wisconsinpress/index.html

Fiction and nonfiction in the Jewish Life in Print series covers a range of authors, from the literary fiction of Rebecca Goldstein and Curt Leviant to Holocaust memoirs, literary criticism, and theology.

University Press of New England

1 Court St., Suite 250
Lebanon, NH 03766
www.upne.com

This consortium of a group of academic presses includes Brandeis University, publisher of the Brandeis Series in American Jewish History, Culture, and Life and the Brandeis Series on Jewish Women.

Awards and Honors

Jewish American authors regularly win the major American literary awards: the National Book Award, the Pulitzer Prize, the Pen/Faulkner Award, etc. These awards are well publicized, and past winners are generally listed on the organizations' Web sites. The H. W. Wilson Company's *Fiction Catalog* and *Public Library Catalog*, and the American Library Association's annual *Notable Books List* are other sources for outstanding titles. These lists can be found in most public libraries. In addition, there are several annual Jewish book awards that interested readers and librarians should be aware of: the National Jewish Book Award, the E. L. Wallant Award, and the Koret Jewish Book Award. In the bibliographic chapters of this book, an icon indicates award-winning titles and the name of the award is listed in the annotation. For ready reference, award-winning titles are listed below. All of these were considered for inclusion based on the criteria for this volume. Finalists, where available, were considered as well.

National Jewish Book Awards

Administered by the Jewish Book Council since 1949, these awards are given in a variety of categories: adult and juvenile fiction, biography/autobiography, Holocaust literature, poetry, and several additional categories of nonfiction. North American and Israeli authors are eligible for the awards. The categories of awards have changed over the years, and not every award has been given every year. Panels in each category select the winners. For many years the awards were given in the spring. In 2002, the date of the awards was changed to the fall, to coincide with National Jewish Book Month, which is scheduled every year for the thirty days leading up to Hanukkah. A listing of award winners in all categories is available from the Jewish Book Council. The categories included here are the ones relevant to the coverage of this guide. The Web site of the Jewish Book Council is www.jewishbookcouncil.org.

Fiction

1949	Howard Fast	*My Glorious Brothers*
1950	John Hersey	*The Wall*
1951	Soma Morgenstern	*The Testament of the Lost Son*
1952	Zelda Popkin	*Quiet Street*
1953	Michael Blankfort	*The Juggler*
1954	Charles Angoff	*In the Morning Light*
1955	Louis Zara	*Blessed is the Land*
1956	No Award	
1957	Leon Feuchtwanger	*Raquel: The Jewess of Toledo*
1958	Bernard Malamud	*The Assistant*
1959	Leon Uris	*Exodus*
1960	Philip Roth	*Goodbye Columbus*
1961	Edward L. Wallant	*The Human Season*
1962	Samuel Yellen	*Wedding Band*
1963	Isaac Bashevis Singer	*The Slave*
1964	Joanne Greenberg	*The King's Persons*
1965	Elie Wiesel	*The Town Beyond the Wall*
1966	Meyer Levin	*The Stronghold*
1967	Chaim Grade	*The Well*
1968	No Award	
1969	Charles Angoff	*Memory of Autumn*
1970	Leo Litwak	*Waiting for the News*
1971	No award	
1972	Cynthia Ozick	*The Pagan Rabbi and Other Stories*
1973	Robert Kotlowitz	*Somewhere Else*
1974	Francine Prose	*Judah the Pious*
1975	Jean Karsavina	*White Eagle, Dark Skies*
1976	Johanna Kaplan	*Other People's Lives*
1977	Cynthia Ozick	*Bloodshed and Three Novellas*
1978	Chaim Grade	*The Yeshiva*
1979	Gloria Goldreich	*Leah's Journey*
1980	Daniel Fuchs	*The Apathetic Bookie Joint*
1981	Johanna Kaplan	*O, My America*
1982	Mark Helprin	*Ellis Island and Other Stories*
1983	Robert Greenfield	*The Temple*
1984	Arthur A. Cohen	*An Admirable Woman*
1985	Frederick Busch	*Invisible Mending*
1986	Arnost Luštig	*The Unloved: From the Diary of Perla S.*

1987	No award	
1988	Philip Roth	*The Counterlife*
1989	Aharon Appelfeld	*The Immortal Bartfuss*
1990	A.B. Yehoshua	*Five Seasons*
1991	Chaim Potok	*The Gift of Asher Lev*
1992	Nathan Shaham	*The Rosendorf Quartet*
1993	A.B. Yehoshua	*Mr. Mani*
1994	Alan Isler	*The Prince of West End Avenue*
1995	Rebecca Goldstein	*Mazel*
1996	Evan Zimroth	*Gangsters*
1997	Saul Bellow	*The Actual*
1998	Aharon Appelfeld	*The Iron Tracks*
1999	Steve Stern	*The Wedding Jester*
2000	Philip Roth	*The Human Stain*
2001	Jonathan Safran Foer	*Everything is Illuminated*
2002	Gary Shteyngart	*The Russian Debutante's Handbook*

First-Time Author Award

2002	Horn, Dara	*In the Image*

Autobiography/Memoir

1989	Natan Sharansky	*Fear No Evil*
1990	Lucy Dawidowicz	*From That Time and Place: A Memoir 1938–1947*
1991	Irving Louis Horowitz	*Daydreams and Nightmares: Reflections of a Harlem Childhood*
1992	Henry Morganthau III	*Mostly Morganthaus: A Family History*
1993	Norman Manea	*On Clowns: The Dictator and the Artist*
1994	Howard A. Schack	*A Spy in Canaan: My Secret Life as a Jewish-American Businessman Spying for Israel*
1995	Louise Kehoe	*In This Dark House: A Memoir*
1996	Benjamin Wilkomirski	*Fragments*
1997	Elizabeth Ehrlich	*Miriam's Kitchen*
1998	Marcel Benabou	*Jacob, Menahem and Mimoun*
1999	Stephen A. Sadow, ed.	*King David's Harp: Autobiographical Essays by Latin American Writers*
2000	Cyrus H. Gordon	*A Scholar's Odyssey*
2001	Malkah Shapiro	*The Rebbe's Daughter*
2002	Hertzberg, Arthur	*A Jew in America: My Life and a People's Struggle for Identity*

Biography

1984	Dan Kurzman	*Ben-Gurion: Prophet of Fire*
1985	Maurice Friedman	*Martin Buber's Life and Works: The Later Years, 1945–1965*
1986	Jehuda Reinharz	*Chaim Weizmann: The Making of a Zionist Leader*

E. L. Wallant Award

This award was established in 1963 in memory of Edward Lewis Wallant, author of *The Pawnbroker* and *The Human Season*. It is given annually for a significant work of Jewish American fiction, preferably to a young, unrecognized author whose work bears some similarity to Wallant's in the opinion of the panel of judges. Awards have not been made every year. The Maurice Greenberg Center for Judaic Studies at the University of Hartford, in Hartford, Connecticut, administers the Wallant Award. The Web site for the Greenberg Center is www.hartford. edu/greenberg.

1963	Norman Fruchter	*Coat Upon a Stick*
1964	Seymour Epstein	*Leah*
1965	Hugh Nissenson	*A Pile of Stones*
1966	Gene Hurwitz	*Home is where You Start From*
1967	Chaim Potok	*The Chosen*
1968	No Award	
1969	Leo Litwak	*Waiting For the News*
1970	No Award	
1971	Cynthia Ozick	*The Pagan Rabbi and Other Stories*
1972	Robert Kotlowitz	*Somewhere Else*
1973	Arthur A. Cohen	*In the Days of Simon Stern*
1974	Susan Fromberg Schaeffer	*Anya*
1975	Anne Bernays	*Growing Up Rich*
1976	No Award	
1977	Curt Leviant	*The Yemenite Girl*
1978	No Award	
1979	No Award	
1980	Johanna Kaplan	*O My America!*
1981	Allen Hoffman	*Kagan's Superfecta*
1982	No Award	
1983	Francine Prose	*Hungry Hearts*
1984	No Award	
1985	Jay Neugeboren	*Before My Life Began*
1986	Daphne Merkin	*Enchantment*

1987	Steve Stern	*Lazar Malkin Enters Heaven*
1988	Tova Reich	*Master of the Return*
1989	Jerome Badanes	*The Final Opus of Leon Solomon*
1990	No Award	
1991	No Award	
1992	Melvin Jules Bukiet	*Stories of an Imaginary Childhood*
1993	Gerald Shapiro	*From Hunger*
1994	No Award	
1995	Rebecca Goldstein	*Mazel*
1996	Thane Rosenbaum	*Elijah Visible*
1997	Harvey Grossinger	*The Quarry*
1998	No Award	
1999	Allegra Goodman	*Kaaterskill Falls*
2000	Judy Budnitz	*If I Told You Once*
2001	Myla Goldberg	*The Bee Season*
2002	Dara Horn	*In the Image*
2003	Joan Leegant	*An Hour in Paradise*

Koret Jewish Book Awards

Beginning in 1999, these awards have been given jointly by the Koret Foundation and the National Foundation for Jewish Culture, for books published in English in the following categories: biography/autobiography/literary studies, fiction, history, and philosophy and thought. A new award was introduced for 2003 that goes to a writer under 35 years of age. The first recipient was Rachel Kadish, for her novel *From a Sealed Room*. All winners are announced in March. The winners in the categories of fiction and biography/autobiography/literary studies are listed below. The Web site for the Foundation is www.koretfoundation.org.

Fiction

1998	Yoel Hoffman	*Katschen and The Book of Joseph*
1999	A.B. Yehoshua	*A Journey to the End of the Millennium*
2000	Philip Roth	*The Human Stain*
2001	Isaac Babel	*The Complete Works of Isaac Babel*
2001	W. G. Sebald	*Austerlitz* (Special Literary Award)
2002	Henryk Grynberg	*Drohobycz, Drohobycz and Other Stories*
2003	Barbara Honigmann	*A Love Made Out of Nothing and Zohara's Journey*
	Aharon Megged	*Foiglman*

Biography, Autobiography, and Literary Studies

1998	Brian Morton	*Starting Out in the Evening*
1999	Steven Nadler	*Spinoza: A Life*
2000	Cynthia Ozick	*Quarrel and Quandary*
2001	Dorothy Gallagher	*How I Came Into My Inheritance*
2002	Frymer-Kensky, Tikva	*Reading the Women of the Bible*
2003	Benjamin Harshav	*Marc Chagall and His Times*

Other Sources for Recommended Titles

Annual "best" and "editor's choice" booklists are published in many review media (*Publishers Weekly, Booklist, Library Journal, The New York Times Book Review*, etc.) and are useful sources for fiction and memoir. Other sources that are worth examining are H. W. Wilson's annual *Fiction Catalog* and *Public Library Catalog*, and the American Library Association's annual *Notable Books List*. At the turn of the current century, the fervor to sum up the previous century's accomplishments produced many "best" lists with the accompanying clamor of support and argument. One of the most interesting for readers of Jewish literature is "100 Greatest Works of Modern Jewish Literature," chosen by a panel sponsored by The National Yiddish Book Center. The list, international in scope, is available on the Center's Web site, www.yiddishbookcenter.org. (For more information about the National Yiddish Book Center see below.)

Organizations and Special Collections

The organizations described below are a few of the most helpful sources for anyone who wishes to keep up with the field of Jewish literature or librarianship. In addition, many communities have Jewish cultural organizations that publish newspapers containing book reviews, offer book discussion groups and lectures, and host book fairs. Libraries in synagogues, universities, Jewish community centers, bureaus of Jewish education, or Holocaust centers are sources of information as well. Universities with Jewish studies departments often sponsor lectures, film festivals, and exhibits.

The Association of Jewish Libraries

www.jewishlibraries.org

The AJL is an international organization of Judaica librarians providing information, support, training, and networking opportunities for its members worldwide. Among their helpful publications are the quarterly *Newsletter* (described above), which reviews new books, and the Bibliography Bank. The listserv HaSafran (the librarian) is a forum for members to communicate about topics of interest. An annual conference is held in June. Membership applications should be directed to the current membership chairperson, available on the organization's Web site.

Center for Jewish History

15 West 16th St.
New York, NY 10011
www.cjh.org

CJH is a library and cultural center comprising five Jewish cultural organizations: the American Jewish Historical Society, American Sephardi Federation, Leo Baeck Institute, Yeshiva University Museum, and the YIVO Institute for Jewish Research. In addition to an excellent research library, which includes the holdings of the member institutions, CJH offers cultural programming and exhibits.

The Jewish Book Council

Jewish Book Council
15 East 26th St.
New York, NY 10010
www.jewishbookcouncil.org

The Council promotes Jewish books by sponsoring the annual National Jewish Book Award, providing recommended lists of books, and offering guidelines for running Jewish book fairs. *Jewish Book World* (described above), published three times each year, is an excellent source for reviews of new books.

The Jewish Community Library of Los Angeles

6505 Wilshire Blvd.
Los Angeles, CA 90048
www.jclla.org

A collection of over 25,000 books that supports the needs of the Jewish community of Los Angeles and provides reference service to the community at large. Their catalog is searchable online.

Jewish Women's Archive

68 Harvard St.
Brookline, MA 02445
www.jwa.org

The mission of this organization is "to uncover, chronicle and transmit the rich legacy of Jewish women and their contributions to our families and communities, to our people and our world." The Web site features virtual exhibits on famous Jewish women, recommendations of books to read, information about traveling exhibits, and opportunities to share stories and ideas.

National Yiddish Book Center

Harry and Jeanette Weinberg Building
1021 West St.
Amherst, MA 01002
www.yiddishbookcenter.org

Started by Aaron Lansky in 1980 to rescue the Yiddish books that were fast disappearing from personal libraries, the Center has an active program promoting Jewish literature and publishes the magazine *Pakn Treger* (*Book Peddler*). The Web site has a number of interesting features, including "The Jewish Reader: A Guide for Book Groups," which features one book—fiction, memoir, or poetry—each month and offers an essay, study questions, selected passages, and often an interview with the author. In 2001, a panel convened by the organization selected "One Hundred Greatest Works of Modern Jewish Literature." Readers will find this list on the Web site.

Note

1. Jim Milliot, "Bowker: Titles Up 19% in 2003," *Publishers Weekly*, May 31, 2004, 7.

Chapter 2

Mysteries and Thrillers

In its best moments, the religious mystery attempts to reflect God at work in the present age, by imagining God's emissaries in the act of sorting sin from crime, meting out responsibility, and bringing justice, punishment, repentance, and restoration.—William David Spencer

Think of Moses—a clandestine Israelite growing up in the court of the pharaoh—maybe history's earliest mole.—S. K. Wolf

Are we thriller/espionage writers to be consigned to the dustbins of history now that détente is here? . . . There are other, neighboring vineyards in which to labor, those of our friends in the Middle East, for example, which can replace the Evil Empire.—Larry Collins

Misfortune can happen to anyone. Only the dead are safe from it.—Harry Kemelman

Introduction

The novels in this chapter offer an escape from the mundane world in which children need babysitters, jobs offer only a few weeks of vacation, and the bills need to be paid on time. Mysteries provide readers with the opportunity to solve a puzzle and experience a frisson from a heart-stopping encounter with a murderer. When we read thrillers, we enter a world where treachery, conspiracy, and deceit provoke a hero or heroine to action in a fast-paced adventure.

The perennial appeal of these genres is evident from our earliest literature. We find mystery, mayhem, spying, and courtroom drama even in the Bible. In Genesis, Adam and Eve are the first thieves when they eat the fruit of the forbidden Tree of Knowledge, and Cain commits the first murder. Moses is the first hostage negotiator, calling down the ten plagues against the Egyptians in an effort to win the release of the Israelite slaves. Joshua sends spies into Jericho and they stay at the first safe house, spending the night with the prostitute Rahab. Solomon presides over the first child custody case when he mediates between two women who claim the same child.

Scope

The novels in this chapter fall into two categories: those with a Jewish setting and those with a Jewish theme. Faye Kellerman's *Ritual Bath* is set in an Orthodox community in Los Angeles and focuses on a murder that took place near the *mikveh* (women's bathhouse). The action of Janice Steinberg's *Death in a City of Mystics* takes place in the holy city of Safed, Israel, during the holiday of Lag ba-Omer. In *Zaddik* by David Rosenbaum, a detective's work with the Hasidic community in Brooklyn helps connect him to his mystical Jewish heritage. These are all examples of novels that are included because of a specifically Jewish setting. Mystery and thriller writers are always looking for unusual settings to provide background color for novels or motivation for characters. Jewish history is full of the variety, color, and conflict for such plots. Increasingly, best-selling popular thrillers and mysteries feature the Israeli intelligence services but are not written by Jewish authors. A few of these titles have been included as "Related Titles" because of their popularity.

Mysteries and thrillers with Jewish themes are as varied as Alan Dershowitz's *Just Revenge*, which examines the problem of Holocaust revenge; Neil Gordon's *The Gun Runner's Daughter*, whose heroine is a modern-day Esther; and Rochelle Krich's *Blood Money*, in which Jessie Drake, raised an Episcopalian, comes to terms with her Jewish heritage. In some stories, like Marissa Piesman's series about lawyer Nina Fischman, the Jewish theme is less obvious, more a matter of culture or attitude than religious practice. We recognize that familiar mix of guilt, love, and responsibility that defines Nina's relationship with her family, friends, and job. Though Nina doesn't fret over her lack of ritual observance, her self-identification as a Jew is basic. Some of these novels provide insight into the lives of observant Jews; social issues facing the Jewish community, like intermarriage or anti-Semitism; or Jewish history, law, and customs.

Organization of the Chapter

Mysteries are divided into the following subgenres. Discussion at the beginning of each section provides more information about the subgenre.

Mysteries are divided into:

Anthologies

Amateur detectives

    Humorous mysteries

Private investigators

Police procedurals

Historical mysteries

Thrillers are divided into:

Suspense

Legal thrillers

Political intrigue and espionage

Appeal of the Genre/Advising the Reader

Mysteries and thrillers are the most popular genres among public library patrons. Because they are in heavy demand, mysteries are often shelved separately in libraries. Librarians know that offering a separate section can limit the range of readers' exposure, but doing so makes it easier to satisfy the avid fan. It is hoped that the information in this chapter will help readers find titles and authors of interest in this genre, and point the way to the enjoyment of novels in other genres, literary fiction, and related nonfiction. Sources for general readers' advisory information can be found in chapter 9; the information below will help in identifying the specific appeal of mysteries and thrillers. It is based on the appeal characteristics developed by Joyce Saricks and Nancy Pearl.[1]

The novels in this chapter are generally plot-driven, and therefore they are not the best candidates for book discussion groups. However, a few have been suggested for discussion.

Character

Mysteries and thrillers are dependent on strong protagonists. Readers enjoy identifying with heroes or heroines who need to solve the puzzle of a mystery, put a political situation to rights, or extricate themselves from a dangerous predicament by intelligence or force. The protagonist may have some imperfections, but we are often able to forgive him or her because the ultimate quest is to restore moral balance. Sometimes, the author seems to be saying, justice needs a helping hand in this less-than-perfect world. Because of this, it is rare that we are unable to empathize with the main character. Thus, although not usually written in the first person, stories are often told from the point of view of the main character.

One of the trends in this genre is that personal lives of characters have taken center stage. Relationships with colleagues, families, friends, and lovers intrude and occupy more of the story. In fact, if the heroes' personal lives are messy, so much the better for the author, who can tempt readers with further installments that promise, if not happy endings, then more engrossing personal details. The novel *Strangers at the Gate,* for example, opens with a crime, like a classic police procedural, but the reader quickly becomes just as interested in detective Zack Tobias's life and how his complex personal history will affect the way he conducts his investigation. Reading to the end to find out whodunit is a parallel pleasure to finding out whether Zack will solve his personal problems.

Where once mysteries were almost exclusively male-dominated, female protagonists and female authors have flourished in the last twenty years. Women no longer appear just in genteel mysteries where violence takes place offstage. There are now many mysteries in which women face the same physical dangers as men. Rachel Gold, the lawyer in Michael Kahn's series, is an amateur detective in the traditional mold, with male sidekicks. Since women have now entered professions that once were exclusively male, they are portrayed in every occupation. A woman rabbi is the protagonist in Roger Herst's *Woman of the Cloth* and the murder victim in Joseph Telushkin's *The Unorthodox Murder of Rabbi Wahl*. Women authors share best-sellerdom with men, and they are responsible for the increased emphasis on character that now pervades this genre.

Thrillers are also anchored by strong protagonists, usually loners whose lives have been marked by tragedy. Gabriel Allon, the Mossad agent in Daniel Silva's series, lost his wife and son in an explosion meant to take Allon's life. This kind of history provides motivation for the character as well as weight to the characterization. Deceit and treachery are staples of this genre; plots often depend on who among the secondary characters can be trusted. Gay Courter's *Code Ezra* hinges on which one of three women operatives is a traitor. Thrillers glorify the efficacy of the individual, whose actions may prevent global or national catastrophe. In *The Assistant* by J. Patrick Law, a lawyer is recruited to hunt for a Palestinian terrorist intent on destroying Israel.

A romantic relationship usually adds tension and interest to the plot. As in the mystery genre, women have taken more prominent roles in recent years. In Allan Topol's *Spy Dance*, a female Mossad officer directs the actions of the agent. Women now appear as spymasters and terrorists, heroines and villains, not only as love interests. The type of antagonist may be particularly important in setting the tone and pacing of the thriller. Often ruthless and powerful, with more resources and fewer moral scruples than the hero, the villain may be an individual or a group, a person whose face and personality the reader knows, or the faceless personification of evil. *The Shadow Man* by John Katzenbach is a good example of the thriller as struggle between good and evil.

Plot

Plot is one of the defining elements of mysteries and thrillers; the way the writer makes use of the plot conventions of these genres is what makes readers return to a favorite author. In the traditional formula for mysteries, a murder was committed by a person unknown to the reader and identified by logical deduction. These plots were characteristic of the era known as the Golden Age of mystery writing. Following World War II, mysteries became darker in tone and writers began to make use of historical and social issues. Many of the mysteries in this chapter take their topics from headlines in the daily newspapers: Holocaust assets, child abuse, recovered memory, neo-Nazism, hate crimes, stalkers, date rape, infertility, child custody, etc. Subjects from the headlines in our morning newspapers become more personal in a novel. Some readers may enjoy plots that provide food for thought about social or philosophical issues; others want more traditional whodunit puzzles to solve.

Thriller plots vary widely from the static psychological thriller to the incident-packed espionage novel, but all share a narrative drive toward conclusion. Readers may enjoy suspense novels where the conflict between protagonist and villain is cerebral, like Libby Lazewnik's *The Judge* or Steven Salinger's *White Darkness*. Espionage thrillers tend to be heavily plotted and centered on powerful conflicts, with explosive endings. Protagonists are kept moving, often in headlong flight to or away from a catastrophic situation. Surprises along the way, reversals of good and evil, keep the reader guessing. Allan Topol's *Spy Dance* or Moris Farhi's *The Last of Days* are examples of this type of thriller. Plots may pick up on current or historical political situations, introducing what-if elements. Legal thrillers often have elements of both. Alan Dershowitz's *Advocate's Devil* has tense, psychological courtroom scenes played out like a chess match in parallel with a chilling story that sets up and finishes off the courtroom drama.

Pacing

Pacing is also key to understanding the appeal of this genre. Thrillers are known for brisk pacing that starts on the first page and draws the reader into a maelstrom of escalating tension. Thrillers that center on political intrigue and espionage tend to fit this description. But some thrillers build from a quiet start, involving the reader in character and setting first. Legal thrillers, in which points of law are described and evidence gathered, may build slowly, while the author develops the intellectual framework for the climactic legal scenes. Some thrillers are compressed into a few days while the prospect of terrifying events hangs in the balance. Pacing in mysteries is generally slower than in thrillers, although readers may be no less enthralled. Since mysteries involve solving a puzzle, readers typically enjoy the process of being drawn in, uncovering all the nuances of the situation, trying to guess how and by whom the crime was committed. Writers can take a more leisurely approach to revealing the details of plot and character without losing mystery readers.

In some series mysteries, as the series progresses, the books increase in length without losing readership; in fact, readers may look forward to spending more time with their favorite characters. Pacing varies within the mystery genre depending on the type of mystery. Cozies, in which the action typically takes place offstage, are the most leisurely and cerebral. Hard-boiled and noirish mysteries, with their cynical and emotionally detached protagonists, focus more on action.

Although pacing may not be as important in mysteries as it is in thrillers, readers' advisors should be aware of the pacing of a particular novel to recommend it appropriately. Variations in pacing are found in all subgenres of mysteries. Several of the mysteries listed here in the amateur detective subgenre are leisurely, like the Rabbi Kemelman mysteries, but some do put the protagonist in jeopardy. Asking readers to share examples of titles they have enjoyed will provide a key to their interest in pacing.

Setting

Setting is important in mysteries and thrillers, providing a familiar or exotic frame on which to hang a story. Some readers enjoy books set in familiar places, so they can visualize locations. Other readers enjoy reading stories set in exotic locales. Sometimes setting is so strongly entangled with plot that it is like a secondary character and becomes familiar even to readers who haven't been there. Abe Lieberman's Chicago, Peter Decker's Los Angeles, and Noah Green's New York City are all examples of locations that are intertwined with plot.

While we often like to read about the familiar, the unfamiliar has great appeal as well. Unexpected things can happen in different cultures, and authors are unencumbered by expectations. One difference between mysteries and thrillers is that mysteries are often localized in setting while thrillers are likely to send characters careening across continents. At least once in a series, the author will set a mystery outside of a character's normal locale. Peter Decker and Rina Lazarus find mystery while on their honeymoon in Brooklyn, Nina Fischman encounters murder at a summer share on Fire Island, Rabbi Small solves a crime while on vacation in Israel.

Historical mysteries present challenges to the writer to convey the "feel" of another era while understanding the details of daily life, politics, language, social conditions, etc. Many readers enjoy learning about a different era or the details of an unusual occupation or hobby. Aileen Baron, in *The Fly Has a Hundred Eyes*, sets her mystery among archaeologists on a dig in Israel. Benjamin Weaver, in David Liss's *Conspiracy of Paper*, set in the eighteenth century, takes the reader into the shadowy underworld of the emerging London financial markets. Some readers enjoy seeing what an author can do within the confines of a genre like the police procedural or private investigator.

In thrillers, settings are varied and plots often take characters to multiple locations, spanning continents. Ben Revere, in *Loot*, finds terror in his hometown of Boston and in several European countries. In *The Fury of Rachel Monette*, the trail of murder takes Rachel to Tunisia, where the author uses to advantage suspicious local attitudes toward women and outsiders. In spy thrillers, with plots often involving relations between two or more countries, protagonists may travel frequently, and authors need to quickly establish a sense of place for the reader. In some thrillers, intensity builds in a localized setting. Steve Salinger's *White Darkness*, set in a Brooklyn neighborhood, is filled with menacing evil. The fertility clinic setting of Rochelle Krich's medical thriller, *Fertile Ground*, gives the author an opportunity to discuss the Jewish medical, legal, and moral issues confronted by her protagonist, Dr. Lisa Brockman.

A Note About Series

Many mysteries and thrillers capitalize on the growing interest readers have in characters' lives, and sometimes that means plot takes a back seat to character development, blurring the classic genre definitions. Series have become very popular to meet this demand for ongoing involvement in characters' lives. Librarians are familiar with readers who are hungry for news of the next Faye Kellerman or Stuart Kaminsky mystery, intent on placing reserves as soon as the publisher announces the newest title. One value of readers' advisory services in libraries is to help readers discover new authors and widen their interests while waiting for the next installment of their favorite series.

Mysteries

There is something special about settling down to read a good mystery, and possibly something quintessentially Jewish as well. Solving logical puzzles, interpreting laws, and teasing meaning out of texts is a particularly Jewish endeavor. The Talmud, that enormous and vital compendium of Jewish law and commentary, consists of statements of Jewish law accompanied by the commentary of scholars throughout the centuries, allowing a conversation on the written page among people who were not contemporaneous, and permitting anyone who reads the Talmud to continue that conversation today. Jewish legal compendia, of which the Talmud is only one part, are concerned with ethics and justice. Students of Judaism could be considered detectives of the text, sifting through written clues and pondering ambiguities to extract meaning. It is no wonder that many fictional detectives are Jewish, and no wonder that so many of them are caught up in internal dialogues over right and wrong.

The mystery is typically dated from Edgar Allan Poe's nineteenth-century short stories that set out the familiar plot devices common to the genre. In the Golden Age of the mystery, from the 1920s to the 1940s, both British and American practitioners developed the major subgenres of the field: hard-boiled, cozy, private investigator, amateur sleuth, and police procedural. Many writers of this classic period are still popular, such as Agatha Christie, Dashiell Hammett, Ellery Queen, Erle Stanley Gardner, and Raymond Chandler. Their protagonists are almost exclusively male (Agatha Christie provides the rare exception) and rarely refer to their ethnic backgrounds. The first Jewish protagonist in a mystery series appeared in 1964. Rabbi David Small, a congregational rabbi in a Boston suburb, was the popular creation of Harry Kemelman. The series ran to a dozen novels in which Rabbi Small confronted murder and synagogue politics, applying Talmudic logic and *halachah* (traditional Jewish law) to find solutions. The novels explain aspects of Jewish life and tradition and address some of the social issues in the Jewish community. James Yaffe, author of the "Mom" mysteries, theorizes that there were no Jewish detectives until Rabbi Small because "Jews felt too insecure in the society around them to try and impose their manners and mores on a popular literary form. And if this state of affairs has changed in the last three or four decades, if Jewish detectives have made more frequent appearances, it is probably because Jewish self-confidence has increased since the end of World War II."[2] In addition, over the last decade the growing popularity of religious fiction, and the acceptance of a serious attitude toward religion, has allowed Jewish mystery writers to create Orthodox, observant characters who are empathetic and believable.

Since Harry Kemelman started writing about Rabbi Small, there have been many mysteries in which private investigators, police detectives, or amateur detectives identify themselves as Jewish and in which a Yiddish word or two find their way into the story. Although some of those titles may be included in "Related Titles," the "Mystery" section of this chapter focuses on titles with significant Jewish content. Characters may be observant Jews, like Joseph Telushkin's Rabbi Winter, or Faye Kellerman's Rina Lazarus. In these mysteries we often learn about Jewish practices or Jewish law. In the first Rina Lazarus mystery, *Ritual Bath*, the reader learns about the laws of ritual purity. Other protagonists may not be observant, but Judaism plays a role in their lives and thoughts. Nate Rosen, in Ronald Levitsky's series about a civil rights lawyer, is preoccupied with issues of justice, in some way as a substitute for the Orthodox Judaism he abandoned as a young man. Nate's thoughts about returning to Orthodox Judaism often intrude upon his casework and allow the author to hold out the possibility that another novel in the series will explore this theme.

Judaism may also be a factor in the crime or its solution. *An Eye for an Eye*, in Joseph Telushkin's <u>Rabbi Daniel Winter</u> series, is a study of the concept of revenge in Jewish law. Some of the stories in the two anthologies *Mystery Midrash* and *Criminal Kabbalah* hinge on very specific issues of Jewish law or custom. In some mysteries, the detective is only nominally Jewish but becomes involved in a crime in the Jewish community. Matt Jacob, in *No Saving Grace* by Zachary Klein, has only a tenuous connection with his Jewish upbringing but becomes involved with the Hasidic community when a beloved rabbi is murdered.

Anthologies

***Mystery Midrash: An Anthology of Jewish Mystery and Detective Fiction.* Edited by Lawrence W. Raphael. Jewish Lights, 1999. 299p.** `YA`

A collection of thirteen mystery tales by well-known authors, including Stuart Kaminsky, Faye Kellerman, Janice Steinberg, and Ronald Levitsky. Many of the stories deal with contemporary Jewish problems of identity and assimilation, and several use Jewish law to solve mysteries. (Raphael's Web site, www.jewishmysteries.com, has an extensive bibliography of Jewish mysteries.)

Themes: short stories

Related Titles: Raphael edited a second anthology, *Criminal Kabbalah: An Intriguing Anthology of Jewish Mystery and Detective Fiction*, published in 2001. Readers may also enjoy the following anthologies: *Unholy Orders: Mystery Stories with a Religious Twist*, edited by Sarita Stevens; and *The Ethnic Detectives: Masterpieces of Mystery Fiction*, edited by Bill Pronzini and Martin Greenberg. These collections include Jewish and non-Jewish mysteries.

Amateur Detectives

An amateur detective matches wits with a criminal for compelling personal reasons. Journalist Margo Simon, for example, in *Death in a City of Mystics*, searches for the person who poisoned her mother. Sometimes the amateur detective is a suspect in a crime and needs to clear his name, as Rabbi Small does in *Friday the Rabbi Slept Late*. Sometimes the thrill of the hunt, of outdoing the police or other professionals, is the motivation, as in *Nursery Crimes* by Ayelet Waldman. Amateur detectives often have excellent psychological insight and common sense. Mom, in James Yaffe's mysteries, solves crimes by relating the circumstances to her own life experiences. Jewish amateur detectives come from all walks of life: rabbis, doctors, journalists, professors, and senior citizens. Their occupations or hobbies provide them with the special knowledge that enables them to solve the mystery. Alex Kertesz, in *The Wish to Kill* by Janet Hannah, uses his expertise in biochemistry to trap a killer. The level of violence is generally less than in other types of mysteries. The term "cozy," a subcategory of the amateur detective genre, refers to mysteries in which there is a minimum of sex and vulgarity, and violence takes place primarily offstage. The detective is almost always a woman, often older, and the setting is generally rural or suburban. The "Mom" mysteries by James Yaffe qualify as cozies, and the Rabbi Small mysteries by Harry Kemelman are sometimes defined as cozies. Most humorous mysteries are cozies. To help readers identify lighter mysteries that are short on graphic violence, cozies are identified as "Themes," and humorous mysteries are annotated in a group at the end of this section.

Hannah, Janet

The Wish to Kill. Soho Press, 1999. 228p.

Alex Kertesz, a biochemist at the University of Jerusalem, wishes an un-pleasant colleague dead; seconds later an explosion takes Ilan's life. Since several of Ilan's colleagues wished him harm, is it possible that negative thoughts caused his death? Alex explores the interconnected-ness of thoughts, feelings, and actions as he tries to identify the murderer. (The author's Web site is www.alexkertesz.com/all_mysteries2.html.)

Themes: biochemists; Jerusalem

Related Titles: Readers who enjoyed this thoughtful, literate mystery may also like Barbara Sofer's *The Thirteenth Hour*, a thriller set in Israel that is annotated in the "Political Intrigue and Espionage" section of this chapter.

Hellmann, Libby Fischer

Ellie Forman Mysteries.

A divorced mother and documentary film producer, Ellie has her own troubles with her ex-husband's financial schemes, but her energy, sense of humor, and quick intelligence help her tie up all the loose ends. (The author's Web site is www.hellmann.com/mystery-author.)

Themes: Chicago; fathers and daughters; single mothers

An Eye for Murder. Poisoned Pen Press, 2002. 316p.

When Ellie Foreman's name is found among the papers of nonagenarian Ben Sinclair after his death, her own father provides the link between the dead man, the Holocaust, and the Chicago Jewish community of the 1930s and 1940s.

A Picture of Guilt. Berkeley Prime Crime, 2003. 324p.
An Image of Death. Poisoned Pen Press, 2004. 320p.

Herst, Roger

Woman of the Cloth. Shengold Books, 1998. 395p.

Gabby Lewyn, assistant rabbi in a large Washington, D.C., congregation, is left in charge when the senior rabbi disappears after the revelation of multiple affairs. Then a member of the congregation is accused of rape and wants Gabby as a character witness.

Themes: adultery; rabbi detectives; rape

Kemelman, Harry

Rabbi Small Mysteries. **YA**

In the suburban Massachusetts town of Barnard's Crossing, Rabbi David Small calls on his knowledge of the Talmud to solve mysteries often in-volving members of his Conservative congregation. In this series, the first to feature an observant Jewish protagonist, the reader learns a great deal about Judaism from the reflective Rabbi Small. Issues of synagogue politics and the dilemmas of twentieth-century Jewish life become more prominent as the series progresses.

Themes: cozies; rabbi detectives; synagogue life

Friday the Rabbi Slept Late. **Crown, 1964. 224p.**

A young girl is murdered, and Rabbi Small is a suspect.

Saturday the Rabbi Went Hungry. **Crown, 1966. 224p.**

Yom Kippur is the setting for a death that may be murder or suicide.

Sunday the Rabbi Stayed Home. **Putnam, 1969. 253p.**

College students home for Passover have problems with drugs and race relations. Rabbi Small's job is at risk.

Monday the Rabbi Took Off. **Putnam, 1972. 288p.**

The Rabbi solves a murder while on a trip to Israel.

Tuesday the Rabbi Saw Red. **Fields, 1973. 272p.**

Rabbi Small helps solve a murder when he teaches at a Christian college.

Wednesday the Rabbi Got Wet. **Morrow, 1976. 312p.**

A member of the congregation is murdered, and the Rabbi and the Board of Trustees struggle over matters of principle.

Thursday the Rabbi Walked Out. **Morrow, 1978. 250p.**

When a well-known anti-Semite is murdered, members of the congregation are suspects.

Conversations with Rabbi Small. **Morrow, 1981. 276p.**

The Rabbi counsels a young couple on marriage and conversion.

Someday the Rabbi Will Leave. **Morrow, 1985. 264p.**

Corrupt politicians, a hit-and-run killing, and contentious synagogue factions provide work for Rabbi Small.

One Fine Day the Rabbi Bought a Cross. **Morrow, 1987. 234p.**

On a vacation in Israel, Rabbi Small is involved with a Jewish fundamentalist charged with murder.

The Day the Rabbi Resigned. **Fawcett, 1992. 273p.**

Rabbi Small gives serious consideration to leaving his congregation, but first he helps solve the mystery of a local professor's death.

That Day the Rabbi Left Town. **Fawcett, 1996. 245p.**

Rabbi Small retires and becomes a college professor, and helps solve a murder at the college.

Related Titles: Kemelman won an Edgar for the first book in the series. His earlier Nicky Welt stories, which are not Jewish in subject matter, are collected in *The Nine-Mile Walk.*

Krich, Rochelle

Till Death Do Us Part. **Avon, 1992. 290p.**

Deena's egocentric husband Jake won't give her a Jewish divorce—a *get*—although he's dating another woman. Since Jewish law requires that Jake must initiate the divorce, Deena feels trapped until Jake is unexpectedly killed. The police view her as a suspect, while Deena knows she could be the next victim. (The author's Web site is www.rochellekrich. com.)

Themes: divorce; Orthodox Jews

Related Titles: Elise Katch's husband wanted a *get* when they were divorced; her account of that process and what it meant to her can be found in *The Get: A Spiritual Memoir of a Divorce*, annotated in the "Spiritual Autobiographies" section of chapter 8.

Krich, Rochelle

Molly Blume Mysteries.

Molly Blume is a freelance Los Angeles crime reporter and Orthodox Jew who goes her own way in her personal and professional life, while cherishing her observant lifestyle and her large, close-knit family. She's also trying to decide whether to resume a relationship with an old boyfriend, now a rabbi. (The author's Web site is www.rochellekrich.com.)

Themes: journalists; Orthodox Jews

Blues in the Night. **Ballantine Books, 2002. 337p.**

A newspaper story about the victim of a hit-and-run accident, out on Mulholland Drive late at night in her nightgown, makes Molly suspicious. After interviewing the victim, the situation seems even more ambiguous.

Dream House. **Ballantine Books, 2003. 400p.**

Historic preservation issues cause a flare-up of tempers and acts of vandalism in a ritzy Hollywood neighborhood; when Molly investigates it looks like one of her articles results in the death of an old man and the disappearance of his daughter.

Related Titles: Krich has written another series, about a woman police detective, Jessica Drake, who discovers that she is Jewish during the course of the series. The series is annotated in the "Police Procedurals" section of this chapter.

Raphael, Lev

Nick Hoffman Mysteries.

Nick Hoffman and his partner Stefan Borowski teach at a large university in Michigan, where the politics of tenure and advancement are literally, murder. Both Nick and Stefan are Jewish, and although their feelings toward Judaism are fraught with issues from childhood, they enjoy some of the rituals, like celebrating Shabbat with Stefan's family. Nick's witty and cynical comments on academic life provide a constant thread of humor, and the crises of Nick's personal life are often as important as the crime. (The author's Web site is www.levraphael.com,)

Themes: gays/lesbians/bisexuals; universities and colleges

Let's Get Criminal. **St. Martin's, 1996. 212p.**

Nick is a suspect when his office mate is murdered.

The Edith Wharton Murders. **St. Martin's, 1997. 227p.**

In an effort to bolster his bid for tenure, Nick organizes a conference on campus, but a murder provides the wrong kind of publicity.

Death of a Constant Lover. **Walker, 1999. 276p.**

Nick is a spectator at a melee on campus in which one of his students is murdered.

Little Miss Evil. **Walker, 2000. 184p.**

A controversial faculty appointment has everyone in Nick's department upset, but someone is angry enough to commit murder.

Burning Down the House. **Walker, 2001. 290p.**

Nick still doesn't have tenure, his personal life is in disarray, and murder threats pose other complications.

Related Titles: Raphael has also written a short story collection, *Dancing on Tisha B'Av,* and a coming of age novel, *Winter Eyes.* These titles are annotated in the "Character" section of chapter 6. His collection of autobiographical essays, *Journeys and Arrivals: On Being Gay and Jewish,* is annotated in the "Childhood and Family" section of chapter 8.

Rawlings, Ellen

Rachel Crowne Mysteries.

Rachel Crowne, twice divorced and still in her thirties, is a Jewish investigative reporter living in suburban Maryland who stumbles into murderous situations as a result of her work. She's also on the lookout for a new guy, ideally one with "two little kids and a housekeeper."

Themes: journalists; single women

The Murder Lover. **Fawcett Gold Medal, 1997. 246p.**

A young woman is brutally murdered in her own driveway, the first of a series of murders. Rachel suspects a local white supremacist group.

Deadly Harvest. **Fawcett Gold Medal, 1997. 234p.**

Rachel interviews a special education teacher, and the next day, Dilly Friedman is murdered, the target of someone who wants to eliminate a group of six college friends.

Steinberg, Janice

Death in a City of Mystics. **Berkley Prime Crime, 1998. 268p.**

Margo Simon's mother Alice has been studying kabbalah (mysticism) in Safed, Israel, with a charismatic teacher, when she is poisoned. Cultural and religious differences make it hard for Margo to sort out fact from opinion, and a murder at the communal celebration of Lag ba-Omer complicates matters further. The interaction of the well-drawn characters and the unusual setting in a religious community differentiate this mystery.

Themes: Americans in Israel; kabbalah; mothers and daughters

Related Titles: Earlier books in this series find Margo solving crimes in southern California, but none of these earlier mysteries have Jewish themes.

Telushkin, Joseph

Rabbi Daniel Winter Mysteries.

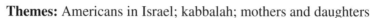

Daniel Winter, rabbi of a large synagogue in Los Angeles, takes on murder and moral issues in these mysteries.

Themes: rabbi detectives; synagogue life

The Unorthodox Murder of Rabbi Wahl. **Bantam, 1987. 180p.**

Janet Wahl, a Reform rabbi and ardent feminist, has offended several people, one of whom may have murdered her after an appearance on Rabbi Winter's radio call-in show.

The Final Analysis of Dr. Stark. **Bantam, 1988. 212p.**

Winter's good friend, psychiatrist Noah Stark, is murdered in his office, and there are too many people with motive and opportunity.

An Eye For an Eye. **Doubleday, 1991. 259p.**

When the daughter of one of Rabbi Winter's congregants is brutally murdered, and the murderer gets off with a light sentence, the girl's outraged father shoots the murderer. An investigation of the Jewish concepts of justice and revenge.

Related Titles: Telushkin is well known for his nonfiction works about Judaism, including *Jewish Wisdom* and *Jewish Literacy*.

Yaffe, James

Mom Mysteries. **YA**

When Dave becomes a widower, he relocates from New York City to a small town in Colorado. His Mom comes too, so she can make sure he is eating properly and help him solve his murder cases. Mom's armchair detective skills are considerable, her insights into human nature right on target, and her roast chicken is delicious.

Themes: cozies; mother and son detectives

A Nice Murder for Mom. **St. Martin's, 1988. 216p.**

>Mom comes for her first visit and helps solve a mystery at the local college.

Mom Meets Her Maker. **St. Martin's, 1990. 249p.**

>Mom helps solve the murder of a much-loved local minister.

Mom Doth Murder Sleep. **St. Martin's, 1991. 230p.**
Mom Among the Liars. **St. Martin's Press, 1992. 218p.**

>The murder of a prostitute has political ramifications.

My Mother the Detective: The Complete "Mom" Short Stories. **Crippen and Landru, 1977. 174p.**

>A collection of the Mom stories originally published in *Ellery Queen's Mystery Magazine.*

Humorous Mysteries

Isaacs, Susan

Judith Singer Mysteries.

>Judith Singer lives on Long Island's North Shore, where her perceptive and funny comments on the lives of men and women enliven these two mysteries. (The author's Web site is www.susanisaacs.com.)

>**Themes:** Long Island, N.Y.; women's lives

Compromising Positions. **Times Books, 1978. 347p.**

>When dentist Marvin Fleckstein is murdered in his office, Judith wonders what he could have done to deserve his fate. Investigating the murder is more interesting than carpooling and arranging play dates for the children, but the consequences endanger her life and marriage.

Long Time No See. **HarperCollins, 2001. 368p.**

>Twenty years later, a widow with a Ph.D. and a college teaching job, Judith still can't resist investigating the murder of a neighbor, even if it involves her with the Mob.

>**Related Titles:** Readers who like Isaacs's particular blend of savvy women and perceptive humor about women's lives may also enjoy her novels *Close Relations,* annotated in chapter 5, or *Lily White,* annotated in the "Legal Thrillers" section of this chapter. Jane Heller also creates Jewish heroines notable for their sass. Readers may enjoy her novels *Cha Cha Cha, Sis Boom Bah,* or *Female Intelligence,* among others.

Kahn, Sharon

Ruby the Rabbi's Wife Mysteries. `YA`

>**Themes:** cozies; rabbis' wives; synagogue life; Texas

>Eternal, Texas, is the setting for mysteries featuring Ruby Rothman, the widow of a rabbi. Stories combine crime with synagogue politics and traditional Jewish foods. Ruby is a self-possessed, perceptive, and independent woman; these character-driven

stories combine humor and insight. (The author's Web site is www. sharonkahn.com.)

Fax Me a Bagel. **Scribner, 1998. 255p.**

Ruby takes on the role of amateur sleuth when the sister of a board member at Temple Rita is poisoned at the bagel shop.

Never Nosh a Matzo Ball. **Scribner, 2000. 300p.**

Lethal matzo balls, an amorous rabbi, and part ownership of the Hot Bagel bakery keep Ruby busy.

Don't Cry for Me, Hot Pastrami. **Scribner, 2001. 298p.**

Ruby finds murder and romance on the Temple Rita-sponsored Caribbean cruise.

Hold the Cream Cheese, Kill the Lox. **Scribner, 2002. 290p.**

Ruby investigates the murder of Herman Guenther, an elderly lox cutter, whose history goes back to Nazi-occupied Denmark.

Related Titles: Readers who enjoy a light touch and a female sleuth may also enjoy the humorous mysteries featuring pharmacist Ruthie Kantor Morris, by Renee B. Horowitz, *Rx for Murder* and *Deadly Rx,* or the <u>Bad Hair Day Mysteries</u> written by Nancy J. Cohen—*Permed to Death*, *Hair Raiser*, *Murder by Manicure*, and *Body Wave*—with Florida hairdresser Marla Shore.

Piesman, Marissa

<u>Nina Fischman Mysteries.</u>

Themes: lawyer detectives; New York City; single women

Nina is a lawyer from New York's Upper West Side, a thirty-something in search of the perfect husband with a sharp eye for the details of the Jewish singles scene. There's always a murder, but it takes second place to the hilarious social commentary, whether it's about a Fire Island summer share or a blind date.

Unorthodox Practices. **Pocket Books, 1989. 222p.**

Nina investigates the murder of two elderly women who lived in desirable apartments, and ponders her attraction to an Orthodox prosecutor.

Personal Effects. **Pocket Books, 1991. 216p.**

When a psychopath murders her oldest friend, Nina puts her life at risk to hunt him down.

Heading Uptown. **Delacorte, 1993. 247p.**

Nina is named executor of the estate of one of her mother's friends, but a murder complicates the settlement.

Close Quarters. **Delacorte, 1994. 247p.**

One of Nina's housemates on Fire Island is killed, and Nina's new boyfriend is a suspect.

Alternate Sides. **Delacorte, 1995. 248p.**

The expression "parking problems" takes on a new meaning, when the doorman is murdered while moving Nina's boyfriend's car.

Survival Instincts. **Delacorte, 1997. 216p.**

Nina goes undercover to clear her brother-in-law of murder, while she tries to put her own life in order after losing her boyfriend.

Related Titles: The last Nina Fischman mystery was published in 1997. Readers who miss Nina's smart, funny voice may enjoy Nora Ephron's novel *Heartburn*, annotated in the "Language" section of chapter 6, or novels by Jane Heller, including *Sis Boom Bah*, *Crystal Clear*, and *Cha Cha Cha*.

Rosen, Dorothy, and Sidney Rosen
Belle Appleman Mysteries. YA

The time is the 1930s in Boston; Depression-era economics and politics serve to fuel the plots of these cozies filled with Yiddish expressions and syntax. An attractive, young widow, Belle is on the lookout for a good job and a good Jewish man, but her curiosity about crime brings trouble.

Themes: Boston; cozies; 1930s; widows

Death and Blintzes. **Academy Chicago, 1985. 174p.**

Belle makes her first appearance as a thirty-six-year-old widow tacking belt loops onto men's pants at the Classic Clothing Company in Boston. When Jeannette, the attractive shop steward, is found murdered, Belle takes over her union position and sets out to find the murderer.

Death and Strudel. **Academy Chicago, 2000. 272p.**

Belle is working in a pharmacy where her detective skills uncover blackmail, murder, and illegal abortions.

Stevens, Serita, and Rayanne Moore
Fanny Zindel Mysteries. YA

Widow and grandmother Fanny Zindel enjoys her trips to Israel and England, but solving murders takes precedence over sightseeing. (Serita Stevens's Web site is www.earthlink.net/~seritas/serita.htm.)

Themes: Americans in Israel; granddaughters; grandmothers

Red Sea, Dead Sea. **St. Martin's, 1993. 214p.**

Fanny accidentally becomes a courier on a trip to Israel, with almost deadly consequences for her beloved granddaughter Susan, but she does get to meet the suave Nathan, a retired Mossad officer.

Bagels for Tea. **St. Martin's, 1993. 264p.**

There's a murder at Susan's English boarding school, and Susan becomes a suspect. Anti-Semitism surfaces and more murders are committed, but Fanny and Nathan help Susan find the murderer.

Related Titles: Young adults who enjoy this series may also want to read the Vivi Hartman mysteries by Harriet K. Feder, starting with *Mystery in Miami Beach*.

Waldman, Ayelet

Mommy Track Mysteries.

Juliet Applebaum reluctantly gave up her dream job as a public defender in Los Angeles to be a stay-at-home mom. The stress and tedium of mothering her lovable but demanding tots, Ruby and Isaac, are relieved by encounters with murder and mayhem. Juliet's lively intelligence and hilarious, unsentimental observations about motherhood and marriage enhance the entertaining, fast-paced stories. (Juliet is supported by her high-powered screenwriter husband Peter; in real life, Ayelet Waldman's husband is best-selling author Michael Chabon. Her Web site is www.ayeletwaldman.com.)

Themes: lawyer detectives; Los Angeles, California; mothers; parents and children

Nursery Crimes. **Berkley, 2000. 215p.**

After Juliet's daughter Ruby is interviewed (and rejected!) by Holly-wood's best preschool, the principal is killed, and Juliet thinks she knows who did it.

The Big Nap. **Berkley, 2001. 227p.**

When babysitter Fraydle Finkelstein vanishes, Juliet takes the children with her to a Hasidic community in Brooklyn to investigate the family of Fraydle's fiancé.

A Playdate with Death. **Berkley Prime Crime, 2002. 229p.**

The police think Juliet's trainer committed suicide, but those close to him believe otherwise, prompting Juliet to probe into his complicated private life.

Death Gets a Time Out. **Berkley Prime Crime, 2003. 314p.**

Juliet is asked by a friend to help her brother, who is accused of raping his stepmother.

Related Titles: In 2003, Waldman published a nonseries title, *Daughter's Keeper*, about a middle-class woman whose pregnant daughter faces prison for her involvement in a drug deal.

Private Investigators

The earliest literary private investigators date to the 1920s. Dashiell Hammett and Raymond Chandler were among the writers who set the characteristics of this subgenre with their hard-boiled mysteries. Many modern PIs are now women and come from every walk of life, ethnicity, and social strata. But they are still mainly the independent, cynical loners, un-fazed by their often-violent profession that we have come to expect from novels, television, and the movies. Unlike the amateur detective, whose foray into detecting could be a one-time experience, private investigators, whose livelihood depends on solving crimes, make great series protagonists. As in so much contemporary genre fiction, character is paramount. Private eyes often have unusual, complicated personal lives that resonate in their cases and make readers eager for the next installment. The lines between personal and professional life may be blurred, as in Zachary Klein's series about the dissipated and depressed Matt Jacob. Cases may take the investigator to exotic locations, as in Reggie Nadelson's series about Artie Cohen, the Russian American detective. Investigators may stray across legal limits, putting their licenses in jeopardy. They all share that characteristic drive to solve the puzzle, to clear up the mystery, to see justice done. As Archie Goodwin, Nero Wolfe's sidekick, noted in the mystery *Some Buried Caesar:* "A detective who minds his own business would be a contradiction in terms."[3]

Black, Cara

Murder in the Marais. **Soho Press, 1999. 354p.**

Aimee LeDuc receives a request from the Jewish community in Paris to decipher an encrypted photograph that puts her in the middle of an ugly murder case going back to Nazi collaborators in World War II. All of her ingenuity is required to solve the case and stay alive in this atmospheric and violent debut mystery. (The author's Web site is www.carablack.com.)

Themes: Holocaust—survivors; World War II—Collaboration

Related Titles: This is the first in a series that continues with *Murder in Belleville* and *Murder in the Sentier.*

Klein, Zachary

No Saving Grace. **Fawcett Columbine, 1993. 322p.**

When a white supremacist group kills a beloved Hasidic rabbi, one of the Rabbi's followers strikes back. Matt Jacob, depressed and drugged out after the death of his wife and child, investigates the hatred on both sides.

Themes: hard-boiled mysteries; Hasidism; hate crimes; rabbis

Related Titles: Two other mysteries in this series, *Still Among the Living* and *Two Way Toll,* feature this down-and-out and very assimilated detective.

Nadelson, Reggie

Artie Cohen Mysteries.

Artie Cohen came to the United States from Russia via Israel when he was nineteen and joined the New York City police force. In these hardboiled mysteries he's left the NYPD and works alone on some very violent cases, often involving other immigrants.

Themes: hard-boiled mysteries; Russian Americans

Red Hot Blues. **St. Martin's, 1995. 264p.**

When a former KGB general, an old family friend, is assassinated on U.S. television, Artie returns to Russia to track the killer and unravel the mysteries in his own past.

Hot Poppies. **St. Martin's, 1997. 240p.**

Artie tracks the killer of a Chinese girl murdered in a Hasidic diamond merchant's office.

Bloody London. **St. Martin's/Thomas Dunne Books, 1999. 308p.**

The Russian Mafia menaces a decadent, rain-soaked London.

Paretsky, Sara

Total Recall: A V. I. Warshawski Novel. **Delacorte, 2001. 414p.**

In an effort to validate the identity of a Holocaust survivor, V. I. is drawn into a web of murder, guilt, and recriminations that involves her friend Lotty Herschel, a survivor with painful memories. Issues of recovered memory, Holocaust assets, and insurance fraud become a volatile and murderous mix in the only title in this series to focus on Jewish issues. (Paretsky's Web site is www.saraparetsky.com.)

Themes: Holocaust—survivors; insurance fraud; recovered memory

Related Titles: Warshawski, a former attorney turned private investigator, is Italian-Jewish on her mother's side; the only link to Judaism in the other mysteries in this popular series is through V. I.'s friend Lotty Herschel.

Siegel, James

Epitaph. **Mysterious Press, 2001. 307p.**

When William Riskin, retired private investigator, attends the funeral of his enigmatic former partner, he learns that Jean was still working on a case when he died. Riskin wants to finish the case for him, but Jean's cryptic notes are dead ends until Riskin realizes the personal and tragic nature of the mystery.

Themes: elderly men; Holocaust—survivors; Queens, N.Y.

Simon, Roger L.

Raising the Dead. **Villard Books, 1988. 228p.**

Moses Wine, a cynical LA private eye, Jewish in name only, finds himself working for an Arab organization and infiltrating a militant Jewish group in search of a murderer. He travels to Israel, where irrational factions on both sides threaten the peace negotiations and Wine's life. (The author's Web site is www.rogerlsimon.com.)

Themes: hard-boiled mysteries; hate crimes; Jewish–Arab relations

Related Titles: *Raising the Dead* is the sixth in the <u>Moses Wine</u> series, but the first one in which the detective faces Jewish issues. The most

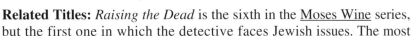

recent, *Director's Cut* (2003), has Wine providing security on a movie set in Prague where Arab terrorists and anti-Semitism make a volatile mix.

Police Procedurals

Police detectives are rarely as glamorous as their private eye counterparts, but the appeal of this subgenre is in the working of a team in a logical, legal, scientific way to solve a crime. Most of these mysteries feature a protagonist who is at odds in some way with his or her superiors, someone who is not quite comfortable with authority, or who encounters discrimination within the organization. Zack Tobias, the police detective in *Strangers at the Gate,* is independently wealthy and well connected to the power elite in San Francisco, much to the dismay of his boss. Jessie Drake, the policewoman in the series by Rochelle Krich, is often hindered in her work by her male colleagues' attitudes toward women. Noah Green, the detective in Nat Hentoff's series, is suspected by Internal Affairs of drug dealing. Since police procedurals are realistic, characters may be involved in more than one case at a time; sometimes characters or situations are carried over into the next title in the series. There is a strong sense of place in these novels, often urban. Abe Lieberman's Chicago, Avram Cohen's Jerusalem, and Noah Green's New York are vividly depicted.

Gordon, Dan
Just Play Dead. St. Martin's, 1997. 227p.

Dani Kahane, the only Jewish cop on the Hawaii police force, watches as Nora Wolfe and her lover Chad plan to kill Nora's rich husband for his insurance money. Dani's wisecracking exterior can't hide the fact that he loves Nora despite her penchant for manipulating everyone around her.

Themes: adultery; hard-boiled mysteries; Hawaii; murder and murderers

Gross, Leonard
Strangers at the Gate. Random House, 1995. 428p.

Zack Tobias, head of the San Francisco police department's Gang Squad, searches for the thugs who attacked popular television journalist Maggie Winehouse, fearful that the political and racial ramifications of this hate crime will forever change his beloved city. Filled with well-drawn characters, especially the empathetic Tobias, whose history and personality drive the plot.

Themes: Asian Americans; 1990s; race relations; San Francisco, California

Related Titles: Gross provides an interesting history of ethnic relations in San Francisco in this novel. He has also written *The Dossier*, coauthored with Pierre Salinger, about an Israeli agent who believes that a French politician was a Gestapo informer during World War II.

Hentoff, Nat
Noah Green Mysteries.

Noah Green works out of the police precinct that serves New York's Alphabet City; in the 1980s it was a grim, drug-infested neighborhood. He tries to do the right thing on the job and in his personal life, but sometimes justice needs a helping hand. (Hentoff is mainly known for his jazz essays and liner notes, and his social commentary in the *Village Voice* newspaper, but these hard-boiled mysteries are no less deserving of note.)

Themes: drug abuse; hard-boiled mysteries; New York City

Blues for Charlie Darwin. **Morrow, 1982. 203p.**
The Man from Internal Affairs. **Mysterious Press, 1985. 215p.**

An anonymous tip has the Internal Affairs Department watching Noah's every move.

Related Titles: Jerome Charyn's mystery series featuring Isaac Sidel, the Jewish police detective, may appeal to readers who enjoy Hentoff's portrayal of the down-and-out, seamy side of urban life. The first title in that series is *Blue Eyes*.

Kaminsky, Stuart

Abe Lieberman Mysteries.

Lieberman is a tough, principled, compassionate, aging cop who isn't above pushing the limits of the law to make things work out right. His Irish partner, Bill Hanrahan, is an alcoholic, and Abe often covers for him. Together, the Rabbi and the Priest, as they are called, work the seamy side of the Chicago crime scene. Lieberman's family life is not easy: his only daughter makes a mess of her marriages, Abe's beloved older brother suffers from depression after his son's death, and the local synagogue pressures Abe to take on responsibilities. Major and minor characters are well developed in this series, and there are several ongoing subplots. (The author's Web site is www.stuartkaminsky.com.)

Themes: Chicago; family relationships

Lieberman's Folly. **St. Martin's, 1991. 216p.**

A prostitute's request for help leads down a ten-year-old murder trail.

Lieberman's Choice. **St. Martin's, 1993. 216p.**

Lieberman negotiates with a rogue cop on a Chicago rooftop.

Lieberman's Day. **Holt, 1994. 260p.**

Abe and Bill have a grueling twenty-four hours that starts with the death of Lieberman's nephew.

Lieberman's Thief. **Holt, 1995. 238p.**

A complicated robbery and murder case.

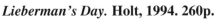

Lieberman's Law. **Holt, 1996. 309p.**

Neo-Nazi skinheads and Arab extremist groups desecrate local synagogues.

Big Silence. **Forge, 2000. 268p.**

Abe has a host of personal and professional crises, as his daughter leaves her second husband and moves back home, a member of Abe's synagogue

is involved in murder, and a key witness is killed before testifying at a mobster's trial.

Not Quite Kosher. **Forge, 2002. 254p.**

Bumbling thieves and two bodies washed up on the shore occupy Abe and Bill, as well as wedding and bar mitzvah preparations.

Related Titles: Kaminsky is a prolific mystery writer, with three more popular series to his credit: the Toby Peters series, which is set in Hollywood in the 1930s and 1940s and includes historical characters; a series about the Russian policeman Porfiry Rostnikov; and a series featuring the process server, Lew Fonseca.

Kellerman, Faye

Peter Decker/Rina Lazarus Mysteries

Kellerman's series offers an empathetic look at the life of a modern Orthodox woman who cherishes her observant lifestyle. As we become more involved with the characters' lives, we also learn about Orthodox Judaism. Despite the religious setting, these mysteries are far from sedate and are filled with graphic sex and violence.

Themes: conversion to Judaism; husband-and wife-detectives; Orthodox Jews

Ritual Bath. **Fawcett, 1986. 277p.**

Rina Lazarus is a widow living in an Orthodox Jewish enclave in Los Angeles. She meets police lieutenant Peter Decker when he is called in after a woman in the community is raped. Despite the differences in their backgrounds, a romance flourishes between them.

Sacred and Profane. **Arbor House, 1987. 311p.**

Peter takes Rina's sons camping and they discover evidence of a brutal murder with connections to the pornographic film industry. Peter and Rina's relationship deepens as Peter studies to become a convert.

Milk and Honey. **Morrow, 1990. 384p.**

While Rina is considering Peter's marriage proposal, Peter becomes involved in a quadruple murder investigation.

Day of Atonement. **Morrow, 1991. 359p.**

When Peter and Rina honeymoon in Brooklyn, they are caught up in the problems of a rebellious Orthodox teenager kidnapped by a psychopath.

False Prophet. **Morrow, 1992. 367p.**

Peter investigates rape and murder at an exclusive spa, while Rina suffers through a difficult pregnancy.

Grievous Sin. **Morrow, 1993. 368p.**

Peter is involved in a baby kidnapping from the same hospital where Rina delivers her baby girl.

Sanctuary. **Morrow, 1994. 396p.**

An old friend of Rina's is caught up in a series of murders involving the international diamond trade.

Justice. **Morrow, 1995. 388p.**

A high school prom queen is found murdered, and one of the suspects is an unusual student musician.

Prayers for the Dead. **Morrow, 1996. 406p.**

The murder of a heart surgeon involves Peter and Rina in the religious and sexual secrets of a troubled family.

Serpent's Tooth. **Morrow, 1997. 400p.**

A trendy Los Angeles restaurant is the scene for multiple murder, as Peter puts his job on the line to solve the case while Rina investigates on her own.

Jupiter's Bones. **Morrow, 1999. 375p.**

Rina's son Jacob experiments with sex and drugs while Peter tries to solve the murder of a cult guru and former astrophysicist.

Stalker. **Morrow, 2000. 406p.**

As a new cop on the Los Angeles police force, Peter's daughter Cindy is working hard to find her own way.

The Forgotten. **Morrow, 2001. 374p.**

When Rina's small Orthodox synagogue is vandalized, Peter's investigation draws him and his stepson Jacob into a world of troubled teenagers, hate crimes, and psychological charlatans.

Stone Kiss. **Warner, 2002. 416p.**

Rina and Peter investigate the murder of Peter's half-brother, Rabbi Jonathan Levin.

Street Dreams. **Warner, 2003. 400p.**

Cindy's life is endangered when she tries to find the mother of an abandoned baby.

Related Titles: Kellerman has also written an historical romance, *The Quality of Mercy*, set in Elizabethan England, annotated in chapter 5.

Kellerman, Jonathan

The Butcher's Theater. **Bantam, 1988. 628p.**

Daniel Sharavi, a chief inspector in the Israeli police force and an observant Jew, is called on to solve a series of grisly murders. Current political issues are combined with a study of the psychopathic mind in a tense and violent story.

Themes: doctors; Jerusalem; serial murders

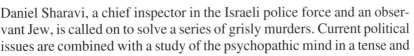

Related Titles: Daniel Sharavi makes an appearance in another of Kellerman's books, *Survival of the Fittest*, where he helps solve the murder of an Israeli diplomat's daughter in the United States. That title is part of Kellerman's <u>Alex Delaware</u> series.

Krich, Rochelle

Jessica Drake Mysteries.

Jessie Drake, an LA homicide detective, has a complicated life on and off the police force. She works well with her detective partner Phil but encounters discrimination on the job. Each story takes on a topical social problem. As the series unfolds Jessie discovers she is Jewish and begins to study with a teacher. Jessie's compassion and thoughtfulness distinguish this traditional police procedural, and graphic violence is kept to a minimum. (The author's Web site is www.rochellekrich.com.)

Themes: Los Angeles, California; social problems

Fair Game. **Mysterious Press, 1993. 342p.**

Jessie searches for a serial killer while she wrestles with a legacy of child abuse.

Angel of Death. **Mysterious Press, 1994. 372p.**

A group of neo-Nazis wants to march in a Jewish neighborhood. Jessie's mother reveals her own Jewish background to her daughters.

Blood Money. **Avon Twilight, 1999. 341p.**

Elderly Holocaust survivors' assets in Swiss accounts are threatened, and Jessie presses her mother for information about relatives who perished in the Holocaust.

Dead Air. **Avon, 2000. 336p.**

A childhood friend, now a radio psychologist, comes to Jessie for help in dealing with a stalker. Jessie tries to sort out her relationship with her former husband Gary and begins to study Judaism seriously.

Shadows of Sin. **Morrow, 2001. 337p.**

Jessie enlists the help of Ezra, her Jewish studies teacher, in dealing with an ultra-Orthodox sect that may be harboring a killer.

Related Titles: Krich has a second series, about crime reporter Molly Blume, annotated in the "Amateur Detectives" section of this chapter.

Rosenberg, Robert

Avram Cohen Mystery Quartet.

Avram Cohen, head of the Criminal Investigations Department of the Jerusalem police, a concentration camp survivor, and weary of the years of war and negotiations, works on the most heinous crimes in the Holy City. These are tensely plotted mysteries with the cynical, bad-tempered Cohen and the high drama of Israeli politics adding to the atmosphere. (Rosenberg's Web site is www.ariga.com/cohen/.)

Themes: hard-boiled mysteries; Holocaust—survivors; Jerusalem

***Crimes of the City.* Simon & Schuster, 1991. 288p.**

In the midst of the Intifada, Cohen tracks the ruthless killer of two Russian nuns. Based on a true crime.

***The Cutting Room.* Simon & Schuster, 1993. 298p.**

Cohen goes to Hollywood to solve the murder of a director found dead in the editing room.

***House of Guilt.* Scribner, 1996. 288p.**

Although retired, Cohen is pressured to investigate the disappearance of a powerful banker's grandson.

***An Accidental Murder* . Scribner, 1999. 283p.**

Cohen attends the Frankfurt Book Fair to promote his autobiography, but when a bomb is planted in his hotel room and a colleague is killed, he must look into his past for an explanation.

Related Titles: Readers may also enjoy the mysteries by the Israeli author Batya Gur featuring the cerebral Israeli police detective Michael Ohayon.

Historical Mysteries

The mysteries in this subgenre share one characteristic: the attempt to bring to life an earlier time. For example, Richard Parrish, writing about Tucson in the 1940s and 1950s, allows us to see how the city's growth was affected by political and social issues of the period. Parrish's intent is clearly to bring an era and a place to life. The characters in historical mysteries are often caught up in well-known historical events.

In a good historical mystery, the characters fit comfortably into the background created by the author's research, and the period comes alive for the reader. Sometimes historical characters make an appearance. The <u>Dutchman</u> series by Maan Meyers involves characters from the major events of American history, from colonial times through the Civil War. In Andrew Bergman's <u>Jack LeVine</u> series, we meet, among others, conductor Arturo Toscanini and gangster Meyer Lansky.

For some readers, learning about a little-known aspect of history while also enjoying the unraveling of a mystery offers great appeal. In David Liss's *Conspiracy of Paper*, we learn, alongside Benjamin Weaver, about the origins of stock market speculation. The precarious position of Jews in Europe in the twelfth century is the basis for Sharan Newman's series, which features the protagonist Catherine LeVendeur.

Although their settings are historical, the emphasis of the novels in this section is mystery; readers who enjoy historical settings should look for additional titles in chapter 3.

Baron, Aileen Garsson

A Fly Has a Hundred Eyes. **Academy Chicago, 2002. 277p.**

In 1938, while the British, Arabs, Jews, and Nazis are fighting for control over Palestine, Lily Sampson, an American archaeologist, searches for the murderer of a fellow archaeologist from the teeming alleys in the Old City of Jerusalem to rural Arab villages in the north. A fast-paced mystery with a tenacious heroine, full of intrigue, and a thoroughly detailed and atmospheric setting.

Themes: archaeologists; Jerusalem; Jewish–Arab relations; Palestine—History

Related Titles: Readers who enjoyed the strong sense of place in this novel may also like Jonathan Wilson's *The Hiding Place*, a literary novel set in post-World War II Palestine with elements of a mystery.

Bergman, Andrew

Jack LeVine Mysteries. `YA`

Bergman was one of the first authors to set mysteries in the recent past and include historical figures. LeVine is a very assimilated Jew, but his cases feature some Jewish characters and settings. The stories parody the hard-boiled mystery genre.

Themes: celebrity mysteries; 1950s; 1940s

The Big Kiss-off of 1944. **Holt, Rinehart & Winston, 1974. 194p.**

LeVine is asked to recover some stag films, but soon finds himself involved in the Roosevelt–Dewey presidential race.

Hollywood and LeVine. **Holt, 1975. 216p.**

LeVine is called on to investigate a murder in Hollywood during the era of the Communist witch hunts.

Tender Is LeVine. **Minotaur, 2001. 289p.**

LeVine learns about a scheme to kidnap the conductor Arturo Toscanini and force NBC to pay millions in ransom. Tracking down the maestro involves outwitting mobsters like Meyer Lansky and Lucky Luciano.

Related Titles: Other light celebrity mysteries, but with minimal Jewish content, are the Groucho mysteries by Ron Goulart, starting with *Elementary My Dear Groucho;* the mysteries written by Ed Koch and Herbert Resnicow, starting with *Murder at City Hall;* and *O Jerusalem: A Mary Russell Novel,* by Laurie King, part of her series pairing Sherlock Holmes with a young woman assistant. Readers of *Tender is LeVine*, who are interested in the lives of Jewish gangsters, may enjoy *Little Man: Meyer Lansky and the Gangster Life* by Robert Lacey, annotated in the "Public Lives" section of chapter 8. *Tough Jews: Fathers, Sons, and Gangster Dreams* by Rich Cohen, about small-time Jewish gangsters, is annotated in the "Collected Biography" section of chapter 8.

Liss, David

Conspiracy of Paper. **Random House, 2000. 442p.** 📖

Benjamin Weaver, a Jew living in London in the eighteenth century, works as a private investigator and bodyguard. He uses his boxing and deductive skills to unravel several murders, including one in his own family. A brutal, fast-paced look at the London criminal underworld, the beginnings of stock speculation, and the status of Jews in eighteenth-century England. (Liss won an Edgar Award from the Mystery Writers of America for this novel. His Web site is www.davidliss.com.)

Themes: anti-Semitism; stock market

Related Titles: In Liss's second novel, *The Coffee Trader*, a Jewish merchant is involved in the shady side of the coffee bean market. It is annotated in the "Dark Ages Through Early Modern History" section of chapter 3. Weaver reappears in Liss's third novel, *A Spectacle of Corruption*, published in 2004. Another historical novel with elements of mystery and intrigue is *The Last Kabbalist of Lisbon*, by Richard Zimler, set in the early sixteenth century, annotated in the same section of chapter 3. Noah Gordon's *The Physician* may be of interest to readers who enjoyed this novel's underworld setting. *Café Berlin* by Harold Nebenzal, annotated in the "Fiction" section of chapter 7, is a novel that will appeal to readers who like empathetic characters with a taste for danger.

Meyers, Maan

The Dutchman Mysteries.

This series follows the Tonneman family for a period of 200 years, starting with Pieter Tonneman, sheriff of New Amsterdam, in the 1660s. Not every book in the series has significant Jewish content. The novels often contain historical figures, and the characters are well drawn. (Maan Meyers is a pseudonym for Martin Meyers and Annette Meyers, who have written mysteries individually. Their Web site is www.meyersmysteries.com/home.html.)

Themes: New York City; sheriffs

The Dutchman. **Doubleday, 1992. 306p.**

Tonneman tries to solve a murder in the days leading up to the English invasion of New Amsterdam, and he falls in love with Racqel Mendoza, a Sephardic Jew.

The Dutchman's Dilemma. **Bantam, 1995. 254p.**

Tonneman and Racqel are happily married, but Racqel is accused of witchcraft and Tonneman is hired to solve a grisly series of mutilations.

The Kingsbridge Plot. **Doubleday, 1993. 321p.**

On the eve of the American Revolution, physician John Tonneman becomes caught up in politics, falls in love with a Sephardic woman, and hunts for a killer of redheads.

The High Constable. **Doubleday, 1994. 307p.**

During Jefferson's presidency John Tonneman is called on to defend his own son, accused of murder.

The House on Mulberry Street. **Bantam, 1996. 305p.**

In 1895, a Tonneman descendant is involved with Jewish immigrant photographer Esther Breslau.

The Lucifer Contract. **Bantam, 1998. 268p.**

Journalist Pete Tonneman is caught up in a Confederate plot that threatens to turn 1864 New York City into an inferno.

Related Titles: *The Books of Rachel* and *The Lives of Rachel* by Joel Gross are other novels that follow the descendants of one family through the centuries. They are annotated in the "Dark Ages Through Early Modern History" section of chapter 3.

Newman, Sharan

Catherine LeVendeur Mysteries. `YA`

Catherine LeVendeur, a young woman of eighteen, lives in the Convent of the Paraclete at the opening of this series. She is a student of philosophy with an inquiring mind and an unfortunate lack of humility. Her close relationship with her secretly Jewish father and his ongoing ties to the Jewish community provide some of the plotlines and allow Newman to paint a well-researched picture of the complex relationship between the Jewish and Christian communities in medieval Europe. The twelfth century is fully brought to life and peopled with well-known historical characters, including Heloise, Abelard, and Bernard of Clairvaux. (The author's Web site is www.sharan/newman.com.)

Themes: Catholic faith; family relationships; Middle Ages

Death Comes as Epiphany. **Tor, 1993. 319p.**

While trying to clear the convent of a fraudulent charge, Catherine learns that her father was born Jewish, and although baptized for his own safety, never officially converted. This revelation and others change Catherine's life in the course of solving the mystery of the changed psalter.

The Devil's Door. **Forge, 1994. 384p.**
The Wandering Arm. **Forge, 1995. 351p.**

A relic is stolen and a Jewish merchant accused; Catherine and her husband Edgar are caught up in an effort to prevent the entire Jewish community in Paris from reprisals.

Strong As Death. **Forge, 1996. 384p.**
Cursed in the Blood. **Forge, 1998. 348p.**
The Difficult Saint. **Tom Doherty Associates/Forge, 1999. 352p.**

In the midst of deteriorating Jewish–Christian relations in France, Catherine and Edgar must go to Germany to save Catherine's sister Agnes, where anti-Semitism is even worse.

To Wear the White Cloak. **Forge, 2000. 367p.**
Heresy. **Forge, 2002. 352p.**

> **Related Titles:** A well-researched novel about Jews in England during this period is Joanne Greenberg's *The King's Persons*, annotated in the "Dark Ages Through Early Modern History" section of chapter 3.

Parrish, Richard

Joshua Rabb Mysteries.

> When a wounded Joshua Rabb returns from World War II, his wife is dead and he has two children to raise on his own. Starting fresh in Tucson, and working as a lawyer for the Bureau of Indian Affairs, he encounters prejudice against Indians, Jews, "pinkos," and others who are different. Rabb is an ethical lawyer, whose strong sense of morality often puts him and his family in danger in these serious, plot-driven mysteries.

> **Themes:** Arizona; Native Americans; physically handicapped

Dividing Line. **Dutton, 1993. 359p.**

> Shortly after Rabb and his children arrive in Tucson, a nun working with the Papago Indian tribe is murdered.

Versions of the Truth. **Dutton, 1994. 309p.**
Nothing But the Truth. **Dutton, 1995. 292p.**

> Rabb becomes involved with gangsters Meyer Lansky and Joe Bonanno in their war with local thugs, and he defends a Papago man accused of murder.

Defending the Truth. **Onyx, 1998. 410p.**

> Communist witch hunters invade the University of Arizona when an Arizona state official with national political ambitions wants to investigate a group of professors.

Roe, Caroline

Chronicles of Isaac of Girona.

> Isaac, the blind Jewish physician, is well known in fourteenth-century Girona, Spain, for his medical and detecting skills. He is assisted by his daughter Raquel and the Arab boy Yusuf, and worried over by his sharp-tongued wife. His friendship with Bishop Berenguer protects him from anti-Semitic harassment. Isaac's compassion for Jews and non-Jews, and the author's sensitive character portrayals, characterize this well-researched series by a medieval scholar.

> **Themes:** blindness; Canadian authors; doctors; Middle Ages; Spain

Remedy for Treason. **Berkley Prime Crime, 1998. 259p.**

> Isaac is involved in a plot against the Spanish monarchy in the shadow of the plague.

Cure for a Charlatan. **Berkley Prime Crime, 1999. 262p.**

Witchcraft threatens to engulf Girona in the wake of three deaths.

Antidote for Avarice. **Berkley Prime Crime, 1999. 277p.**

Isaac's trip to court with Bishop Berenguer involves him in the search for the murderer of the Pope's messengers.

Solace for a Sinner. **Berkley Prime Crime, 2000. 277p.**

Isaac investigates the murder of a wealthy merchant who thought he had found the Holy Grail.

A Potion for a Widow. **Berkley Prime Crime, 2001. 269p.**

The death of a young cleric sets in motion a chain of events that takes Yusuf to Sardinia.

A Draught for a Dead Man. **Berkley Prime Crime, 2002. 336p.**

A wedding brings Isaac to the house of his old friend Jacob, in Perpignan, and to the assistance of a Christian nobleman.

A Poultice for a Healer. **Berkley Prime Crime, 2003. 320p.**

Related Titles: Canadian author Roe has written another mystery series, set in and around Toronto, under the name Medora Sale.

Thrillers

Thrillers are the books that keep us reading until the small hours of the morning. Fast-paced, suspenseful, and full of action, we just can't put them down. Thriller is an ambiguous term, often applied to any book with adventure and quick pacing. It is a category that ranges over many subgenres: legal, espionage, political, corporate, medical, historical, psychological, technological, military, etc. Joyce Saricks, in *The Readers' Advisory Guide to Genre Fiction*, identifies the basic elements of the thriller: "Basically this genre focuses on a particular profession . . . and tells an action-packed story that reveals the intricacies of that profession and the potential dangers faced by those involved in it."[4] Often there are secrets that drive the plot; information must quickly be obtained before a person, organization, or country will be destroyed. Time is short, and it is urgent that the secrets be uncovered or protected. The reader is drawn in by the increase of tension, which is maintained by violence, and the threat of violence. It is not unusual for thrillers to be hefty, but the best authors build and maintain tension so the reader is oblivious of length. Jewish history, present and past, affords many sources of plot and setting for the thriller writer.

Suspense

These are the novels that make us feel that there's danger lurking all around us, even if we're curled up safe and sound on the sofa. There's no consistency in setting or plot; it's the effect the author has on our emotions that ties these novels together. Readers enjoy suspense novels for the intense anticipation of terror they evoke. Pacing is the key appeal characteristic. A few of these novels feature Nazis as villains, playing on the idea that decades after the

Holocaust, its unimaginable evil persists. *The Shadow Man* by John Katzenbach exploits the frightening idea that Nazis are still hunting Jews, even in sunny Florida. Other suspense novels, like Libby Lazewnik's *The Judge*, prey on our fears for children, whose innocence makes them easy targets for sociopaths.

Abrahams, Peter

The Fury of Rachel Monette. **Macmillan, 1980. 310p.**

> Rachel returns home from work to find her husband dead and her son kidnapped. When the police are unwilling to pursue the leads in her husband's research into French collaboration with the Nazis, she travels to Morocco, Paris, and Israel, literally digging up secrets that threaten the Israeli government, as she repeatedly risks her own life to find her son, in this dark, fast-paced thriller. (The author's Web site is www.peterabrahams.com.)
>
> **Themes:** Holocaust; kidnapping; mothers; World War II—Collaboration

Elkins, Aaron

Loot. **Morrow, 1999. 354p.**

> When a Jewish pawnbroker calls on Ben Revere to identify a painting, Ben is drawn into a network of murder and international crime reaching back to the Nazi theft of Old Masters. Elkins provides interesting details about the art world and the fate of art stolen during World War II. (The author's Web site is www.aaronelkins.com.)
>
> **Themes:** art collectors; Nazi plunder

> **Related Titles:** Elkins is the author of *Turncoat,* another thriller with roots in World War II, about Nazi collaborators and resistance fighters in France. A nonfiction account of the theft of Jewish property during World War II can be found in Richard Z. Chesnoff's *Pack of Thieves: How Hitler and Europe Plundered the Jews and Committed the Greatest Theft in History.*

Kanfer, Stefan

Fear Itself. **Putnam, 1981. 215p.**

> Niccolo Levi, an actor in war-torn Italy, vows revenge on the Nazis for killing his wife and child and also on President Roosevelt for failing to rescue Jews from the Holocaust.
>
> **Themes:** actors and acting; Holocaust—Italy; revenge

> **Related Titles:** Kanfer wrote an earlier novel, *The Eighth Sin,* about the experience of a Gypsy boy who survives the Holocaust and is adopted by a Jewish couple in New York.

Katzenbach, John

The Shadow Man. **Ballantine Books, 1995. 468p.**

> Retired homicide detective Simon Winter is living a quiet life in Florida when his neighbor Sophie Millstein is murdered after seeing *Der*

Schattenmann, a notorious "catcher" for the Nazis and the personification of evil to his victims. Sophie's Holocaust survivor friends fear that they are his next targets and implore Simon to track down the killer.

Themes: Holocaust—survivors; Nazis; serial murders

Krich, Rochelle

Fertile Ground. **Avon, 1998. 342p.**

Problems develop at a prestigious Los Angeles fertility clinic when an egg donor is murdered and the clinic is accused of switching eggs. When one of the doctors disappears, his fiancée, Dr. Lisa Brockman, uncovers a network of fraud. Lisa's work with an Orthodox couple undergoing in vitro fertilization brings into relief her misgivings about her secular lifestyle. (The author's Web site is www. rochellekrich.com.)

Themes: doctors; in vitro fertilization; Orthodox Jews

Related Titles: Readers who enjoy Krich's novels for their thoughtful, empathetic characters should look for her other mysteries and thrillers, annotated in various sections of this chapter.

Lazewnik, Libby

The Judge. **Shaar Press, 2000. 476p.**

Orthodox judge David Newman is trying to live a quiet life with his two teenaged children after his wife's death in a hit-and-run accident five years earlier. An anonymous death threat puts his children at risk from a determined killer, as the tension spirals up to a heart-stopping showdown.

Themes: Internet; kidnapping; murder and murderers; teenagers

Levin, Ira

The Boys from Brazil. **Random House, 1976. 280p.**

Josef Mengele, the infamous Nazi doctor, now living in Brazil, plots to re-create the Third Reich by means of a diabolical medical experiment while the Nazi hunter Yakov Liebermann tries to stop him.

Themes: cloning; Nazi hunters; Nazis

Related Titles: Other novels about the persistence of the Nazi menace after World War II include Harry Patterson's *The Valhalla Exchange*, Robert Fish's *Pursuit*, Ignacio Padilla's *Shadow Without a Name*, and Stan Pottinger's *The Last Nazi*. Readers may also be interested in Robert Harris's *Fatherland*, an alternate history thriller in which the victorious Nazis have erased knowledge of the Holocaust.

Rosenbaum, David

Sasha's Trick. **Mysterious Press, 1995. 387p.**

Sasha, a Russian-Jewish thief, makes the transition from a Soviet prison camp to Brighton Beach, Brooklyn, where his interest in stolen art puts him at odds with the violent Russian Mafia, in this dark and fast-paced portrait of a hustler and survivor.

Themes: art theft; Mafia, Russian; Russian Americans

***Zaddik.* Mysterious Press, 1993. 438p.**

A diamond dealer is brutally killed by a thief looking for a fabled 72-carat stone destined to be the dowry in a wedding uniting two rival Hasidic groups. When Dov Taylor, a former policeman and newly religious, agrees to search for the diamond, he discovers in his own ancestry a link to a great Polish *zaddik*, or sage, with whom he establishes a mystical connection.

Themes: diamonds; Hasidism; Nazis

Related Titles: Although this is a fast-paced thriller in the traditional mold, there is a mystical element in Dov Taylor's connection to his ancestral *zaddik*. Readers who enjoy unusual characters and plotlines in their thrillers may also like *The Last Kabbalist of Lisbon*, annotated in the "Dark Ages Through Early Modern History" section of chapter 3.

Salinger, Steven D.

White Darkness. **Crown, 2001. 362p.**

Moe Rosen continues to run the family jewelry store in Brooklyn, despite the fact that his clientele is no longer white middle-class, but poor Haitian immigrants. When Moe saves a Haitian neighbor from a mugger, the grateful Haitian community welcomes him, but the violent world of voodoo ritual and illegal immigration threatens him and the woman he loves.

Themes: Haitians; immigrants; psychological thrillers

Stevens, Shane

The Anvil Chorus. **Delacorte, 1985. 370p.**

Cesar Dreyfus, inspector in the French police and Holocaust survivor, investigates the murder of a former SS officer, unlocking a secret Nazi plan dating back to the end of World War II.

Themes: conspiracies; Nazi plunder

Wilentz, Amy

Martyr's Crossing. **Simon & Schuster, 2001. 311p.**

Palestinian Marina Hajimi, trying to take her son to the hospital, is turned back at the Israeli checkpoint by Ari Doron. When her son dies, Ari and Marina become pawns in an ugly political confrontation, exploited by both sides. Told alternately from Marina and Ari's point of view.

Themes: Arabs; Israel; Palestinians; soldiers; terrorism

Legal Thrillers

The legal thriller has never been as popular as it is now, thanks in part to the novels of John Grisham and Scott Turow, whose courtroom dramas have been best sellers since the late 1980s. Unlike the earlier generation of legal thrillers, typified by the Perry Mason mysteries, this new breed focuses on the psychology and personal lives of the participants. The excitement of these novels may hinge on a particular point of law, as in Alan Dershowitz's novel *Advocate's Devil*; on the events leading up to the trial, as in Jean Hanff Korelitz's *Sabbathday River*; or on the drama of the trial itself.

Dershowitz, Alan

Abe Ringel Series.

Abe Ringel is a high-profile Boston lawyer whose cases combine issues of law and ethics.

Advocate's Devil. Warner, 1994. 342p. 📖

Ringel takes the case of a basketball player accused of date rape. Issues of lawyer–client confidentiality complicate what seems at first to be an open-and-shut case. Ringel finds that discussing relevant points from the Talmud with his old mentor Haskell Levine helps him clarify the issues of the case.

Themes: basketball and basketball players; fathers and daughters; rape

Just Revenge. Warner, 1999. 322p. **YA** 📖

Max Menuchen, survivor of a Holocaust massacre, sees the murderer years later in Boston. Max's trial for his attempt to avenge the deaths of his family members enables Dershowitz to explore questions of Holocaust guilt and revenge.

Themes: Holocaust—survivors; revenge

Related Titles: Dershowitz's autobiography, *Chutzpah*, is annotated in the "Public Lives" section of chapter 8. Another novel of Holocaust revenge is Irving R. Cohen's *The Passover Commando*. Readers may also enjoy Leon Uris's *QBVII*, an intricate, suspenseful courtroom thriller about a Polish doctor accused of murder in the concentration camps.

Isaacs, Susan

Lily White. HarperCollins, 1996. 459p. **YA**

Lily White, savvy Long Island lawyer, is hired to defend Norman Torkelson, a charming con artist who makes love to rich women and then fleeces them. Lily's personal life has also been filled with love and betrayal. (The author's Web site is www.susanisaacs.com.)

Themes: family relationships; marriage; swindlers

Related Titles: Many of the heroines in Isaacs's books are smart, funny, independent, and caught up in the social issues that changed women's lives in the 1980s and 1990s. Other novels by this author that readers may enjoy are *Compromising Positions* and *Long Time No See,* annotated in the "Humorous Mysteries" section of this chapter. Readers who enjoy novels about spirited heroines may also like *The Book of Candy*, by Susan Dworkin, annotated in the "Character" section of chapter 6.

Kahn, Michael A.

Rachel Gold Series.
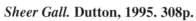

When we first meet Rachel Gold, she's left a prestigious Chicago law firm to start her own practice. Rachel's cases are never as simple as they seem, and she is often at risk from unpleasant and violent characters. Her law professor friend Benny Goldberg, and various boyfriends, including an Orthodox widower, assist her. Although Rachel is a lawyer, the emphasis in these fast-paced novels is often on detecting rather than courtroom work.

Themes: lawyer detectives

Grave Designs. **Dutton, 1992. 351p.**

Rachel's former law firm hires her to take on a sensitive investigation involving the trust fund set up by a senior partner, recently found dead in a call girl's apartment.

Death Benefits. **Dutton, 1992. 308p.**

The same firm hires her to investigate the apparent suicide of a partner in their St. Louis office.

Firm Ambitions. **Dutton, 1994. 309p.**

Rachel relocates to St. Louis, her childhood home, where her mother and sister still live, and where she investigates the death of a local fitness guru.

Due Diligence. **Dutton, 1995. 326p.**

Killers threaten Rachel when she is involved in a politically motivated murder.

Sheer Gall. **Dutton, 1995. 308p.**

Rachel is involved with domestic violence issues.

Bearing Witness. **Forge, 2000. 316p.**

Rachel battles a group of companies involved in anti-Semitic crimes reaching back to World War II.

Trophy Widow. **Forge, 2002. 397p.**

Rachel suspects her high-profile client has been framed and the murderer is still at large. She continues to date Orthodox lawyer Jonathan Wolf.

Korelitz, Jean Hanff

The Sabbathday River. **Farrar, Straus & Giroux, 1999. 504p.**

Naomi Roth came to the small town of Goddard, New Hampshire, ten years ago as a VISTA volunteer, and stayed on to start a women's craft cooperative, although her status as outsider has never changed. When she discovers the body of an infant in the Sabbathday River, she is first a suspect, then the defender of the young woman the community believes to be the murderer.

Themes: adultery; infanticide; single mothers; small town life

Related Titles: Two other mysteries characterized by a strong sense of place that deal with local prejudices in small towns are *Catskill*, by John Hayes, about an attack on Jews vacationing in the Catskills in the 1920s, and Susan R. Sloan's *An Isolated Incident*, set in a small town in the state of Washington.

Krich, Rochelle

Speak No Evil. **Mysterious Press, 1996. 402p.**

Los Angeles attorney Debra Laslow, defending a man accused of date rape, finds herself both a suspect and a potential victim of a serial killer. Her Orthodox background provides her with ethical guidance, but as other women lawyers are murdered, she becomes suspicious of everyone around her. (The author's Web site is www.rochellekrich.com.)

Themes: lawyer detectives; Orthodox Jews; rape; serial murders

Related Titles: Krich, like Faye Kellerman, writes with respect and empathy about Orthodox Jewish women. The characters in her novels struggle with issues of faith in a secular world. Krich has created another likable Orthodox heroine in Molly Blume, an amateur detective who stars in her own series, annotated in this chapter.

Levitsky, Ronald

Nate Rosen Series.

Lawyer Nate Rosen travels around the country defending the civil rights of clients whose views he may abhor. He wrestles with his rejection of his Orthodox Jewish upbringing, his estrangement from his father, and his guilt over the divorce that separated him from his teenaged daughter. Nate doesn't hesitate to confront unpleasant situations and characters, and his cases sometimes put him in physical danger.

Themes: civil rights; Orthodox Jews; social problems

The Love That Kills. **Scribner, 1991. 249p.**

Nate defends a neo-Nazi accused of murdering a young Vietnamese woman.

The Wisdom of Serpents. **Scribner, 1992. 274p.**

When a rattlesnake bites a member of an evangelical church during a worship service, Nate takes on the issue of religious tolerance.

Stone Boy. **Scribner, 1993. 245p.**

Nate travels to South Dakota to defend a Native American accused of murder.

The Innocence That Kills. **Scribner, 1994. 254p.**

Back home in Chicago, Nate tries to solve the murder of a young girl who may have been molested by a teacher, while learning some unpleasant things about his daughter's friends.

Yastrow, Shelby

Undue Influence. **Contemporary Books, 1990. 353p.**

> Benjamin Stillman, a Roman Catholic bookkeeper, dies, leaving his multimillion-dollar estate to a local synagogue, setting off a legal battle among several very interested parties.

> **Themes:** Holocaust—survivors; inheritance and succession

Political Intrigue and Espionage

This has long been the most popular of the thriller subgenres, with John LeCarre, Len Deighton, Jack Higgins, and many others appearing with regularity on best-seller lists. Following World War II, Cold War rivalries and the ever-present threat of nuclear warfare, provided an endless source of plots. With the close of the Cold War in the early 1990s, authors turned to other areas of conflict, which were unfortunately not hard to find. The volatile Middle East with its centuries-old religious and geopolitical conflicts, has become fertile ground for novels in this genre by Jewish and non-Jewish authors. Starting before the War of Independence in 1948, the Israeli intelligence services have been legendary for their audacity and fearlessness. The Haganah, Irgun, Palmach, and Stern Gang were notorious for their exploits under the very noses of the British along with their own internecine rivalries. The Mossad, Israel's current secret service, carries on that tradition; the sexy, ruthless Mossad agent single-handedly preventing the collapse of Israeli–Arab peace negotiations is a staple of spy fiction. Barbara Sofer's *The Thirteenth Hour* is a particularly good example of the mystique of the Mossad agent, as well as a frightening look at how the conflict between Israelis and Palestinians affects individual lives. Most deal with matters of Middle East politics and the survival of the state of Israel. The increase in terrorist activities since the millennium has brought the Middle East conflict to the American public in a very personal way. Events that were the stuff of fiction, movies, and overseas news reports, devastating but remote, became possible at home.

Bar-Zohar, Michael

Brothers. **Fawcett Columbine, 1993. 424p.**

> Two brothers, separated in childhood, one remaining in the Soviet Union, the other sent to his mother's Jewish family in Brooklyn, become deadly adversaries in the Cold War espionage game.

> **Themes:** brothers; Communism; Soviet Union—Intelligence services

Chafets, Zev

> Chafets' American upbringing and his experience in Israeli politics (he was Menachem Begin's press secretary) give him an excellent vantage point from which to write about Middle East politics. He has also written nonfiction about Israel and contemporary Jewish issues.

Hang Time. **Warner, 1996. 305p.**

> Two popular American basketball players and their coach, Digger Dawkins, are kidnapped by Palestinian terrorists, who demand that the

U.S. government apologize for its anti-Islamic policies or the hostages will be mutilated and killed. When the kidnappers begin to carry out their threats, Rasheed Hollinan, the brother of one of the hostages, mounts his own rescue effort.

Themes: Americans in Israel; basketball and basketball players; kidnapping; terrorism

Related Titles: Another Chafets novel, *Inherit the Mob*, mixes humor with suspense; it is annotated in the "Story" section of chapter 6.

The Project. **Warner, 1997. 261p.**

When the prime minister of Israel fails to support the reelection campaign of the first Jewish U.S. president, journalist Charlie Walker is dispatched to Israel to uncover the reasons. It's up to Charlie to derail a plan that threatens the international balance of power. The emphasis here is on unraveling international intrigue rather than on violence.

Themes: conspiracies; Israel—Politics and government; U.S.—Politics and government

Courter, Gay
Code Ezra. **Houghton Mifflin, 1986. 607p.**

Eli Katzar, a Mossad operative, works with a team of three women to neutralize nuclear threats to Israel. When one of their missions results in the murder of an Israeli, Eli must find out which of the women has betrayed him after thirty years of loyalty. (The author's Web site is www.gaycourter.com.)

Themes: betrayal; Israel—Intelligence services; women spies

Related Titles: Courter has also written the historical novels *The Midwife* and *The Midwife's Advice*, set in early twentieth-century New York City, annotated in the "Modern Period, United States and Canada" section of chapter 3. Readers may also enjoy her historical romance *Flowers in the Blood,* set among the Jewish communities in India and annotated in chapter 5.

Elon, Amos
Timetable. **Doubleday, 1980. 349p.**

In the spring of 1944, the Nazis are desperate for supplies and offer Joel Brand of the Hungarian Jewish Rescue Committee a deal: For every truck he can provide, 100 Jews will be saved from the death camps. Based on historical evidence, using real names and documents, Brand's frantic mission is told at a relentless pace.

Themes: Holocaust—resistance and rescue; Hungary; Nazis; World War II

Related Titles: Other thrillers about the rescue of Jews during the Holocaust are *The Mission* by Hans Habe, *The Parachutists* by Edward Klein, and Greg Iles's *Black Cross.*

Farhi, Moris
The Last of Days. **Crown, 1983. 538p.**

The head of a radical Islamic group believes that he has been chosen to destroy Israel and fulfill a Koranic prophecy bringing on the end of days. In this frightening page-turner, still as timely as when it was written, Boaz Ben-Ya'ir, top Mossad operative, joins with a Jordanian intelligence officer and an Ethiopian Israeli woman to stop the Warriors of Jihad from detonating a nuclear device over the Middle East.

Themes: Islam; Israel—Intelligence services; Jewish–Arab relations; nuclear warfare; terrorism

Related Titles: Another still timely, edge-of-the-seat thriller involving Israelis and radical Islamic terrorists, with lots of technical details, is Nelson DeMille's *By the Rivers of Babylon*.

Fisher, David E.

The Wrong Man. **Random House, 1993. 400p.**

A Nazi hunter and Holocaust survivor mistakenly planning to assassinate the German prime minister for his support of neo-Nazism is hunted by Mossad agent David Melnik and two Americans intent on unraveling the layers of double-dealing before the wrong man is killed.

Themes: assassination; Israel—Intelligence services; neo-Nazism

Related Titles: Melnik is a character in an earlier thriller, *Hostage One*, by Fisher and Randolph Albertazzie.

Gordon, Neil

Sacrifice of Isaac. **Random House, 1996. 304p.**

Brothers Luke and Danni Benami are pitted against each other in their efforts to understand themselves and their famous father, an Israeli general who smuggled Jews out of Europe during the Holocaust.

Themes: brothers; fathers and sons; Paris

The Gun-Runner's Daughter. **Random House, 1998. 316p.**

The U.S. government unexpectedly arrests Allison Rosenthal's father, an international arms dealer working for Israel. When her former lover is appointed as her father's prosecutor and a radical journalist with his own agenda stalks her, this modern Esther must chart a path among conflicting loyalties.

Themes: arms trade; betrayal; fathers and daughters

Harris, Leonard

The Masada Plan. **Crown, 1976. 314p.**

What would the Israeli government do if the Arab nations mounted an attack that was certain to destroy Israel? Harris suggests they would use the threat of a nuclear doomsday plan to coerce the nations of the world into guaranteeing Israeli peace. The suspense is in the relationships among the characters, as they manipulate, bluff, and spy their way down to the final hour.

Themes: conspiracies; nuclear warfare

Related Titles: Another thriller in which nuclear warfare is threatened is Joel C. Rosenberg's *The Last Jihad*.

Harris, Thomas

Black Sunday. **Putnam, 1975. 318p.**

Angry Vietnam veteran Michael Lander and the ruthless Black September wing of the PLO plot to blow up the stadium on Super Bowl Sunday to punish the United States for supporting Israel. David Kabakov, Israeli intelligence officer, works to identify the plotters and their target before it's too late, in this fast-paced nail-biter that was made into a movie. (The author's Web site is www.randomhouse. com/features/thomasharris/home.html.)

Themes: Israel—Intelligence services; Super Bowl Game (football); terrorists, Arab

Related Titles: Harris went on from this first novel to write the best seller *Silence of the Lambs*.

Hartov, Steven

Eckstein and Baum Series.

Hartov's experiences as an Israeli intelligence agent are put to good use in these intense and violent novels, which pit Israeli agents Benni Baum and Eytan Eckstein against Middle East terrorists.

Themes: Israel—Intelligence services; terrorism

The Heat of Ramadan. **Harcourt, Brace, Jovanovich, 1992. 513p.**

Baum and Eckstein track a Palestinian terrorist intent on revenge after a botched Israeli assassination attempt.

Nylon Hand of God. **Morrow, 1996. 468p.**

Baum, sent to New York to investigate the bombing of the Israeli consulate, is pitted against the beautiful Martina Klump, an old and deadly adversary.

The Devil's Shepherd. **Morrow, 2000. 323p.**

A Czech defector who promises to divulge the name of an Israeli mole involves Baum and Eckstein in the rescue of Ethiopian Jewish children.

Jordan, Eric

Operation Hebron. **Mosaic Press, 2000. 370p.**

A fast-paced, violent game of international intrigue between Brenda Straus, an ambitious Jewish FBI agent, and Jackie Markovic, a sexy, ruthless, freelance assassin. When the United States threatens to cut off all aid to Israel unless a peace agreement is reached with the Palestinians, the Israelis launch a plan to elect one of their top agents to the U.S. presidency. (The author is a former U.S. intelligence officer and diplomat. The novel's Web site is www.operationhebron.com.)

Themes: Israel—Intelligence services; U.S.—Intelligence services; women spies

Law, J. Patrick

The Assistant. **Simon & Schuster, 2000. 414p.**

Ben Poltarek, lawyer and amateur magician, is accidentally drawn into the world of the *sayanim,* civilian recruits to the Israeli secret service. He and his girlfriend Rachel become crucial players in the hunt for a Palestinian terrorist whose goal is the downfall of the state of Israel.

Themes: Israel—Intelligence services; terrorism

Related Titles: John Le Carre's *The Little Drummer Girl* is another example of a spy thriller in which a nonprofessional is drawn into international espionage for Israel.

Mendels, Ora

A Taste For Treason. **Carol Publishing Group, 1990. 273p.**

Eliahu Golan, an Israeli mole inside the Palestinian movement for nearly twenty years, is now at risk. He must continue to convince the Palestinians he is Tewfik while the Israelis mount a complicated scheme to rescue him.

Themes: Israel—Intelligence services; Palestinians

Related Titles: Mendels was born in Jerusalem, grew up in South Africa, and now lives in the United States. She has also written the novel *Mandela's Children.* Readers who enjoy thrillers about undercover agents may like *The Tower of Babel,* set just before the Six-Day War, by the Australian author Morris West.

Ostrovsky, Victor

Lion of Judah. **St. Martin's, 1993. 313p.**

Natan Stone, veteran Mossad officer, is called in to lead a special team to find a mole planted in the Mossad by the Syrians and neutralize a new Palestinian terrorist cell, but his job is complicated by internal rivalries and his suspicions that he is being set up.

Themes: Israel—Intelligence services; terrorism

Related Titles: Ostrovsky was a Mossad agent who became disillusioned and left the organization. Readers may enjoy his two books about the Mossad's methods: *By Way of Deception* (with Claire Hoy) and *The Other Side of Deception.*

Rosenbaum, Ray

Condors. **Presidio Press, 1995. 340p.**

In 1946, veteran combat pilot Ross Colyer, struggling to keep his air freight business afloat, is offered a lucrative contract by the Jewish Relief Foundation, the cover for an organization bringing arms and ammunition to the Haganah in Palestine. Lots of detail about flying, and the changes in the U.S. military and intelligence services that followed World War II.

Themes: Americans in Israel; Israel–Arab War, 1948–1949; Israel—History; Palestine

Related Titles: Readers who enjoy thrillers that feature details of military operations may also like *The Last Liberator* by Jerry Yulsman, about an American pilot who smuggles arms to the Jewish resistance movement during World War II.

Shagan, Steve

Pillars of Fire. Pocket Books, 1989. 371p.

Tom Lawford, sometime spy for the CIA, uses his journalist's cover and the assistance of an attractive Mossad agent to locate the launch site of nuclear missiles built jointly by Pakistan, Libya, and Germany and aimed at Israel.

Themes: Israel—Intelligence services; journalists; nuclear warfare

Silva, Daniel

Gabriel Allon Series.

Gabriel Allon, undercover Mossad agent, lives in England and works as an art restorer in these fast-paced and violent thrillers. Several involve unfinished business from the Holocaust and reflect serious research and historical insight. (Silva has written several earlier thrillers that do not involve the Middle East or Jewish protagonists. The author's Web site is www.danielsilvabooks.com.)

Themes: art restorers; Holocaust; Israel—Intelligence services; Nazi plunder; World War II—Collaboration

The Kill Artist. Random House, 2000. 425p.

Allon is recruited to assassinate Tariq, the man who killed Allon's wife and child years ago, and now wants to derail the Middle East peace negotiations by assassinating Yasir Arafat.

The English Assassin, Putnam, 2002. 400p.

In Switzerland to restore a painting in a private collection, Allon becomes involved with art theft dating back to Swiss collaboration with Nazi Germany in World War II.

The Confessor. Putnam, 2003. 401p.

Allon is called on to expose a group planning to assassinate the Pope to prevent exposure of Nazi collaborators in the Vatican. Silva draws on the research of historian Susan Zuccotti for this provocative and timely plot.

A Death in Vienna. Putnam, 2004. 416p.

The search for the bomber of the Austrian Wartime Claims and Inquiries office turns personal for Allon when he reads his mother's account of her time in the camps.

Related Titles: Another novel about Jewish-owned art that fell into the hands of the Nazis is *The Girl in Hyacinth Blue*. Readers interested in nonfiction on the theft of Jewish property during World War II may be interested in Richard Z. Chesnoff's *Pack of Thieves: How Hitler and Europe Plundered the Jews and Committed the Greatest Theft in History*.

Sofer, Barbara

The Thirteenth Hour. **Dutton, 1996. 340p.**

Deborah Stern, a Jewish biology researcher and almost-divorced mother of two, and Raba Alhassan, a middle-class Palestinian woman, become agents of the Mossad and a Palestinian terrorist group, respectively, against their better judgment. A fast-paced thriller with excellent characterization about the ways in which conflict affects ordinary people trying to live quiet lives in desperate situations. (The author's Web site is www.barbarasofer.com.)

Themes: family relationships; Israel—Intelligence services; Palestinians; terrorism

Related Titles: Another novel in which ordinary Israeli citizens are drawn into political events is *Quiet Street* by Zelda Popkin, annotated in the "Modern Period, Middle East" section of chapter 3. Readers may also enjoy *Shula, Code Name the Pearl*, by Aviezer Golan and Danny Pinkas, a true story about an Israeli woman who spied for the Mossad.

Topol, Allan

A Woman of Valor. **Morrow, 1980. 324p.**

When all Jews were forced to leave Egypt in 1956, Leora Baruch's family lost everything. In Israel, Leora joined an elite antiterrorist unit of Israeli intelligence to avenge the ruin of her family.

Themes: Israel—Intelligence services; women spies

Spy Dance. **Onyx, 2001. 423p.**

Greg Nielsen, on the run from the CIA, thought his new life in Israel was secure, until a phone call and a kidnapping put him back into the spy game working for the Mossad. (The author's Web site is www.allantopol.com.)

Themes: betrayal; Israel—Intelligence services; kidnapping; spies; U.S.—Intelligence services

Victor, Barbara

Friends, Lovers, Enemies. **D.I. Fine, 1991. 327p.**

Journalist Sasha Beale is next door when Palestinian terrorists bomb an Alitalia office in Rome. When she arranges to interview the Palestinian leader whose group is responsible, the Mossad recruits her to help them infiltrate the terrorist's household.

Themes: Israel—Intelligence services

Sources for Additional Information

There are many sources in print and on the Internet for information about mysteries and thrillers, but only a few that are specifically Jewish. Readers may find additional general information in chapter 9, "Readers' Advisory Resources."

Breen, Jon, and others, eds. *Synod of Sleuths: Essays on Judeo-Christian Detective Fiction.* Metuchen, NJ: Scarecrow Press, 1990.

James Yaffe's essay, "Is This Any Job for a Nice Jewish Boy?," gives an overview of the Jewish detective, from Harry Kemelman to Faye Kellerman.

Raphael, Lawrence W., ed. *Mystery Midrash: An Anthology of Jewish Mystery and Detective Fiction.* Woodstock, VT: Jewish Lights, 1999.

The introduction to this collection is a good discussion of what makes a mystery Jewish. Raphael's Jewish mystery site (www.jewishmysteries.com) contains an extensive bibliography of Jewish mysteries through 2001.

Roth, Laurence. *Inspecting Jews: American Jewish Detective Stories.* New Brunswick, NJ: Rutgers University Press, 2004.

Roth writes about how Jewish mysteries reveal the complex acculturation process of American Jews. He discusses mysteries by Harry Kemmelman, Rochelle Krich, Stuart Kaminsky, and Faye Kellerman, among others.

Notes

1. Joyce G. Saricks, *The Readers' Advisory Guide to Genre Fiction* (Chicago: American Library Association, 2001); Nancy Pearl, *Now Read This: A Guide to Mainstream Fiction, 1978–1998* (Englewood, CO: Libraries Unlimited, 1999).

2. James Yaffe, "Is This Any Job for a Nice Jewish Boy? (Jews in Detective Fiction)," in *Synod of Sleuths: Essays on Judeo-Christian Detective Fiction*, ed. Jon L. Breen and Martin H. Greenberg (Metuchen, NJ: Scarecrow Press, 1990), 22–23.

3. Rex Stout, *Some Buried Caesar* (New York: Bantam, 1994), 183.

4. Joyce G. Saricks, *The Readers' Advisory Guide to Genre Fiction* (Chicago: American Library Association, 2001), 312.

Chapter 3

Historical Fiction

Some say that history is dry, while the novel is juicy.—Sonia Levitin

There is no such thing as a short historical novel.—Max Byrd

I knew the facts. I had to give them a good story.—William Martin

Introduction

Who among us has not tried to imagine what it was like to live in another time and be involved in momentous events? Historical fiction gives us the opportunity to experience history vicariously. Historical fiction fleshes out the dry facts of history to provide a window into life in another era.

For the writer, the challenge is to find an opening for the imagination in the historical record. Beyond that, there are as many ways as there are novelists to manipulate elements of character, story, and setting. The diversity of this genre is its strength; almost any reader can find something to enjoy.

Historical fiction lives in the spaces among the recorded facts of history, but novelists are free to take liberties with facts for the uses of fiction. Cynthia Ozick reminds us in no uncertain terms:

> Imagination owes nothing to what we call reality; it owes nothing to history. The phrase "historical novel" is mainly an oxymoron. History is rooted in document and archive. History is what we make out of memory. Fiction flees libraries and loves lies.[1]

In the best historical fiction, the author honors the truth of the historical record and the people involved. Readers and librarians need to be mindful of the author's intention, sometimes apparent from prefaces or notes, of how much liberty has been taken with the historical record.

Scope

Historical fiction has been defined in several ways. Some reference sources specify that the events of a novel must take place fifty or seventy-five years before the writing, but this guide uses a more flexible definition. The novels in this chapter are those in which an author deliberately re-creates an earlier time period; specifically, a story set before 1950 and written at a later date. Thus novels set before 1950 but written contemporaneously are not considered historical fiction. For example, Abraham Cahan's classic *The Rise of David Levinsky*, about the conflicts in the lives of early twentieth century immigrants, written in 1917, may be read now for its depiction of an earlier era, but Cahan was writing about his own times. (*The Rise of David Levinsky* appears in the "Classics and Major Authors" section of chapter 6.) On the other hand, Francine Prose's *Hungry Hearts*, set in the same era, but published in 1983, fits the definition of an historical novel. Some readers who are interested in a particular period of time may not care if a novel is considered historical fiction. These readers will find additional novels of interest in the "Classics and Major Authors" section of chapter 6. The reader can also find titles listed under chronological subject headings in the subject index, for example, 1920s, U.S.—History—Depression.

All the novels in this chapter were written with an eye for the details of daily life and the historical "feel" of an era. If the historical setting is secondary to plot or character, the novel may not be found in this chapter. For example, in the coming-of-age novel *Allegra Maud Goldman*, by Edith Konecky, Allegra's distinctive wry voice and efforts to understand the world around her are far more vivid than the 1930s setting. Readers will find this novel in chapter 6.

Holocaust fiction, although typically set during the 1930s and 1940s, is not included in this chapter. The Holocaust fiction in this guide was written by survivors of those years and is closely tied to memoir and the burden of horrific memories. It cannot be considered genre fiction in the same way as the titles in this chapter; therefore, the reader will find these novels in chapter 7 along with Holocaust memoirs.

Historical settings can be found in all genres: mystery, romance, thriller, etc. Although readers may have different opinions about the grouping of some novels, when the conventions of another genre dominate the plot, the novel has been placed in that genre rather than historical fiction. Aileen Barron's novel *A Fly Has a Hundred Eyes*, about an archaeological dig near Jerusalem in the late 1930s, is found in chapter 2, since the plot focuses on the intrigue and danger involved in tracking a murderer. Along the way, readers will enjoy the well-defined setting and learn some political history. Gay Courter's novel *Flowers in the Blood*, set in Victorian India, has a wonderfully detailed setting describing the different Jewish groups that settled in India, but the romantic thread drives the novel.

Novels in this chapter are not limited to those set in the Americas. Jewish American writers have written about all periods of time through the lens of their own experience and research. Jewish history is rich in themes, personalities, events, and conflicts in every era and every part of the world. The novels in this chapter reflect the fact that Jews have lived all over the world and played important roles in every historical period.

Readers may be surprised to find a few graphic novels in this chapter, but it is becoming difficult to ignore their presence. Since the term "graphic novel" refers to format and not content, they will be found in the appropriate chapter. Readers who have never read a graphic novel may enjoy the ones by Will Eisner, Ben Katchor, and James Sturm that are annotated here. Readers can identify all the graphic novels in this guide by checking the subject index under that term.

Organization of the Chapter

Historical fiction titles are divided into three main time periods to facilitate readers' advisory work. The most recent time period is subdivided geographically. Divisions are as follows:

Biblical and Ancient Worlds

Dark Ages Through Early Modern History (400–1840)

Modern Period (1840–1950)

> Europe
>
> Eastern Europe and Russia
>
> The Middle East
>
> Latin America
>
> The United States and Canada

Introductory text describes the scope of each subsection. Subject headings (themes) visible in each entry, and additional subject headings that appear only in the index, will help readers find other books about particular topics.

Appeal of the Genre/Advising the Reader

Sources for general readers' advisory information can be found in chapter 9, but the information below will be helpful for librarians providing readers' advisory assistance for this genre, and for readers in identifying the kinds of historical fiction they enjoy.

Setting

A well-defined setting is a basic feature of this genre. Many readers are specifically looking for a realistic setting, well researched, full of the detail that makes another era come to life. These readers expect to learn more about history and anticipate that the writer has been accurate in its depiction. Some want to learn about a particular period in Jewish history or the history of a place as it applies to the Jews who lived there. David Raphael's novels *The Cavalier of Malaga* and *The Alhambra Decree*, about Inquisition-era Spain, are good examples of well-researched novels, rich with factual detail. Other novels, like Anita Diamant's *The Red Tent* and Howard Fast's *All My Brothers,* flesh out times where there is scant detail in the historical or biblical record about people's daily lives. For some authors, the setting may be a jumping off point for a story that creates a reality that never quite existed. Frances Sherwood's *The Book of Splendor,* set in seventeenth-century Prague, falls into this category. The author has provided a well-researched historical framework and then created a plot that combines realistic and legendary elements. What might-have-been-but-never-was provides food for thought for both writer and reader. The setting may become the background for the artistic interpretation of the lives of ordinary people in interesting historical times, as in Nancy Richler's *Your Mouth is Lovely*, set in early twentieth-century Russia at the very beginning of the Russian Revolution.

With this genre, it is important for readers' advisors to understand how much realism and accuracy the reader expects.

Character

The lives of characters in historical fiction are often affected by events known to the reader. The author isn't starting out fresh. In Gloria Goldreich's *West to Eden*, we know that Emma Coen and her husband will suffer problems with their business during the Depression. We may know that Rabbi Elisha ben Abuyah, in Milton Steinberg's *As a Driven Leaf,* will be excommunicated for his heretical views. It is how the characters face these events that make historical fiction compelling for readers interested in character-driven fiction. The way the writer brings the characters to life and motivates them interests these readers.

The use of voice has an effect on the sense of immediacy in historical fiction. Readers to whom character is important may enjoy novels written in the first person. Jacqueline Park's *The Secret Book of Grazia dei Rossi*, written as a set of letters to her son in fifteenth-century Italy, draws the reader in immediately. In E. L. Doctorow's *World's Fair*, we see the Bronx in the 1930s through the eyes of a very young boy.

Authors of historical fiction have several choices in creating character. They can portray historical people using their own accounts of themselves or the historical record. Since history is filled with great personalities, the author has the opportunity to use characters who already have weight and substance in readers' minds. In *God Knows*, Joseph Heller takes the character of King David and gives us a funny and irreverent depiction of one of the most well-known biblical figures. Heller's David is all the more amusing for the way we try to anticipate the author's explanations for events we know will occur. But an author who plays too fast and loose with the facts will lose many readers of this genre, particularly those who want to make the acquaintance of the character in the historical record.

Authors may choose to write about ordinary people caught up in the great events of history, like the women in Meredith Tax's novels *Rivington Street* and *Union Square*, or people living their lives against a historical backdrop. Leo Haber's *The Red Heifer* is a vivid coming-of-age novel set against a background of the Lower East Side of New York during the Depression and World War II.

Writing historical fiction allows an author to bring to the forefront groups of people whose voices have traditionally not been heard in recorded history. Two novels in this chapter, for example, focus on women who are mentioned only briefly in the Bible: Dinah in Anita Diamant's *The Red Tent* and Avishag in Yael Lotan's novel of that name. Will Eisner's graphic novels set on Dropsie Avenue in the Bronx record the lives of immigrants who struggled and often did not succeed in their new country. Judith Katz's novel *The Escape Artist* depicts the life of a woman who was forced into prostitution in Latin America in the early 1900s, a very real occurrence but one rarely treated in the history books.

Story

One of the most fascinating and appealing aspects of historical fiction is the opportunity it provides to explore why events may have occurred. The author can work within the confines of historical events to create an interpretation that's not in the history books but rings true to the characters and situations created. Bernard Malamud, in *The Fixer*, takes the trial of Mendel Beiliss and creates a life that Mendel could have lived that led to his arrest, although the known details of Mendel's life are quite different. Joanne Greenberg, in her novel *The King's Persons*, imagined how anti-Semitic fervor grew in England in the twelfth century by examining the relationship between the Jewish and non-Jewish communities in one town.

Sometimes plot follows the broad sweep of historical events and the reader is caught up in a saga that covers many years and several generations. Anne Roiphe's *The Pursuit of Happiness* takes a family from the shtetls of Eastern Europe to the Lower East Side of New York, through World War II and the establishment of the State of Israel. Other novels treat history on a small scale, covering a few characters and a short amount of time. In Gloria Goldreich's *That Year of Our War*, one teen-aged girl living in Brooklyn feels the effects of World War II and learns some difficult lessons about herself and the world.

Pacing

Some readers may like historical novels that are leisurely, with dense prose that gives them a chance to spend time in a detailed world the author creates. Often these novels are long, but readers don't mind, since the point is escape and edification. Marge Piercy's gripping novel *Gone to Soldiers* follows many characters as it slowly builds up a picture of World War II on several fronts. Chava Rosenfarb's *Bociany*, set in a shtetl prior to World War II, is a study of a community that draws the reader into the characters' struggles.

Other historical novels are almost like thrillers, set in tempestuous times for Jews. *The Last Kabbalist of Lisbon* is filled with the violence of massacres in Inquisition-era Lisbon. David Mamet's *The Old Religion* is a stark retelling of the Leo Frank case, in which the known outcome doesn't prevent the reader from getting caught up in the tension.

Historical Fiction

Biblical and Ancient Worlds

Despite the wealth of possibilities for historical fiction in biblical sources, there are comparatively few novels set in the biblical period that meet the criteria for this chapter. There is, however, a long and rich tradition of biblical interpretation in Judaism, including folklore, legend, and Midrash. Midrash refers to the texts written by sages and scholars, oral in origin, that interpret the Bible, filling in the empty spaces in the spare narrative. Midrash is not historical fiction, since its intent is to discern God's purpose, but it allows us to imagine ourselves into the text to interpret it. Midrash is still being written and told; it is one of the ways scripture is interpreted and made meaningful in the Jewish community in every age.

Diamant, Anita

The Red Tent. St. Martin's, 1997. 321p. YA

From a single line in Genesis, Diamant has created a full life story for Dinah, daughter of Jacob and Leah, bringing to life the ancient world in which she lived. In slow, rich detail, Dinah tells a story of love, jealousy, tribal hatreds, ritual, and superstition learned from Jacob's wives in the women's tent. (The author's Web site is www.anitadiamant.com.)

Themes: biblical stories; family relationships; women in the Bible; women's lives

Related Titles: Readers may be interested in Diamant's essay "Midrash—or Not," about *The Red Tent*, in her collection of essays *Pitching My Tent: Marriage, Motherhood, Friendship, and Other Leaps of Faith.* Diamant's second novel, *Good Harbor,* is annotated in the "Character" section of chapter 6. Another novel about Dinah is Deena Metzger's *What Dinah Thought.* Readers may also enjoy *Only Human* by the British author Jenny Diski, about Abraham and Sarah, and their relationship with God. *The Red Tent* offers a vivid picture of the ancient, seminomadic way of life. Readers interested in this period may enjoy two recent nonfiction works: *Walking the Bible* and *Abraham*, both by Bruce Feiler. Readers may also enjoy two collections that provide a woman's perspective on biblical stories: *Miriam's Well: Stories About Women in the Bible,* by Alice Bach and J. Cheryl Exum, or *Out of the Garden: Women Writers on the Bible,* edited by Christina Buchmann and Celina Spiegel.

Fast, Howard

My Glorious Brothers. Little, Brown. 1949. 280p. YA

When the Syrians tried to impose the worship of pagan gods on the Jews of Judea in the second century B.C.E., Mattathias and his five sons gathered a small army and fled to the wilderness to fight. Simon, the only one of the brothers to survive into old age, tells the story of his brother Judah's leadership and the war they waged together against a succession of Syrian armies. (Winner of the National Jewish Book Award.)

Themes: brothers; Maccabees; war

Related Titles: The story of the Maccabean Revolt is recorded in Maccabees I and II, texts that are part of the *Apocrypha*, a collection of writings from the last two centuries B.C.E. and the first century C.E. Fast is a prolific writer, well-known for his historical fiction set during the American Revolution.

Heller, Joseph

God Knows. Alfred A. Knopf,1984. 353p.

King David addresses the modern reader directly in this colloquially written, humorous version of his life and relationship to God, filling in the spaces in the biblical narrative with his own explanations. Heller's David is ribald, combative, and philosophical by turns, the entertaining star of his own life, who, in his own words "built an empire the size of Maine."

Themes: biblical stories; David, king of Israel; humorous fiction

Related Titles: Readers who enjoyed Heller's irreverent comic voice here and in *Catch-22* may also enjoy *Good as Gold*, a political satire. His autobiography, *Now and Then: From Coney Island to Here*, is annotated in the "Childhood and Family" section of chapter 8.

Lotan, Yael

Avishag. **The Toby Press, 2002. 226p.**

When the young girl Avishag the Shunnamite is summoned to the court of King David to provide companionship and warmth to the dying king, she becomes involved in palace intrigue and the fight over the succession when David dies. The wealth of realistic detail in this well-researched novel brings the characters and the times to life.

Themes: biblical stories; David, king of Israel; kings and rulers

Related Titles: Other novels based on biblical stories told from a woman's point of view are *Solomon and Sheba* by Faye Levine and *Queenmaker, a Novel of King David's Queen* by India Edghill.

Steinberg, Milton

As a Driven Leaf. **1939; reprint, Berhrman House, 1996. 480p.**

In Roman Palestine at the end of the first century C.E., Rabbi Elisha ben Abuyah, struggling with a loss of faith, turns to the study of Greek philosophy and is excommunicated by the Sanhedrin. The anguish of a scholar driven to uncover purpose in the universe is compellingly portrayed in a restrained style, rewarding the patient reader. Historical and fictional characters populate this novel of ideas. (Steinberg, a brilliant rabbi active in the development of Reconstructionist Judaism, died in 1950 at the age of forty-six. This was his only novel.) A discussion guide is available at www.behrmanhouse.com.

Themes: Akiva ben Joseph (ca. 40–135 C.E.); Elisha ben Abuyah; Hellenism; heretics; rabbis

Related Titles: Although this is primarily a novel of ideas, Steinberg's characterizations are superb. Readers may also enjoy Chaim Potok's novels, annotated in the "Classics and Major Authors" section of chapter 6, which combine the exploration of religious beliefs with vivid characterization.

Zelitch, Simone

Moses in Sinai. **Black Heron Press, 2002. 268p.**

Zelitch's account of Moses's life from the time the princess Bityah takes him from the river as an infant to his death on Mount Nebo is set in an atmospheric world of witches and superstition and explores questions of theology and faith.

Themes: Bible—Exodus; Egypt; Moses (biblical figure)

Related Titles: Zelitch's first novel, *Louisa*, a modern retelling of the Book of Ruth set in the aftermath of the Holocaust, is annotated in the "Setting" section of chapter 6.

Dark Ages Through Early Modern History (400–1840)

This period of time, as Jews spread throughout Europe, around the Mediterranean, into Asia, across the Atlantic, and into the Americas, offers dramatic material for historical fiction. Conditions for Jews varied widely from place to place and changed often and abruptly, depending on political and social conditions. Tolerance was often the best that could be hoped for; persecution was often what occurred.

Several of the novels in this section are set in late fifteenth-century Spain, where conditions for the Jewish community underwent a dramatic change. Jews had lived in relative tranquility under Moorish governments from the eighth to the thirteenth centuries. Art and literature flourished in this Golden Age; it is an era known for great Jewish philosophers and religious scholars. The Jews known as Sephardim are descended from this community. But beginning in the twelfth and thirteenth centuries, Moorish rule declined, and persecution by Dominican friars signaled the beginning of the end of the Golden Age. Jewish communities were attacked, and thousands of Jews were massacred. Many underwent baptism and forced conversion. As New Christians, many practiced Judaism secretly and lived in fear of exposure. In 1480, King Ferdinand and Queen Isabella brought the Inquisition to Spain and put the Dominican monk Torquemada in charge, a zealot in search of heretics. The New Christians were targets of the Inquisition, and thousands were tortured and killed. In 1492, all remaining Jews were given an ultimatum: accept baptism or leave Spain. More than 100,000 Jews left, resettling mainly in countries around the Mediterranean.[2] Those that went to Portugal suffered similar persecutions, culminating in an edict of expulsion a few years later. The terrifying and dramatic events of these years are recalled in *The Last Kabbalist of Lisbon* by David Zimler, *The Last Jew* by Noah Gordon, and David Raphael's historically detailed novels *The Cavalier of Malaga* and *The Alhambra Decree*, among others.

Gordon, Noah

The Last Jew. St. Martin's, 2000. 348p.

> Teenaged Yonah Toledano, separated from the remnants of his family after they are murdered or expelled from Spain by the Inquisition, travels the countryside on his donkey Moises, hoping to avenge his brother's death, and leading a double life as Ramon Callico, Old Christian. Engrossing and well researched regarding the experience of *conversos* and filled with details of life in that era. (The author's Web site is www.noahgordonbooks.com.)

> **Themes:** *conversos*; doctors; Inquisition; picaresque novels; Sephardim

> **Related Titles:** Gordon also wrote *The Physician*, set in the eleventh century, in which a young man pretends to be Jewish to gain admittance to an Arab medical school. Another novel set in this same time period, about a family torn apart by the Inquisition, is Lewis Weinstein's *The Heretic*. Readers who enjoy picaresque

novels may want to try *Pinto and Sons* by Leslie Epstein, an historical novel set in the Old West in the mid-nineteenth century.

Greenberg, Joanne

The King's Persons. **Holt, Rinehart & Winston, 1964. 284p.**

Misunderstood, despised, and feared by their gentile neighbors, the Jews of England in the twelfth century were protected by the king so they could survive as tradesmen and moneylenders. In York, the small Jewish community watches with apprehension as calls for a new Crusade inflame the populace to violence against infidels. Historically accurate, with excellent characterizations, and based on a real incident. (Winner of the National Jewish Book Award.)

Themes: England; Jewish–Christian relations; Jews—persecutions; moneylenders

Related Titles: Of Greenberg's many novels, this is the only one not set in the twentieth century. Another novel, *A Season of Delight,* is annotated in the "Character" section of chapter 6.

Gross, Joel

Rachel Series.

Themes: diamonds; family sagas; Jews—persecutions

The Books of Rachel. **Seaview, 1979. 440p.**

Starting with Rachel Cuhena, from a wealthy family of diamond merchants in fifteenth-century Spain, in each generation a girl named Rachel experiences the travails of the Jewish people, from the Inquisition to the Holocaust, and shares possession of a beautiful diamond.

The Lives of Rachel. **NAL, 1984. 424p.**

In a prequel we follow the Rachels in the family from the period of the Maccabees to the Crusades.

Isler, Alan

The Bacon Fancier. **Viking, 1997. 214p.**

In four witty, poignant, and very literary stories set in different time periods, Jews come into conflict with the larger gentile world. In "The Monster," Shylock reveals a different side of his life in the Venetian ghetto. In the title novella, a Jewish violinmaker finds happiness with a non-Jewish woman who endures the scorn of the community for her choice.

Themes: Jewish identity; short stories

Related Titles: Two other Isler novels, *The Prince of West End Avenue* and *Kraven Images,* are annotated in the "Character" section of chapter 6. Another view of the Shylock story can be found in the young adult novel *Shylock's Daughter* by Mirjam Pressler.

Leviant, Curt

The Man Who Thought He Was Messiah. **Jewish Publication Society, 1990. 222p.**

Reb Nachman of Bratslav (1770–1811) was a beloved Hasidic leader and story-teller, the great-grandson of the Baal Shem Tov, the founder of Hasidism. In this biographical novel, Nachman, although he believes he may be the Messiah, falls in love with a gentile girl and undertakes a pilgrimage to Vienna, Turkey, and Palestine to test his faith. Among his many adventures, he studies music with Beethoven.

Themes: Hasidim; magical realism; rabbis

Related Titles: A few of Reb Nachman's famous stories are included in this novel; others can be found in Howard Schwartz's collection *The Captive Soul of the Messiah: New Tales About Reb Nachman.* Leviant has captured some of the same qualities of magical realism that infuse the stories of Isaac Bashevis Singer, whose works are annotated in the "Classics and Major Authors" section chapter 6. Readers can also find this particular mix of reality and fantasy in Joseph Skibell's *A Blessing on the Moon*, annotated in the "Setting" section of chapter 6, and parts of Jonathan Safran Foer's *Everything Is Illuminated*, annotated in the "Language" section of chapter 6. Other novels and novellas by Leviant are also annotated in the "Language" section of chapter 6.

Liss, David

Coffee Trader. **Random House, 2003. 384p.**

When Miguel Lienzo, a Portuguese *converso* living in 1650s Amsterdam, begins to trade in coffee bean futures to recoup his fortune and pay his debts, he becomes vulnerable to his enemies, including those in the Jewish community. (The author's Web site is www.davidliss.com.)

Themes: *conversos*; fraud; Holland; seventeenth century; stock market

Related Titles: Liss's first novel, the mystery *Conspiracy of Paper*, is set in eighteenth-century London and involves Lienzo's descendants. It is annotated in the "Historical Mysteries" section of chapter 2.

Michener, James

The Source. **1965. Reprint. Random House, 2002. 909p.** 📖

As archaeologists excavate the layers of civilizations that make up the site Tel Makor in Northern Israel, Michener brings to life the people and cultures that inhabited it for 12,000 years, from the ancient Canaanites, Hebrews, Egyptians, Babylonians, and Romans to the modern Turks, British, and Israelis.

Themes: archaeology; Israel—History; Middle East—History

Park, Jacqueline

The Secret Book of Grazia dei Rossi. **Simon & Schuster, 1997. 572p.**

Although the Italian Jews were spared the terrors of the Spanish Inquisition, they were persecuted by the aristocracy and clergy and lived in fear of losing their livelihoods. Grazia dei Rossi, from a wealthy Jewish moneylending family, endured the capricious benevolence of her patron, the Lady Isabella d'Este, and was tempted by love to abandon Judaism for a more secure life as a Catholic. In this well-researched novel, cast as Grazia's memoir, we see how the corruption, greed, and prejudices of the ruling classes affected the lives of Renaissance-era Jews.

Themes: fifteenth century; Italy; Jewish–Christian relations; mothers and sons; sixteenth century; women—social conditions

Related Titles: This account is based on an historical exchange of letters between an Italian noblewoman and a young Jewish girl in the Renaissance. Readers who like historical novels told from the point of view of minor characters may also enjoy Philippa Gregory's *The Queen's Fool*, about a young Jewish girl caught up in the intrigue of Queen Mary's court.

Prose, Francine

 Judah the Pious. **Atheneum, 1973. 279p.**

In this tale within a tale told by Rabbi Eliezer to Casimir, the boy-king of Poland, a young Jewish boy lives in the woods to study what he believes is the orderly, rational world of nature, only to find that his life is invaded by the magical and the miraculous. (Winner of the National Jewish Book Award.)

Themes: magic; magical realism; shtetl life

Related Titles: Readers who enjoy the floating, timeless quality of this tale may also enjoy Lillian Nattel's novel *The River Midnight*, annotated in the "Language" section of chapter 6, and Isaac Bashevis Singer's short stories and novels set in Poland, annotated in the "Classics and Major Authors" section of chapter 6. Prose has also written several children's books based on Jewish folk tales. Her novella *Guided Tours of Hell* is annotated in the "Setting" section of chapter 6.

Raphael, David

A turbulent era comes to life in these lively, thoroughly researched novels set during the Inquisition, filled with action and conflict, historical figures, details of daily life, Jewish ritual, and Spanish politics with vivid characterizations of both influential and ordinary citizens. Historical notes and bibliographies offer avenues for further exploration.

The Alhambra Decree. **Carmi House, 1988. 358p.**

Neither Don Abraham Senior, wealthy tax collector and royal advisor, nor the powerful statesman and philosopher Don Isaac Abravanel, can persuade King Ferdinand and Queen Isabella to rescind the order of Jewish expulsion in 1492. The escaping Jews encounter pirates, disease, and forced conversion as they flee Spain.

Themes: Abravanel, Don Isaac (1437–1508); *conversos*; Inquisition; Jews—persecutions; Spain

Related Titles: Don Isaac Abravanel, a key figure in this novel, was a great scholar and leader of Spanish Jewry. Readers who want to learn more about him may enjoy the biography *Don Isaac Abravanel* by Benzion Netanyahu. Another novel about Spanish Jews that draws heavily on political history is *The Marrano Prince* by Avner Gold, set in the late 1600s.

The Cavalier of Malaga. **Carmi House, 1989. 186p.**

Alberto Galante, a *converso*, distinguishes himself in battle at the siege of Málaga but is denounced by a rival as a Judaizer and forced to flee under a new identity. He spends his life on the run from the ever-vigilant Inquisition.

Themes: Abravanel, Don Isaac (1437–1508); *conversos*; Inquisition; Jews—persecutions; Spain

Sackville, Raphael

Prince of Akko. **Tamar Books, 1992. 269p.**

Against the advice of his father, Chaim Farhi becomes financial advisor to the Pasha of Akko in the late 1700s, knowing that the cost of the Pasha's displeasure is death. Chaim weathers far-reaching political changes, including Napoleon's attack on Akko, and is able to use his influence to help the Jewish communities under Turkish rule, in this well-researched story.

Themes: Palestine—History; Sephardim; Turkey

Sherwood, Frances

The Book of Splendor. **W. W. Norton, 2002. 352p.** `YA`

In this rich stew of history, legend, and romance set in seventeenth-century Prague's Jewish ghetto and Emperor Rudolf II's castle, the mad emperor's desire for immortality, the anti-Semitism of the populace, and turbulent political issues intersect in unexpected ways in the life of Rochel, the orphan seamstress. While astronomy and the pseudo-science of alchemy entertain the court, Rabbi Judah Loewe creates a *golem*, Yossel, to protect the Jews from a rumored pogrom, but as often happens, the *golem* is not the soulless creature his creator expected.

Themes: anti-Semitism; Czechoslovakia; *golem*; magical realism; seventeenth century

Zimler, Richard

The Last Kabbalist of Lisbon. **Overlook Press, 2000. 318p.** 📖

Young Berekiah Zarco, a scribe and student of Kabbalah, searches for his uncle's murderer in the aftermath of the massacre of Lisbon's Jews in 1506. He confronts Christians and *conversos* (secret Jews), using his knowledge of Kabbalah to penetrate the Portuguese Inquisition's nightmarish world of death and persecution. A well-researched story based on historical events, dark and violent in tone. (Zimler's Web site is www.zimler.com.)

Themes: *conversos*; Inquisition; Kabbalah; murder and murderers; Sephardim

Related Titles: The descriptions of torture methods used by the Inquisition come from detailed records left by the Inquisitors themselves. Sensitive readers can often skip these descriptions without losing the narrative thread. Another novel of the Inquisition, based on the experiences of the author's family, is *Siguiriya* by Sylvia Lopez-Medina. In Zimler's next novel, *Hunting Midnight*, set in early nineteenth-century Portugal and America, the protagonist is a descendant of Berekiah Zarco.

Modern Period (1840–1950)

The first group of Jews to settle in the United States arrived in 1654 from Recife, Brazil, and were given grudging entry to New Amsterdam by Governor Peter Stuyvesant. These early settlers were Sephardim of Spanish and Portuguese origin. Although Jews were active participants in colonial life and the early republic, there are few novels in this chapter set in the Americas before 1840. The period from 1840 to 1950 includes the time when millions of Jews arrived in America, first from Germany, then from Eastern Europe. Jews left Europe because of the difficult political and social conditions. They were restricted in where they could live or travel, what occupations they could choose, and whether or not they could own land. Quotas restricted access to secular education. In vicious pogroms, peasants murdered and raped, burned synagogues, and ransacked homes, all with impunity. Religious persecution was often sanctioned by the government as a way for the peasantry to relieve their frustrations.

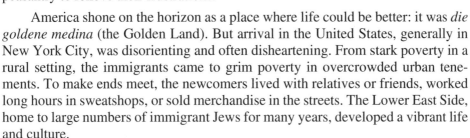

America shone on the horizon as a place where life could be better: it was *die goldene medina* (the Golden Land). But arrival in the United States, generally in New York City, was disorienting and often disheartening. From stark poverty in a rural setting, the immigrants came to grim poverty in overcrowded urban tenements. To make ends meet, the newcomers lived with relatives or friends, worked long hours in sweatshops, or sold merchandise in the streets. The Lower East Side, home to large numbers of immigrant Jews for many years, developed a vibrant life and culture.

Other immigrants settled in Boston or other East Coast cities, and even, due to a settlement scheme of the German Jewish community, in Galveston, Texas. Following a tradition of itinerant peddling, many Jews struck out into rural areas with packs on their backs, or with horse and buggy, to sell dry goods and notions. Many ended up settling in small towns throughout the country, trading in their packs to open dry goods stores. The "Jew store" became a fixture of small town life. Through hard work many achieved success. There were no guarantees, but at least there was opportunity where there had been none before.

The drama in the novels in this section derives from cultural dislocation. The religious observances that had sustained community and family in the Old World were difficult to maintain here. For some this was liberating; for others, anathema. How the immigrant generation and their children related to each other and the larger culture over these issues fueled novels for decades. It was, for most of the twentieth century, the primary subject matter of Jewish American literature.

Not all the novels in this section are set in the American immigrant community. Nomi Eve writes about the generations of a family that settled in Palestine in *The Family Orchard.* Gina Barkhordar Nahai tells a story about Iranian Jews in *The Cry of the Peacock.* Marge Piercy writes about Jewish participation in World War

II in *Gone to Soldiers*. Other novels are set in South America, Palestine, and Eastern Europe. This section has been subdivided geographically to reflect this diversity.

Europe

Epstein, Leslie
Pandaemonium. **St. Martin's, 1997. 398p.**

Actor Peter Lorre is glad of a respite from playing Mr. Moto to join the charismatic director Rudoph Von Beckmann in staging *Antigone* in Austria on the eve of the Anschluss. Historical and fictional characters combine in this inventive, satiric brew that mixes Hollywood and Holocaust-era politics with an abundance of characters and subplots.

Themes: actors and acting; Austria; Lorre, Peter; motion picture directors; Nazis

Related Titles: An earlier comic novel by Epstein, *Pinto and Sons*, follows the adventures of a Jewish medical student in California in the Gold Rush era. An autobiographical novel published in 2003, *San Remo Drive*, is based on Epstein's childhood in Los Angeles, where his father and uncle were successful screenwriters. *King of the Jews*, set in a small town at the beginning of the Holocaust, is annotated in the "Fiction, Individual Stories" section of chapter 7.

Piercy, Marge
Gone to Soldiers. **Summit Books, 1987. 703p.** 📖

A sweeping saga of World War II combining action, suspense, and absorbing personal drama, told from many points of view and locations, often focusing on women's experiences. Plotlines include Jewish resistance fighters in France, refugees in the United States, pilots, codebreakers, and war correspondents.

Themes: family relationships; Holocaust—resistance and rescue; women's lives; World War II

Related Titles: Piercy's novels are full of the social issues of the twentieth century from a feminist point of view. Readers who enjoy her fully realized, empathetic characters may also like her novel *Three Women*, annotated in the "Character" section of chapter 6, or her autobiography, *Sleeping with Cats*, annotated in the "Public Lives" section of chapter 8. (Her Web site is archer-books. com/Piercy/.)

Eastern Europe and Russia

Hoffman, Allen
Small Worlds Series.

Small Worlds. **Abbeville Press, 1996. 280p.** 📖

As the Hasids of the Polish village of Krimsk usher in the holiday of Tisha b'Av, their Rebbe tells the story of a supernatural frog, setting off a chain of events that mingles Talmudic disputation, the villagers' mystical beliefs, and the aggressive anti-Semitism of their Polish neighbors. Short chapters move back and forth among various characters and levels of Krimsk society, with a captivating combination of humor, realism, and fantasy.

Themes: 1900s; rabbis; shtetl life; Tisha B'Av

Big League Dreams. **Abbeville Press, 1997. 294p.** 📖

When the Krimsker Rebbe immigrated to St. Louis, he was followed by many of his flock, including the prodigy Matti Sternweiss, now grown and a catcher for the St. Louis Browns baseball team. On one particular Sabbath, we enter the thoughts of the former Krimskers as they are seduced by the wonders and temptations of America.

Themes: baseball and baseball players; 1920s; rabbis; Sabbath

Two for the Devil. **Abbeville Press, 1998. 254p.** 📖

The series concludes with two novellas, *Royal Garments* and *The Strength of Stones*, both dark in tone and set on Rosh Hashanah and Yom Kippur, respectively. In *Royal Garments*, Grisha Schwartzman, married to the Krimsker Rebbe's daughter and a member of the Soviet secret police, realizes that he has given his life to a cruel and immoral vision. In *The Strength of Stones*, Yechiel Katzman, who was cursed by the Krimsker Rebbe years earlier, stands in a cattle car on his way to Treblinka, where he has a redemptive meeting with Itzik, the Krimsk village idiot.

Themes: Holocaust; Holocaust—concentration camps; police; Soviet Union

Related Titles: Hoffman's *Kagan's Superfecta*, a collection containing the title novella and four short stories, won the Wallant Award in 1981. Readers who enjoyed Hoffman's depiction of Krimsk, laced with superstition and folklore, may also enjoy Isaac Bashevis Singer's early short stories, annotated in the "Classics and Major Authors" section of chapter 6. His memoir *In My Father's Court* is annotated in the "Childhood and Family" section of chapter 8.

Kornblatt, Joyce Reiser

The Reason for Wings. **Syracuse University Press, 1999. 233p.**

Rachael Silver, writing a family history for her unborn granddaughter, tells of their endurance in the face of persecution from Europe to Argentina, in lyrical prose with elements of magical realism. Memorable characterizations include the grandfather who may have flown away with the pelicans and the one-eyed gypsy who became a Jew.

Themes: family sagas; granddaughters; grandmothers; magicians; Ukraine

Related Titles: An earlier title by Kornblatt, *Breaking Bread,* a collection of fictionalized portraits of family members and friends remembered from childhood, is annotated in the "Character" section of chapter 6 along with a collection of stories, *Nothing to Do with Love*.

Malamud, Bernard

 The Fixer. **1966; reprint, Penguin Books, 1994. 299p.** 🟥**YA** 📖

After his wife runs off, destitute Yakov Bok leaves his village to try his luck in the city. At his new job he incurs the enmity of his anti-Semitic coworkers, who accuse him of the ritual murder of a young boy. Thrown into jail, Bok suffers constant humiliation by the authorities as they try to extract a confession. Based on the historical Mendel Beiliss case of 1911. (Winner of the Pulitzer Prize and the National Book Award.)

Themes: anti-Semitism; historical novels; Russia; trials

Related Titles: Malamud is one of the most noteworthy and critically acclaimed writers of the twentieth century. His novels and short stories are annotated in the "Classics and Major Authors" section of chapter 6.

Richler, Nancy

Your Mouth Is Lovely. **Ecco Press, 2002. 357p.** 🟥**YA** 📖

Miriam records her life story for her daughter from a prison in Siberia in the early 1900s, telling of her lonely childhood in a rural village after her mother died, and how she came to participate in the early years of the Russian Revolution. A satisfying combination of absorbing plot, well-researched historical background, and vivid characters. (Winner of the Canadian Jewish Book Award.)

Themes: Canadian authors; radicals and radicalism; Russia; shtetl life; women's lives

Related Titles: Another novel that mixes happiness and grief, about a woman who comes to a deeper understanding of herself, is Carole Glickfeld's *Swimming Toward the Ocean*, annotated in the "Character" section of chapter 6.

Rosenfarb, Chava

Bociany. **Syracuse University Press, 2000. 430p.**

A vivid and unsentimentalized portrait of a shtetl in Poland, in the early twentieth century, where Hindele, the scribe's widow, her children, and her neighbors do their best to survive the disease and poverty in which they live, taking pleasure in their natural surroundings and the comforting round of religious rituals. (Originally written in Yiddish and translated into English by the author, a survivor of the Lodz Ghetto.)

Themes: Canadian authors; family relationships; shtetl life

Related Titles: Another evocative portrayal of shtetl life in the early twentieth century can be found in Canadian Yiddish author Yehuda Elberg's *The Empire of Kalman the Cripple*.

Singer, Isaac Bashevis

The Family Moskat. **Alfred A. Knopf, 1950. 611p.**

A panoramic, bustling novel set in Warsaw, with a large cast of characters, centering on the family of the wealthy Meshulam Moskat in the first four decades of the twentieth century as a traditional culture is challenged by the modern world and the impending Holocaust. Translated by A. H. Gross.

Themes: assimilation; family sagas; Hasidism; Zionism

Related Titles: Readers may also enjoy *The Manor* and *The Estate*, which precede *The Family Moskat* chronologically. Together, these novels provide a broad picture of Jewish life in Eastern Europe from 1863 to the eve of World War II. Readers will find other novels by this master storyteller annotated in the "Classics and Major Authors" section of chapter 6.

The Middle East

Eve, Nomi

The Family Orchard. **Alfred A. Knopf, 2000. 316p.** **YA** 📖

Follows the branches of an Israeli family beginning with Esther and Yochanan, from mid-nineteenth-century Palestine to the Israel of today, through an episodic, poetic narrative accompanied by pictures, letters, and texts about fruit tree cultivation. Family stories are told from the point of view of the author and her father. (The author's Web site is www.nomieve.com.)

Themes: experimental fiction; family sagas; Israel; Palestine

Related Titles: Readers who enjoyed Eve's experimental style, disturbing the usual relationship between author and readers, may also enjoy *Diary of an Adulterous Woman* by Curt Leviant, annotated in the "Language" section of chapter 6.

Gross, Joel

This Year in Jerusalem. **Putnam, 1983. 304p.**

Diana Mann, an American reporter in Israel in 1947, falls in love with Jewish resistance fighter David Stern and agrees to become involved in obtaining weapons for the Haganah.

Themes: Israel—Intelligence services; Israel–Arab War, 1948–1949; love affairs; smuggling

Related Titles: Gross also wrote *The Books of Rachel* and *The Lives of Rachel*, annotated in the "Dark Ages Through Early Modern History" section of this chapter.

Nahai, Gina Barkhordar

The Cry of the Peacock. **Crown, 1991. 341p.**

Peacock, 116 years old, tells the harrowing story of the Jews in Iran for the last 200 years through her family's bitter history, in a style reminiscent of *Arabian Nights*, blending poetic imagery, exotic characters, and historical detail.

Themes: Iran; magical realism; Muslims and Jews; women's lives

Related Titles: Nahai's second novel, *Moonlight on the Avenue of Faith*, also about Iranian Jews, and similarly magical realist in style, is annotated in the "Setting" section of chapter 6.

Popkin, Zelda

 Quiet Street. **1951; reprint, University of Nebraska Press, 2002. 382p.**

Follows the Hirsch family and other Jewish residents of a street in Rehavia, a neighborhood of Jerusalem, during the Arab siege of the city in 1948. Tension builds slowly and steadily to an almost unbearable pitch, as the families cope with snipers, bombings, treason, food shortages, death, and their fears for the future of the newly created state of Israel. (Winner of the National Jewish Book Award.)

Themes: family relationships; friendship; Israel–Arab War, 1948–1949; Jerusalem

Related Titles: Popkin's strength is in her sensitive depiction of relationships, as evidenced further in two other novels, *"Dear Once"*, a multigenerational family saga, and *Herman Had Two Daughters*, an autobiographical novel. Two other novels set in Palestine in the time just before statehood with some of the same understated authority are Shulamith Hareven's *City of Many Days* and Linda Grant's *When I Lived in Modern Times*.

Uris, Leon

Exodus. **Doubleday, 1958. 626p.**

A sweeping, emotional narrative that captures the saga of the birth of Israel from the point of view of participants and spectators: refugees, Holocaust survivors, *sabras*, Americans, Arabs, and the British. Conflict, romance, details of military operations, and the charismatic protagonist Ari ben Canaan, make this a page-turner. (Winner of the National Jewish Book Award.)

Themes: Israel–Arab War, 1948–1949; Jewish–Arab relations; love affairs; Zionism

Related Titles: Readers who are interested in the story of the British attempts to turn away boatloads of Holocaust survivors may want to read the true account in Ruth Gruber's *Exodus 1947: The Ship That Launched a Nation*. Readers who want to learn more of the historical background should check the "Jewish History Sources" at the end of this chapter.

Mitla Pass. **Doubleday, 1988. 435p.**

Ambitious American novelist Gideon Zadok receives permission to parachute into the treacherous Mitla Pass in the Sinai desert with Israeli troops during the war with Egypt in 1956. Tightly plotted, with Uris's trademark driving narrative style, preparations for the battle alternate with the history of Gideon's immigrant forebears and his own tempestuous life story.

Themes: family relationships; Israel—Sinai Campaign, 1956; love affairs; war stories

Wouk, Herman

Historical figures interact with Wouk's characters in this colorful, panoramic history of the state of Israel, starting with its creation in 1948 and ending with the celebration of the fortieth anniversary of statehood.

The Hope. Little, Brown, 1993. 693p.

The struggles of Israel's early years, from the war that began as soon as statehood was announced to the Six-Day War in 1967, are reflected in the lives of four army officers and their women.

Themes: Israel—armed forces; Israel—History; Israel–Arab War, 1948–1949; Jewish–Arab relations; Six-Day War, 1967; soldiers

The Glory. Little, Brown, 1994. 685p.

The next generation begins to assume responsibilities for the survival of Israel, participating in such pivotal events as the Yom Kippur War in 1973 and the raid on Entebbe Airport.

Themes: Entebbe Airport Raid, 1976; Israel—Armed Forces; Israel—History; Jewish–Arab relations; soldiers; Yom Kippur War, 1983

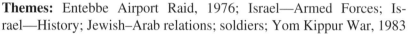

Related Titles: Wouk's two earlier novels about World War II, *Winds of War* and *War and Remembrance*, deal with the Holocaust and serve as a prologue to these novels about Israel. Other Wouk novels with Jewish themes are *Marjorie Morningstar*, *City Boy*, and *Inside, Outside*. The last title is annotated in the Story section of chapter 6. Wouk's commitment to Judaism and Israel is evident in two nonfiction works: *This is My God* and *The Will to Live On*. Another historical novel set in Palestine around the time of World War I, combining historical and fictional characters, is *Promise the Earth*, by the British author Clive Irving.

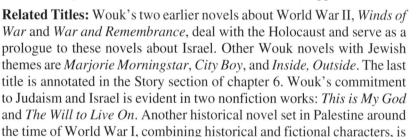

Latin America

Alcala, Kathleen

Spirits of the Ordinary: A Tale of Casas Grandes. Chronicle Books, 1997. 244p.

When the Inquisition came to Mexico from Spain in the 1600s, Jews were forced to convert, but many secretly retained their religious traditions and encouraged their children to marry other secret Jews. Zacarias, a *converso* living in Mexico in the 1870s, leaves his family in search of adventure but cannot escape the force of his Jewish heritage and its mystical traditions. (The author's Web site is www.kathleenalcala.com.)

Themes: *conversos*; family relationships; Mexico; mysticism

Related Titles: Readers who would like to know more about the history of hidden Jews in the Western hemisphere may enjoy Trudi Alexy's *The Mezuzah in the Madonna's Foot: Marranos and Other Secret Jews*, annotated in the "Memoirs, Personal Narratives" section of chapter 7 or *Suddenly Jewish: Jews Raised as Gentles Discover Their Jewish Roots* by Barbara Kessel, annotated in the "Collected Biography" section of chapter 8, or the young adult historical novel *Out of Many Waters* by Jacqueline Dembar Greene, which tells the story of how the first Jews came to North America.

Katz, Judith

The Escape Artist. **Firebrand Books, 1997. 283p.**

Instead of marriage to a South American diamond merchant, Sofia finds herself sold into prostitution in Argentina, where she endures the squalid brothel life until she escapes with the woman who is her true love. Based on research into the stories of Eastern European girls who were abducted into prostitution in the early twentieth century.

Themes: gays/lesbians/bisexuals; magicians; 1900s; prostitution

Related Titles: Katz has written an earlier novel, *Running Fiercely toward a High Thin Sound,* about the lives of Jewish lesbians.

Prose, Francine

 Hungry Hearts. **Pantheon Books, 1983. 213p.**

Dinah Rappoport tells how she became a star of the Yiddish theater in the 1920s and became possessed by a dybbuk in South America. Historical detail, humor, and elements of folklore combine with wonder-working rabbis, prostitutes, and pilots in a very theatrical tale. (Winner of the E. L. Wallant Award.)

Themes: dybbuks; Latin America; Yiddish theater

Related Titles: Two other novels by Prose with Jewish themes are *Judah the Pious*, annotated in the "Dark Ages through Early Modern History" section of this chapter and *Guided Tours of Hell*, annotated in the "Setting" section of chapter 6. Readers wishing to learn more about the Yiddish theater may be interested in Nahma Sandrow's *Vagabond Stars: A World History of Yiddish Theater* or *A Life on the Stage* the autobiography of the celebrated actor Jacob Adler, annotated in the "Public Lives" section of chapter 8. The dybbuk that possesses Dinah in this novel has often appeared in Jewish literature, most famously in Solomon Ansky's play *The Dybbuk*. Readers can learn more about the dybbuk and its appearances in Yiddish literature in Joachim Neugroschel's *The Dybbuk and the Yiddish Imagination: A Haunted Reader*. Another novel with a combination of history and magical realism is Lillian Nattel's *The River Midnight*, annotated in the "Language" section of chapter 6.

Rabinovich, Dalia

Flora's Suitcase. **HarperCollins, 1998. 238p.**

When Flora marries Dave Grossenberg and travels with him to Colombia, she becomes part of his contentious and overbearing Russian family, and enters a world where reality is tempered by magic and superstition.

Themes: brothers and sisters; Colombia; magical realism; women's lives

United States and Canada

Birmingham, Stephen

The Auerbach Will. **Little, Brown, 1983. 430p.**

When Essie marries into the fashionable, wealthy Auerbach family, she becomes part of a social milieu where proper behavior counts for everything. Although Essie and Jake achieve stunning financial success in the mail-order business, their lives are afflicted with discord and deception.

Themes: family secrets; merchants; wealth

Related Titles: Birmingham has written several other novels in which family members struggle with scandal and secrets and clash over control of businesses, including *Carriage Trade* and *The Rothman Scandal*. For the background of Birmingham's novels, readers may enjoy his history of the great German–Jewish merchant families, *"Our Crowd"*, annotated in the "Collected Biography" section of chapter 8. Readers may also enjoy Michael Korda's novel *Worldly Goods*, in which greed and family secrets collide against a background of high finance.

Chabon, Michael

The Amazing Adventures of Kavalier and Clay. **Random House, 2000. 639p.**

Joe Kavalier escapes from the Nazis by hiding in the coffin of the Prague *golem*, joining with his cousin Sammy Clay in New York to create a popular comic book superhero, *The Escapist*. Their artistic creation gives them the chance to explore the unresolved themes of exile, revenge, and sexual identity in their own lives. (Winner of the Pulitzer Prize and an ALA Notable Book. The author's Web site is www.michaelchabon.com.)

Themes: Arctic regions; artists; comic books; Holocaust; New York City; 1940s; sexual identity

Related Titles: When the National Yiddish Book Center released its list, *100 Great Works of Modern Jewish Literature*, this was the only title included that was published after 1990. Chabon's earlier novels include *The Mysteries of Pittsburgh* and *Wonderboys*. The *golem*, a fascinating figure of Jewish folklore, appears in a number of recent novels in a variety of ways. Among the titles in which a *golem* figure makes an appearance are *The Book of Splendor* by Frances Sherwood, annotated in the "Dark Ages through Early Modern History" section of this chapter; *The Alchemist's Door* by Lisa Goldstein, annotated in chapter 4; *Consent* by Ben Schrank, annotated in the "Character" section of chapter 6; and *Snow in August* by Pete Hamill, annotated in the "Story" section of chapter 6.

Courter, Gay

The Midwife Series.

In two well-researched novels, Courter captures the struggles of immigrants in New York in the early 1900s from the perspective of a woman involved in health care and social issues. The empathetic Hannah grows in self-confidence about her own skills, but her work is hampered by prejudice against women in the health care field and ignorance about the treatment of women's illnesses. (The author's Web site is www.gaycourter.com.)

Themes: medicine; midwives; radicals and radicalism; women's lives

The Midwife. **Houghton Mifflin, 1981. 559p.** `YA` 📖

Hannah becomes a certified midwife in Russia, but when the political situation for Jews becomes dangerous, she and her family go to New York, where she works hard to make a living and keep her marriage together.

The Midwife's Advice. **Dutton, 1992. 598p.** `YA` 📖

Hannah, now the head midwife at Bellevue Hospital, finds a second career advising women who have sexual problems and becomes involved with political issues through her activist husband, Lazar.

Related Titles: Courter has also written a thriller, *Code Ezra*, annotated in the "Political Intrigue and Espionage" section of chapter 2. The Jewish women portrayed in the historical novels of Courter and Meredith Tax (annotated in this section) were based on the early Jewish feminists in Eastern Europe who strove to educate themselves, live independent lives, and participate in the radical social movements of the nineteenth century. Readers may enjoy the autobiography of one of these early Jewish feminists, *My Life as a Radical Jewish Woman: Memoirs of a Zionist Feminist in Poland,* by Puah Rakovsky.

Doctorow, E. L.

🎗 *Ragtime.* **1974; reprint, Modern Library, 1994. 320p.** `YA` 📖

A Jewish immigrant and his daughter, an African American moved to violent action by racial injustice, and a family living a privileged but shallow existence in the suburbs find their lives colliding and changing in the early 1900s. Historical figures from all walks of life turn up to advance the plot, including Houdini and J. P. Morgan. Doctorow uses a variety of stylistic devices to push the boundaries of the traditional historical novel. (Winner of the National Book Critics Circle Award.)

Themes: African Americans; immigrants; race relations; radicals and radicalism

Related Titles: Readers who are looking less for historical information and more for imaginative uses of historical material may enjoy other novels by Doctorow, annotated in the "Classics and Major Authors" section of chapter 6.

🎗 *World's Fair.* **Random House, 1985. 288p.** `YA` 📖

Four-year-old Edgar is our guide through the sights, sounds, and smells of a Bronx neighborhood in the 1930s. Filled with vivid details and perceptive insights into the process of growing up and learning about self, family, and the outside world, culminating in the fantasy world of the 1939 World's Fair, this reads more like autobiography than fiction. (Winner of the National Book Award and an ALA Notable Book.)

Themes: boys; family relationships; New York World's Fair, 1939–1940; 1930s

Related Titles: Readers may enjoy *Fourth Street East: A Novel of How it Was* by Jerome Weidman, another novel written from the point of view of a young boy growing up in New York City.

Eisner, Will

The Will Eisner Library.

Eisner is one of the pioneers in the field of comic art. He began selling his comics in 1936 after finishing high school in the Bronx. Comic books were new and wildly popular; to meet the demand Eisner and Jerry Iger opened a studio that produced comics for publishers in an assembly-line fashion. Many well-known comic artists trained with Eisner, including Jules Feiffer. In 1940 Eisner created the popular comic strip *The Spirit*, about a masked detective superhero character. *The Spirit* ran in newspapers until 1952. In 1978, ever an innovator, Eisner pushed the limits of comic art to create the first graphic novel, *A Contract with God*, the first in a series of graphic novels set in a particular tenement in the Bronx, portraying the lives of working-class immigrants in the 1930s. (The author's Web site is www.willeisner.com.)

Themes: Bronx, N.Y.; family relationships; graphic novels; immigrants; poverty; U.S.—History—Depression

A Contract with God. **1978; reprint, DC Comics, 2000. 181p.**

Vignettes of the difficult lives of the residents of 55 Dropsie Avenue. In the title story, Frimme Hersh has a hard time understanding God's ways.

New York, the Big City. **1986; reprint, DC Comics, 144p.**
The Dreamer. **Kitchen Sink Press, 1986. 46p.**
City People Notebook. **1989; reprint, DC Comics, 2000. 88p.**
To the Heart of the Storm. **1991; reprint, DC Comics, 2000. 208p.**

Will Eisner Reader: Seven Graphic Stories by a Comics Master. **1991; reprint, DC Comics, 2000. 88p.**

In "A Sunset in Sunshine City," aging widower Henry Klop is the victim of family greed. These stories originally appeared in issues of *Will Eisner's Quarterly*, published by Kitchen Sink Press.

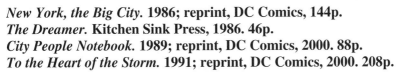

Invisible People. **1993; reprint, DC Comics, 2000. 117p.**
Dropsie Avenue: The Neighborhood. **1995; reprint, DC Comics, 2000. 170p.**

Minor Miracles. DC Comics. **Kitchen Sink Press, 1995. 128p.**

Four tales of good fortune and bad luck, of smart and foolish people. "The Miracle of Dignity" tells how standing on his dignity made Uncle

Amos rich, then poor again. In "A Special Wedding Ring," an unlikely couple ultimately come to value each other.

The Building. **Kitchen Sink Press, 1996. 80p.**
Family Matters. **Kitchen Sink Press, 1998. 68p.**
Life on Another Planet. **DC Comics, 2000. 136p.**
The Name of the Game. **DC Comics, 2001. 168p.**

In tracing the Arnheim family and their marriages, Eisner gives us the history of the immigrant Jewish community from the mid-nineteenth century to the 1950s.

A Life Force. **DC Comics, 2001. 139p.**

The Depression and the growing Nazi menace in Germany affect the lives of the residents of 55 Dropsie Avenue in the Bronx.

Related Titles: Readers looking for other novels with working-class settings may enjoy Michael Gold's *Jews Without Money*, annotated in the "Classics and Major Authors" section of chapter 6. In 2003, in a change from his Dropsie Avenue setting, Eisner published the graphic novel *Fagin the Jew*, an apologia for the thieves' ringleader in Dickens's *Oliver Twist*.

Fast, Howard

Max. **Houghton Mifflin, 1982. 395p.**

Max Britsky was only twelve when his father died, but he took on the support of his family. He became an entrepreneur in the fledgling motion picture business, starting as a distributor of the earliest Edison moving pictures and eventually controlling an empire in Hollywood. Character takes a back seat to plot in this vivid re-creation of an era and an industry.

Themes: immigrants; men's lives; motion picture industry; teenaged boys

Related Titles: Max's story is the fictional version of the lives of many early twentieth-century immigrants, forced into adult roles early in life, cultivating a sharp eye for opportunity. A classic novel in this vein is *What Makes Sammy Run?* by Budd Schullberg, annotated in the "Character" section of chapter 6.

The Bridge Builder's Story. **M. E. Sharpe, 1995. 210p.** **YA** 📖

When Scott and Martha Waring stop off in Berlin on their honeymoon in 1939, a series of innocuous events culminates in tragedy, changing Scott's life forever. It is not until years later, when Scott falls in love with a Holocaust survivor, that he comes to terms with his past.

Themes: Holocaust; Holocaust—survivors; Jewish–Christian relations; World War II

Related Titles: Fast is a prolific writer who has written novels, plays, essays, and nonfiction under his own name and also as E. V. Cunningham.

Gold, Herbert

🎗 ***Fathers: A Novel in the Form of Memoir.*** **Random House, 1967. 308p.**

Sam Gold's life, in colorful, colloquial detail, from Russian village to New York's Lower East Side, and then to the Midwest, where he was a grocer. He saved to bring over his brothers and sisters, then to raise a family and cope with racketeers, the Depression, and anti-Semitism. (An ALA Notable Book.)

Themes: fathers and sons; immigrants; merchants; 1940s; 1930s

Goldreich, Gloria

Goldreich's novels of the immigrant experience feature strong women who know their own minds and find compromise difficult, even if it means that family relationships will suffer. Social and political conditions provide an authentic backdrop, affecting her characters' lives and decisions and providing fuel for the plot.

Leah's Journey. **Harcourt Brace Jovanovich, 1978. 404p. YA**

Fleeing persecution in Russia, Leah and David Goldfeder settle in New York's Lower East Side, where the strong-willed, independent Leah works in sweatshops, while David studies medicine and they raise three children, against a background of international social and political events from the 1920s through the 1940s. (Winner of the National Jewish Book Award.)

Themes: artists; family relationships; immigrants; Lower East Side, N.Y.; marriage

Related Titles: Readers who enjoy Goldreich's strong characters may like Norma Harris's *Trumpets of Silver*, also about an immigrant family.

Leah's Children. **Macmillan, 1985. 329p. YA**

Leah has become a successful artist, while her children and grandchildren are caught up in world events from the 1940s to the 1960s: the Hungarian uprising, the creation of the State of Israel, and the U.S. civil rights movement.

Themes: artists; immigrants; Lower East Side, N.Y.; 1950s; 1940s; 1960s; parents and children

Related Titles: Readers may also enjoy Rose Cohen's autobiography about her childhood on the Lower East Side working in sweatshops, *Out of the Shadows*, annotated in the "Childhood and Family" section of chapter 8. Other stories of immigrant women who struggled to express their artistic talents can be found in the novels and short stories of Anzia Yezierska, annotated in the "Classics and Major Authors" section of chapter 6. Another panoramic family saga set against the backdrop of twentieth-century social and political events is Erica Jong's *Inventing Memory: A Novel of Mothers and Daughters*.

That Year of Our War. **Little, Brown, 1994. 356p. YA**

In 1942 fifteen-year-old Sharon Grossberg's mother dies while her father is overseas in the army, so her aunts take her in. As everyone waits for news of loved ones in the war, Sharon grows older and wiser, learning about love, death, and betrayal.

Themes: coming-of-age stories; family relationships; World War II

Related Titles: Readers who enjoyed the nostalgic portrayal of family relationships in this novel may also enjoy Zelda Popkin's novel *"Dear Once"*. Another novel told from the point of view of a teenaged girl going through family upheavals is *Growing Up Rich* by Anne Bernays. Another novel about family relationships with a strong sense of time and place is Gary Glickman's *Years from Now*. Herman Wouk's classic *Marjorie Morningstar* tells about a young woman in the 1930s trying to reconcile her family's expectations with her own romantic ambitions.

West to Eden. Macmillan, 1987. 418p. YA

In 1897, Emma Coen is left penniless by her father's death and leaves Amsterdam to seek her fortune, vowing to be independent. In Galveston, Texas, she marries Isaac Lewin, and they move to Phoenix, raising a family, building a successful department store business, but struggling all the while with their own fragile relationship. A panorama of American life in the first four decades of the twentieth century, from a Western perspective.

Themes: Arizona; family sagas; frontier and pioneer life; immigrants

Related Titles: *West to Eden* includes a description of the devastating hurricane that hit Galveston in 1900. For a nonfiction account of this storm, readers may enjoy *Isaac's Storm: A Man, a Time, and the Deadliest Hurricane in History* by Erik Larson. Many of the major department stores were started in the way Goldreich recounts in this novel. A nonfiction account of the great merchant families is *Merchant Princes: An Intimate History of Jewish Families Who Built Great Department Stores* by Leon Harris, annotated in the "Collected Biography" section of chapter 8.

Greenberg, Eric Rolfe

The Celebrant. Everest House, 1983. 272p. YA

Jack Kapp is offered a baseball contract by a Pennsylvania team, but his horrified parents keep him in the family jewelry business. His continuing love of baseball brings him into contact with Christy Mathewson, who exemplifies for Jack all the nobility of the sport, and he designs a ring for the ballplayer, opening a connection between the two men that enriches Jack's life.

Themes: baseball and baseball players; brothers; immigrants; Mathewson, Christy; 1900s; 1910s

Haber, Leo

The Red Heifer. Syracuse University Press, 2001. 289p. YA

Linked stories about life on the Lower East Side of New York in the 1930s and 1940s as seen through the perceptive eyes of a young boy whose gradual loss of innocence the reader shares. Rich in *Yiddishkeit*, with memorable secondary characters, and a vivid setting, this is an unsentimentalized portrait of a teeming immigrant community.

Themes: boys; coming-of-age stories; immigrants; Lower East Side, N.Y.; 1940s; 1930s

Related Titles: Readers may also enjoy *Fourth Street East: A Novel of How it Was*, by Jerome Weidman, about a young boy growing up on the Lower East Side in the 1920s, filled with memorable characters and incidents. Another novel set in the same time and place and told from the point of view of a young boy trying to understand the world around him is Henry Roth's *Call It Sleep*, annotated in the "Classics and Major Authors" section of chapter 6.

Katchor, Ben

The Jew of New York. **Pantheon Books, 1998. 104p.**

Dreamers, schemers, playwrights, and businessmen collide in New York City in the early nineteenth century in this graphic novel that mixes history and fantasy. In one of several threads, based in fact, characters attempt to start a utopian Jewish community in upstate New York. (The author's Web site is www.katchor.com.)

Themes: fantasy; graphic novels; immigrants; nineteenth century; utopian communities

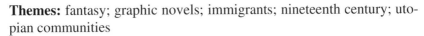

Related Titles: Katchor, a popular graphic artist, has a long-running comic strip in the weekly *Forward* newspaper. Readers who appreciate his monochromatic art and convoluted plots may also enjoy *Julius Knipl, Real Estate Photographer: The Beauty Supply District.*

Kluger, Steve

Last Days of Summer. **Avon, 1998. 353p.** `YA`

As Joey Margolis's family life disintegrates and anti-Semitic neighborhood boys attack him, he writes increasingly urgent letters to New York Giants third baseman Charlie Banks, changing both their lives in the process. Joey's letters, newspaper clippings, and scorecards add immediacy to this story filled with nostalgia for Brooklyn during the 1940s. (The author's Web site is www.stevekluger.com.)

Themes: baseball and baseball players; boys; Brooklyn, N.Y.; fathers and sons; World War II

Related Titles: Another novel filled with childhood nostalgia and love of baseball is Alan Lelchuk's *Brooklyn Boy*, annotated in the "Setting" section of chapter 6.

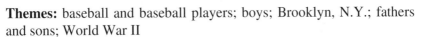

Kotlowitz, Robert

Sea Changes. **North Point Press, 1986. 275p.**

Manfred Vogel, a German teenager, is adopted by the Gordon family in Baltimore in the late 1930s. As the news from Germany gets worse, Manfred struggles to make sense of American family relationships, high school, and his growing attraction to the Gordon's daughter. Wryly narrated from Manfred's point of view, a literate and unsentimental study of identity in exile.

Themes: coming-of-age stories; immigrants; teenaged boys

Related Titles: Another perceptive character study by Kotlowitz is *The Board-walk*, about a teenaged boy vacationing in Atlantic City, New Jersey, in the weeks before the outbreak of World War II. Kotlowitz has also written a memoir about his experiences as a soldier in an infantry platoon in World War II, *Before Their Time*.

Mamet, David
The Old Religion. **The Free Press, 1997. 194p.**

A spare, impressionistic study of Leo Frank, the Georgia factory owner who was wrongfully convicted of the rape and murder of a young girl in 1914, and lynched by an anti-Semitic mob. Through Frank's interior monologues and conversations with friends and family, the author builds a picture of life in the South for Jews before World War I.

Themes: anti-Semitism; Ku Klux Klan; lynching

Related Titles: Another fictional account of the Frank case is *Member of the Tribe* by Richard Kluger. Readers who would like a nonfiction account of the crime and the trial may enjoy *And the Dead Shall Rise: The Murder of Mary Phagan and the Lynching of Leo Frank* by Steve Oney.

Nissenson, Hugh
My Own Ground. **Farrar, Straus & Giroux, 1976. 181p.**

Fifteen-year-old Jake Brody is an orphan, scraping by on his own on the Lower East Side, when he is befriended by the pimp Schlifka, who seeks his help in adding the beautiful Hannah Isaacs to his stable of prostitutes. An unusual coming-of-age story, set in a starkly rendered, violent setting.

Themes: coming-of-age stories; immigrants; Lower East Side, N.Y.; 1910s; prostitution

Related Titles: Readers who appreciated the realism of this gritty historical novel may also enjoy Bernard Malamud's *The Assistant*, annotated in the "Classics and Major Authors" section of chapter 6 or Lewis Wallant's *The Pawnbroker*, annotated in the "Character" section of chapter 6.

Raboy, Isaac
Jewish Cowboy. **Tradition Books, 1989. 297p.** **YA**

An autobiographical novel about Isaac, a Russian immigrant in the early 1900s, who takes a job as a ranch hand in North Dakota to further his dream of living off the land and working with horses. Translated from the Yiddish by Nathaniel Shapiro.

Themes: cowboys; immigrants; men's lives

Related Titles: Readers interested in the Jewish experience on the plains may enjoy *Rachel Calof's Story: Jewish Homesteader on the Northern Plains*, annotated in the "Childhood and Family" section of chapter 8, the autobiography of a pioneer woman in North Dakota at the same time period. An unusual memoir about another Jewish cowboy is Argentinean Albert Gerchunoff's *The Jewish Gauchos* *of the Pampas*, first published in Spanish in 1910, and recently reissued in English by the University of New Mexico Press. Gerchunoff and his family came to Argentina in the mid-nineteenth century as part of Baron de Hirsch's Jewish Colonization Association.

Rochlin, Harriet

Desert Dwellers Trilogy. YA

Rochlin's extensive knowledge of the Jewish communities of the Old West enlivens this series, as we follow her spirited heroine, Frieda Levie, from San Francisco to the Arizona Territory at the end of the nineteenth century. Readers will enjoy the details of pioneer life, the colorful characters, and Frieda's development from naïve schoolgirl to resourceful, independent rancher.

Themes: Arizona; frontier and pioneer life; marriage

The Reformer's Apprentice: A Novel of Old San Francisco. **Fithian Press, 1996. 224p.**

Frieda wants to go to high school and become a schoolteacher, against the wishes of her immigrant father. By marrying Bennie Goldson, a colorful Jewish rancher from Arizona Territory, she gains her independence and a chance for adventure.

The First Lady of Dos Cacahuates. **Fithian Press, 1998. 229p.**

Frieda finds life in Arizona Territory is filled with natural disasters, murder, and creative ways to remain Jewish.

On Her Way Home. **Fithian Press, 2001. 270p.**

When her youngest sister Ida is kidnapped, Frieda leaves her infant daughter at home to search for her.

Related Titles: Rochlin's interest and expertise in this period is evidenced by her coauthorship of the book *Pioneer Jews: A New Life in the Far West*. A true story of the challenge of maintaining Jewish traditions in primitive frontier conditions can also be found in *Rachel Calof's Story*, the autobiography of a Russian mail-order bride in 1890s North Dakota, annotated in the "Childhood and Family" section of chapter 8. Another view of San Francisco in the nineteenth century can be found in Harriet Lane Levy's autobiography *920 O'Farrell Street*, annotated in the same section.

Roiphe, Anne Richardson

The Pursuit of Happiness. **Summit Books, 1991. 473p.**

This panoramic novel moves back and forth in time across four generations of the Gruenbaum family from Poland to New York to Israel, chronicling their successes, failures, loves, and losses in search of the American Dream.

Themes: family relationships; family sagas; immigrants

Related Titles: Readers of Roiphe's autobiography *1185 Park Avenue*, annotated in the "Childhood and Family" section of chapter 8, may be able to identify some of the autobiographical elements in this novel. Intergenerational issues are also the subject of Roiphe's novel *Lovingkindness*, annotated in the "Character" section of chapter 6. Another multigenerational saga with multiple story lines and well-drawn characters is Silvia Tennenbaum's *Yesterday's Streets*.

Rosen, Charley

The House of Moses All-Stars. Seven Stories Press, 1996. 490p. **YA**

A pick-up team of Jewish basketball players tours the country in an old hearse, playing in small towns, hoping to make some money and redeem their lives from their personal demons. A sweetly melancholic tale told by one of the players and set against a realistic backdrop of Depression-era hardships and the expansion of Nazism in Germany.

Themes: anti-Semitism; basketball and basketball players; 1930s

Related Titles: Rosen, a former coach and player, wrote another sports novel, *Barney Polan's Game*, about the 1951 college basketball scandals. Two other sports novels with historical frameworks are *The Rabbi of Swat* by Peter Levine, about baseball in the 1920s, and *Haymon's Crowd*, by Robert Greenfield, a basketball novel.

Silbert, Layle

The Free Thinkers: Two Novellas. Seven Stories Press, 2000. 317p.

Two psychological studies of the lives of Eastern European immigrants to the United States. In the title novella, Ida, a single woman, envisions a nontraditional role for herself and attempts to change her life.

Themes: Chicago; immigrants; women's lives

Related Titles: Readers may also enjoy *Leah*, by Seymour Epstein, another novel about a woman who questions how she can live her life on her own terms; winner of the E. L. Wallant Award.

Stern, Steve

Harry Kaplan's Adventures Underground. Ticknor & Fields, 1991. 310p.

Fifteen-year-old Harry Kaplan's quiet life in Memphis, Tennessee, reading and working in his father's pawnshop, is changed forever by his grandmother's death and a 1930s flood that turns Beale Street into a fantastic floating world. Evading his contentious family in the company of a pair of African American twins, Harry floats off to explore a seamy and forbidden part of the city.

Themes: African Americans; coming-of-age stories; grandmothers; Memphis, Tennessee; twins

Sturm, James

The Golem's Mighty Swing. Drawn and Quarterly Books, 2001. 100p. **YA**

In the 1920s, The Stars of David, a barnstorming Jewish baseball team, play a circuit of small towns, often encountering anti-Semitism, but gamely trying to make a living. A promoter encourages one of the players to wear a *golem* costume to increase the team's appeal. Noah Strauss, the Zion Lion, third baseman and manager, tells the story. (Winner of the Ignatz Award for Outstanding Graphic Album.)

Themes: anti-Semitism; baseball and baseball players; *golem*; graphic novels

Tax, Meredith

Tax writes about the strong, independent women on New York's Lower East Side who became union organizers and suffragists. The wealth of historical details about public events and private lives paints a vivid picture of the period from the early 1900s the end of the 1930s.

Rivington Street. **1982; reprint, University of Chicago Press, 2001. 431p.** YA

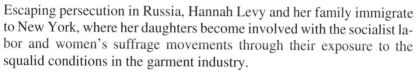

Escaping persecution in Russia, Hannah Levy and her family immigrate to New York, where her daughters become involved with the socialist labor and women's suffrage movements through their exposure to the squalid conditions in the garment industry.

Themes: labor unions; Lower East Side, N.Y.; 1900s; 1910s; women's lives

Related Titles: Abraham Cahan, editor of the influential Yiddish newspaper *The Forward*, makes an appearance in *Rivington Street*. Readers may be interested in Cahan's own novel of the immigrant experience, *The Rise of David Levinsky*, annotated in the "Classics and Major Authors" section of chapter 6. One of the characters in *Rivington Street* writes to the advice column in *The Forward*, a column that helped immigrants with the transition to American life. Letters to that column are collected in the volume *A Bintel Brief: Sixty Years of Letters From the Lower East Side to the Jewish Daily Forward.* (The Yiddish title means "a bundle of letters.") Readers may enjoy *All for One*, the autobiography of Rose Schneiderman, who was involved in the union movement, much like Sarah in Tax's books. That title is annotated in the "Public Lives" section of chapter 8. Readers may also enjoy *Half a Heart* by Rosellen Brown, also about the difficult choices women make in life. It is annotated in the "Story" section of chapter 6.

Union Square. **1988; reprint, University of Chicago Press, 2001. 437p.** YA

The sequel follows Hannah's daughters and their friends Rachel and Tish through the 1920s and 1930s as they marry or explore other lifestyles and prosper in their careers.

Themes: labor unions; Lower East Side, N.Y.; socialism; women's lives

Related Titles: Another view of the lives of Russian immigrants caught up in political movements of the late nineteenth and early twentieth centuries can be found in Peter Glassgold's historical novel *The Angel Max*, which features historical characters like Emma Goldman and Sasha

Berkman. Readers may also enjoy the biography *Joe Rapoport: The Life of a Jewish Radical* by Kenneth Kann. Rapoport started his activist career as a youth in Russia and was involved in union organizing in the garment industry; he remained involved in socialist causes all his life.

Taylor, Benjamin

Tales Out of School. **Turtle Point Press, 1995. 283p.**

In the steamy climate of Galveston, Texas, at the turn of the twentieth century, the wealthy Mehmel family suffers losses both financial and spiritual, forever changing the life of the teenaged Felix. Languid, mannered prose describes the events leading up to the summer of Felix's sexual coming of age.

Themes: coming-of-age stories; gays/lesbians/bisexuals; immigrants; teenaged boys

Jewish History Sources

Often after reading a historical novel, readers want to turn to the historical record to learn more about an era. Since the novels in this chapter cover Jewish history from ancient to modern times, the sources below are not confined to American Jewish history. There are many popular and scholarly works on Jewish history; this list covers a few of the titles likely to be readily available in public and synagogue libraries. Readers' advisory sources for historical fiction in general can be found in chapter 9.

Abella, Irving. *A Coat of Many Colours: Two Centuries of Jewish Life in Canada.* Toronto: Key Porter Books, 1990.

Cowan, Neil M., and Ruth Schwartz Cowan. *Our Parents' Lives: The Americanization of Eastern European Jews.* New York: Basic Books, 1989.
Recounts the experiences of Eastern European immigrant Jews born between 1895 and 1915 and how they adapted to American culture.

Dimont, Max I. *Jews, God and History.* Rev. and updated ed.. New York: Penguin Books, 1994.
A panoramic history of the Jews from the biblical era to modern times.

Diner, Hasia. *Lower East Side Memories: A Jewish Place in America.* Princeton, NJ: Princeton University Press, 2000.
An exploration of what the Lower East Side means in the collective Jewish memory.

Gerber, Jane S. *The Jews of Spain: A History of the Sephardic Experience.* New York: The Free Press. 1992.
A history of the Sephardic Jews from the Golden Age in Spain to the twentieth century.

Gilbert, Martin. *Israel: A History.* New York: Morrow, 1998.
Issued for the fiftieth anniversary of Israel, this history includes the political events in the first half of the twentieth century leading up to statehood and an account of the development of Israel through the Oslo accords.

Gilbert, Martin. *Letters to Auntie Fori: The 5,000–Year History of the Jewish People and Their Faith.* New York: Schocken Books, 2002.
This is a compilation of letters that Gilbert wrote to Auntie Fori, an old friend in India, that comprise a history of the Jewish people.

Grayzel, Solomon**.** *A History of the Jews: From the Babylonian Exile to the Present.* 2nd ed. Philadelphia: Jewish Publication Society, 1968.

Gribetz, Judah, et al. *The Timetables of Jewish History: A Chronology of the Most Important People and Events in Jewish History.* New York: Simon & Schuster, 1993.

Hoffman, Eva. *Shtetl: The Life and Death of a Small Town and the World of Polish Jews.* Boston: Houghton Mifflin, 1997.
Hoffman uses the Polish village of Brask as a microcosm of the relationship between the Polish and Jewish communities.

Howe, Irving, with the assistance of Kenneth Libo. *World of Our Fathers: The Journey of the East European Jews to America and the Life They Found and Made.* New York: Harcourt Brace Jovanovich, 1976.
An extensive and illuminating account of the wave of immigration that brought two million Eastern European Jews to the United States; how it transformed the immigrants, and how the immigrants transformed the United States, particularly the Lower East Side of New York. Full of information about people, social and political issues, culture, mores, and *Yiddishkeit.*

Johnson, Paul**.** *A History of the Jews.* New York: Harper & Row. 1987.

Joselit, Jenna Weissman. *The Wonders of America: Reinventing Jewish Culture, 1880–1950.* New York: Hill and Wang, 1994.
A social history of the Jewish cultural world created by the American Jewish community during the course of three crucial generations.

Karp, Abraham. *Haven and Home: A History of the Jews in America.* New York: Schocken Books, 1986.

Korn, Bertram Wallace. *American Jewry and the Civil War.* Philadelphia: Jewish Publication Society, 2001.
An exhaustive study of the Jewish involvement in the Civil War, first published in 1951.

Laqueur, Walter. *A History of Zionism: From the French Revolution to the Establishment of the State of Israel.* With a new preface by the author. New York: Schocken Books, 2003.

Lewis, Bernard. *The Jews of Islam.* Princeton, NJ: Princeton University Press, 1984.
A history of the Jewish communities in Muslim countries.

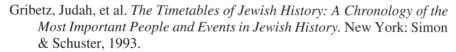

Salamander, Rachel, ed. *The Jewish World of Yesterday, 1860–1938*. New York: Rizzoli, 1990.
An illustrated overview of life in Central and Eastern Europe leading up to the Holocaust.

Sarna, Jonathan D. *American Judaism: A History*. New Haven, CT: Yale University Press, 2004.

Schoener, Allon. *The American Jewish Album: 1654 to the Present*. New York: Rizzoli, 1983.

Sharp, Rosalie, Irving Abella, and Edwin Goodman, eds. *Growing Up Jewish: Canadians Tell Their Own Stories*. Toronto: McClelland & Stewart, 1997.

Notes

1. Cynthia Ozick, "The Rights of History and the Rights of Imagination," *Commentary* 107, no. 3 (1999): 22.

2. Abba Eban, *Heritage: Civilization and the Jews* (New York: Summit Books, 1984), 170–74.

Chapter 4

Fantasy and Science Fiction

In chapters 2 and 3 of Genesis, you have the story of Adam and Eve, which, it is clear to anyone, is the first story ever told in good detail of how human beings colonized a new world.—Isaac Asimov

Now the world is so corrupted that the demons just keep hidden. —Isaac Bashevis Singer

Introduction

Sometimes we wish to explore worlds beyond reality as we know it. That's when we head for the writers in this chapter, all of whom are willing to loosen up the metaphysical moorings of our universe. Because these writers work at the edges of reality, hard and fast definitions and distinctions among their works are hard to come by. Reference books hedge and point out ambiguities. Science fiction can shade over into fantasy, and fantasy turns up in almost every genre. The lack of clear-cut definitions gives writers freedom to do almost anything. Science fiction takes us to a world—future or past—that never was or will be, but could have been, at least scientifically speaking. Fantasy takes us to places that only exist courtesy of authors' imaginations. Suspension of disbelief, tolerance for speculation, and acceptance of alternate ways of thinking are requirements for readers of these genres.

Scope

Although there are a number of American science fiction writers who are Jewish, most of their novels do not reflect obviously Jewish themes or settings. The handful of titles in this chapter come from a small group of authors; their thought-provoking novels and short stories represent some of the traditional subgenres of science fiction. It is interesting that while SF novels with Jewish themes are scarce, SF short stories with Jewish themes are not.

A comprehensive Jewish science fiction Web site that indexes anthologies and science fiction magazines is listed in the "Sources for Further Reading" section.

Although traditional science fiction is not plentiful in Jewish American fiction, fantasy is a different matter. There are many Jewish American writers who use fantastic elements in their fiction: Cynthia Ozick, Woody Allen, Steve Stern, Bernard Malamud, Isaac Bashevis Singer, Lillian Nattel, and Moacyr Scliar to name a few. Jewish religious literature is filled with fables and legends; many, like the story of Jonah and the whale, are familiar to us all.

As in all cultures, Jewish folktales have a strong fantastic element and often include out-of-body experiences, demons, witches, and sorcerers. Many fantastic stories come from the Jewish mystical tradition and have their roots in the Talmud, Kabbalah, Zohar, and folk literature associated with the Hasidic movement, especially with the Baal Shem Tov and his great-grandson Reb Nachman of Bratslav. Their presence pervades Jewish fiction in every era and language. They are the source and justification for the strain of fantasy, folklore, and magic realism in contemporary Jewish fiction.

The novels selected for this chapter are ones that have more than just elements of fantasy. If, as in *The Puttermesser Papers*, the narrative is basically realistic, the book will be found in another genre. Checking under the subject heading "magical realism" in the index will allow the reader to find these novels in whatever genre they appear.

Appeal of the Genre/Advising the Reader

This genre is a special interest, and readers often have strong feelings about whether they like it or not. True fans often read nothing else. It is hard to convert someone who likes realistic fiction into a science fiction or fantasy reader. Nevertheless, the titles in this chapter are well worth exploring by the reader who is not usually a fan of the genre. Like interesting literature of any type, they offer food for thought, in this case, about Jewish issues of ethics, community, traditions, and lore.

The small number of titles in this chapter means it is difficult to find illustrative examples of genre characteristics. For those who are interested in exploring the nature of the genre, the titles listed in chapter 9 will be of help in pointing out some specific appeal characteristics.

Science Fiction and Fantasy

Science fiction owes its origins in the late 1920s to the expansion of technology and the sense it gave that through science we could make substantive changes in our world. It freed the author to explore changes in every aspect of society. The science fiction in this chapter participates enthusiastically in this exploration. Along with interesting technological developments, "what if" in Jewish science fiction extends to reimagining gender stereotypes, as in Marge Piercy's *He, She and It,* or changing Jewish political history, as in Philip Graubart's *Planet of the Jews.*

Fantasy is generally of two kinds: set in an entirely fantastic world, or set in a world that is initially recognizable, but turns out to be governed by the irrational. The Jewish fantasy listed here is mainly of the second kind. Lisa Goldstein's *The Alchemist's Door* is set against the real background of sixteenth-century Prague, where *golem*s and charlatans converge at the court of the mad Emperor Rudolf. In one of Avram Davidson's stories we find an elderly couple in sunny California encountering a *golem*-gardener.

Dann, Jack

Jubilee. Tor, 2003. 441p. **YA**

Among the seventeen stories in this collection are several that feature Jewish characters and themes. In "Fairy Tale," a Borscht Belt comedian finds a fantasy land in the Catskill forests; "Tattoos" describes an artist whose tattoos redeem and save his clients as he takes on their pain, and "Jumping the Road" is set on the Jewish planet of Tobias. A highly literate and varied collection spanning the range of science fiction subgenres. (The author's Web site is eidolon.net/homesite.html?author=jack_dann.)

Themes: short stories

Davidson, Avram

Davidson's (1923–1993) many short stories and novels span the genre from fantasy to science fiction to magic realism and into a dimension uniquely his own. He edited the magazine *Fantasy and Science Fiction* in the early 1960s, fought for the United States during World War II, and fought in Israel in the 1948–1949 Israel–Arab War. A committed Orthodox Jew, he was notoriously cranky and idealistic, and ended his days in poverty. (The author's Web site is www.avramdavidson.org.)

Everybody Has Somebody in Heaven: Essential Tales of the Jewish Spirit. Edited by Jack Dann and Grania Davidson Davis. Devora Publishing, 2000. 285p. **YA**

A collection of Davidson's Jewish stories and poems, with additional material about him by writers who knew and appreciated his work. It includes the often-anthologized story "The *Golem*," a modern and hilarious Southern California version of the old legend, and "Dr. Morris Goldpepper Returns," a follow-up to the original story about the dentist who was abducted by aliens. Davidson's concerns with Jewish law, lore, and ethics permeate these stories, as does his unique voice.

Themes: humorous fiction; poetry; short stories

The Avram Davidson Treasury: A Tribute Collection. Edited by Robert Silverberg and Grania Davis. Tom Doherty Associates, 1998. 447p. **YA**

Themes: short stories

The Other Nineteenth Century: A Story Collection. Edited by Grania Davis and Henry Wessells. Tor, 2001. 327p. **YA**

Themes: short stories

Dunn, J. R.

Days of Cain. Avon, 1997. 328p. **YA** 📖

Gaspar James, a monitor who preserves the continuity of history for the Moiety, is assigned to return to the twentieth century to stop a renegade mission to abort the Holocaust. The renegades are led by his protégé, the saintly, strong-willed Alma Lewin, who has infiltrated Auschwitz as a Jewish prisoner. Gaspar's hatred for the Nazis, his duty to the Moiety, and his feelings for Alma are all in conflict in this dark and fast-paced time-travel tale.

Themes: Holocaust—concentration camps; time travel

Related Titles: Another science fiction work with a Holocaust setting is the <u>Madagascar Manifesto</u> trilogy beginning with *Children of the Light*, by George Guthridge and Janet Berliner, based on the historical plan of the German High Command to resettle Jews on the island of Madagascar.

Goldstein, Lisa

The Alchemist's Door. Tor, 2002. 286p. **YA**

Sixteenth-century Prague is the setting for this fantasy that exploits the desire of rational men and women for forbidden knowledge and power. Rabbi Judah Loew, creator of a *golem* to protect the Jews from persecution, joins forces with the English scientist and alchemist John Dee to prevent Emperor Rudolf from finding the thirty-sixth righteous man and gaining control of the universe. (The author's Web site is www.brazenhussies.net/goldstein.)

Themes: Czechoslovakia; *golem*; magic; sixteenth century

Related Titles: An earlier fantasy by Goldstein, *The Red Magician*, set in Eastern Europe before and during the Holocaust, would be suitable for young adults.

Graubart, Philip

Planet of the Jews. Creative Arts Book, 1999. 201p.

In this story within a story, a Hasidic couple bring a manuscript to comic book editor Judah Loeb about how the Jewish people escape a future Holocaust by relocating to a distant planet. The published stories have a miraculous effect on readers, bringing about mass conversions to Judaism.

Themes: conversion to Judaism; Jews—persecutions; space colonies

Piercy, Marge

He, She, and It. Alfred A. Knopf, 1991. 446p.

In 2059, Shira, employee of one of the huge, faceless "multis" that run the world, loses custody of her son and rejoins her grandmother Malkah in the free town of Tikva, where she trains Yod, a male cyborg. As Shira plots her revenge on the "multis," her relationship with Yod deepens. The *golem* story, told by Malkah in alternating chapters, comments on the problems inherent in technology that attempts to create life. (The author's Web site is archer-books.com/Piercy.)

Themes: artificial intelligence; *golem*; grandmothers; women's lives

Related Titles: Piercy explores gender roles in this unusual novel, which may appeal to readers who do not ordinarily read science fiction. Readers may enjoy Piercy's autobiography, *Sleeping with Cats*, about her unconventional life, annotated in the "Public Lives" section of chapter 8. Another retelling of the *golem* story is found in Frances Sherwood's *The Book of Splendor*, annotated in the "Dark Ages Through Early Modern History" section of chapter 3.

Singer, Isaac Bashevis

The Golem. **Illustrations by Uri Shulevitz. Farrar, Straus & Giroux, 1982. 83p. YA**

Rabbi Leib, in old Prague, creates a *golem* to aid a member of the Jewish community falsely accused of kidnapping and killing a Polish nobleman's daughter. Later, the Rabbi loses his power over the *golem*, and it is only when it falls in love with a young woman that the Rabbi is able to lay the *golem* to rest. Marketed as a children's book, but readers from teens on up will appreciate this tale by a master storyteller.

Themes: Czechoslovakia; *golem*; rabbis

*The Stars of David: Jewish Science Fiction***. Edited by D. J. Kessler. DLZ Media, 1996. 414p. YA**

In the first novella in this collection, *Can Androids Be Jewish?* by Jo Sampliner, Josh Kominski is posted to the Galilee Colony; as the only human he oversees a giant mine worked by androids who practice Judaism in deference to him. In *Miriam's World*, by Sol Weiss, Ben Goldberg, commander of Starship Eitan, on a routine supply drop-off mission at Miriam's World, the newest and most distant of Israel's planets, finds that unknown invaders have destroyed this beautiful, peaceful colony.

Themes: androids; space colonies

*Wandering Stars: An Anthology of Jewish Fantasy & Science Fiction***. Edited by Jack Dann. 1974; reprint, Jewish Lights, 1998. 239p. YA**

Although the settings of theses hilarious, poignant, and unique stories may be Venus, Mars, or Earth in a few centuries from now, and the characters lumpy brown aliens, they explore perennial Jewish themes of identity, assimilation, and exile. Includes stories by Harlan Ellison, Robert Silverberg, Pamela Sargent, Bernard Malamud, and others.

Themes: short stories

Related Titles: Dann edited a second compilation called *More Wandering Stars,* with stories by Barry Malzberg, Woody Allen, Cynthia Ozick, Hugh Nissenson, Isaac Bashevis Singer, and others. Another compilation of Jewish fantasy tales, although not necessarily American, is *Great Tales of Jewish Fantasy and the Occult*, compiled, translated, and introduced by Joachim Neugroschel. There have been several editions, with varying titles. (Dann's Web site is eidolon.net/homesite.html?author=jack_dann.)

With Signs and Wonders: An International Anthology of Jewish Fabulist Fiction. **Edited by Daniel Jaffe. Invisible Cities Press, 2001. 333p.** YA

> A diverse compilation of stories from twenty-five authors with elements of fantasy, folklore, mysticism, and the supernatural. Editor Jaffe sets the stage with an introduction about the fabulist tradition in Jewish fiction. A man becomes possessed by the prophets, a rabbi explains to his students how the Jews named the dinosaurs, and a Memphis businessman watches in dismay as an Orthodox rabbi flies, in stories by Moacyr Scliar, Steven Sher, and Steve Stern, among others.
>
> **Themes:** fantasy; folklore
>
> **Related Titles:** Some of these authors are not traditionally associated with fantasy. Readers encountering and enjoying these authors for the first time in this anthology will find it worthwhile to look for their novels.

Yolen, Jane

Briar Rose. **1972; reprint, Starscape. 2002. 241p.** YA

> Becca's beloved grandmother Gemma has always told her own dark version of the story of Sleeping Beauty. When Gemma dies, after saying that she is the princess Briar Rose, Becca finds mementos that help her uncover the true story of her grandmother's life and help her to understand her own. (The author's Web site is www.janeyolen.com.)
>
> **Themes:** family secrets; granddaughters; grandmothers; Holocaust—refugees and displaced persons; Holocaust—survivors
>
> **Related Titles:** This is part of the *Fairy Tale* series edited by Terry Windling and marketed for young adults, but adult readers will enjoy the story of the compassionate Becca and the way Yolen weaves the two women's stories together. Another transformation of fairy tale into Holocaust novel is Louise Murphy's *The True Story of Hansel and Gretel.* A dark and unusual novel that combines fantasy with a Holocaust theme is *A Blessing on the Moon* by Joseph Skibell, annotated in the "Setting" section of chapter 6.

Sources for Further Reading

The titles below will help readers and librarians who want to explore Jewish fantasy, folklore, and legend. The Web site will be of interest to readers who are looking for additional science fiction and fantasy with a Jewish theme. General sources on science fiction and fantasy are found in chapter 9.

Ginzberg, Louis. *Legends of the Jews.* 2 vols. Philadelphia: Jewish Publication Society, 2003.
> A classic and exhaustive collection, originally published in seven volumes starting in 1901.

Jewish Science Fiction and Fantasy, sfsite.com/~silverag/jewishsf.html
> An ongoing bibliography of novels, anthologies, and short stories appearing in magazines and anthologies. This is a wide-ranging bibliography that includes

works with some Jewish content by authors who are not Jewish, and works by Jewish authors with minimal Jewish content.

Schwartz, Howard, reteller. *Elijah's Violin and Other Jewish Fairy Tales.* New York: Oxford University Press, 1994.
Jewish fairy tales from around the world.

Schwartz, Howard, reteller. *Gabriel's Palace: Jewish Mystical Tales.* New York: Oxford University Press, 1993.
A collection of 150 tales of mystical experiences from Jewish folklore, the Talmud, and the Zohar.

Schwartz, Howard, reteller. *Lilith's Cave: Jewish Tales of the Supernatural.* San Francisco: Harper & Row, 1988.
Fifty classic tales with supernatural elements, from the Middle East, Germany, and Eastern Europe.

Schwartz, Howard, reteller. *Miriam's Tambourine: Jewish Folktales from Around the World.* NY: Oxford University Press, 1988.

Chapter 5

Stories of Love and Romance

Introduction

Romance is an extremely popular and varied genre, with a large and eager group of readers. Since romance is an approach to storytelling in which the focus is on a love story, it can be found in every genre. Joyce Saricks provides a good definition of the traditional romance:

> First, in romances, the plot revolves around the love relationship and its inevitable happy ending; all else that happens is secondary . . . Secondly, these stories are told in such a way that the reader is involved in the outcome of the Romance; the reader participates on an emotional level and experiences genuine satisfaction at the inevitable happy ending.[1]

Love stories have universal appeal; they appear in the earliest written and oral literature. The Bible is filled with archetypal stories of relationships between men and women: Isaac's tender feelings for Rachel and his devotion despite her father's trickery; the complexity and pain in Abraham and Sarah's long marriage; David's lust for Bathsheba with its fateful consequences for his empire. These stories affirm the strength of our fundamental needs and desires. They are also very satisfying reading. Often maligned as escapist literature, they appear on best-seller lists with regularity, much to the delight of their many fans.

Scope

Only a few of the popular mass-market romance series that fill the racks in supermarkets and bookstores are Jewish in content, setting, or theme. Julie Ellis and Belva Plain are the best-known Jewish authors of these popular romances. Their novels are set mainly in the United States and often focus on the struggles of the immigrant generation. Other novels range from contemporary romance, like Judith Arnold's *Love in Bloom's*; to historical romance, like Gay Courter's *Flowers in the Blood*; to Dora Levy Mossanen's racy *Harem*.

To offer readers more suggestions for novels in the romantic style, this chapter includes additional authors that romance readers may enjoy. In these novels the love interest is still important, but the plot may not conform to the traditional pattern. Some of these novels, like Susan Isaacs's *Close Relations* or Eileen Pollack's *Paradise, New York,* shade over into the developing genre of women's fiction, in which family relationships play an important role.

Organization of the Chapter

Due to the small number of titles in this chapter, they are not subdivided into subgenres. Indication of whether they fit into such subgenres as humor, historical fiction, or suspense is provided in the annotation and themes listings.

Appeal of the Genre/Advising the Reader

Romance is filled with longings, secrets, misunderstandings, and protagonists who overcome problems. Readers become caught up in the lives of characters who make the wrong choices and suffer for it, are led astray by deceitful people, or refuse to recognize their own failings. Belva Plain makes good use of deceit in her novel *Legacy of Silence*. In *Only Yesterday* by Syrell Rogovin Leahy, a misunderstanding with a lover sets Lee Stein's life on a different course.

Stories may take place in exotic or familiar settings. Faye Kellerman's *The Quality of Mercy* is set in Elizabethan London, where the reader meets Shakespeare and a lively Jewish heroine who is involved in saving the lives of Jews fleeing persecution. Gay Courter's historical romance *Flowers in the Blood* takes readers into the Jewish community in Calcutta in the Victorian era, providing a picture of a little-known Jewish community. The promise of redemptive love, no matter how delayed, is the appeal of this fiction. As Kristin Ramsdell put it in *Romance Fiction: A Guide to the Genre*:

> Finally, one of the most basic reasons for the enduring appeal of the romance is simply that it is the most optimistic and hopeful of all the fiction genres. It celebrates life and love with abandon and reaffirms one of the most basic of all fantasies, the triumph of true love against all odds.[2]

General information about romance readers' advisory work will be found in chapter 9.

Stories of Love and Romance

Arnold, Judith

Love in Bloom's. **Mira, 2002. 379p.** `YA`

When the matriarch of the Bloom family, owners of a Jewish delicatessen that's become a New York City institution, orders her granddaughter Julia to take over the business, the young woman must learn to cope with flaky and intrusive relatives; a sexy, snooping reporter; and her own fears of inadequacy. Humorous and fast-paced, filled with the messy truths of family relationships. (The author's Web site is www.juditharnold.com.)

Themes: family relationships; grandmothers; humorous romances; women's lives

Related Titles: Readers can follow Julia's further adventures in the sequel, *Blooming All Over.*

Blair, Leona

A Woman's Place. **Delacorte, 1981. 397p.**

The consequences of love, forbidden and sanctioned, animate this family saga about the Fursten children and their spouses, whose lives are intertwined with the growth of Palestine and Israel from the days of the British Mandate to the Six-Day War in 1967 and the creation of a multimillion dollar cosmetics business.

Themes: family sagas; family relationships; Israel—History; love affairs

Related Titles: Readers may enjoy two other multigenerational family sagas: Aviva Hellman's *To Touch a Dream* and Norma Harris's *Trumpets of Silver.*

Courter, Gay

Flowers in the Blood. **Dutton, 1990. 615p.** 📖

The scandalous murder of Dinah Sassoon's mother reverberates through Dinah's life, making it difficult for her to find a husband in the close-knit Jewish community of Calcutta. Through her search for love and fulfillment the reader learns about the opium trade, the history of the different Indian Jewish communities, and life in Victorian India. (The author's Web site is www.gaycourter.com.)

Themes: historical romance; India; opium trade; women's lives

Related Titles: Another historical novel about a Jewish woman in an exotic setting is Julie Ellis's *East Wind*, set in Hong Kong. Readers may also enjoy Courter's two historical novels set in Russia and early twentieth-century New York City: *The Midwife* and *The Midwife's Advice*, annotated in the "Modern Period, United States and Canada" section of chapter 3.

Denker, Henry

Horowitz and Mrs. Washington. **Morrow, 1991. 409p.** YA

When the elderly Samuel Horowitz suffers a stroke, Harriet Washington, a widowed African American nurse and physical therapist, bullies and cajoles him into complete recovery, setting up the dynamics of a friendship that sustains them both.

Themes: elderly men; friendship; humorous romances; Jews—Relations with African Americans; physically handicapped

Mrs. Washington and Horowitz, Too. **Morrow, 1993. 333p.** YA

When Mrs. Washington recognizes signs of depression in Samuel Horowitz, she arranges for him to volunteer at the hospital as part of a far-reaching plan to cheer him up.

Themes: depression, mental; elderly men; friendship; humorous romances; Jews—Relations with African Americans

Related Titles: Denker has also written *Payment in Full*, about a Jewish couple who adopt an African American child during the Depression. Readers who enjoy the gentle humor in this series may also like the Belle Appleman mystery series by Dorothy and Sidney Rosen, annotated in the "Humorous Mysteries" section of chapter 2.

Ellis, Julie

Ellis's heroines are spirited, intelligent, likable women who make the best of bad situations, which include difficult marriages as well as sudden changes of social and economic status. They often encounter anti-Semitism, which helps them define their Jewish identity. Strong bonds of friendship and devotion to family help them survive. All the novels are set against historical backgrounds, but they are primarily about family relationships affected by historical events. Several of Ellis's later novels are annotated below; readers may enjoy her earlier novels with Jewish heroines: *Rich Is Best, Maison Jennie, East Wind, Glorious Morning*, and *The Only Sin.* (The author's Web site is www.julieellis.net.)

A Daughter's Promise. **Arbor House/ Morrow, 1988. 470p.**

Laura and Iris Roth leave the town of Magnolia after their father is lynched by the Ku Klux Klan for a crime he didn't commit, hoping to start new lives in New York City, but Laura is unable to give up her dream of clearing her father's name.

Themes: anti-Semitism; lawyers; 1950s; 1940s; 1930s; 1920s; sisters

An Uncommon Woman. **Kensington Books, 1997. 410p.**

On Kristallnacht, thirteen-year-old Vera Mueller loses her parents; due to the kindness of a Christian neighbor she survives the war in Copenhagen and London. Marriage to Paul, an American soldier, takes her to America, where strength and courage help her navigate the rocky shores of family relationships, including the secret sorrows of Paul's family.

Themes: family relationships; historical romances; Holocaust—survivors; 1950s; 1940s; 1960s

Far to Go. **Kensington Books, 1995. 486p.**

> Growing up in a provincial Southern town in the 1930s, Fran Goldman broke away from the restrictions on women's lives to work in the union movement and marry Northerner Bernie Garfield. In her search for a meaningful life, Fran weathers unexpected hardships with grace and energy, and lives to see her descendants' successes.

> **Themes:** businesswomen; family relationships; friendship; mothers and daughters

Lasting Treasures. **Putnam, 1993. 446p.**

> Viktoria Gunsburg escapes the war on the Russian front and comes to Paris in 1917, where she meets and marries American soldier Gary Barton, much to the dismay of his gentile family, heirs to the Barton tobacco empire in Virginia.

> **Themes:** anti-Semitism; businesswomen; family sagas; immigrants; Russian Americans

Trespassing Hearts. **Putnam, 1992. 366p.**

> Betsy Bernstein's dreams seem fulfilled when she and wealthy, gentile socialite Paul Forrest fall in love, but her domineering, unstable mother-in-law cannot accept a Jew in the family. A Cinderella story set against the background of World War II and the glittering social life of New York and the Hamptons.

> **Themes:** interfaith marriage; interior decorators; orphans; widows; World War II

Fast, Howard

Redemption. **Harcourt, Brace, 1999. 276p.**

> When seventy-eight-year old Ike Goldman stops on the George Washington Bridge to rescue a woman intent on committing suicide, it is the beginning of a May–December romance. But when Elizabeth is accused of murdering her abusive ex-husband, Ike realizes he may have taken on more than he bargained for, in this gentle novel of psychological suspense.

> **Themes:** domestic violence; May–December romance; trials (murder)

> **Related Titles:** Fast is a prolific writer, well-known for his historical novels, many set in biblical times; among them is *My Glorious Brothers*, annotated in the "Biblical and Ancient Worlds" section of chapter 3.

Freeman, Cynthia

A World Full of Strangers. **Arbor House, 1981. 450p.**

> When Katie marries the secretive and ambitious David, she becomes an unwilling partner in his rejection of Judaism. They leave the Lower East Side for San Francisco, where David achieves financial success, but Katie's life lacks happiness and spiritual contentment.

Themes: historical romances; immigrants; Jewish identity; marriage; 1940s; 1930s

Related Titles: Freeman has also written *Portraits,* a multigenerational saga about the colorful Sandsonitsky family's odyssey from Eastern Europe to America. Another historical romance about a young woman in the early part of the century, making decisions about her life, is *Journey Home* by Janet C. Robertson.

Gordon, Noah
Jerusalem Diamond. **Random House, 1979. 304p.**

When a large diamond is found that may have been part of the sacred objects of the ancient Temple, Harry Hopeman, the latest in a long line of diamond merchants, is asked to purchase it from its secretive Egyptian owner, but all three of the major religions have emotional claims on the stone and may be willing to kill for it. (The author's Web site is www.noahgordon.com.)

Themes: diamonds; Israel—Intelligence services; love affairs

Related Titles: Another novel by Gordon, *The Last Jew*, set in Inquisition-era Spain, is annotated in the "Dark Ages Through Early Modern History" section of chapter 3.

Isaacs, Susan
Close Relations. **Lippincott & Crowell, 1980. 270p.**

Marcia Green, speechwriter for a New York City politician, thirty-five years old, and single, endures her family's disapproval of her Irish boyfriend and their attempts to find her a suitable Jewish husband. (The author's Web site is www.susanisaacs.com.)

Themes: family relationships; single women; women in politics

Related Titles: Susan Isaacs's lively, offbeat novels about women whose lives take unexpected turns combine insight and humor. Readers who enjoyed *Close Relations* may also like another Isaacs novel, *Lily White*, a legal thriller annotated in chapter 2.

Red, White and Blue. **HarperCollins, 1998. 407p.**

Journalist Lauren Miller travels to Wyoming to investigate Wrath, a white supremacist group that may have been responsible for an anti-Semitic crime, while Charlie Blair, an FBI agent, volunteers to go undercover to investigate the group. In addition to exploring the psychology of hate groups, Isaacs traces the heritage that brought Charlie and Lauren from the same immigrant ancestor to the very different lives they live today.

Themes: anti-Semitism; FBI agents; hate crimes; journalists

Shining Through. **Harper & Row, 1988. 402p.**

In 1941, Linda Voss longs to escape from her humdrum life as a Wall Street secretary and caretaker of her alcoholic mother. When her handsome boss proposes, it seems like a dream come true, but marriage to WASP John Berringer is not easy. She volunteers for a spy mission in Germany, an adventure that will change her life in dramatic ways.

Themes: secretaries; women spies; World War II

Related Titles: Jane Heller also creates Jewish heroines notable for their sass and savvy. Readers may enjoy her novels *Cha Cha Cha, Sis Boom Bah*, or *Female Intelligence,* among others. Other titles by Isaacs can be found in chapter 2.

Katkov, Norman

The Judas Kiss. **Dutton, 1991. 423p.**

In 1937 Vienna, two men are in love with Carly Siefermann: Nick, a Jewish architect, and Fritz, a German count. As the Nazis close in on Nick and his family, Carly makes a dangerous bargain to save Nick's life.

Themes: Holocaust—resistance and rescue; love stories; Nazis; revenge

Kellerman, Faye

The Quality of Mercy. **Morrow, 1989. 607p.**

The Lopez family, living in Elizabethan London, practice their Judaism secretly, while smuggling *conversos* (secret Jews) out of Spain. Daughter Rebecca, impatient with the restrictions on women's lives, becomes involved in the criminal underworld and Elizabethan politics while pursuing a romance with William Shakespeare.

Themes: *conversos*; England; historical romances; sixteenth century

Related Titles: Kellerman is well-known for the Peter Decker/Rina Lazarus series of mysteries, annotated in the "Police Detectives" section of chapter 2, which are set in the present day. Readers who like historical romances with strong heroines caught up in dangerous situations may enjoy Liliane Webb's novel *The Marranos,* set in Inquisition-era Spain.

Leahy, Syrell Rogovin

Circle of Love. **Putnam, 1980. 273p.**

At the close of World War II, Anna Kleinberger sets off from Paris to find her parents, but she meets and falls in love with Anton, who is on the same search; the few days they spend together echo throughout their lives.

Themes: Holocaust—survivors; love affairs

Only Yesterday. **Putnam, 1989. 222p.** **YA**

When Lee Stein visits Germany on a Fulbright scholarship, her life is changed by the family she stays with and by a romance with an American professor, but it isn't until twenty years later that all the threads begun that year are finally tied together, in this portrait of a straightforward young woman who goes her own way in love and marriage.

Themes: family secrets; Germany; Holocaust—survivors; love affairs; women's lives

Related Titles: Another novel about lovers who are separated by circumstances is Elaine Kagan's *Somebody's Baby*.

Lipman, Eleanor

The Inn at Lake Devine. **Random House, 1998. 253p. YA**

A romantic comedy in which teenaged Natalie Marx, angered to learn that a certain hotel won't accept Jewish guests, arranges to visit in the company of a non-Jewish family. Natalie's life becomes intertwined with the hotel and its owners in unexpected ways.

Themes: anti-Semitism; love stories; women's lives

Related Titles: Lipman's heroines are often attracted to unsuitable men, and her novels are filled with insights into the relationship between the sexes. Among her other novels, readers may enjoy *Then She Found Me* or *Isabel's Bed*. Other novels exploring male/female relationships with a light touch are Jennifer Weiner's *Good in Bed* and *In Her Shoes* and Thisbe Nissen's *The Good People of New York*.

Mossanen, Dora Levy

Harem. **Scribner, 2002. 378p.** 📖

Three generations of passionate, strong-willed Jewish women—Rebekah, Gold Dust, and Raven—challenge their fate in exotic fourteenth-century Persia, among courtesans, eunuchs, and shahs. In this book, carefully researched and intricately plotted with lush descriptions, Mossanen brings to life an opulent and treacherous milieu. (The author's Web site, www.doralevymossanen.com, has a discussion guide.)

Themes: harems; historical romances; women—social conditions; women's lives

Plain, Belva

Blessings. **Delacorte, 1989. 340p.**

Jennie is happily engaged to Jay until she is contacted by the child she gave up for adoption nineteen years before, bringing back all the insecurities of that time and her fears that her upper-class fiancé and his family will reject her. (The author's Web site is www.belvaplain.com.)

Themes: adopted children; children of Holocaust survivors; mothers and daughters

Related Titles: In *Swimming Across the Hudson*, by Joshua Henkin, annotated in the "Character" section of chapter 6, a young man has to face the needs of his biological mother. Another novel about an adoptee who searches for her parents is Elaine Kagan's *Somebody's Baby*.

Crescent City. **Delacorte, 1984. 429p. YA**

Brought up amid wealth in New Orleans, Miriam Raphael is married at sixteen to an older man. But her life is turned upside down when she falls in love with someone else and her brother David becomes an abolitionist. (The author's Web site is www.belvaplain.com.)

Themes: abolitionists; historical romances; New Orleans; U.S.—History—Civil War; women's lives

Related Titles: For a glimpse into the life of a Southern Jewish woman in the same era, try Helen Jacobus Apte's *Heart of a Wife: The Diary of a Southern Jewish Woman*, annotated in the "Childhood and Family" section of chapter 8.

Legacy of Silence. Delacorte, 1998. 344p. **YA** 📖

In 1938, eighteen-year-old Caroline flees Germany with her adopted sister Lore and her unborn child, making her way to New York. Forced to marry Joel Hirsch, her life is always shadowed by her painful past.

Themes: family secrets; historical romances; Holocaust; immigrants; marriage

Plain, Belva

Werner Family Saga.

This saga of the Werner, Friedman, and Roth families follows the political and social issues of the twentieth century. The story lines are parallel rather than chronological, each novel focusing on a particular family or character. (The author's Web site is www.belvaplain.com.)

Themes: family sagas; family secrets; immigrants; love affairs; women's lives

Evergreen. Delacorte, 1978. 593p.

Shortly before World War I, teenaged Anna comes to New York from Poland, marries Joseph, and starts a family, all the while in love with Paul Werner, son of a wealthy Jewish family.

The Golden Cup. Delacorte, 1986. 399p.

The story of Henrietta De Rivera, Paul's aunt, her marriage to Daniel Roth, and their involvement in the social causes of the day.

Tapestry. Delacorte, 1988. 554p.

Although Paul's marriage is unhappy, he has a successful career in banking, and he is able to help the Jewish community in Europe during World War II.

Harvest. Delacorte, 1990. 409p.

Anna's daughter Iris and her family have a difficult time in the turbulent 1960s, and Paul is drawn to help them.

Related Titles: Readers who enjoy romantic family sagas may also like the novels by British writer Maisie Mosco.

Pollack, Eileen

Paradise, New York. Temple University Press, 1998. 251p.

Lucy Appelbaum grew up spending summers at her family's resort hotel in the Catskills, but by the late 1970s the hotel is seedy and the area unpopular. In an effort to make sense of her life, Lucy takes over the resort with Thomas Jefferson, the black handyman she loves. A tender and nostalgic story of self-discovery and family dynamics, filled with unusual characters and subplots.

Themes: coming-of-age stories; family relationships; hotels; interracial romance

Related Titles: Pollack's earlier collection of stories, *The Rabbi in the Attic and Other Stories,* also focuses on defining moments in the lives of young Jewish women.

Notes

1. Joyce G. Saricks, *The Readers' Advisory Guide to Genre Fiction* (Chicago: American Library Assoc., 2001), 202–3.

2. Kristin Ramsdell, *Romance Fiction: A Guide to the Genre* (Englewood, CO: Libraries Unlimited, 1999), 20.

Chapter 6

Literary Fiction

I like the real stuff, inside information, the sight and bristling sound of other people's dramas, especially when the plots are taken from family life and its fractious heart, the snarled bloodnest of fathers, sons, and everyone else; there lies the source of every clue about ourselves.—Robert Kotlowitz

Like many other young, affluent American families, they had embraced their ethnicity. The overassimilation issue that Philip Roth and Wendy Wasserstein struggled with on paper and stage seemed to be passé. Being a self-acknowledged Jew was hot these days. Especially if you were a man. People magazine was filled with photos of yarmulked studio executives and banking moguls rediscovering their roots. And some of their wives had even converted.—Marissa Piesman

Introduction

Literary fiction is the literature by which we judge cultures. These are the books that are studied in literature courses and are the subjects of literary criticism. Most Jewish American fiction falls into this category. Magazines like *Commentary, Tikkun,* and *The New York Review of Books* are filled with debates about trends and definitions in Jewish American literary fiction. This chapter avoids debates in favor of offering the reader the opportunity to form his or her own opinions. Browsing here reveals how rich the world of Jewish American literature is. Unlike genre fiction, there are no formulas or expectations; open one of these novels and anything is possible. From the experimental novels and stories of Jonathan Safran Foer, Curt Leviant, and Gabriel Brownstein; to the more traditional storytelling of Allegra Goodman, Jay Neugeboren, and Paul Hond, the range is breathtaking. These novels remind us of the delights of reading, of spending time inside someone else's worldview, examining philosophical questions, and meeting compelling characters that step off the page and enrich our lives.

Scope

This chapter includes the largest number of titles published before 1980. It would be a disservice to readers to omit some of the early classic works, like Abraham Cahan's *The Rise of David Levinsky*, or the early novels of Singer, Bellow, Malamud, and the Roths (Philip and Henry). These authors have had a significant influence on American literature and cannot be ignored in any discussion of Jewish American fiction. Their novels are found in the "Classics and Major Authors" section of the chapter.

It has been a pleasure to discover and include fiction by Canadian and Latin American authors who deserve to be better known in the United States. Readers will enjoy making the acquaintance of Lillian Nattel, Cary Fagan, Moacyr Scliar, and Sabina Berman, among others. It is hoped that the anthologies will introduce readers to new authors and titles.

The Canadian authors included are those whose novels have been published in the United States. Latin American Jewish literature is becoming more available in English translation, thanks especially to the University of New Mexico Press and the efforts of Ilan Stavans and Marjorie Agosín. Some of the novels by Latin American authors were written by Sephardic Jews. They are descendants of the Spanish and Portuguese Jews who spread out into the Ottoman Empire and around the Mediterranean in the fifteenth century after expulsion from Spain. The Sephardim came to the Americas in the seventeenth century and again in the late nineteenth century and throughout the twentieth century. Other Latin American authors are from Ashkenazi families who came to Latin America between the two World Wars.

There are a number of collections of linked stories in this chapter, an interesting recent trend in literary fiction. Readers who enjoy this cross between the novel and the short story can find them by looking in the subject index under the term "linked stories."

Organization of the Chapter

Literary fiction does not lend itself well to categorization. In an effort to provide some guidance to readers trying to find novels and short stories they will enjoy, the chapter is arranged as follows:

Anthologies

Classics and Major Authors

Character

Story

Language

Setting

The last four categories reflect the groundbreaking work done by Joyce Saricks in *The Readers' Advisory Guide to Genre Fiction* and adapted to literary fiction by Nancy Pearl in her guides *Now Read This* and *Now Read This II*. Discussion at the beginning of each section defines the appeal characteristics, but anyone who wants to learn more about their use is enthusiastically referred to Saricks's book.

Appeal of the Genre/Advising the Reader

The pleasure of reading literary fiction lies in its complexity, ambiguity, and variety; without constraints on the writer, anything can happen. Readers of genre fiction have some expectations about the novels they read; readers of literary fiction enjoy the unexpected.

The appeal characteristics provide a convenient shorthand for readers' advisors to initiate conversation about what a reader enjoys in a book. Since readers have different responses to literature, the appeal characteristics should be considered handy guidelines, not fixed categories. They will also help readers choose books based on their current mood or current interest. Readers may want a book with a compelling story line at one time, but at another prefer a novel rich in character development. It is hoped that by using the appeal characteristics and the "Related Titles" feature, readers will be encouraged to expand their reading interests. The appeal characteristics are noted with the caveat that each reader responds differently to a novel. There is no database of assigned appeal characteristics to rely on; readers are encouraged to disagree and decide on their own interpretation.

The novels in the "Classics and Major Authors" section are listed separately for several reasons. Sometimes librarians, students, or reading groups are looking specifically for a list of classic titles. It is also difficult to assign these titles to one appeal characteristic as they are often rich in all of them.

Readers and readers' advisors who are using this guide to find read-alikes in literary fiction can try several different approaches. Additional titles by the same author, if not annotated, are listed in the "Related Titles" part of the annotation. Themes that are listed for each novel can be searched in the subject index. Suggestions in "Related Titles" will send readers to literary fiction by other authors in other parts of the chapter or to other genres. When working with fans of literary fiction, the readers' advisory interview becomes very important. Listening to what readers say about why they enjoyed a book can provide clues for further questions about whether story, character, setting, or language are important. Some literary fiction readers like to read award winners or best-selling titles that are the "talk of the town." Some prefer the tried and true classics, well-established in the canon. The novels annotated in the "Classics and Major Authors" section and the award icon will be helpful for these readers. The "Anthologies" section can be valuable as a way to introduce a variety of voices to readers who aren't sure of their interests.

6

Literary Fiction

Anthologies

These collections give readers an opportunity to make the acquaintance of writers whose stories have appeared primarily in literary magazines. They also showcase the diversity of Jewish American fiction and the way that Jewish American literature reflects its unique heritage and influences. Because Jews have been spread out around the globe for so many centuries, Jewish literature has richly benefited from cross-pollination with the literature of all the countries and languages in which Jews have settled. As the pace of translation grows, Jewish writers everywhere have access to these traditions. The literary conversation is also enriched by Israeli and Yiddish literature.

America and I: Short Stories by American Jewish Women Writers. **Edited and with an introduction by Joyce Antler. Beacon Press, 1990. 355p.** **YA** 📖

A collection that showcases the changing issues in Jewish women's fiction through its chronological divisions: From the Ghetto and Beyond: 1900–1929; Troubles in the New World: 1930–1959; Wider Glimpses: 1960–1979; The Past as Present: The 1980s. Stories are by Edna Ferber, Hortense Calisher, Joanne Greenberg, Lynne Sharon Schwartz, Grace Paley, and others.

Themes: Jewish identity; women—literary collections; women's lives

American Jewish Fiction: A Century of Stories. **Edited by Gerald Shapiro. University of Nebraska Press, 1998. 445p.** **YA** 📖

A chronologically arranged collection of stories from a range of writers: the immigrant generation from early in the century (Abraham Cahan, Anzia Yezierska), the major writers at mid-century (Saul Bellow, Bernard Malamud, Isaac Bashevis Singer, Grace Paley), and the stars of the younger generation (Steve Stern, Allegra Goodman and others).

Related Titles: Readers may also want to read *Jewish-American Stories,* edited by Irving Howe, the groundbreaking first anthology of American Jewish stories, published in 1977.

Best Contemporary Jewish Writing. **Edited by Michael Lerner. Jossey-Bass, 2001. 436p.**

This first volume in a projected annual series includes essays, short fiction, and poetry that address aspects of spirituality, healing, and contemporary Jewish issues published between 1944 and 2000. (Subsequent volumes will cover one to two years.) The volume concludes with the editor's own list of the 100 most significant Jewish books written in English since 1985.

Themes: Holocaust; Israel; Jewish identity; spiritual life

Jewish American Literature: A Norton Anthology. **Compiled and edied by Jules Chametzky and others. W. W. Norton, 2001. 1221p.** **YA** 📖

A comprehensive, almost encyclopedic compendium of Jewish American literature that includes stories, excerpts from novels, poetry, cartoons, diaries, sermons, letters, speeches, plays, and prayers written in English or translated from Yiddish, beginning with the arrival of the Jews in New Amsterdam in 1654. Arranged chronologically, with excellent introductions, author notes, and bibliographies; an ideal volume for browsing or study.

Themes: diaries; essays; poetry; short stories

Related Titles: The first groundbreaking anthology of stories by Jewish American authors, *Jewish American Stories*, edited by Irving Howe, was published in 1977. Another excellent collection that includes stories, poetry, and essays is *The Prairie*

Schooner Anthology of Contemporary Jewish American Writing, a reprint of a special issue of the literary magazine.

Neurotica: Jewish Writers on Sex. Edited by Melvin Jules Bukiet. W. W. Norton, 1999. 360p.

Short stories and excerpts from novels, most from well-known writers—Saul Bellow, Cynthia Ozick, Erica Jong, Thane Rosenbaum, Isaac Bashevis Singer, and Henry Roth among them—on sex of the Jewish variety.

Themes: love; sex

Nothing Makes You Free: Writings by Descendants of Jewish Holocaust Survivors. Edited by Melvin Jules Bukiet. W. W. Norton, 2002. 394p. `YA`

An international collection of short stories, excerpts from novels, and essays, by writers who capture the pain of growing up as children of survivors. The introduction by Bukiet asks the question, "How do you cope when the most important events of your life occurred before you were born?"

Themes: children of Holocaust survivors; essays; parents and children; short stories

Related Titles: The title of this collection is a chilling echo of the words inscribed on the gate at Auschwitz: *Arbeit Macht Frei* (work makes you free). Bukiet's own fiction is mostly set in the years before and after the Holocaust and is annotated in the "Language" section of this chapter.

Oxford Book of Jewish Stories. Edited and with an introduction by Ilan Stavans. Oxford University Press, 1998. 493p. `YA`

A collection of fifty-two stories from around the world, showcasing the diversity of Jewish literature. Arranged roughly in chronological order, the collection starts with a mid-nineteenth-century story from the great Polish Hasidic storyteller Reb Nachman of Bratslav, and finishes with American Allegra Goodman. In between are translations from Yiddish, Hebrew, Spanish, Italian, and French, among others. Stavans provides an excellent introduction discussing the role that language and dispersion have played in Jewish literature.

Related Titles: Another contemporary international anthology is *Here I Am: Jewish Stories from Around the World*, from the Jewish Publication Society.

Sephardic-American Voices: Two Hundred Years of a Literary Legacy. Edited by Diane Matza. Brandeis University Press, 1996. 363p.

A collection of stories, personal essays, plays, and poems showcasing the experiences and concerns of those Jews who came to the Western hemisphere from Spain, Greece, and the countries of the Middle East. Matza has contributed chapter notes and biographical information about the authors represented.

Themes: essays; Latin American authors; poetry; Sephardim; short stories

Related Titles: Another excellent and comprehensive anthology of literature written by Sephardim is *The Scroll and the Cross: 1,000 Years of Jewish-Hispanic Literature,* edited by Ilan Stavans.

***The House of Memory: Stories by Jewish Women Writers of Latin America.* Edited by Marjorie Agosín. The Feminist Press, 1999. 246p.**

This varied collection of twenty-two stories and excerpts from novels is an excellent introduction to the rich cultural heritage of Latin American Jewish women. Includes stories by Clarice Lispector, Teresa Porzecanski, Margo Glantz, Angelina Muniz-Huberman and others, from all over Latin America. Agosín's introduction provides history and context for the reader.

Themes: Latin American fiction; women's lives

Related Titles: Agosín has also edited an anthology of poetry, *Miriam's Daughters: Jewish Latin American Women Poets.* Readers interested in the Latin American perspective may enjoy *Tropical Synagogues: Short Stories by Jewish-Latin American Writers,* edited by Ilan Stavans. Agosín's autobiography and biographies of her parents are annotated in the "Childhood and Family" section of chapter 8.

***The Schocken Book of Contemporary Jewish Fiction.* Edited by Ted Solotaroff and Nessa Rapoport. Schocken Books, 1996. 380p. `YA` 📖**

A collection of twenty-four stories all published after 1967, when Israel's victory in the Six-Day War, the emergence of Holocaust testimony, and the social upheavals in the United States created major changes in the American Jewish community's perspective about itself. Stories from already established major writers are included, like Bellow, Roth, Malamud, and Singer, but there are also stories from newer voices: Allegra Goodman, Max Apple, and Michael Chabon. (Originally published in 1992 as *Writing Our Way Home: Contemporary Stories by American Jewish Writers.*)

Themes: assimilation; Jewish identity

Related Titles: Young adult readers may also enjoy the collection, *With All My Heart, With All My Mind: Thirteen Stories About Growing Up Jewish,* edited by Sandy Asher.

Classics and Major Authors

Picking a list of classic titles or major writers is always risky; readers and critics have strong feelings about which authors they admire. Listing in this section does not guarantee enjoyment, but these novels bear reading and rereading because they have something valuable to say about the Jewish experience in America and the experience of all Americans in the twentieth century. The best fiction helps us understand who we are and where we've collectively been. Anyone looking to understand the social and political forces active in American life in the last half of the twentieth century will find no more enlightening and entertaining source than *American Pastoral, I Married a Communist,* and *The Human Stain* by Philip Roth. The novels of Abraham Cahan, Anzia Yezierska, and Henry Roth will give the reader a visceral description of the dislocation and anxiety of the immigrant in the New World.

Bellow, Saul

When Saul Bellow won the Nobel Prize for Literature in 1976, he was cited for the way his work displays "the human understanding and subtle analysis of contemporary culture." Bellow's novels and stories are filled with observations about his characters' states of mind and depictions of the urban landscape. As Chick, the author's surrogate in *Ravelstein*, says, "Taking note is part of my job description." Bellow was born in Canada but has lived most of his life in the United States. Many of his novels and stories are set in Chicago. He received the National Jewish Book Award and the Pulitzer Prize and is a three-time winner of the National Book Award.

Dangling Man. 1944; Reprint, Penguin, 1988. 191p.

Joseph's journal of the eighteen months he spends, unemployed, waiting to be inducted into the army paints a picture of a man literally dangling between eras in his life, using his enforced idleness to examine his emotions, his aimlessness, and the human condition.

Themes: diaries; men—psychology; men's lives

Herzog. Viking, 1964. 341p. **YA** 📖

Moses Herzog, on the verge of insanity and violence after his second wife leaves him for his best friend, spends his time writing unsent letters to famous people (living and dead), friends, and family, arguing, justifying, and explaining. The narrative, veering from third person to first person, is filled with rich characterizations and language that moves at a headlong pace. (Winner of the National Book Award and an ALA Notable Book.)

Themes: adultery; insanity; marriage; men's lives

Related Titles: Bellow's earlier novel, the picaresque *The Adventures of Augie March*, also has a larger-than-life hero.

Mr. Sammler's Planet. 1993; reprint, Penguin, 1970. 313p. 📖

Artur Sammler, an elderly Holocaust survivor, is an intellectual who sees the moral and spiritual decay of late 1960s New York City epitomized in his humiliating encounter with a pickpocket. During the course of three days, these events and others give the urbane and civilized Sammler the chance to reflect on the nature of modern urban life. (Winner of the National Book Award and an ALA Notable Book.)

Themes: Holocaust—survivors; men's lives; urban life

Related Titles: Readers who enjoyed this novel may be interested in Elie Wiesel's *The Accident* for its reflections on contemporary morality.

★ *The Actual.* **Viking, 1997. 103p.**

Although Harry Trellman has always been an outsider, presenting a façade to the world, he carries a torch for Amy Wustrin, his high school sweetheart. Now older, and both divorced, Harry and Amy are once more brought together by their relationship with the perceptive billionaire Sigmund Adletsky. (Winner of the National Jewish Book Award.)

Themes: businessmen; Chicago; love affairs

Ravelstein. **Viking, 2000. 233p.**

Abe Ravelstein, larger-than-life university professor, political philosopher, and author of a best seller about the state of American education, is lovingly described by Chick, a close friend (and stand-in for Bellow, as Ravelstein is a stand-in for Allan Bloom, author of *The Closing of the American Mind*). Chick writes about Ravelstein's last months, their shared confidences about friends, women, illness, and death in an elegiac and tender memoir of a most extraordinary person.

Themes: authors; friendship; illness

Related Titles: Readers may also enjoy Arthur A. Cohen's *An Admirable Woman*, a character study of another strong-willed, successful intellectual historian.

Collected Stories. **Viking, 2001. 442p.** 📖

Bellow chose the stories for this volume, which includes the two novellas *A Theft* and *The Bellarosa Connection,* originally published separately. They exemplify his exceptional descriptive powers and ability to illuminate character with a telling detail or episode. As in many of his novels, the setting is urban, and characters look back on their lives, reflecting on death, complex family relationships, and choices made long ago. In "A Silver Dish," Woody Selbst remembers an unpleasant experience with his manipulative father in a moment of intense grief after his father's death. In "The Bellarosa Connection," the unnamed narrator, a memory expert, recounts his involvement with a man who was rescued from the Holocaust by the impresario Billy Rose.

Themes: novellas; short stories

Related Titles: Earlier collections of Bellow's stories and novellas are *Seize the Day, Mosby's Memoirs and Other Stories*, *Him With His Foot in His Mouth and Other Stories*, and *Something to Remember Me By*.

Cahan, Abraham

Cahan was born in Lithuania in 1860 and came to America in 1882, at the beginning of the great wave of immigration. He settled on the Lower East Side of New York and became active in the socialist movement there. He early recognized the importance of Yiddish in communicating with the Jewish immigrant community and was one of the founders of the Yiddish newspaper, *The Jewish Daily Forward*, in 1897. Under Cahan's editorship, from 1903 to 1951, *The Forward* became very successful and made Cahan an influential figure in the Jewish community. Part of *The Forward*'s popularity lay in Cahan's sensitivity to the dilemmas faced by the immigrants in making the change from a largely rural, tradition-bound culture, to the wide-open, secular society they found in America. In his advice column, *Bintel Brief* (a bundle of letters), Cahan answered questions that illustrated the extent of disorientation and anxiety in the community. In addition to his career as a journalist and social activist, Cahan's reputation is based on his short stories and the novel *The Rise of David Levinsky*, which address these same themes.

The Imported Bridegroom and Other Stories of the New York Ghetto. Penguin, 1996. 254p. 📖

The tenement and sweatshop world of the Lower East Side is the setting for poignant tales of immigrants in late nineteenth-century New York, and their feelings of dislocation. The novella *Yekl, a Tale of the New York Ghetto*, about a man who brings his wife and son to New York only to find that he has changed too much to pick up the old relationship, was the basis for the movie *Hester Street*.

Themes:; garment industry; love affairs; Lower East Side, N.Y.; marriage; short stories

Related Titles: *Yekl* was originally published separately in 1896, and the remaining stories were published in 1898 under the current title.

The Rise of David Levinsky. 1917; reprint, Penguin USA, 1993. 538p. **YA**
📖

David Levinsky reflects on his rise to wealth and security as a cloak-and-suit manufacturer after his arrival in New York as a penniless Russian immigrant in 1885. The classic account of the immigrant who achieves material success but in the process loses his soul. "My past and my present do not comport well" is Levinsky's understated, haunting comment on the emptiness of a life spent running after the American Dream.

Themes: garment industry; Jewish identity; love affairs; Lower East Side, N.Y.; men's lives

Related Titles: Readers who want to learn more about Cahan's life in the context of Lower East Side Yiddish culture may enjoy Ronald Sanders's *The Downtown Jews: Portraits of an Immigrant Generation,* or Irving Howe's comprehensive *World of Our Fathers*. Cahan's own memoir was published in English in 1960 as *The Education of Abraham Cahan*. Samuel Ornitz's novel *Haunch, Paunch, and Jowl*, published in 1923, is another early novel of the immigrant experience.

Doctorow, E. L.

Doctorow's novels are stylistically varied and characterized by a strong sense for the "feel" of an era. He has a wonderful ability to portray the American experience from various points of view and incorporate historical characters into his novels in unusual ways. In setting, his novels range from the early twentieth century New York depicted in *Ragtime* to the same city in the 1990s, in *City of God*. His characters are often emblematic of social groups, or function like mythological figures, giving his novels a touch of magical realism. Two of his novels, *Ragtime* and *World's Fair,* are annotated in the "Modern Period" section of chapter 3.

The Book of Daniel. **Random House, 1971. 303p.** 📖

An imaginative re-creation of what life might have been like for two children whose Communist parents were executed for treason in the 1950s, based loosely on the Rosenberg case, and set against a background of the Cold War era. Point of view alternates between the author and the older sibling, Daniel, as he and his sister Susan struggle with the legacy of their parents' martyrdom. (An ALA Notable Book.)

Themes: Bronx, N.Y.; Communists; parents and children; treason; trials (espionage)

Related Titles: For other fiction based on the Rosenberg case, readers may enjoy Tema Nason's well-researched novel *Ethel: The Fictional Autobiography of Ethel Rosenberg.* For nonfiction about the Rosenbergs, see the entry for *The Rosenberg File: A Search for the Truth* by Robert Radosh and Joyce Milton, in the "Public Lives" section of chapter 8.

The City of God. **Random House, 2000. 272p.**

When Father Tom Pemberton finds his church's stolen cross on the roof of the Synagogue of Evolutionary Judaism across town, he joins forces with two rabbis to uncover the reason for this unusual crime, examining as well the nature of spirituality and religion at the end of the millennium. Written in an unusual style, ranging over many subjects, the process of novel writing joins the story itself, rewarding the reader who is patient at unraveling the various threads.

Themes: Catholic priests; New York City; rabbis; spiritual life

Gold, Michael

Jews Without Money. **1930; reprint, Carroll & Graf, 1996. 309p.** 📖

All the sights, sounds, and smells of the Lower East Side are brought to life in this classic novel of social protest in which we see the tenement world through the eyes of a young boy in the early twentieth century. Pimps, prostitutes, thieves, and gangsters provide a different and often more useful kind of education than public schools and parents.

Themes: boys; immigrants; Lower East Side, N.Y.; 1930s; poverty

Related Titles: For another very realistic treatment of life on the Lower East Side, readers may enjoy Hugh Nissenson's *My Own Ground*, annotated in the "Modern Period, United States and Canada" section of chapter 3.

Malamud, Bernard

Malamud's beautifully crafted novels and stories have earned him a major place in the pantheon of twentieth-century Jewish American writers, one of the triumvirate of literary giants that includes Bellow and Philip Roth. His plots are played out on the small scale of individual lives and relationships, but his themes are the great philosophical questions. His protagonists are usually males, and although they try to be compassionate and ethical, they often fall into sin and experience redemption, though not necessarily through religion. Reality and fantasy frequently combine in playful ways, as in his novels *God's Grace* and *The Natural*, or the short story "The Jewbird." Readers may enjoy Philip Roth's depiction of Malamud in his novel *The Ghost Writer*.

 The Assistant. **Farrar, Straus & Cudahy, 1957. 246p.** **YA**

Morris Bober, barely able to make a living from his grocery store, is the victim of a robbery; in an act of charity he later unknowingly accepts one of the thieves—Frank Alpine—as his assistant. In Malamud's hands, Frank's efforts at self-understanding, his guilt and shame over his crime, and his attraction to Morris's daughter take on biblical symbolism. (Winner of the National Jewish Book Award.)

Themes: fathers and daughters; grocers; Jewish–Christian relations

Related Titles: In a later novel, *The Tenants*, Malamud depicts another relationship between two people with very different moral codes; in this case, two writers, one Jewish, the other African American.

Dubin's Lives. **Farrar, Straus & Giroux. 1979. 361p.**

William Dubin, successful biographer, fails to put as much effort into his marriage and his relationship with his children as he does into his work. When he has difficulty writing about D. H. Lawrence, he discovers a passion for the young woman who cleans his house, with tragicomic results.

Themes: adultery; authors; May–December romance; 1970s

God's Grace. **1982; reprint, Penguin, 1995. 201p.**

In this witty fable, Calvin Cohn finds himself the last man on earth, warned by God that his survival was an oversight and his time is limited. With chimps for company, he settles on a tropical island and tries to create a rational society, but untamed forces are at work.

Themes: castaways; fables; humorous fiction; monkeys

The Complete Stories of Bernard Malamud. **Farrar, Straus & Giroux. 1997. 634p.** **YA**

This collection brings together all fifty-five of Malamud's stories; those published separately and those appearing in the collections *The Magic Barrel*, *Idiots First*, *Pictures of Fidelman*, and *Rembrandt's Hat*, giving the reader a chance to experience the range and development of his art, from the stories of poor Jews in New York to the hilarious fable of "The Jewbird." (*The Magic Barrel* won the National Book Award.)

Themes: short stories

Olsen, Tillie

Tell Me a Riddle. **Delta, 1994. 116p.**

The often-anthologized title story in this collection concerns an older woman who experiences conflict with her husband and children when she tries to redefine her role. Wanting something more, she is unable to break free of the destructive patterns in her marriage.

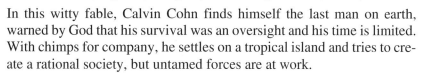

Related Titles: *Tell Me a Riddle* was originally published in a collection with that title in 1961.

Ozick, Cynthia

Cynthia Ozick's highly literate novels, essays, poetry, and literary criticism have won her a loyal following among serious readers who value her writing for its intelligence, wit, and insight.

The Pagan Rabbi and Other Stories. Alfred A. Knopf, 1971. 270p. 📖

This collection includes two of Ozick's most celebrated stories. When Isaac Kornfeld, a brilliant rabbinical student, hangs himself, a friend sets out to learn why and finds that Isaac had turned to a different kind of worship, in "The Pagan Rabbi." "Envy; or, Yiddish in America" is full of the rivalries among American Yiddish authors, who worry about the survival of Yiddish literature among the younger generation.

Themes: authors; rabbis; short stories

The Cannibal Galaxy. Alfred A. Knopf, 1983. 161p. 📖

Holocaust survivor Joseph Brill starts the Edmund Fleg school in the Midwest, which offers a rigorous curriculum of Jewish studies and the traditional literary canon of Western civilization, but Fleg is frustrated by the lack of committed students, until he meets Hester Lilt, a famous philosopher, and her daughter, the phlegmatic but brilliant Beulah.

Themes: Holocaust—survivors; Midwest; teacher–student relationships

Related Titles: This novel is based on an earlier short story, "The Laughter of Akiva," published in *The New Yorker* magazine.

The Messiah of Stockholm. Alfred A. Knopf, 1987. 141p. 📖

Lars Andemening, a third-rate book reviewer for a Stockholm newspaper, is obsessed by the idea that he is the son of Bruno Schulz, the great Polish-Jewish author murdered by the Nazis in 1942. When a manuscript turns up that may be Schulz's last unpublished work, *The Messiah*, Lars is forced to face all his illusions.

Themes: authors; fathers and sons; obsessions; Schulz, Bruno

Related Titles: Readers who enjoyed the shifting reality in this story may also like Curt Leviant's novel *The Yemenite Girl*, annotated in the "Language" section of this chapter.

The Shawl. Alfred A. Knopf, 1989. 69p. **YA** 📖

In this most heartbreaking of stories, Rosa unsuccessfully tries to protect her infant daughter Magda from death in a concentration camp by wrapping her in a shawl; in the companion novella, *Rosa*, she is living in Miami near her niece Stella, impoverished and desolate.

Themes: Holocaust—concentration camps; Holocaust—survivors; infants; mothers

The Puttermesser Papers. **Alfred A. Knopf, 1997. 235p.**

In two short stories and three novellas, we follow the adult life of lawyer Ruth Puttermesser, a seeker of paradise and an optimist in the face of anti-Semitism, urban decay, and men's indifference. In the novella *Puttermesser and Xanthippe*, she creates a female *golem* who helps her become mayor of New York City, briefly creating a paradise where crime is nonexistent and the streets bloom with flowers.

Themes: *golem*; picaresque novels; single women

Related Titles: Readers who enjoyed Ozick's unconventional heroine and satirical humor may like Johanna Kaplan's short stories, collected in *O, My America,* or Lore Segal's *Her First American*, annotated in the "Story" section of this chapter.

Potok, Chaim

Potok (1929–2002) was a scholar, rabbi, and novelist who wrote about the conflict between Judaism and the secular world and the discord within Judaism. His novels portrayed observant Jewish communities and families in a loving and respectful way, opening a window onto that insular world for many readers. The strength of his writing was in his ability to dramatize universal questions of faith, commitment, and identity.

 The Chosen. **1967; reprint, Alfred A. Knopf, 1996. 284p.** **YA**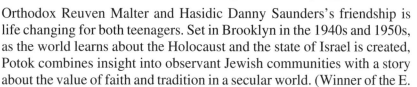

Orthodox Reuven Malter and Hasidic Danny Saunders's friendship is life changing for both teenagers. Set in Brooklyn in the 1940s and 1950s, as the world learns about the Holocaust and the state of Israel is created, Potok combines insight into observant Jewish communities with a story about the value of faith and tradition in a secular world. (Winner of the E. L. Wallant Award and an ALA Notable Book.)

Themes: fathers and sons; friendship; Hasidism; Orthodox Judaism; rabbis; Zionism

Related Titles: *The Promise*, a sequel to *The Chosen*, follows Danny and Reuven as they move into adulthood. Potok writes about difficult religious and emotional issues in a compelling and universal fashion, appealing to Jewish and non-Jewish readers alike. Readers who enjoyed this glimpse into the Hasidic community may be interested in reading Gerry Albarelli's account of his time spent teaching English as a second language in a Hasidic grade school, *Teacha: Stories from a Yeshiva*. Readers may also enjoy Jo Sinclair's *The Changelings*, about a socially unacceptable friendship between two teenaged girls, annotated in the "Story" section of this chapter.

My Name Is Asher Lev. **Alfred A. Knopf, 1972. 369p.** **YA**

As a child growing up in Brooklyn in the 1950s, Asher Lev's artistic talent brings him into conflict with his parents and his Hasidic community, but he is unable to stop drawing.

Themes: artists; coming-of-age stories; Hasidism; parents and children

In the Beginning. **Alfred A. Knopf, 1975. 407p.** **YA** 📖

In a narrative that grows ever more intense and mesmerizing, the reader follows sickly, sensitive David Lurie in the 1920s and 1930s, as he grows in scholarship and comes to understand the world around him, especially the dangers to Jews at home in his Bronx neighborhood and abroad.

Themes: anti-Semitism; coming-of-age stories; immigrants; parents and children

Related Titles: A memoir in which the joys of intellectual development are as vividly portrayed as they are in Potok's novel is Cyrus H. Gordon's *A Scholar's Odyssey*, annotated in the "Public Lives" section of chapter 8.

The Book of Lights. **Alfred A. Knopf, 1981. 369p.** **YA** 📖

Gershon Loran, a troubled and lonely rabbinical student who experiences visions, becomes interested in Kabbalah, but before he can pursue his studies further, he is sent to Korea as a chaplain, where his faith is tested by contact with modern warfare.

Themes: faith; Kabbalah; Korean war, 1950–1953; mysticism; rabbis

Related Titles: Potok's only secular novel, *I Am the Clay*, is about the effects of the Korean War on one family.

Davita's Harp. **Alfred A. Knopf, 1985. 371p.** **YA** 📖

Davita's search for a spiritual home leads her to reject the Communism of her father and the Christianity of her aunt for the Judaism of her mother's family; along the way she has several mentors and experiences both anti-Semitism and the problems women face in the Orthodox community. Political events in Europe in the late 1930s and early 1940s provide background and motivation for characters.

Themes: Christianity; Communism; family relationships; Orthodox Judaism; women—religious life

Related Titles: Davita also appears in *Old Men at Midnight,* in which she hears the stories of three men with very different experiences, at different stages of her own life.

🎗 ***The Gift of Asher Lev.*** **Alfred A. Knopf, 1990. 370p.** **YA** 📖

At forty-five and a renowned artist, Asher Lev returns from self-imposed exile in Europe to his childhood Hasidic community in Brooklyn, where he is forced once again to make a painful choice between his family and his art. (Winner of the National Jewish Book Award, the E. L. Wallant Award, and an ALA Notable Book.)

Themes: artists; family relationships; fathers and sons; Hasidism; men—religious life; rabbis

Related Titles: Readers may also enjoy Allegra Goodman's novel *Kaaterskill Falls*, about the conflicts in the life of an Orthodox woman. It is annotated in the "Character" section of this chapter.

Richler, Mordecai

Richler was born in 1931 in the Jewish St. Urbain section of Montreal. He became one of the most prominent Canadian authors in the twentieth century, with novels that satirize Canadians and the Canadian Jewish community. His first successful novel was *The Apprenticeship of Duddy Kravitz* in 1959, which introduced the Richler antihero: a garrulous extrovert trying to be a *mensch*, but failing for various reasons, often blaming outside forces. Richler's protagonists have complicated lives: they marry often and usually badly, have strained relationships with their children, and despite their good intentions, often deceive their friends. The narratives are filled with humor and satire, often with hilarious set pieces, and the narrative structure often wanders back and forth in time, taking a while for the full picture to develop. Richler was also an essayist, scriptwriter, children's book author, and journalist. Richler died in 2001.

Barney's Version: With Footnotes and an Afterword by Michael Panofsky. Alfred A. Knopf, 1997. 355p.

In this fast-paced, irreverent, satirical novel, Barney Panofsky defends his life and adventures, from his bohemian days in Paris in the early 1950s and three marriages, to his trial for the murder of an old friend.

Themes: Canadian authors; friendship; men's lives; Montreal, Quebec; satirical novels; trials

Solomon Gursky Was Here. Alfred A. Knopf, 1990. 413p.

The story of the wealthy Canadian Gursky family as pieced together by Moses Berger, who becomes obsessed with chronicling its quirky, larger-than-life family members and their battles for control of the family fortune. With an enormous cast of characters, a time span of 150 years, and Richler's trademark ribald humor, the novel weaves back and forth in time through Canadian history from polar expeditions in the late nineteenth century to the present day.

Themes: Arctic regions; bootlegging; Canadian authors; family sagas; family secrets; humorous fiction; immigrants; liquor business

Roth, Henry

Call It Sleep. 1934; reprint, Farrar, Straus & Giroux, 1991. 462p. **YA**

The bond between David Schearl and his mother Genya cannot completely protect them from the fury of David's father and the terrors of life for a small boy on the Lower East Side in the early 1900s, which we see, hear, and smell through David's frightened eyes. An absorbing and powerful first novel vividly rendered in two kinds of prose: the fractured English of the immigrants and the eloquent Yiddish of David's parents. Although it was well-received when it was published in 1934, it wasn't until it was reissued in 1964 that *Call it Sleep* received widespread critical acclaim.

Themes: boys; coming-of-age stories; family relationships; immigrants; mothers and sons

Related Titles: Another novel told from the point of view of a very young child living in a dysfunctional family is *The Kingdom of Brooklyn* by Merrill Joan Gerber, annotated in the "Character" section of the this chapter.

Roth, Henry

Mercy of a Rude Stream. 📖

After the publication of *Call it Sleep*, Roth did not publish another novel for sixty years. *A Star Shines Over Mt. Morris Park*, the first in a series continuing the life of the young boy readers met in *Call It Sleep*, was published shortly after the author's death. His writer's block may have been due to the intensely personal incidents he reveals in the novels. The narrative voice alternates between Ira Stigman as a young man and Roth as an octogenarian writer addressing his computer, Ecclesias.

Themes: coming-of-age stories; immigrants; incest; intellectuals; teenaged boys

A Star Shines Over Mt. Morris Park. St. Martin's, 1994. 290p.

Ira and his parents, in the traditional immigrant journey, arrive on New York's Lower East Side but eventually move to Harlem in hopes of bettering themselves. While his father has a difficult time making a living, Ira learns how to defend himself against anti-Semitism despite his own ambivalence about his Jewishness.

A Diving Rock in the Hudson. St. Martin's, 1995. 418p.

Ira's adolescence and early years in college reveal him struggling with issues of identity and sex, particularly the shame of his sexual relationship with his sister Minnie and his cousin Stella.

From Bondage. St. Martin's, 1996. 432p.

While at college, Ira finds a lover and mentor in Edith Welles, an English professor, who introduces him to intellectuals like Margaret Meade and Louise Bogan. As his horizons widen, he becomes more certain of his vocation as a writer. The older Henry examines the psychological ramifications of his incestuous relationships.

Requiem for Harlem. St. Martin's, 1998. 304p.

Ira, still involved in sexual relationships with his cousin Stella and his English professor, manages to break free of his family and move to Greenwich Village. .

Roth, Philip

Philip Roth burst on the literary scene in 1959 with *Goodbye Columbus and Five Short Stories*, winning the National Book Award and the National Jewish Book Award, but provoking mixed reactions in the Jewish community for his less-than-flattering characterizations of Jews. With these stories, Roth began his lifelong work of probing the uncomfortable contradictions of Jewish life following the Holocaust. It is unusual for readers to be neutral about Roth's work. For over four decades he has been one of a handful of writers dominating literary fiction in the United States, continuing to win prizes and critical acclaim, despite the controversy that often follows him. The titles annotated below are a selection from a remarkable body of work filled with humor, eroticism, and social commentary.

🎗 *Goodbye, Columbus and Five Short Stories.* **1959; reprint, Modern Library, 1995. 298p. 1959** `YA` 📖

In these disquieting stories Roth delineates many aspects of the problems of assimilation in the post-World War II American Jewish community. In "Eli the Fanatic," when a group of Holocaust survivors moves into town, the Jewish community is afraid the immigrants' "otherness" will jeopardize their hard-won acceptance. In "Defender of the Faith," a Jewish soldier appeals to his assimilated Jewish sergeant for special treatment. The title novella is a hilarious and painful love story that takes place in a wealthy New Jersey suburb. It was made into a movie in 1967. (Winner of the National Jewish Book Award and the National Book Award.)

Themes: family relationships; Jewish identity; short stories

🎗 *Portnoy's Complaint.* **1969; reprint, Random House, 2002. 288p.**

Graphic sex scenes and frank language made the publication of this novel a cultural event. Alexander Portnoy's comic, erotic monologue is directed at his analyst. Portnoy traces his obsessive preoccupation with masturbation, sex, guilt, and repression to his childhood relationship with his mother. (An ALA Notable Book.)

Themes: Jewish identity; picaresque novels; psychiatrists and psychologists; sexuality

Roth, Philip

Zuckerman novels.

Nathan Zuckerman first appears in *My Life as a Man*, a character in the stories written by Roth's creation, the author Peter Tarnopol. In the succeeding three Zuckerman novels, published separately and also in the collection *Zuckerman Bound* (with the addition of the novella *The Prague Orgy*), Zuckerman's life parallels Roth's in ways that allow Roth to comment on the writing life and the accompanying problems of celebrity. In these early Zuckerman novels, plot takes a backseat to the development of Zuckerman's character. These novels take Zuckerman from his early twenties to his mid-forties. *The Counterlife* uses Zuckerman and his brother Henry to explore the role of narrative in life and art. The subsequent Zuckerman novels take a wider scope, examining the major social and political issues of the last half of the twentieth century. In these novels, Zuckerman is no longer the protagonist; he recounts other people's stories. The last three novels showcase Roth the master prose stylist, storyteller, and chronicler of the American experience.

6

The Ghost Writer. **Farrar, Straus & Giroux, 1979. 179p.**

The young Zuckerman, just beginning to gain attention for his fiction, pays a visit to the reclusive older writer E. I. Lonoff, hoping to find a spiritual father for his artistic vision. In the Lonoff household, a delicately unbalanced ménage à trois, Zuckerman learns some lessons about the realities of the writing life and meets a young woman who may be Anne Frank.

Themes: authors; literary life; men's lives

Zuckerman Unbound. **Farrar, Straus & Giroux. 1981. 225p.**

Now a celebrity after publishing a popular novel filled with graphic sex and Jewish angst, Zuckerman is alternately praised and reviled by family, friends, and strangers. In tender, hilarious, and painful scenes, he coaches his mother on how to talk to the press, takes calls from a would-be kidnapper, and confronts the damage he may have done to family relationships by his writing.

Themes: authors; family relationships; literary life; men's lives

The Anatomy Lesson. **Farrar, Straus & Giroux. 1983. 291p.**

Zuckerman, suffering from a mysterious, intractable neck pain, and unable to write, seeks relief in the ministrations of various women and doctors, and in contemplating a change of career.

Themes: authors; illness; love affairs; men's lives; middle age

The Prague Orgy. **Vintage International, 1985. 86p.**

In this novella, an epilogue to the previous three novels, Zuckerman visits Prague in the mid-1970s, attempts to retrieve the unpublished manuscript of a Yiddish writer, and encounters the literary repression of the Communist regime.

Themes: authors; censorship; Communists; Czechoslovakia

The Counterlife. **Farrar, Straus & Giroux. 1986. 324.**

Nathan and his brother Henry exchange identities and fates repeatedly as Roth manipulates the reader's expectations about whose life is the central subject of this experimental novel, as they engage in discussions about family relationships, Jewish survival, Israel, and literature. (Winner of the National Jewish Book Award and the National Book Critics Circle Award.)

Themes: brothers; experimental fiction; transformations (personal)

Operation Shylock: a Confession. **Simon & Schuster, 1993. 398p.**

In this meditation on illusion, reality, fame, and Jewish identity, the author discovers that someone in Israel is impersonating him and proposing a fantastic scheme to repatriate Holocaust survivors in Europe. When Roth visits Israel, he is drawn into a world where nothing is what is seems, most of all for the reader. (Winner of the Pen/Faulker Award.)

Themes: impersonations; Israel—Politics and government; Jewish identity

American Pastoral. **Houghton Mifflin, 1997. 423p.**

Zuckerman tells the story of Seymour "Swede" Levov, his high school classmate, who confounded the Jewish stereotype with his blond good looks and athletic prowess. When he married Miss New Jersey, he seemed to have it all, but misfortune struck, in ways that mirror the events and mores of the late twentieth century. (Winner of the Pulitzer Prize.)

Themes: fathers and daughters; interfaith marriage; Newark, N.J.; 1960s; radicals and radicalism

I Married a Communist. **Houghton Mifflin, 1998. 323p.**

Zuckerman encounters his old high school English teacher, Murray Ringgold, and during the course of several nights, listens to the tragic story of his boyhood idol, Murray's brother Ira, aka Iron Rinn, a radio personality who was exposed as a Communist by his actress wife in the McCarthy-era 1950s. As Zuckerman reflects on the influence the idealistic Ira had on him as a precocious teenager, Roth paints a vivid picture of the political turmoil of post-World War II America and Newark from the Depression through the early 1950s.

Themes: betrayal; brothers; Communists; marriage

Related Titles: Roth grew up in the Weequahic section of Newark, New Jersey, and while his novels often chart the decline of that city, they display a loving nostalgia for the old boisterous, thriving immigrant neighborhoods. Another novel with a strong sense of nostalgia is Alan Lelchuk's *Brooklyn Boy*, annotated in the "Setting" section of this chapter. Readers who enjoy the way Roth combines personal and social issues may also enjoy Frederick Busch's novels and stories, particularly: *Invisible Mending*, *Don't Tell Anyone*, and *A Memory of War*.

The Human Stain. **Houghton Mifflin, 2000. 361p.**

Zuckerman relates the story of his friend Coleman Silk, classics professor at Athena College, accused of racism and forced to resign. Silk's life, with its secrets about race and religion, and his affair with a young illiterate woman, combine to form a complex story of human imperfection and the search for identity in the aftermath of the civil rights movement and the Vietnam War. (Winner of the National Jewish Book Award, the Pen/Faulkner Award, and the Koret Jewish Book Award.)

Themes: Jewish identity; love affairs; racism; satirical novels; Vietnam War veterans

Related Titles: Another novel with a mix of academic satire and personal identity issues is Michael Blumenthal's *Weinstock Among the Dying*.

Singer, Isaac Bashevis

Through Singer's novels, stories, and memoirs we are able to enter a world that vanished in the Holocaust. Singer was born in Poland in 1904 and spent his early childhood in Warsaw, where his father, a Hasidic rabbi, established a *bet din*, a rabbinical court, where the precocious Isaac heard his father rule on all aspects of law, many relating to intimate details of people's lives. His mother was descended from a line of distinguished rabbis and tempered his father's ecstatic approach with her own rationalism and practicality. The family was materially poor but spiritually rich. As he writes in *A Little Boy in Search of God*, "in our house Jewishness wasn't some diluted formal religion but one that contained all the flavors, all the vitamins, the entire mysticism of faith." His parents sent him to rabbinical school at seventeen, but Singer left to become a writer, immersing himself in the heady Yiddish intellectual circles of the 1920s, inspired by his older brother, the writer Israel Joshua Singer. In 1935, due to personal considerations and the deteriorating conditions in Eastern Europe, he left Warsaw for the United States. He began contributing to *The Jewish Daily Forward*, the popular Yiddish newspaper. *The Forward* published most of his stories and serialized many of his novels. Singer wrote in Yiddish his entire life; his writing is suffused with *Yiddishkeit*, providing a poignant reminder of what was lost in the Holocaust. His novels and stories do not sentimentalize Eastern European life; they are filled with fallible characters who lose faith, commit adultery, and are otherwise tempted from good into evil, sometimes by demons and spirits. Although Singer does not write directly about the Holocaust, it is always a presence, lending the stories, memoirs, and novels set in the prewar period an elegiac quality. The Holocaust survivors who appear in his later works are disconsolate, shattered, and homeless in a very literal way. Nonetheless, fantasy and humor abound in his work; love is explored in all its varieties; and piety is seen as a way to redemption. In addition to his novels and memoirs, he published children's stories, essays, and reviews and translated novels into Yiddish. Singer won the Nobel Prize for Literature in 1978. He died in 1991.

Satan in Goray. **Noonday Press, 1955. 239p.**

In the 1660s, after the Jewish population of Poland was decimated by the Cossack uprisings, news of the false Messiah, Shabbatai Zevi, reaches Jews in the isolated town of Goray, bringing hope of redemption to a fever pitch, letting loose demons and dybbuks, and creating hysteria among the residents. A dark story, almost gothic in tone, about the conflict between good and evil. Translated by Jacob Sloan.

Themes: Kabbalah; Messiah, false; Shabbetai Zevi; shtetl life

Related Titles: A novel about a modern-day Messiah figure is Arthur A. Cohen's *In the Days of Simon Stern*. Readers who are interested in learning more about Shabbetai Zevi can look for the book *Shabbetai Tzevi* by the great scholar of mysticism Gershom Scholem.

The Magician of Lublin. **Noonday Press, 1960. 246p.**

Yasha Mazur, magician, hypnotist, lover of women both Jewish and gentile, is spiritually empty and bored with life. After years of juggling multiple love affairs, disaster strikes, and Yasha has a spiritual rebirth. Translated by Elaine Gottlieb and Joseph Singer.

Themes: love affairs; magicians; men—religious life; Poland

The Slave. **Farrar, Straus & Cudahy, 1962. 311p.**

Jacob of Josefov loses his wife and children in one of the Cossack uprisings of the mid-seventeenth century and becomes the slave of a Polish family in a primitive mountain town. He tries to keep God's commandments, but falls in love with the gentile Wanda. Translated by the author and Cecil Hemley. (Winner of the National Jewish Book Award and an ALA Notable Book.)

Themes: love stories; Poland

Related Titles: Singer's pessimistic view of man's nature is further developed in *The King of the Fields*, set in an indeterminate, barbaric period of Poland's history.

Enemies: A Love Story. **Farrar, Straus & Giroux, 1972. 280p.** 📖

Believing that his wife and children are dead, Herman Broder marries Yadwiga, the peasant girl who hid him during the War, and they come to New York, where Herman has an affair with another survivor and discovers that his wife is alive. Singer blends elements of farce with the serious theme of the effects of the Holocaust on the survivors in his first novel set in America. Translated by Aliza Shevrin and Elizabeth Shub. (An ALA Notable Book.)

Themes: adultery; Holocaust—refugees and displaced persons; Holocaust—survivors; marriage

Shosha. **Farrar, Straus & Giroux, 1978. 277p.**

Told in the first person by Aaron Greidinger, and set in pre-World War II Warsaw, where Aaron is brought up in a traditional Hasidic household but prefers to spend time with Shosha, a beautiful but simple-minded girl, with whom he is free to indulge his artistic, storytelling temperament. Aaron becomes a writer and a libertine but rediscovers his love for the childlike Shosha as the Holocaust closes in on Polish Jewry.

Themes: authors; Holocaust; love affairs; Poland; Yiddish culture

Related Titles: Aaron Greidinger, Singer's alter ego, is the protagonist in a later novel, *Meshugah*, set in New York in the 1950s among Holocaust survivors, where Aaron continues his writing career and love affairs.

The Penitent. **Farrar, Straus & Giroux, 1983. 169p.**

Framed as a story told to Singer by a man he encounters at the Western Wall, an American named Joseph Shapiro, who was dissatisfied with his promiscuous and materialistic life in the United States and came to Israel to take up a life of faith. A poignant depiction of the conflict between traditional Judaism and the modern, secular world.

Themes: Holocaust—survivors; Jewish identity; teshuvah

Scum. **Farrar, Straus & Giroux, 1991. 217p.**

Max Barabander returns to Warsaw, the city of his birth, from Argentina where he has become a successful but assimilated and shallow businessman. He yearns to live a pious life but instead makes impossible promises to several women and becomes involved in shady business deals. Translated by Rosaline Dukalsky Schwartz.

Themes: crime and criminals; love affairs; prostitution

Related Titles: Many of Singer's male characters are running from complications with women, usually of their own making. Krochmalna Street appears with regularity in Singer's writing; it is where he grew up in

Warsaw, and some of his characters, who can be suspected of being the author's alter ego, spend time on Krochmalna Street.

The Certificate. **Farrar, Straus & Giroux, 1992. 231p.**

Dreamy David Bendiger, an eighteen-year-old aspiring writer, recounts his penniless arrival in Warsaw in 1922. He falls into complicated love affairs and schemes with three women, makes tentative contact with other writers through his older brother, and fantasizes about his future, all the while musing about man's relationship to God. Translated by Leonard Wolf.

Themes: authors; love affairs; 1920s; Poland

Related Titles: *The Certificate* was published after Singer's death but was written much earlier, and serialized in Yiddish in 1967. In many respects it parallels Singer's own life as it appears in his memoir *A Young Man in Search of Love.*

Shadows on the Hudson. **Farrar, Straus & Giroux, 1998. 548p.**

A group of Jewish refugees in New York, centered around the religious Boris Makaver, search for meaning in the shadows cast by the Holocaust. One adulterous affair among the group sets off a chain of unexpected events that leads to betrayal. Laced with Singer's trademark eye for the comic in human relationships, filled with absorbing portraits of major and minor characters, this is also a bleak novel of human failings and questioning. Translated by Joseph Sherman.

Themes: Holocaust—refugees and displaced persons; Holocaust—survivors; love affairs; 1940s

Related Titles: *Shadows on the Hudson* was originally serialized in Yiddish in *The Forward* in 1957–1958.

Singer, Isaac Bashevis

Short Stories.

Singer was a gifted and original storyteller, a master at combining the rational and the mystical, the real and the fantastic. The early stories are set in rural Poland or Warsaw. Demons and spirits intrude on everyday life, leading the pious astray. Many stories are recounted as straight narrative, but others are told by demons, or even unborn souls. The strongest emotions—lust, greed, desire for power—lead individuals and sometimes entire villages into disaster and hysteria. The later stories are often set in America, among Holocaust survivors and refugees, and are told in the first person, as events that happened to Singer himself. Those who enjoy reading Singer for a glimpse of a vanished world may also enjoy Yehuda Elberg's *The Empire of Kalman the Cripple*, set in Poland on the eve of Hitler's takeover of Germany.

Themes: fantasy; Holocaust—survivors; love stories; Poland; shtetl life; short stories

Gimpel the Fool and Other Stories. **Noonday Press, 1955. 205p.**

The title story was the first of Singer's short stories to appear in English. It was translated by Saul Bellow and appeared in *Partisan Review* in 1953, to great acclaim. A whole village conspires against the naïve Gimpel, who may or may not be a fool. The stories are set in rural villages where poverty, superstition, and faith converge in miraculous ways. Translated by Saul Bellow, Elaine Gottlieb, and others.

***The Spinoza of Market Street.* Farrar, Straus & Cudahy, 1961. 214p.**

Translated by Martha Glicklich and others.

***Short Friday and Other Stories.* Farrar, Straus & Giroux, 1964. 243p.**

Translated by Joseph Singer and others.

***The Séance and Other Stories.* Farrar, Straus & Giroux, 1968. 276p.**

Translated by Roger H. Klein and others.

***A Friend of Kafka and Other Stories.* Farrar, Straus & Giroux, 1970. 311p.**

Stories of Holocaust survivors, immigrants, and refugees. Includes *The Cafeteria*, set in Singer's own Upper West Side New York neighborhood. Translated by Isaac Bashevis Singer and others.

***A Crown of Feathers and Other Stories.* Farrar, Straus & Giroux, 1973. 342p.**

Translated by Isaac Bashevis Singer and others. (Winner of the National Book Award.)

***Passions and Other Stories.* Farrar, Straus & Giroux, 1975. 312p.**

Translated by Isaac Bashevis Singer and others.

***Old Love.* Farrar, Straus & Giroux, 1979. 273p.**

Translated by Joseph Singer and others.

***Collected Stories.* Farrar, Straus & Giroux, 1982. 610p.**

Stories selected by the author from the previous collections, including many of the best and most well known.

***The Image and Other Stories.* Farrar, Straus & Giroux, 1985. 310p.**

***The Death of Methuselah and Other Stories.* Farrar, Straus & Giroux, 1988. 244p.**

Yezierska, Anzia

Yezierska came to New York from Poland in 1898 as a teenager, living on the Lower East Side with her family. Her novels and stories record the struggles and dreams of Jewish immigrant women. Although her prose has a Yiddish cadence, and her style is unadorned, her stories are far from naïve; they shrewdly capture the dilemmas of immigrants caught between the old and the new in authentic language, and they burst with emotion.

***Bread Givers: A Struggle Between a Father of the Old World and a Daughter of the New.* 1925; reprint, Persea Books, 1999. 297p.**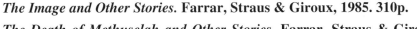

Sara Smolinsky struggles to free herself of her father's expectations, still rooted in the shtetl they left behind, where women's opportunities for education, work, and marriage were limited.

Themes: fathers and daughters; immigrants; Lower East Side, N.Y.; New York City; 1910s; 1920s; women's lives

Hungry Hearts and Other Stories. **1920; reprint, Signet, 1996. 239p.** YA 📖

Yezierska's earliest stories about immigrant women record their anguish and sense of dislocation.

Themes: immigrants; Lower East Side, N.Y.; New York City; 1910s; short stories; women's lives

Red Ribbon on a White Horse. **1950; reprint, Persea Books, 1988. 228p.**

A semiautobiographical account of Yezierska's time in Hollywood after her novel *The Bread Givers* was optioned by Samuel Goldwyn.

Themes: authors; Hollywood; 1920s

The Open Cage: An Anzia Yezierska Collection. **Edited by Alice Kessler Harris. 1979; reprint, Persea Books, 1994. 262p.** YA 📖

Selected short stories and excerpts from the novels.

Themes: immigrants; Lower East Side, N.Y.; New York City; women's lives

Related Titles: Readers who enjoy novels and stories that read like nonfiction, may also like Gloria Goldreich's historical novel *That Year of Our War*, annotated in the "Modern Period" section of chapter 3, or *Swimming Toward the Ocean*, by Carole Glickfeld, annotated in the "Character" section of this chapter. A novel, *John and Anzia: An American Romance* by Norma Rosen is based on the real-life relationship between Yezierska and the philosopher John Dewey.

Character

These are the novels from which the characters step off the page and spend time with us, whose actions we find troubling, pleasing, or even mystifying. The elderly man in Lesléa Newman's *A Letter to Harvey Milk*, the troubled student in Ben Schrank's *Consent*, and the intense Ruth Rothwax in Lily Brett's *Too Many Men* may haunt us long after we have finished reading about them.

These novels give us the chance to identify with characters who struggle with issues we recognize from our own lives. Or, we can enjoy reading about characters entirely different from us, and through them experience thoughts and lives far from our own. Often the author uses first person narration, making the reader feel like a friend hearing a story. In *Funny Accent*, Anna Schopenhauer tells us about her affairs with older men, and we share her efforts to understand herself. In Carole L. Glickfeld's *Swimming Toward the Ocean*, Chenia's daughter Devorah tells the story of her mother's life, providing the perspective of a child involved in the events yet not always understanding them. Andrew Bergman uses first person narration in *Sleepless Nights*, which helps us identify with the unusual trials of his narrator, Robbie Weisglass. Other novels are written from characters' points of view. In *What Remains*, by Nicholas Delbanco, point of view shifts from one character to another, providing an empathetic portrait of several generations. Whatever type of individual is portrayed, whether amusing or tormented, young or old—the characters in these novels are people the reader will long remember.

Badanes, Jerome

 The Final Opus of Leon Solomon. **Alfred A. Knopf, 1989. 272p.**

In the days before he plans to commit suicide, Leon Solomon records his life story in a seedy Manhattan hotel. He writes about his German childhood, experiences in Auschwitz, marriage, and love affairs, culminating in his strange career of stealing historical documents from the public library. (Winner of the E. L. Wallant Award.)

Themes: Holocaust—survivors; love affairs; men's lives; suicide

Related Titles: Another novel in which the memories of Holocaust survivors fracture their present lives is Lynne Alexander's *Safe Houses.*

Bergman, Andrew

Sleepless Nights. **D. I. Fine, 1994. 218p.**

Growing up in Queens, New York, in the 1950s with an overbearing mother and detached father, Robbie Weisglass's childhood is difficult, especially when his mother and sister initiate him into sex before his bar mitzvah. Robbie becomes unable to separate himself from the family dynamics and form stable relationships. Moving back and forth in time from the 1950s to the 1990s, Robbie recalls the events of his life for the reader and his psychiatrist.

Themes: dysfunctional families; incest; psychiatrists and psychologists

Bloch, Alice

The Law of Return. **Alyson Publications, 1983. 249p.**

A casual suggestion sends Ellen to Israel after college, where she becomes Elisheva and starts a journey toward understanding herself as a Jewish woman and a lesbian, in this very personal story set in the 1970s.

Themes: Americans in Israel; gays/lesbians/bisexuals; Jewish identity; women—religious life

Bloom, Stephen

No New Jokes. **W. W. Norton, 1997. 187p.**

At Bald Sam's luncheonette, Izzy and his friends gather to kibitz, gripe, and trade jokes, in this character study told mostly in telegraphic dialogue that vividly captures the place and time: Brownsville, Brooklyn, in 1949. Humor functions as a survival mechanism for Izzy, a desolate war veteran haunted by tragedies in his past, using casual sex to assuage his emotional hunger.

Themes: Brooklyn, N.Y.; fathers and sons; humorous fiction; men's lives; 1940s

Brett, Lily

Too Many Men. Morrow. 2001. 531p. 📖

Ruth Rothwax, self-sufficient, everything-under-control career woman, meets her Holocaust-survivor father, Edek, in Poland where they revisit his childhood haunts and the Auschwitz-Birkenau camp where he and Ruth's mother were prisoners. Written in a deceptively straightforward, conversational style, filled with humor and the pain of being the child of Holocaust survivors, this is a story of self-discovery.

Themes: children of Holocaust survivors; family secrets; fathers and daughters; women's lives

Related Titles: The conversational and humorous tone of *Too Many Men* belies its seriousness as a novel about the nature of Holocaust memory. Brett is an Australian now living in New York, the child of Holocaust survivors. Her collection of linked stories, *What God Wants*, published in the United States, is set in the Jewish community in Melbourne, Australia.

Canin, Ethan

Carry Me Across the Water. Random House, 2001. 206p. 📖

August Kleinman, now a seventy-eight-year-old wealthy widower, reviews events in his life and choices he made, especially his encounter with a Japanese soldier in World War II, in this gracefully written meditation on loss.

Themes: elderly men; family relationships; World War II

Related Titles: Canin has also written the novel *For Kings and Planets* and the short story collections *The Palace Thief* and *Emperor of the Air*.

Carter, Dori

Beautiful WASPs Having Sex. Morrow, 2000. 320p.

Frankie Jordan's successful husband has left her, her scripts aren't getting read, and she's feeling like a failure until she meets Jonathan Prince, an agent wannabe who seems to have her interests at heart. Sharp and funny in its portrayal of a variety of Hollywood types, with an insider's look at the way movies are made and the contrast between the Jews who write and produce the movies and the WASPs who act in them.

Themes: authors; betrayal; Hollywood; women's lives

Related Titles: Another novel in which a woman learns through her husband's betrayal what she really wants is *Heartburn*, a humorous novel by Nora Ephron, annotated in the "Language" section of this chapter.

Diamant, Anita

Good Harbor. Scribner, 2001. 253p.

Kathleen Levine and Joyce Tabachnik, at different stages of their lives, meet and find nourishment in their friendship in a seaside town in Massachusetts. (The author's Web site is www.anitadiamant.com.)

Themes: cancer; conversion to Judaism; family relationships; friendship; love affairs; women's lives

Related Titles: Diamant's first novel was the extremely popular *The Red Tent*, annotated in the "Biblical and Ancient Worlds" section of chapter 3. Another novel about an enduring friendship between women is *The Book Borrower* by Alice Mattison.

Dworkin, Susan

The Book of Candy. **Four Walls Eight Windows, 1997. 359p.**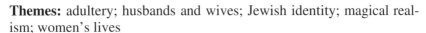

Candy Shapiro is jolted out of her traditional Long Island Jewish housewife role when she learns that her husband Marty is having an affair. Seeking revenge, Candy finds herself following paths she never anticipated, including trafficking with the Mafia and falling in love with an Israeli moving man. (The author's Web site is www.susandworkin.com.)

Themes: adultery; husbands and wives; Jewish identity; magical realism; women's lives

Elkin, Stanley

🎗 *Mrs. Ted Bliss*. **Hyperion, 1995. 292p.**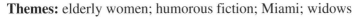

Widowed, living in a high-rise condominium in Miami, Dorothy Bliss spends her declining years amid the anxieties and degeneration of old age, in this humorous novel that concludes with the arrival of Hurricane Andrew. (Winner of the National Book Critics Circle Award.)

Themes: elderly women; humorous fiction; Miami; widows

Related Titles: Elkin was a prolific writer with a unique comic voice. Readers may enjoy two earlier works by him: *The Rabbi of Lud*, a novel, and *Criers and Kibitzers, Kibitzers and Criers*, a collection of short stories.

Englander, Nathan

🎗 *For the Relief of Unbearable Urges*. **Alfred A. Knopf. 1999. 205p.**

Nine short stories, many about conflicts in the lives of Orthodox Jews. In the title story, a man with a marital problem consults his rabbi and is given unexpected advice; in "The Tumblers," a group of Hasidim become acrobats to escape the Nazis; in "The Gilgul of Park Avenue," a man discovers while in a taxi that he has a Jewish soul. (An ALA Notable Book.)

Themes: Jewish identity; Orthodox Jews

Epstein, Leslie

Ice, Fire, Water: A Leib Goldkorn Cocktail. **W. W. Norton, 1999. 264p.**

The inimitable Leib Goldkorn, from the vantage point of his nineties, looks back on his romantic adventures in three tales, starting in the late 1930s. Sonja Henie, Carmen Miranda, Darryl Zanuck, and *The New York*

Times book critic Michiko Kakutani mingle with fictional characters in this sexual romp.

Themes: elderly men; Holocaust—survivors; love affairs; men's lives; musicians

Related Titles: Leib Goldkorn first appeared in the title novella of *The Steinway Quintet: Plus Four* as a garrulous musician involved in a holdup, then in the collection *Goldkorn Tales.*

Fagan, Cary

The Animals' Waltz. St. Martin's, 1996. 277p.

At thirty-one, Sheila Hersh has only recently moved out of her father's house and is still working in the family mattress business by day and cruising the Toronto party scene at night. In an effort to start afresh and take her father away from an unsuitable girlfriend, they travel to Vienna, where Sheila hopes to learn about a Jewish girl whose poems have haunted her since she found them among her late mother's books.

Themes: Canadian authors; fathers and daughters; poets

Feinberg, David B.

Eighty-Sixed. Viking, 1989. 326p.

In this irreverent and satirical novel, B. J. Rosenthal is living in early 1980s Manhattan, enjoying the freedom of the post-Stonewall gay community, cruising the bars and baths, until the advent of AIDS changes all the rules.

Themes: AIDS; gays/lesbians/bisexuals; men's lives; New York City

Related Titles: Feinberg's second novel, *Spontaneous Combustion*, follows the same protagonist after he tests positive for HIV.

Ferber, Edna

Fanny Herself. 1917; reprint, University of Illinois Press, 2001. 323p. **YA** 📖

Fanny Brandeis, growing up in small-town Winnebago, Wisconsin, before World War I, is determined not to waste her talents running the family store and supporting her violin-playing brother in Europe. Through her intelligence and energy, she builds a successful career in a large Chicago mail-order company, but learns that material success does not always bring contentment.

Themes: coming-of-age stories; mothers and daughters; women's lives

Related Titles: Ferber (1885–1968) was a very popular author; several of her novels became successful films. She grew up in the Midwest, daughter of a storekeeper, like Fanny Brandeis, with an awareness of social issues that spilled over into her writing. Many of her novels depict strong women succeeding in nontraditional careers. *Fanny Herself* is the most autobiographical of her novels and the only one with a Jewish heroine. She wrote two volumes of autobiography: *A Peculiar Treasure* and *A Kind of Magic*. Another novel about a woman's determination to succeed is *West to Eden* by Gloria Goldreich, annotated in the "Modern Period, United States and Canada" section of chapter 3.

Friedman, Bruce Jay

Stern. **1962; reprint, Grove Press, 2001. 191p.**

Stern suffers from feelings of despair and alienation in his new suburban home when an anti-Semitic neighbor calls his wife a "kike" and he is unable to respond to the insult. A classic novel of black humor and insight.

Themes: anti-Semitism; black humor; men's lives; 1950s; suburban life

Related Titles: Although *Stern* was not well received initially, it has had a long life as a cult classic. Friedman has written several other novels, including *A Mother's Kisses* and *About Harry Towns,* and the plays *Scuba Duba* and *Steambath. The Collected Short Fiction of Bruce Jay Friedman* brings together short stories written between 1953 and 1995.

Gerber, Merrill Joan

The Kingdom of Brooklyn. **1992; reprint, Syracuse University Press, 2000. 239p.** **YA**

Three-year-old Issa tells about her dysfunctional world, filled with the tantrums and threats of her mother, unspoken conflicts among relatives, and the mysterious dangers of World War II. Issa navigates this fearful place, trying to find allies and understand herself apart from her mother.

Themes: Brooklyn, N.Y.; dysfunctional families; girls; mothers and daughters

Related Titles: Gerber takes the reader inside the mind of her characters in a very intimate way. Another novel told from the point of view of a child trying to make sense of a complex adult world is Henry Roth's *Call It Sleep,* annotated in the "Classics and Major Authors" section of this chapter.

Gerber, Merrill Joan

The Anna Series.

Themes: aging; death; elderly women; family relationships

Anna in Chains. **Syracuse University Press, 1998. 139p.** **YA**

Eleven stories told by Anna Goldman, nearing eighty, feisty and irreverent, enduring the indignities of an aging body with wit and as much grace as she can muster in her vibrant multiethnic Los Angeles neighborhood.

Anna in the Afterlife. **Syracuse University Press, 2002. 123p.** **YA**

Anna looks back on her life from the point of her death with the same sharp tongue.

Glickfeld, Carole L.

Swimming Toward the Ocean. **Alfred A. Knopf, 2001. 387p.**

When Chenia Arnow, pregnant with an unwanted third child, wades into the surf at Coney Island, she sets in motion events that ultimately free her from an adulterous husband and unlock the secrets of her own heart. A character study filled with *Yiddishkeit* and told mainly from the viewpoint of her precocious daughter Devorah. (The author's Web site is www.caroleglickfeld. com.)

Themes: immigrants; mothers and daughters; 1950s; urban life; women's lives

Related Titles: Glickfeld's earlier collection of linked stories, *Useful Gifts*, won the Flannery O'Connor Award for Short Fiction. Glickfeld's heroine is a descendant of Anzia Yezierska—still wanting America to "want what's in me," but prevented by a traditional role and lack of opportunity. Yezierska's novels are annotated in the "Classics and Major Authors" section of this chapter. Another novel about a woman stifled in an unhappy marriage is *Home Is Where You Start From*, by Gene Horowitz, winner of the E. L. Wallant Award.

Goldstein, Rebecca

Strange Attractors. **Viking Press, 1993. 276p.**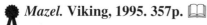

A collection of nine stories in which character is foremost, often exploring how we are similar and different from our parents, and how their legacies affect our lives. In the powerful story "The Legacy of Raizel Kadish," the daughter of a Holocaust survivor learns some unexpected lessons about morality. In "Rabbinical Eyes," the daughter of a rabbi finds that abandoning Judaism doesn't exempt her from suffering.

Themes: family relationships; short stories

Related Titles: Readers who enjoy Goldstein's stories for their insight into character may also like Sharon Solwitz's collection *Blood and Milk*.

Mazel. **Viking, 1995. 357p.**

Phoebe's conventional marriage and life in suburban New Jersey are a surprise to her flamboyant grandmother Sasha, who chose to defy convention by becoming an actress in the Yiddish theater in 1930s Poland. Sasha's philosophy of *mazel* (luck) is confirmed by her own adventurous life story. (Winner of the National Jewish Book Award and the E. L. Wallant Award.)

Themes: granddaughters; grandmothers; scientists; Yiddish theater

Related Titles: Another novel with an unusual grandmother–granddaughter relationship is *He, She and It* by Marge Piercy, annotated in chapter 4. Goldstein, an intelligent and subtle writer, often explores questions of philosophy and physics and their effect on our lives. Her other novels are *The Dark Sister*, *The Mind-Body Problem*, *The Late-Summer Passion of a Woman of Mind*, and *Properties of Light*.

Goodman, Allegra

Goodman published her first story in the magazine *Commentary* during her freshman year at Harvard; the collection *Total Immersion* was published when she was twenty-one. Her stories and novels deal with issues of faith in a secular world, particularly for women, and span the United States from Hawaii, where she grew up, to New York and Boston. (The author's Web site is theory.lcs.mit.edu/~karger/allegra.html.)

Total Immersion. **Harper & Row, 1989. 260p.**

Goodman's first collection of stories depicts contemporary Jewish life in California and Hawaii. In "Oral History," a young woman collecting oral histories from elderly Jewish women is frustrated by her inability to control her subjects' rambling memories. The retired rabbi at Martin Buber Temple has trouble adjusting to his replacement, who was hired to inspire the younger members, in "The Succession." In some of the stories, we meet characters who reappear in *The Family Markowitz.*

Themes: Jewish identity; short stories

The Family Markowitz. **Farrar, Straus & Giroux. 1996. 262p.** **YA**

A gently satirical collection of linked stories about three generations of the Markowitz family as their mother ages and moves from Brooklyn to California. Stories are told by different family members at times when their lives intersect.

Themes: aging; family relationships; short stories

Related Titles: Another collection of linked intergenerational stories is Maxine Rodburg's *The Law of Return*. Readers may also enjoy Enid Shomer's collection *Imaginary Men*, for her often wryly narrated stories about family relationships.

Kaaterskill Falls. **Dial, 1998. 324p.** **YA**

Set in an Orthodox Jewish summer enclave in upstate New York, where Elizabeth Schulman, devout mother of five, longs to expand her horizons within the expectations of her religious community. A poignant picture of the joys and frustrations of the observant life. (Winner of the E. L. Wallant Award and an ALA Notable Book.)

Themes: Orthodox Jews; rabbis; women—religious life

Paradise Park. **Dial, 2001. 360p.** **YA**

Sharon Spiegelman, abandoned in Honolulu by her dancing partner, embarks on a chaotic spiritual quest that leads her to the study of science, Christianity, Buddhism, and various forms of Judaism. Ever faithful to herself, Sharon ultimately finds love and fulfillment where she least expects it. (Winner of the E. L. Wallant Award.)

Themes: coming-of-age stories; Hawaii; Jewish identity; women—religious life

Related Titles: Readers may also enjoy Nessa Rapoport's novel *Preparing for Sabbath*, about a young Orthodox woman on a journey of self-discovery, or Cathleen Schine's novel *The Evolution of Jane,* about a young woman who travels far from home to find herself.

Goodman, Eric

In Days of Awe. **Alfred A. Knopf, 1991. 288p.**

When Joe Singer, a star major league pitcher, is suspended from baseball for attempting to throw a game, his wife leaves him, fans insult him in the street, and his girlfriend's husband tries to kill him. Between Rosh Hashanah and Yom Kippur, Joe tries to put his life in order, atone for his sins, and find forgiveness in this darkly humorous story set in a very Southern California milieu.

Themes: baseball and baseball players; men's lives; repentance

Related Titles: Zachary Klein's mystery series featuring the detective Matt Jacob, annotated in the "Private Investigators" section of chapter 2, is also about a down-and-out character who suffers for past mistakes. Temptation and atonement also play a part in the title novella of Allen Hoffman's short story collection *Kagan's Superfecta*, about a compulsive gambler on Yom Kippur.

Greenberg, Joanne

A Season of Delight. **Holt, Rinehart & Winston, 1981. 244p.**

In a peaceful, rural Pennsylvania town, Grace Dowben mourns the choices made by her two grown children, lost to their Jewish faith, and takes comfort in her work on the fire and rescue squad. Her unexpected attachment to a young man on the rescue squad forces Grace to make some difficult decisions.

Themes: cults; family relationships; May–December romance, 1970s; rescue work

Related Titles: Greenberg has also written *The King's Persons*, an historical novel annotated in the "Dark Ages and Early Modern History" section of chapter 3. Greenberg is known for her ability to portray difficult emotional states. Her novel, *I Never Promised You a Rose Garden* (published under the name Hannah Green) was written from the point of view of a young mentally ill girl.

Greene, Bette

Summer of My German Soldier. **1973; reprint, Dial, 2003. 230p.** YA

Patty Bergen, a Jewish teenager living near a POW camp in Arkansas during World War II, hides Anton, an escaped German prisoner. Their relationship provides the love missing in their lives. (An ALA Notable Book.)

Themes: family relationships; love stories; prejudice; prisoners of war; teenaged girls

Related Titles: This poignant story is well loved by teenagers and adults. The sequel, *Morning Is a Long Time Coming*, picks up when Patty graduates from high school and travels to Germany, still missing Anton.

Havazelet, Ehud

Like Never Before. Farrar, Straus & Giroux. 1998. 268p.

A collection of linked stories about an Orthodox family, focusing on the son, David, and the gradual deterioration of his relationship with his father, a Holocaust survivor. Various family members recount the stories at different times in their lives, with an eye for the telling detail of characterization and the texture of family life.

Themes: coming-of-age stories; family relationships; fathers and sons

Related Titles: Another collection with shifting perspectives on family relationships is *Esther Stories* by Peter Orner.

Henkin, Joshua

Swimming Across the Hudson. Putnam, 1997. 230p.

When adoptee Ben Suskind's birth mother contacts him, he begins to reexamine the choices he's made and his relationships with his family and girlfriend, in this gracefully written story about the fragility of identity and the persistence of religious traditions.

Themes: adopted children; Jewish identity; men's lives; parents and children

Related Titles: Another novel about an introspective young man trying to understand himself and the adults around him is *The Lost Legends of New Jersey* by Frederick Reiken.

Horn, Dara

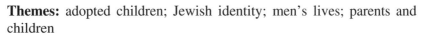 *In the Image.* W. W. Norton, 2002. 278p. YA

When Leora loses her best friend Naomi in a hit-and-run accident, Naomi's grandfather Bill Landsmann tries to interest her in his unusual slide collection. Leora rebuffs him, but threads of fate, coincidence, and Jewish history connect their lives in an almost mystical way. (Winner of the E. L. Wallant Award and the National Jewish Book Award. The author's Web site is www.darahorn.com.)

Themes: grandfathers; journalists; photographers; women's lives

Horowitz, Eve

Plain Jane. Random House, 1992. 261p. YA

Jane's life is shaken up when her sister Caroline changes from promiscuous bohemian to devout Orthodox wife, forcing Jane, her parents, and her brother to reexamine their lives. A humorous and tender coming-of-age story of how family relationships affect our sense of identity.

Themes: brothers and sisters; coming-of-age stories; humorous fiction; sisters; women's lives

Isler, Alan

 The Prince of West End Avenue. **Bridge Works Publishing, 1994. 246p.** 📖

In the Emma Lazarus retirement home, Holocaust survivor Otto Korner confronts the guilt he bears from his actions in Auschwitz, as the residents rehearse Hamlet. An elegantly written character study, filled with humor, the indignities of growing old, and the consequences of self-deception. (Winner of the National Jewish Book Award.)

Themes: actors and acting; elderly men; Holocaust—survivors; men's lives

Related Titles: Readers who like Isler's literary style may also enjoy his collection of four novellas, *The Bacon Fancier*, annotated in the "Dark Ages through Early Modern Period" section of chapter 3.

Kraven Images. **Bridge Works Publishing, 1996. 264p.**

Filled with wordplay and literary allusion, this satire of academic life and the human condition finds Nicholas Kraven, professor of English at an inner-city college, coping with ardent lovers, sexy students, self-important colleagues, and the family demons that have killed off all his Kraven relatives.

Themes: adultery; college life; family curses; men's lives; professors

Related Titles: Readers who enjoyed the academic satire in this novel may like Philip Roth's *The Human Stain*, annotated in the "Classics and Major Authors" section of this chapter.

Kadish, Rachel

From a Sealed Room. **Putnam, 1998. 356p.** `YA` 📖

In this quietly affecting first novel, Maya, an American student involved in an abusive relationship; Shifra, a Holocaust survivor paralyzed by guilt; and Tami, a mother unable to express emotion, find their lives intertwined as they seek redemption and forgiveness during a tense time in Israeli politics. (The title refers to the room in Israeli households where families were sequestered in 1991 during Iraqi missile attacks.)

Themes: domestic violence; Israel; mothers and daughters; women's lives

Related Titles: Readers who enjoyed Kadish's well-developed, empathetic characters and the realistic Israeli setting may also enjoy Linda Grant's *When I Lived in Modern Times*. Another novel about women's roles in Israel is E. M. Broner's *A Weave of Women*.

Kalman, Judith

The County of Birches. **St. Martin's Griffin, 2000. 183p.** `YA` 📖

An absorbing, richly textured collection of linked stories that follows a family from wealth in pre-World War II Hungary, through unimaginable losses in the Holocaust, to a new life in Montreal, Canada, in the 1950s. Many of the stories are told from the point of view of the youngest daughter, Dana Weisz, as she struggles to make sense of her parents' lives and establish her own identity.

Themes: Canada; family relationships; Holocaust—survivors

Kirchheimer, Gloria DeVidas

Goodbye, Evil Eye: Stories. Holmes & Meier, 2000. 150p. **YA**

Short stories, some of them linked, with the feel of memoir, about Sephardic families in and around New York. The older generation regrets the loss of tradition in their children, the children feel the rueful pull of traditions that have become attenuated in their American lives. A bittersweet collection with insight into the special traditions of this community.

Themes: family relationships; immigrants; Sephardim

Related Titles: Faye Moskowitz's autobiographical collection *A Leak in the Heart*, about her childhood and young adult years in the Midwest, has the same poignant tone of time past and lessons learned from family members.

Kirshenbaum, Binnie

Hester Among the Ruins. W. W. Norton, 2002. 286p.

Historian Hester Rosenfeld, looking for a subject for her next book, decides to study her lover, a German professor born during World War II. As research and love affair progress, we uncover suppressed aspects of the lovers' relationships with their families.

Themes: historians; Jewish–German relations; Nazis; women's lives

Related Titles: The theme of Jewish–German relationships after the Holocaust occurs in two of Kirschenbaum's earlier books: *Pure Poetry* and *History on a Personal Note*. Kirshenbaum's edgy and unusual novels confront issues of female sexuality in provocative ways. In *An Almost Perfect Moment*, published in 2004, a Jewish teenager becomes obsessed with the Virgin Mary.

Konecky, Edith

Allegra Maud Goldman. 1976; reprint, Feminist Press, 2001. 224p. **YA**

Allegra's insights into growing up female in Brooklyn in the 1930s are delivered in a wise and funny voice, as she refuses to fit into the role expected of her.

Themes: coming-of-age stories; family relationships; teenaged girls, women—social conditions

Related Titles: Konecky wrote another novel, *A Place at the Table*, about Rachel Levin, a middle-aged woman who refuses to mold her life to other people's expectations. Readers may enjoy speculating whether Rachel is the grown-up Allegra. Another novel about family roles and expectations is *The Changelings* by Jo Sinclair, annotated in the "Story" section of this chapter, or *The Sweetheart Is In*, a collection of linked stories by S. L. Wisenberg, annotated in the "Language" section of this chapter. Anne Bernays's *Growing Up Rich* is another novel told in the distinctive voice of a teenaged girl.

Kornblatt, Joyce Reiser

Nothing to Do with Love. **Viking, 1981. 298p.**

A novella and seven stories that explore the impact of family dynamics and friends on our lives in Kornblatt's lyrical, introspective style. In the title novella, geneticist Janet Sorokin, whose fifteen-year-old daughter has run away, searches her own past for the seeds of this calamity.

Themes: children; mothers and daughters; women's lives

Baking Bread. **Dutton, 1987. 206p.** `YA`

A collection of linked stories about five people who meant a great deal to the narrator, among them her grandfather and friends from childhood and adulthood. The stories portray the facts of their lives and the author's imaginative re-creation of their feelings.

Themes: family relationships; friendship; grandfathers; linked stories; women's lives

Related Titles: Kornblatt's magical realist novel *The Reason for Wings* is annotated in chapter 3 in the "Modern Period, Eastern Europe and Russia" section.

Kotlowitz, Robert

His Master's Voice. **Alfred A. Knopf, 1992. 337p.**

In the summer of 1944, Sigmund Safer, cantor of a large Baltimore congregation, prepares for the all-important Rosh Hashanah and Yom Kippur services, as he worries about synagogue politics, his daughter's Catholic boyfriend, and the fate of his remaining family in Poland.

Themes: cantors; men—religious life; synagogue life

Related Titles: Another novel about a man whose efforts to do the right thing cause problems is Paul Hond's novel *The Baker*, annotated in the "Story" section of this chapter.

Lowenthal, Michael

The Same Embrace. **Dutton, 1998. 289p.**

Jacob and Jonathan, identical twins, go their separate ways as young adults, each one unaware of the loss the other one feels. In flashbacks seen from Jacob's point of view, we see how the dark secrets of their Holocaust-survivor grandparents split the family and make their reconciliation difficult.

Themes: family secrets; gays/lesbians/bisexuals; Jewish identity; men's lives; twins

Magun, Carol

Circling Eden. **Academy Chicago Publishers, 1995. 182p.**

Looking for an opportunity to shake up her life, Rebecca Harrison decides to spend her junior year abroad in Israel instead of Paris. Landladies, lovers, teachers, and friends offer her glimpses into Israeli society, but she feels like an outsider, trying hard to understand language and culture and find acceptance, until she meets Avner.

Themes: Americans in Israel; women's lives; Yom Kippur War, 1973

Mekler, Eva

Sunrise Shows Late. **Bridge Works Publishing, 1997. 272p.**

Manya Gerson survived the war by passing as a Pole and fighting in the resistance, but afterward she finds herself under attack as a Jew and a Communist. In the limbo of a German DP camp, waiting for a visa, her attraction to two very different men forces her to think about the future of the Jewish people as it affects her own life. A sensitive and insightful portrait of the circumstances of survivors, fraught with difficulties.

Themes: Holocaust—refugees and displaced persons; Holocaust—survivors; Israel; women's lives

Related Titles: Readers who enjoyed Manya's complex character may also enjoy *The Hiding Room* by Jonathan Wilson, about an enigmatic Englishwoman and her dangerous love affair in Palestine in the aftermath of World War II.

Merkin, Daphne

🎗 *Enchantment.* **Harcourt Brace Jovanovich, 1986. 288p.**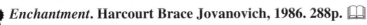

Growing up in a family of six children, self-absorbed Hannah Lehman often felt neglected by her wealthy, German-born mother, whose detachment left Hannah feeling abandoned and dependent. Plot is minimal in this intense scrutiny of the mother–daughter relationship filled with wit, insight, and the texture of life in an Orthodox family in New York in the 1950s. (Winner of the E. L. Wallant Award.)

Themes: family relationships; mothers and daughters; 1950s; women's lives

Related Titles: Merkin has also published a collection of very personal essays, *Dreaming of Hitler*. Readers who enjoyed this sensitive portrayal of the rough edges of a mother–daughter relationship from the daughter's point of view may enjoy Vivian Gornick's memoir *Fierce Attachments*, annotated in the "Childhood and Family" section of chapter 8, or Edith Chevat's novel *Love Lesson*.

Newman, Lesléa

A Letter to Harvey Milk. **Firebrand Books, 1988. 173p.**

A collection of stories that map the intersection of lesbian love and Jewish faith. In "The Gift," Ellen has ambivalent feelings about being Jewish as she grows up, but finds that Judaism is a necessary part of her identity as an adult. In the much-anthologized "A Letter to Harvey Milk," an elderly Jewish man takes a creative writing class, and when the teacher encourages him to write about his friendship with Harvey Milk, the memories summoned up are too difficult to bear. (The author's Web site is www.lesleanewman.com.)

Themes: gays/lesbians/bisexuals; short stories

Related Titles: Newman's stories are filled with the warmth of community and the angst of relationships. Additional short stories can be found in her collections *She Loves Me, She Loves Me Not* and the recently published *The Best Short Stories of Lesléa Newman*. She is also known for her poetry and children's books. Readers may also enjoy *Nice Jewish Girls: A Lesbian Anthology*, a collection of fiction and nonfiction, annotated in the "Collected Biography" section of chapter 8.

Nissenson, Hugh

***The Elephant and My Jewish Problem: Selected Stories and Journals, 1957–1987.* Harper & Row, 1988. 211p.**

A collection of short stories, previously published in other collections, and several journal pieces. The stories present Jews in different eras and places, struggling with difficult issues: anti-Semitism, death of a loved one, the value of religious belief. One of the journal entries is an account of the Eichmann trial, another of the trial of Klaus Barbie.

Themes: essays; Israel; Poland; short stories

Related Titles: Nissenson's novel *My Own Ground*, set on the Lower East Side, is annotated in the "Modern Period, United States and Canada" section of chapter 3.

Paley, Grace

Paley's short stories are critically acclaimed and widely anthologized. Her vividly drawn characters express themselves with energy and passion; they are immersed in family and love relationships; and they argue about ideas and ideals of a political, literary, or feminist nature. Paley is also well known as a political activist, a legacy from her upbringing as the daughter of immigrant parents who fled Russia because of their political activities. The earliest of her three short story collections is the one that focuses on the lives and concerns of Jewish Eastern European immigrants.

Themes: short stories; women's lives

***The Little Disturbances of Man: Stories of Women and Men at Love.* Doubleday, 1959. 189p.**

In one of the most well-known stories in this collection, "Goodbye and Good Luck," Rose Lieber explains to her niece how, despite her failure to follow the path prescribed for Jewish women of her generation, she has led a rich and fulfilling life.

***Enormous Changes at the Last Minute.* Farrar, Straus & Giroux, 1974. 198p.**
***Later That Same Day.* Farrar, Straus & Giroux, 1985. 211p.**
***Collected Stories.* Farrar, Straus & Giroux, 1994. 386p.**

Contains all the stories from Paley's three collections.

Related Titles: Paley is also a poet, essayist, and teacher. Readers who want to explore more of Paley's works may enjoy *Long Walks and Intimate Talks*, which contains poems and stories, or *Just As I Thought*, a volume of essays.

Piercy, Marge

Three Women. Morrow, 1999. 309p.

Suzanne Blume, a law professor, twice divorced, enjoys the freedom of her highly organized single life, her only romance being over the Internet, until her erratic older daughter and ailing mother move in with her, and her Internet boyfriend comes to visit. Sparks fly among these three women, whose different life stages, lifestyles, and expectations are in conflict. (The author's Web site is archer-books.com/Piercy.)

Themes: aging; drug abuse; family sagas; illness; love affairs; mothers and daughters

Related Titles: Piercy's fifteenth novel, like many of her earlier ones, is filled with insights about women's lives in the last half of the twentieth century. Readers may enjoy her autobiography, *Sleeping with Cats*, annotated in the "Public Lives" section of chapter 8, or her novels *Small Change* and *The Longings of Women*.

Pilcer, Sonia

The Holocaust Kid. Persea Books, 2001. 180p.

A set of edgy, autobiographical, linked stories that explore the territory of "2G," the children of Holocaust survivors. Zosha acts out as a teenager by joining a Latina gang, dating a German boy, and reading her emotional poems at a Holocaust conference, as she deals with her feelings of guilt and anger toward her parents and the survivor community. (The Web site for the book is www.holocaustkid.com.)

Themes: children of Holocaust survivors; Holocaust—refugees and displaced persons; linked stories; parents and children

Related Titles: Pilcer's in-your-face style may remind readers of the fiction of Melvin Jules Bukiet, annotated in the "Language" section of this chapter. Another approach to the second-generation story can be found in Joseph Berger's *Displaced Persons*, annotated in the "Memoirs, the Next Generation" section of chapter 7.

Pogrebin, Letty Cottin

Three Daughters. Farrar, Straus & Giroux, 2002. 388p.

Sisters Shoshanna, Leah, and Rachel Wasserman share a complex history of family secrets and betrayals, intensified by their very different personalities; their conflicts come to a boil as they prepare to celebrate the arrival of the millennium with their widowed father, Rabbi Sam. Full of crackling dialogue, feminist themes, well-drawn characters, and the messy truths of family relationships.

Themes: family relationships; fathers and daughters; New York City; sisters; women's lives

Related Titles: Some of the source material for the Wasserman family relationships can be found in Pogrebin's own autobiography, *Deborah,*

Golda, and Me. Pogrebin is a well-known feminist, the cofounder of *Ms. Magazine*, and author of several works of nonfiction. Another novel about a large, contentious family is Elizabeth Klein's *Reconciliations*. Readers who like family novels may also enjoy Lynne Sharon Schwartz's novels, like her recent *In the Family Way*.

Raeff, Anne

Clara Mondschein's Melancholia. **MacAdam/Cage Publishing, 2002. 258p.**

The grim legacy of the Holocaust is explored through its effect on three generations: Ruth, who gave birth in the camps to Clara; Clara herself; and Clara's teenage daughter Deborah, born in suburban New Jersey. The story is told alternately by grandmother and granddaughter, as they try to make sense of their own lives in the shadow of Clara's depression.

Themes: AIDS; depression; mental; grandmothers; mothers and daughters

Raphael, Frederic

All His Sons: A Novella and Nine Stories. **Catbird Press, 2001. 187p.**

In the title novella, Stanley and Sidney, two very different brothers, confront the possibility that a young African American they befriended has murdered their father, turning their family history upside down. Written in a cinematic style with parts of the story in screenplay format, the brothers' conflict is simultaneously funny and touching.

Themes: brothers; fathers and sons; Jews—relations with African Americans

Related Titles: Raphael, a prolific novelist, has written several well-known screenplays and is a translator of classical Greek and Roman literature.

Raphael, Lev

Dancing on Tisha B'Av. **St. Martin's, 1990. 231p.** 📖

The nineteen compelling and very personal stories in this collection deal with issues of being Jewish and gay, and with the meaning of Judaism for children of Holocaust survivors. (The author's Web site is www.levraphael.com.)

Themes: children of Holocaust survivors; short stories

Related Titles: Raphael is the author of a series of mysteries set on a Midwestern college campus; they are annotated in the "Amateur Detectives" section of chapter 2. Readers may enjoy his autobiography, *Journeys and Arrivals: On Being Gay and Jewish,* annotated in the "Childhood and Family" section of chapter 8. *Found Tribe: Jewish Coming Out Stories*, a collection of essays by gay Jewish men, is annotated in the "Collected Biography" section of chapter 8.

Winter Eyes. **St. Martin's, 1992. 245p.**

Stefan Borowski grows up in New York City in the 1950s and 1960s unaware that his parents and uncle are Holocaust survivors, or even that they are Jewish. Their inability to communicate as a family leaves Stefan angry and confused about who he is.

Themes: coming-of-age stories; family secrets; gays/lesbians/bisexuals; parents and children; uncles

Related Titles: Raphael has also written the autobiography *Journeys and Arrivals: Being Gay and Jewish*, annotated in the "Childhood and Family" section of chapter 8, and the Nick Hoffman mystery series, annotated in the "Amateur Detectives" section of chapter 2. Another novel about a teenaged boy who feels like an outsider is Robert Kotlowitz's *Sea Changes*, annotated in the "Modern Period, United States and Canada" section of chapter 3.

Roiphe, Anne Richardson

Lovingkindness. **Summit Books, 1987. 279p.** YA

When Annie, daughter of a liberal, assimilated Jewish mother, joins an ultra-Orthodox yeshiva in Israel, her mother finds it just as hard to accept as Annie's earlier excursions into dope addiction and promiscuity.

Themes: Americans in Israel; Jewish identity; mothers and daughters; Orthodox Judaism

Related Titles: An autobiographical account of a mother who finds it difficult to accept her son's commitment to Buddhism is Rosie Rosenzweig's *A Jewish Mother in Shangri-La*. Readers may also enjoy Chaim Potok's novels for the way they deal with issues of religious commitment. They are annotated in the "Classics and Major Authors" section of this chapter.

Rosen, Jonathan

Eve's Apple. **Random House, 1997. 309p.**

Joseph Zimmerman becomes obsessed with trying to understand his lover, Ruth, and her eating disorder. Memories of his relationship with his sister, who committed suicide, mix with his fears for Ruth.

Themes: brothers and sisters; eating disorders; love

Related Titles: Rosen has also written a nonfiction work, *The Talmud and the Internet*, annotated in the "Spiritual Autobiographies" section of chapter 8.

Schrank, Ben

Consent. **Random House, 2002. 255p.**

In the spring of 1999, while the stock market is in free fall, Mike Zabusky's life spins out of control as he struggles to complete his graduate dissertation on the *golem*; hold onto Katherine, his troubled lover; and make sense of his father's suicide. An insightful picture of troubled relationships in the twenty-something crowd among the trendy bars and restaurants of New York City.

Themes: fathers and sons; *golem*; love affairs; men's lives; teacher–student relationships

Schulberg, Budd

What Makes Sammy Run? **1941; reprint, Random House, 1991. 328p.** **YA** 📖

Driven by ambition, Sammy Glick rises from copy boy to Hollywood mogul, offending and alienating his would-be mentors and friends. The narrator, cynical writer Al Manheim, watches Sammy and recounts his soulless and obsessive climb to power.

Themes: authors; friendship; men's lives; motion picture industry

Related Titles: *What Makes Sammy Run?* became an immediate best seller when it was published, although the author was reviled in Hollywood. Read sixty years later, Sammy remains the same unpleasant but compelling figure. The fiftieth anniversary edition contains the original two stories that became the novel. Another Hollywood novel by a Jewish author, written in the same period, is *The Day of the Locust* by Nathaniel West. Another novel about a schemer like Sammy, who uses his friends for his own gain, is the classic *I Can Get It for You Wholesale* by Jerome Weidman, written in 1937.

Schulman, Helen

The Revisionist. **Crown, 1998. 246p.**

When an old friend becomes involved with the Holocaust denial movement, neurologist David Hershleder recognizes his own denial of the important people and events in his life, from his Holocaust-survivor mother to his wife and children. Comedy and tragedy accompany David on a physical and spiritual journey to reassessment and possible redemption.

Themes: children of Holocaust survivors; Holocaust denial; Holocaust—survivors; marriage; men's lives

Related Titles: Another novel that mixes comedy with themes of identity and responsibility for Jewish survival is Frederick Busch's *Invisible Mending*, winner of a National Jewish Book Award for fiction.

Shapiro, Dani

Picturing the Wreck. **Doubleday, 1996. 244p.**

Solomon Grossman, Holocaust survivor and respected New York psychiatrist, has an affair with a patient, ruining his career and his marriage. His son grows up without him, but thirty years later their paths cross by chance, giving Solomon an opportunity to redeem himself, in this sensitive study of a man haunted by past mistakes. (The author's Web site is www.danishapiro.com.)

Themes: adultery; fathers and sons; men's lives; psychiatrists and psychologists

Related Titles: Shapiro also writes about the explosive nature of sexual relationships in the novel *Playing with Fire* and an autobiography, *Slow Motion*, annotated in the "Childhood and Family" section of chapter 8.

Shapiro, Gerald

 From Hunger. **University of Missouri Press, 1993. 168p.**

Shapiro's protagonists in these edgy stories are antiheroes, men who have lost their way in life, in exile from the Jewish community and their own feelings. In the title story, a man takes in his dying, obese uncle, whose insatiable physical hunger matches his own spiritual emptiness. The character Levidow, in another story, is always fixing things and making them worse, until God sends him on a journey. (Winner of the E. L. Wallant Award.)

Themes: men's lives; spiritual life

Related Titles: Shapiro's second collection of stories is *Bad Jews*. Readers may also enjoy Allen Hoffman's short stories in the collection *Kagan's Superfecta*, also an E. L.Wallant Award winner.

Shulgasser-Parker, Barbara

Funny Accent. **Picador USA, 2001. 198p.**

Anna Schopenhauer publishes a short story that reveals how a kiss from her parents' friend Misha when she was thirteen initiated a ten-year sexual relationship. Told from multiple points of view, the author muses with humor and poignancy on the writing process, her attraction to older men, and her complicated relationship with her Holocaust-survivor parents and their Lithuanian friends.

Themes: authors; fathers and daughters; love affairs; sexual abuse; women's lives

Related Titles: Readers who liked Anna's self-aware and self-deprecating humor in this novel may also enjoy the short story collection *Foreign Brides* by Elena Lappin or the novel *Pure Poetry* by Binnie Kirshenbaum.

 6

Sinclair, Jo

Anna Teller. **1960; reprint, Feminist Press, 1992. 612p.**

Anna Teller, matriarch of her family and support of those around her, known as "The General" for her fierce tenacity, survives World War II and the 1956 Hungarian uprising, but finds that she must change the way she relates to her family to survive in America. A study of an unconventional woman and the social forces that shape her life.

Themes: Holocaust—survivors; Hungary; mothers and sons; refugees, Hungarian; women's lives

Related Titles: Jo Sinclair is a pseudonym for Ruth Seid. Readers may enjoy *Tell Me a Riddle* by Tillie Olsen, another story about a woman who feels out of place at the end of her life. It is annotated in the "Classics and Major Authors" section of this chapter.

Singer, Katie

The Wholeness of a Broken Heart. **Riverhead Books, 1999. 369p.**

Devastated when her beloved mother Celia turns away from her, Hannah Felber tries to heal herself by writing and teaching. Told in multiple first person voices from the point of view of Hannah, her mother, and her immigrant grandmothers, this quiet novel probes the way women survive and love. (The author's Web site is www.katiesinger.com.)

Themes: family relationships; family secrets; mothers and daughters; sexual abuse; single women

Related Titles: Another novel in which secrets disrupt a mother–daughter relationship is Judy Goldman's *The Slow Way Back*. Readers may also enjoy *Love Lesson* by Edith Chevat, about a complex mother–daughter relationship.

Stracher, Cameron

The Laws of Return. **Morrow, 1996. 245p.**

A darkly comic blend of wit and allusion enlivens this tale of self-discovery as Colin Stone, first-born son of intellectual and very assimilated parents, finds himself singled out as a Jew wherever he goes, but it takes a series of painful events for him to accept his birthright.

Themes: anti-Semitism; coming-of-age stories; humorous fiction; Jewish identity; lawyers; men's lives

Sucher, Cheryl Pearl

The Rescue of Memory. **Scribner, 1997. 283p.** 📖

Rachel Wallfisch, caught up in planning her wedding and producing her first film, receives news that her beloved Tante Tsenyah has died in Israel. The novel shifts back and forth in time as Rachel is overwhelmed with memories of her childhood, the psychological and physical pain suffered by her survivor parents, and her own haunted dreams.

Themes: aunts; children of Holocaust survivors; Holocaust—survivors; memory; parents and children

Swados, Elizabeth

Flamboyánt. **Picador USA, 1998. 244p.**

Orthodox Chana Landau takes a job teaching at Harvey Milk High School in Manhattan without telling her fiancé about the largely homosexual and drug-addicted student population. She befriends the aptly named student Flamboyánt, a prostitute, and in journal entries by student and teacher, we learn how they are both tested by the relationship.

Themes: gays/lesbians/bisexuals; Orthodox Jews; prostitution; teacher–student relationships

Related Titles: Readers who enjoyed the cultural conflict in *Flamboyánt* may also enjoy *Teacha: Stories from a Yeshiva* by Gerry Albarelli, a true story about a young non-Jewish man who teaches English as a second language in an Orthodox yeshiva.

Teleky, Richard

***The Paris Years of Rosie Kamin*. Steerforth Press, 1998. 218p.**

Rosie Kamin left the United States after college, tired of caring for her ungrateful father after her Holocaust-survivor mother committed suicide. In Paris for twenty years, she is still a passive participant in her own life until her lover dies and she is forced to face the way she has denied her own emotional life.

Themes: children of Holocaust survivors; family relationships; Jewish identity; Paris; women's lives

Related Titles: Readers may enjoy another novel set in Paris about a woman who is out of place, *The Mark of the Angel* by Canadian novelist Nancy Huston.

Wallant, Edward Lewis

***The Human Season*. 1960; reprint, Syracuse University Press, 1998. 192p.**

An absorbing character study of Joseph Berman, whose grief over the death of his wife leads him to rage against God. In his struggle with loneliness, Berman movingly recalls his childhood in Russia and his courtship and marriage, and considers his daughter's offer of a new home.

Themes: death; elderly men; men's lives

Related Titles: Two other novels with sensitive portraits of the elderly are Norman Fruchter's *Coat Upon a Stick*, winner of an E. L. Wallant Award, and Michelle Herman's *Missing*.

***The Pawnbroker*. 1961; reprint, Harcourt Brace Jovanovich, 1978. 279p.**

Sol Nazerman survived the Holocaust but lost his wife and children. A pawnbroker now in Harlem, he is haunted by cruel memories of his former life and existential questions that seem to have no answer, until a brutal act changes everything.

Themes: Holocaust—survivors; Jews–Relations with African Americans; men's lives

Wenner, Kate

***Setting Fires*. Scribner, 2000. 301p.**

A touching and introspective first novel about the love we owe to our families and our responsibility to face down evil. In the course of one year, Annie Fishman Waldmas puts her personal life on hold to tend to her dying father and search for answers to why her country home was torched in an act of anti-Semitic arson. (The Web site for the book is www.settingfires.com.)

Themes: anti-Semitism; arson; cancer; fathers and daughters; women's lives

Related Titles: Wenner's second novel, *Dancing with Einstein*, is about a young woman who is haunted by her Holocaust-survivor father's work with the Manhattan Project.

Story

In literary fiction, there's no common denominator in story line. Each author finds a different way to engage the reader in the action. Readers who are interested in plot want to be carried along by situations and events. They are interested in the author's point of view and eager to know how he or she will bring the threads of the narrative to a conclusion. Pacing will vary in plot-driven novels from leisurely and descriptive to quick and action-oriented. It is important for readers' advisors to understand what kind of pacing readers enjoy.

Writers play with a profusion of narrative devices and voices. Tova Mirvis uses an unusual group narrator to express the judgment of the community in her novel *The Ladies' Auxiliary*. The story may be told in a linear fashion, like Thane Rosenbaum's *The Golems of Gotham;* in flashbacks, like Marcie Hershman's *Safe in America;* or by multiple characters, like Rosellen Brown's *Half a Heart*. Plot may be layered and complex, like Hortense Calisher's *Sunday Jews*, or realistic and funny, like Ze'ev Chafets's *Inherit the Mob*. Endings are often ambiguous or bittersweet. The novels in this section feature compelling stories that draw readers in and maintain their interest. Whether the plot is simple or complex, whether pacing is fast or slow, readers will want to follow the story to its resolution.

Appel, Allan

The Rabbi of Casino Boulevard. **St. Martin's, 1986. 287p.**

> To the gambling members of Rabbi Arthur Bloom's Las Vegas congregation, the Rabbi is a lucky charm, particularly after he falls in love with a Japanese woman, in this humorous and existential novel.

> **Themes:** gambling; interracial marriage; love affairs; men's lives; rabbis

High Holiday Sutra. **Coffee House Press, 1997. 240p.**

> In a funny and touching Yom Kippur sermon, Rabbi Jonah Grief, sometime Buddhist, tells the Hebrew Meditation Circle the story of his search for love and meaning.

> **Themes:** Buddhism; death; marriage; men's lives; rabbis; Yom Kippur

Club Revelation. **Coffee House Press, 2001. 335p.**

> The lives of three interfaith couples, living on the Upper West Side in Manhattan, are disrupted when an evangelical Christian opens a cafeteria in their building, hoping to convert Jews.

> **Themes:** humorous fiction; interfaith marriage; Jewish–Christian relations

Bache, Ellen

The Activist's Daughter. Spinster's Ink, 1997. 256p. YA 📖

> In 1963, embarrassed by her mother's activism in the civil rights movement, Beryl defiantly enrolls in college in the South, where she is caught up in social and political change and works hard to find her own way, in this tale of self-discovery.

Themes: civil rights movement; college life; coming-of-age stories; mothers and daughters

Related Titles: Another novel about women coming to terms with the legacies of the previous generation is Marge Piercy's *Three Women*, annotated in the "Character" section of this chapter.

Black, David

An Impossible Life: A Bobeh Myseh. Moyer Bell, 1998. 183p.

When Leo Polishook begins to delve into a dark family history that includes Jewish gangsters, his relatives resist his need to know his origins. He pieces together a story that wanders back and forth across seven generations and two centuries, set in Poland, the Lower East Side, and elsewhere, filled with family legends that mirror biblical themes.

Themes: family secrets; fathers and sons; gangsters; shtetl life

Related Titles: A *bobeh myseh* is literally a grandmother's tale; here the term refers to the stories that Leo extracts from his relatives, some factual, some almost mythical. Black calls this novel "a fictional family history," and cites bibliographical sources, some of which are imaginary. Readers who like novels that straddle the borders of fiction and nonfiction may also enjoy Robert Rand's *My Suburban Shtetl: A Novel About Life in a Twentieth-Century Jewish-American Village*. A very dark and violent novel set in the same underworld of Jewish gangsters on the Lower East Side is Kevin Baker's *Dreamland*. In addition to novels, Black is well-known as a screenwriter and author of several well-received nonfiction works, including *The King of Fifth Avenue: The Fortunes of August Belmont*, the biography of the immigrant who climbed to the top of the Jewish social ladder in nineteenth-century New York.

Brown, Rosellen

Half a Heart. Farrar, Straus & Giroux, 2000. 402p.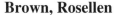

Miriam Vener is living a comfortable upper-middle-class life in Houston in the 1980s with her husband and three children, when she is shaken out of her complacency by the arrival of her rebellious eighteen-year-old daughter Veronica, the child she abandoned after an affair with a black college professor in the 1960s. Alternating from Miriam to Veronica's point of view, mother and daughter are forced to reassess their lives.

Themes: biracial children; civil rights movement; Jews–Relations with African Americans; mothers and daughters

Related Titles: Another novel about a mother–daughter reunion, from the daughter's point of view, is *Then She Found Me* by Elinor Lipman. Readers may also be interested in Rebecca Walker's autobiography, *Black, White and Jewish: Autobiography of a Shifting Self*, a poignant account of the multiple problems of growing up the daughter of an African American mother and a white Jewish father.

Budnitz, Judy

 If I Told You Once. **Picador USA, 1999. 294p.**

When Ilana leaves her village to escape a domineering mother and a life of brutal poverty, she finds the outside world full of dangers to spirit and flesh in the form of witches, beasts, soldiers, and lovers. In America she becomes the matriarch of three generations of women who struggle with their own demons. (Winner of the E. L. Wallant Award.)

Themes: grandmothers; immigrants; magical realism; mothers and daughters; shtetl life; women's lives

Related Titles: Budnitz wrote *Flying Leap*, a collection of unusual, thought-provoking short stories in a magical realist style. Another novel with powerful women whose magic changes the natural order is Lillian Nattel's *The River Midnight*, annotated in the "Language" section of this chapter. Other novels of rich relationships among several generations of women, also with magical realist overtones, are *Four Women* by Shifra Horn and *Beyond the Pale* by Elana Dykewomon.

Calisher, Hortense

Sunday Jews. **Harcourt, 2002. 694p.**

Calisher's typically analytical style is trained on the large family of anthropologist Zipporah Zangwill and Peter Duffy, who have an ambivalent relationship to the Judaism inherited from their mother. Zipporah is forced to retire when Peter becomes ill; a nurse who cares for him sets in motion events that allow Calisher to examine the varieties of modern Jewish experience as displayed by a diverse cast of characters.

Themes: assimilation; family relationships; intellectuals; Jewish identity

Related Titles: Calisher has written fourteen novels and many novellas and short stories; only occasionally have her characters or themes been Jewish. Readers who enjoy novels in which language and ideas are important may like Saul Bellow's *Ravelstein* or Cynthia Ozick's *The Cannibal Galaxy*, both annotated in the "Classics and Major Authors" section of this chapter.

Chafets, Zev

Inherit the Mob. **Random House, 1991. 272p.**

When William Gordon's uncle Max dies, William inherits Max's estate share in an organized crime family. In this humorous crime caper, William needs to decide whether or not to take on the Mob and assert his claim to a legacy that could leave him dead if he's not clever.

Themes: funerals; humorous fiction; journalists; Mafia

Chefitz, Mitchell

The Seventh Telling: The Kabbalah of Moshe Katan. **St. Martin's, 2001. 422p.** 📖

Stephanie and Sidney Lee teach Kabbalah by telling stories from the lives of their friends Rabbi Moshe Katan and his wife Rivke. In the process, they learn as much about themselves as their students learn from them. (The author's Web site is www.mitchellchefitz.com.)

Themes: cancer; husbands and wives; Kabbalah; teachers

The Thirty-Third Hour of Moshe Katan. St. Martin's, 2002. 288p.

When a congregant makes a serious accusation against Rabbi Moshe Katan, a second Rabbi is brought in to assess the charges. The new Rabbi has thirty-three hours to understand Rabbi Katan's unique approach to Jewish education and accuse or exonerate him. (Chefitz provides discussion guides and an opportunity for feedback on his Web site, www.mitchellchefitz.com.)

Themes: rabbis; synagogue life; teacher–student relationships

Cohen, Martin S.
The Truth About Marvin Kalish. Ben-Simon, 1992. 280p. **YA**

Marvin Kalish, a young stand-up comic in New York, is starting to have some success in the clubs when he finds himself the target of violence. At the same time, Bunny and Lawrence Luft receive some information about a baby Bunny put up for adoption many years ago. The connection between Marvin and the Lufts turns out to be mystical in nature, and may affect the survival of the Jewish community.

Themes: adopted children; Canadian authors; magical realism; Messiah

Cohen, Robert
The Here and Now. Scribner, 1996. 351p.

When Samuel Karnish, a disaffected thirty-something journalist, meets a Hasidic couple on a plane, he is forced to take stock of his life and its lack of focus. A humorous and perceptive look at the clash between secularism and religion at the end of the twentieth century.

Themes: Hasidism; Jewish identity; journalists; men's lives

Related Titles: Cohen has also written two other novels, *The Organ Builder* and *Inspired Sleep*, and the short story collection *Varieties of Romantic Experience*.

Delbanco, Nicholas
What Remains. Warner, 2000. 200p.

Loss and adjustment to changed circumstances permeate this thoughtful autobiographical novel about Karl and Gustave, two Jewish brothers who leave Germany before 1939 and settle in London, then later the United States, turning to art, music, and literature for solace. Three generations of family members, from children to grandparents, provide shifting points of view.

Themes: art dealers; artists; family relationships; parents and children

Related Titles: Readers who enjoyed this novel's reflective tone may enjoy Ethan Canin's *Carry Me Across the Water*, annotated in the "Character" section of this chapter.

Dezenhall, Eric
Money Wanders. St. Martin's, 2002. 338p.

Jonah Eastman, out of favor as a Washington pollster, is called back to Atlantic City by his dying mobster grandfather Mickey, who asks him to put a new spin on his old Mafia crony Mario Vanni and make him a pillar of respectability. Jonah has a wacky and nostalgic tour though the New Jersey gangster world among the likes of Bobby "the Toaster" and Irv the Curve as he sets up opportunities to clean up Vanni's image.

Themes: gangsters; grandfathers; humorous fiction; public opinion polls

Edelman, Gwen
War Story. Riverhead Books, 2001. 168p.

In spare and haunting prose, Kitty recalls her intense May–December love affair with Joseph as she takes the train to Amsterdam for his funeral years later. In his old hotel room, Kitty relives the madness and tragedy of the war and the anguish that was Joseph's constant companion.

Themes: authors; Holocaust—survivors; love affairs

Fast, Howard
The Outsider. Houghton Mifflin, 1984. 249p.

Fresh from an army chaplaincy and newly married to Lucy, David Hartman becomes the rabbi of a new congregation in Connecticut. The forces of social change and history sweep through the lives of the rabbi, his family, his congregation, and his community from the late 1940s to the early 1970s.

Themes: anti-Semitism; Jewish–Christian relations; rabbis; small town life; synagogue life

Related Titles: Fast effortlessly incorporates current events and trends into *The Outsider*, from McCarthyism to the civil rights movement to the feminist movement. Another novel in which readers feel the sweep of history is Anne Roiphe's *The Pursuit of Happiness*, annotated in the "Modern Period, United States and Canada" section of chapter 3.

Friedman, Donald
The Hand Before the Eye. Mid-List Press, 2000. 266p.

Lawyer David Farbman's life is in disarray: His shady practice is on the verge of bankruptcy, his marriage is on the rocks, and his children are strangers to him. A chance encounter with a charismatic rebbe and a beautiful actress help him to re-evaluate his life and see the redemptive power of religion.

Themes: adultery; husbands and wives; lawyers; men's lives; repentance

Goldberg, Myla

The Bee Season. Doubleday, 2000. 276p. YA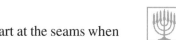

The fragile fabric of the Naumann family comes apart at the seams when younger daughter Eliza is found to have an extraordinary talent for spelling. A unique coming-of-age story that combines Kabbalah, cults, mental illness, and spelling bees. (Winner of the E. L. Wallant Award.)

Themes: coming-of-age stories; family relationships; fathers and daughters; mysticism; spelling bees

Related Titles: Another novel in which mental illness affects family relationships is *Like Normal People* by Karen Bender. The effects of claustrophobic family relationships are well drawn by Barbara Finkelstein in her novel *Summer Long-a-Coming*. Frederick Reiken's *The Lost Legends of New Jersey* is also about a dysfunctional family and the effect of the parents' problems on their teenaged son and daughter.

Greenfield, Robert

The Temple. Summit Books, 1982. 411p.

Sometime graduate student Paulie Bindel abandons a dissolute life with his girlfriend in Boston and returns to his family in Brooklyn during the Days of Awe between Rosh Hashanah and Yom Kippur. Shifting from first to third person narration, a well-drawn cast of characters, from Paulie's gentle Holocaust-survivor grandfather to the members of the local synagogue, share Paulie's search for answers to life's eternal questions. (Winner of the National Jewish Book Award.)

Themes: family relationships; grandfathers; Jewish identity; rabbis

Grossinger, Harvey

The Quarry. University of Georgia Press, 1997. 263p.

Five short stories and a novella filled with the authentic texture of family relationships, especially between fathers and sons, in affectionate and sometimes rueful detail. In "Dinosaurs," Lenny returns home for the funeral of his beloved grandfather Zolly and learns some hard truths about his family and himself. In "Home Burial," Noah looks forward to his father's return from the Korean War, but the shell-shocked man who arrives is a stranger. The title novella is about the nature of Holocaust memory for survivors and the next generation. (Winner of the E. L. Wallant Award.)

Themes: family relationships; fathers and sons; Jewish identity

Related Titles: Readers may enjoy *Radiance* by John J. Clayton, another short story collection about Jewish men's lives and relationships.

Hall, Richard

Family Fictions. **Viking, 1991. 273p.**

When Margaret Barish marries wealthy clothing manufacturer Judah Schanberg, she systematically eradicates all evidence of their Jewishness, changing the family name and joining a church so she and her children won't suffer the prejudice she experienced in her rural Texas childhood. Told from shifting points of view, starting with Margaret and Judah, then the children, as they move into adulthood.

Themes: family relationships; gays/lesbians/bisexuals; Jewish identity; mothers and sons

Hamill, Pete

Snow in August. **Little, Brown, 1997. 327p.** **YA**

In this perceptive coming-of-age story about our need for heroes in difficult times, eleven-year-old altar boy Michael Devlin, living in a working-class Brooklyn neighborhood in 1947, befriends a recent immigrant, Rabbi Judah Hirsch. They trade English and Yiddish lessons while following the progress of Jackie Robinson's first season with the Brooklyn Dodgers. Michael's friendship with the Rabbi enables him to transcend the anti-Semitism of the neighborhood gangs, with terrible and miraculous consequences. (The author's Web site is www.petehamill.com.)

Themes: anti-Semitism; baseball and baseball players; Catholic faith; coming-of-age stories; friendship; *golem*

Related Titles: A young adult novel that explores the relationship between a young boy and a Holocaust survivor is Robert Cormier's *Tunes for Bears to Dance to*.

Hershman, Marcie

Safe in America. **HarperCollins, 1995. 285p.**

Evan and Vera Eichenbaum left the anti-Semitism of Eastern Europe for an American city they believed would be a safe place to work and raise a family, but they are unable to protect their children or their Hungarian relatives from events beyond their control. This novel's strength is in portraying the relationship between parents and children and how the parents' fears affected their children's life choices. Told from the point of view of the strong-minded Vera and her daughter Joy, moving back and forth from the 1930s to the 1990s.

Themes: Cleveland, Ohio; family relationships; Holocaust; immigrants

Related Titles: Hershman's collection of linked stories, *Tales of the Master Race*, annotated in the "Fiction" section of chapter 7, is set in a town in Germany in the 1930s and 1940s, and deals with guilt and responsibility. Another novel in which parents have a powerful effect on their children's lives is *The Speed of Light* by Elizabeth Rosner, annotated in the "Language" section of this chapter.

Hond, Paul

The Baker. **Random House, 1997. 360p.**

Images of breadmaking and gardening enrich this compelling and realistic tale of how inner-city conflict between African Americans and Jews affects the family of baker Mickey Lerner in Baltimore.

Themes: Baltimore, Md.; family secrets; fathers and sons; men's lives; race relations

Related Titles: Readers who enjoyed the social realism of *The Baker* may also enjoy Bernard Malamud's novels, especially *The Tenants* and *The Assistant*, annotated in the "Classics and Major Authors" section of this chapter.

Kane, Andrew

Rabbi, Rabbi. **St. Martin's, 1995. 306p.** **YA**

Sparks fly when Yakov and Rebecca meet as teenagers in a Catskill Mountains resort, but Rebecca's parents forbid her to see him. Yakov, son of a famous Orthodox rabbi, is torn between following his father's expectations for him to continue his Talmudic studies and his own yearning for a more secular education. When he and Rebecca meet again as adults on New York's Upper West Side, she challenges him to make his own decisions, putting their revived relationship in jeopardy.

Themes: family secrets; love stories; men—religious life; Orthodox Jews; rabbis

Related Titles: In several of Chaim Potok's novels young men struggle with the religious traditions of their fathers, notably *The Chosen* and *The Promise*. Potok's novels are annotated in the "Classics and Major Authors" section of this chapter.

Lerman, Rhoda

God's Ear. **Holt, Rinehart & Winston, 1989. 309p.**

Yussel Fetner abandoned the family rabbinic tradition to sell insurance, counting himself successful and content until his father convinces him to invest all his money in an Indian reservation near Kansas City and face the Fetner heritage. Laced with humor and Hasidic tales.

Themes: fathers and sons; rabbis; satirical novels

Related Titles: In an earlier novel, *Call Me Ishtar*, Lerman brings the demonic Babylonian mother-goddess Ishtar into the twentieth century, in the guise of a suburban Jewish housewife.

Levin, Meyer

 The Old Bunch. **1937; reprint, Citadel Press, 1985. 964p.** **YA**

Follows the lives of a group of young Jewish men and women from the day of their high school graduation in 1921 to Jewish Day at the Chicago World's Fair in 1934. In between, they move into adulthood, each struggling in his or her own way with issues of family, assimilation, identity, and material success, buffeted by the political and economic forces of the era. (An ALA Notable Book.)

Themes: Chicago; coming-of-age stories; 1930s; 1920s

Related Titles: Readers who enjoyed this look at young people finding their way may also enjoy Herman Wouk's *Marjorie Morningstar.*

Manus, Willard
The Pigskin Rabbi. Breakaway Books, 1999. 300p.

Ezekiel "Ziggy" Cantor was ordained a rabbi to please his father, but his first love is football, where his skills as a kicker land him a spot with the New York Giants. Ziggy's joyful approach to the game and his grandmother's chicken soup win over most of the players, but there are still some anti-Semites who wish him ill. A zany, lecherous, and highly implausible romp.

Themes: football and football players; Orthodox Jews; rabbis

Mirvis, Tova
The Ladies' Auxiliary. W. W. Norton, 1999. 352p. **YA** 📖

When Batsheva, a widow and a convert to Judaism, moves to Memphis, the close-knit, insular, Orthodox community is first welcoming, then feels threatened by her individualistic approach to traditional rituals, and accuses her of enticing the younger generation away from Orthodoxy. In an unusual stylistic device, the women of the community speak in one voice. (The author's Web site is www.tovamirvis.com.)

Themes: Orthodox Judaism; women—religious life

Related Titles: Mirvis's second novel, *The Outside World*, is also about friction in the Orthodox community, this time between parents and children. Readers who enjoyed *The Ladies' Auxiliary* may also like *The Romance Reader* and *Giving Up America* by Pearl Abraham, annotated in the "Setting" section of this chapter, for their insight into Orthodox life.

Neugeboren, Jay
The Stolen Jew. 1981; reprint, Syracuse University Press, 1999. 322p.

Nathan Malkin, a wealthy sixty-four-year-old businessman, returns to his childhood neighborhood in Brooklyn when his beloved but mentally unstable brother Nachman commits suicide. In comforting the family, Nathan finds himself caught up in old quarrels and secrets; his nephew Michael's scheme to save Russian refuseniks; and the way his old best-selling novel, *The Stolen Jew,* parallels his life.

Themes: authors; brothers; family relationships; 1970s; refuseniks

Related Titles: In this novel, close relationships between male relatives influence the plot and help the characters define their identity. Other novels in which a strong bond between siblings is important are *The Sacrifice of Isaac* by Neil Gordon, annotated in the "Political Intrigue and Espionage" section of chapter 2;

The Speed of Light by Elizabeth Rosner, annotated in the "Language" section of this chapter; and *The Book of Daniel* by E. L. Doctorow, annotated in the "Classics and Major Authors" section of this chapter. The story-within-a-story device is used extensively by Philip Roth; several of his Zuckerman novels, annotated in the "Classics and Major Authors" section of this chapter, are told to Zuckerman by old friends.

 ***Before My Life Began*. Simon & Schuster, 1985. 391p.**

David Voloshin follows in the footsteps of his gangster uncle Abe, a boss in the Brooklyn Jewish underworld, making choices that lead him to betray his talent and family and change his identity. A richly detailed picture of multiethnic Brooklyn following World War II, combined with a suspenseful, compelling plot. (Winner of the E. L. Wallant Award.)

Themes: coming-of-age stories; family relationships; gangsters; 1950s; 1960s; teenaged boys

Related Titles: Neugeboren's novels and stories display some common themes: They are often set in the Brooklyn neighborhood where he grew up; they reflect his passion for sports; there is often a troubling sibling relationship; and characters debate specifically Jewish issues of ethics, morality, and responsibility. The earlier novels are *Big Man*, *Listen Ruben Fontanez*, *Corky's Brother*, and *Sam's Legacy*. The sources of these themes can be found in his memoir, *Parentheses: An Autobiographical Journey*.

Ragen, Naomi

One of the first authors to write about the lives of Hasidic women in a realistic way, Ragen's novels are extremely popular in Israel and the United States. The Toby Press editions are bound with a readers' guide for discussion groups. (The author's Web site is www.naomiragen.com.)

6

Jephte's Daughter. **1989; reprint, Toby Press, 2002. 447p.**

Batsheva Ha-Levi, a modern Orthodox girl brought up in Los Angeles, agrees to an arranged marriage to an ultra-Orthodox Israeli Torah scholar, but discovers that his piety is a cover for abusive behavior.

Themes: domestic violence; Israel; marriage; Orthodox Jews

Sotah. **1992; reprint, Toby Press, 2002. 493p.**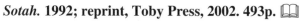

Dina Reich, brought up in the ultra-Orthodox community in Jerusalem, marries the man her father chose, but succumbs to a flirtation and becomes a *sotah*, a woman suspected of adultery.

Themes: adultery; marriage; Orthodox Judaism; women—religious life

The Sacrifice of Tamar. **1994; reprint, Toby Press, 2002. 445p.**

Tamar Finegold, an ultra-Orthodox married woman living in Brooklyn, is raped by a black man. Fearing her community will ostracize her, she keeps the rape secret, and is relieved when she gives birth to a white child. But twenty years later, history catches up to her.

Themes: Orthodox Judaism; rape; women—religious life

The Ghost of Hannah Mendes. **Simon & Schuster, 1998. 384p.** 📖

Catherine da Costa, diagnosed with a fatal illness, regrets that her family has no interest in their Jewish heritage. Inspired by the ghost of her famous ancestor, Dona Gracia (Hannah) Mendes, she sends her two granddaughters on a search for an old manuscript that takes them through several countries and out of their self-absorbed, secular lives. Dona Gracia's own fascinating story of the role her faith played in escaping the Inquisition is told in parallel to the young women's realization of the importance of tradition and continuity.

Themes: family relationships; Inquisition; Nasi, Gracia, ca. 1510–1569; Sephardim; women's lives

Related Titles: Dona Gracia Mendes was a remarkable historical figure who fled the Inquisition in Portugal and became a wealthy, influential businesswoman and philanthropist in sixteenth-century Turkey. Readers may enjoy Cecil Roth's classic biography *The House of Nasi: Dona Gracia* or the new biography, *The Woman Who Defied Kings: The Life and Times of Dona Gracia Nasi—A Jewish Leader During the Renaissance* by Andrée Aelion Brooks.

Chains Around the Grass. **Toby Press, 2001. 253p.**

When six-year-old Sara Markowitz's father dies during a routine operation, it forces each member of the family to find their own way of coping with loss. A semiautobiographical novel rich in detail, set in a housing project in Queens in the 1950s.

Themes: death; family relationships; girls

Reich, Tova

The Jewish War. **Pantheon Books, 1996. 269p.**

In Camp Ziona in the Catskills, Jerry Goldberg and Herbie Levy forged a friendship that brought them and their wives to Israel. Now, as Yehudi HaGoel and Hoshea HaLevi, they establish the Kingdom of Judah and Samaria with the charismatic HaGoel as its king, precipitating a confrontation with the Israeli government. Nothing in modern-day Judaism is sacred in this hilarious satire of American Jews and their relationship to Israel.

Themes: Americans in Israel; Israel; religious extremism; satirical novels; Zionism

Rosenbaum, Thane

Rosenbaum surveys the world from the point of view of the child of Holocaust survivors. The titles below form a loosely related trilogy. In *Elijah Visible*, the children of survivors live with the burden of their parents' experiences, suffering at second hand their losses and torments. *Second Hand Smoke* deals with the need to avenge the parents' experiences in the Holocaust. How to move on, honoring Holocaust victims without jeopardizing one's own life and children, is the theme of *The Golems of Gotham*. Rosenbaum makes vivid use of colloquialisms and popular culture motifs to pose questions about the nature of Holocaust memory.

Elijah Visible. **St. Martin's, 1996. 205p.**

A collection of nine linked stories about Adam Posner, son of Holocaust survivors, that explores how the suffering of the parents is internalized by their children. Although Adam has no firsthand experience of the camps, when he is trapped in a stalled elevator he experiences the terror of the Nazi transports, in the story *Cattle Car Complex*. The title story illustrates how parents who were unable to transfer to their children a sense of Jewish identity have condemned them to seders that Elijah will never visit. (Winner of the E. L. Wallant Award.)

Themes: children of Holocaust survivors; Holocaust—survivors; Jewish identity; short stories

Second Hand Smoke. **St. Martin's, 1999. 303p.**

Duncan Katz, who takes on his Holocaust-survivor mother's rage against the Nazis, becomes a Nazi hunter for the U.S. government. It is not until he meets a long-lost brother in Poland that he can start to heal his life.

Themes: brothers; children of Holocaust survivors; mothers and sons; Nazi hunters

The Golems of Gotham. **HarperCollins, 2002. 367p.**

Ariel Levin, trying to cure her father Oliver writer's block, summons up the ghosts of his parents and six writers, all Holocaust survivors who committed suicide, including Primo Levi and Jerzy Kosinski. The ghosts teach Oliver how to accept and transform the stifling emotional legacy of the children of Holocaust survivors; their humor and rage transform New York City.

Themes: children of Holocaust survivors; fathers and daughters; ghosts; magical realism; musicians; New York City

Sasson, Jean

Ester's Child. **Windsor-Brooke Books, 2001. 445p.**

Joseph and Ester Gale survive the Warsaw Ghetto invasion, and in 1948 they travel to Palestine, where they find their lives entwined in heartbreaking and unexpected ways with the Palestinian Antoun family and the German Kleists. The legacies of war and hatred follow them across three decades of Israeli–Palestinian conflict in this elaborately plotted and historically detailed saga told from multiple viewpoints. (The author's Web site is www.jeansasson.com.)

Themes: children of Nazis; Holocaust—survivors; Israel; Jewish–Arab relations; Palestinians

Related Titles: Sasson has also written *Princess: A True Story of Life Behind the Veil in Saudi Arabia*.

Segal, Lore

Her First American. **Alfred A. Knopf, 1985. 287p.**

At the age of twenty-one, after surviving the Holocaust, Ilka Weissnix arrives in New York City courtesy of her cousin Fishgoppel. Ilka's drive to become an American and her lack of inhibition bring her unusual experiences, including the friendship of Carter Bayoux, a down-and-out African American intellectual; their offbeat relationship enriches Ilka's American experience.

Themes: African Americans; cousins; immigrants; love stories

Related Titles: Segal wrote an earlier novel, *Other People's Houses*, about the experiences of a young girl who spends the Holocaust years living with the various families who are willing to take her in.

Sinclair, Jo

The Changelings. **1955; reprint, The Feminist Press, 1985. 352p.** **YA** 📖

The Jewish and Italian families living on an urban street in the 1950s are concerned that vacant apartments will be rented to African American tenants, changing the nature of the community they have worked hard to create. In this charged atmosphere, Judy Vincent and Clara Jackson, two thirteen-year old girls, one Jewish and one African American, become friends, defying the anger of the neighborhood and learning about prejudice and themselves in the process. A multilayered novel with a large cast of fully realized characters.

Themes: family relationships; friendship; 1950s; race relations; teenaged girls; urban life

Related Titles: Jo Sinclair is the pseudonym of Ruth Seid. Another novel in which a teenage girl defies the prejudices of her community is *Summer of My German Soldier* by Bette Greene, annotated in the "Character" section of this chapter. Another novelist who writes in a thoughtful way about social problems is Norma Rosen. Readers may enjoy her novels *At the Center* and *Touching Evil.*

Stern, Steve

The Wedding Jester. **Graywolf Press, 1999. 223p.**

Set mostly in the Pinch, an immigrant Jewish neighborhood of Memphis, Tennessee, in the period between World War I and World War II, these stories, with their wonderful, vivid descriptions, explore the conflicts Jews faced living in the New World and particularly in the South. Dreamers and schemers, fathers and sons, secular and Orthodox Jews struggled for acceptance and success. (Winner of the National Jewish Book Award.)

Themes: immigrants; Jewish identity; Memphis, Tenn.; 1930s; short stories

Related Titles: An earlier collection of stories, *Lazar Malkin Enters Heaven,* and the novellas collected as *A Plague of Dreamers* also take place in the Pinch, with the same rich texture and combination of the real and the miraculous. Stern won the E. L. Wallant Award for *Lazar Malkin Enters Heaven.* Stern's novel *Harry Kaplan's Adventures Underground* is annotated in chapter 3 in the "Modern Period, United States and Canada" section.

Wouk, Herman

Inside, Outside. Little, Brown, 1985. 644p. `YA`

In the early 1970s, David Goodkind, special assistant to the president, reflects on the history that brought him success, retelling in leisurely fashion the quintessential Jewish immigrant story, from shtetl to the Lower East Side, contrasting the "inside" of Jewish family life with the "outside" of secular American society.

Themes: family sagas; immigrants; Jewish identity; men's lives

Related Titles: Wouk is mainly known for his sweeping historical sagas. Readers will find *The Hope* and *The Glory*, about the birth and early history of the State of Israel, in chapter 3 in the "Modern Period, Middle East" section.

Language

Novels with language as the primary appeal characteristic are extremely varied, but they are distinguished by the voice in which they are told. Woody Allen and Nora Ephron's hilarious stories and novels are listed here, as well as Arthur Miller's stark and serious novel *Focus*. Jonathan Safran Foer's *Everything Is Illuminated* and Gary Shteyngart's *The Russian Debutante's Handbook* share verbal pyrotechnics, but Aryeh Lev Stollman's novels are equally appropriate in this section for their elegiac elegance. What unites these novels is that readers will exclaim that they love the way they are written, whether for poetic, humorous, or haunting language.

Allen, Woody

The humor in Allen's stories owes much to the New York Jewish milieu and from his juxtaposition of the abstract and the mundane. As he writes in "Examining Psychic Phenomena" from the collection *Without Feathers*: "There is no question that there is an unseen world. The problem is, how far is it from midtown and how late is it open?" Allen started his career as a writer for some of the great television comedians (Sid Caesar, Herb Shriner) in the 1950s and then began delivering his own lines as a stand-up comic in the 1960s. As a playwright, he had two long-running Broadway hits, *Don't Drink the Water* and *Play It Again, Sam*. But it is in film, as actor, writer, director, and producer that he is best known to audiences outside of New York. Films like *Annie Hall*, *Sleeper*, and *Manhattan*, to mention only a few from a large and varied list, have brought Allen international popularity.

Themes: humorous fiction; short stories

Getting Even. Random House, 1971. 151p.

The oft-quoted "Not only is there no God, but try getting a plumber on weekends" is found in the story "My Philosophy" in this collection that also includes imagined conversations with famous people.

***Without Feathers.* 1975; reissue, Ballantine Books, 1990. 210p.** *YA*

Includes the story "The Whore of Mensa," about women who discuss literature for money, and two one-act plays, *God* and *Death.*

***Side Effects.* Random House, 1980. 149p.**

"The Kugelmass Episode," often anthologized, appears in this collection, as well as other stories satirizing academic pretensions.

Related Titles: For readers interested in Allen's life, Eric Lax's biography is annotated in the "Public Lives" section of chapter 8.

Ari, Mark

***The Shoemaker's Tale.* Zephyr Press, 1993. 245p.**

Meir, the poor shoemaker, leaves his village in Poland to seek his fortune and find the meaning of life. In traditional folktale fashion, along the way he meets wise and foolish characters, like the Baal Shem Tov and Luckshinkopf (Noodlehead) the Fool; their stories teach him the lessons he needs to learn.

Themes: Baal Shem Tov; folklore; magical realism; Poland; shoemakers

Related Titles: Readers who want to learn more about the Baal Shem Tov, father of Hasidism, may enjoy Isaac Bashevis Singer's *Reaches of Heaven: A Story of the Baal Shem Tov.*

Berman, Sabina

***Bubbeh.* Latin American Literary Review Press, 1998. 90p.**

Sabita reflects on her childhood relationship with her grandmother, whose mystical Old World wisdom contrasted with her mother's secular, analytical explanations. A low-keyed coming-of-age novel that feels autobiographical, set in Mexico City, tracing the currents of love and anger that connected three generations of the Glickman family. Translated by Andrea G. Labinger.

Themes: death; grandmothers; Latin American fiction; mothers and daughters

Brownstein, Gabriel

***The Curious Case of Benjamin Button, Apt. 3W.* W. W. Norton, 2002. 223p.**

A strong sense of place and a sharp eye for the telling details of character animate these nine stories set in the 1970s and 1980s. Five of the stories take place in an Upper West Side apartment building and incorporate elements from well-known stories by Auden, Fitzgerald, Hawthorne, Kafka, and Singer. In the title story, Benjamin Button is born old and grows young.

Themes: apartment houses; boys; friendship; short stories; urban life

Related Titles: Frederick Reiken's novel *The Lost Legends of New Jersey* also has a strong sense of place and insight into the way our feelings change as we grow up.

Bukiet, Melvin Jules

After. St. Martin's, 1996. 384p.

A darkly humorous and cynical vision of life after liberation for three concentration camp survivors—a dentist, a scholar, and a scoundrel—as they use the skills that kept them alive during the war to prosper on the black market, in an amoral vision of the post-Holocaust world.

Themes: forgers and forgery; fraud; Holocaust—survivors; satirical novels; soldiers

Signs and Wonders. Picador USA, 1999. 376p. 📖

When a storm destroys a prison ship, the surviving prisoners follow the mysterious Ben Alef, a Messiah figure, through Germany, as he performs miracles and picks up followers for his new religion.

Themes: Messiah, false; parables; prisoners and prisons; religion

Related Titles: Another novel about a messiah-figure in the wake of the Holocaust is Arthur A. Cohen's *In the Days of Simon Stern.*

Strange Fire. W.W. Norton, 2001. 337p.

Nathan Kazakov, the blind speechwriter for the right-wing Israeli prime minister, is injured in an assassination attempt. Uncertain who the real target was, Nathan's investigations take him into dangerous and lunatic territory in a suspenseful and hilarious combination of events.

Themes: conspiracies; gays/lesbians/bisexuals; Israel—Politics and government

🎗 *Stories of an Imaginary Childhood.* 1991; reprint, Northwestern University Press, 2002. 201p.

The Holocaust shadows these dark, linked stories about a boy of twelve in a traditional Polish shtetl in 1928 as he explores the limits of independence and develops his talents as a writer. In "The Virtuoso," he reluctantly takes music lessons on an ancient violin that embodies the history of the Jewish people. In "Sincerely, Yours," he graduates from writing advertisements for his father's herring store to plagiarizing Shakespeare for Isaac the Millionaire's love letters. (Winner of the E. L. Wallant Award.)

Themes: boys; family relationships; Poland; shtetl life

Ephron, Nora

Heartburn. Alfred A. Knopf, 1983. 179p.

Rachel Samstat, successful cookbook author, is seven months pregnant with her second child when she learns that her husband is having an affair and plans to leave her. Food, therapists, friends, family, and politics all come into hilarious focus as Rachel matures and learns some lessons about love. Recipes included.

Themes: adultery; divorce; humorous fiction; marriage; women's lives

Related Titles: Readers may also enjoy *Crazy Salad: Some Things About Women* and *Wallflower at the Orgy*, both collections of Ephron's humorous essays. Ephron is also known for her screenplays, including *Silkwood*, *Sleepless in Seattle*, and *You've Got Mail*.

Foer, Jonathan Safran

Everything Is Illuminated. **Houghton Mifflin, 2002. 276p.** 📖

"We are being very nomadic with the truth, yes?" says Alex, a young Russian, the translator on a strange trip into the past, whose fractured English provides humorous and insightful commentary. As Alex and his cantankerous grandfather guide an American named Jonathan Safran Foer through the Ukraine in search of the woman who may have saved his grandfather from the Nazis, the author reconstructs his ancestors' lives in the shtetl of Trachimbrod. Multiple points of view and English-language pyrotechnics combine in a moving work of memory and guilt. (The author's Web site is www.jonathansafranfoer.com.)

Themes: children of Holocaust survivors; experimental fiction; grandfathers; grandmothers; Holocaust

Handler, Daniel

Watch Your Mouth. **Thomas Dunne Books, 2002. 232p.**

An outrageous, erotic, and satirical story of the ultimate dysfunctional family, cast first as an opera, then as a twelve-step program. When Joseph moves in with his girlfriend Cynthia's family for the summer, he becomes tangled up in a surrealistic mix of sex, murder, and *golems*. (The author's Web site is www.danielhandler.com.)

Themes: family relationships; incest; satirical novels

Related Titles: Handler is the author of a popular series of children's books under the pseudonym Lemony Snicket.

Helprin, Mark

Refiner's Fire: The Life and Adventures of Marshall Pearl, a Foundling. **Alfred A. Knopf, 1977. 377p.**

Orphan Marshall Pearl's life comes full circle in this *bildungsroman*, from his birth on a ship of immigrants bound for Palestine, to a freewheeling upbringing in a wealthy home in New York State, and back to Israel during the October War. Light, both literal and figurative, illuminates Marshall's adventures in search of his origins.

Themes: fathers and sons; Israel—History; magical realism; orphans

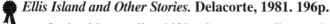 *Ellis Island and Other Stories*. **Delacorte, 1981. 196p.**

In the title novella, shifting between realism and magical realism, an immigrant arriving in New York finds it a city of mysterious women, Hasidic rabbis, and ice-melting machinery. (Winner of the National Jewish Book Award.)

Themes: immigrants; magical realism; short stories

Leviant, Curt

 The Yemenite Girl. **Bobbs-Merrill, 1977. 187p.**

Ezra Shultish, a writer and literary critic, admires the Israeli writer Yehiel Bar-Nun and is infatuated with a character in his story, "The Yemenite Girl." Shultish's efforts to become close to Bar-Nun and obtain a tape of the story are frustrated by the wily old writer and by Ezra's own insecurities. (Winner of the E. L. Wallant Award.)

Themes: authors; Israel

Related Titles: Readers who enjoyed the surrealistic quality of this novel may enjoy the three novellas by Michael Bornstein collected in the book *Sand Devil*.

***Diary of an Adulterous Woman, Including an ABC Directory That Offers Alphabetical Tidbits and Surprises*. Syracuse University Press, 2000. 389p.; 111p.**

At a reunion of their Jewish day school, the elegant womanizing Guido tells Charlie about his latest affair with the beautiful cellist, Aviva. Charlie becomes involved with Aviva too, setting up a potent and ultimately deadly triangle. An index of commentary on the relationships adds a postmodern twist.

Themes: adultery; experimental fiction; friendship; psychiatrists and psychologists

Related Titles: Leviant's characters are often seekers on mystical quests, and his unique, literate style pushes the boundaries of the novel. Readers may also enjoy his *Ladies and Gentleman, the Original Music of the Hebrew Alphabet* and *Weekend in Mustara*, two novellas Leviant published together in 2002. Another novel that explores the boundaries of traditional narrative is *A Guide for the Perplexed* by Jonathan Levi.

Markfield, Wallace

To an Early Grave. **Simon & Schuster, 1964. 255p.**

Leslie Braverman's death brings four of his friends together in an old Volkswagen, bumbling and arguing their way across Brooklyn for the funeral, in this satirical tale about lost youth and the writing life.

Themes: death; friendship; funerals; satirical novels

Related Titles: *To an Early Grave* was made into the movie *Bye Bye Braverman*. Markfield's absurdist humor was most often trained on Brooklyn Jews. He also wrote the novels *You Could Live If They Let You*, *Teitelbaum's Window*, and *Radical Surgery*.

Miller, Arthur

Focus. **1984; reprint, Syracuse University Press, 1997. 217p.** `YA`

When Lawrence Newman begins to wear eyeglasses, he is mistaken for a Jew and becomes a target for anti-Semites, losing his job, becoming a pariah in his neighborhood, and forced to confront the consequences of a life of unthinking conformity. The novel is set against the background of World War II and the hysteria created by those seeking to blame Jews for the War.

Themes: anti-Semitism; men's lives; 1940s; prejudice

Related Titles: *Focus* is Miller's only novel, written early in his career, an example of his brilliance in using the individual story to represent universal truths. His plays are classics of the postwar American theater, especially *Death of a Salesman*, *All My Sons*, *A View from the Bridge*, and *The Crucible*. Readers may also be interested in Laura Z. Hobson's *Gentleman's Agreement*, a classic novel of anti-Semitism set just after World War II in New York City. A later novel by Hobson, *First Papers*, is an account of a Jewish intellectual who is harassed in the 1950s for his political beliefs.

Nattel, Lilian

The River Midnight. Scribner, 1999. 414p. 📖

In the imaginary shtetl of Blaszka, midwife Misha startles everyone when she becomes pregnant but refuses to name the father. An absorbing, magical account of the intertwined lives of the village men and women, with memorable characterizations. (The author's Web site is www.liliannattel.com.)

Themes:; adultery; Canadian authors; friendship; magical realism; shtetl life

Related Titles: Nattel's second novel, *The Singing Fire*, focuses on a group of immigrant women in London's East End

Pinkwater, Daniel

Uncle Boris in the Yukon and Other Shaggy Dog Stories. Simon & Schuster, 2001. 203p. `YA`

Starting with Uncle Boris's talking dog Jake, we learn about Pinkwater's life from stories about the animals, chiefly dogs that he has known and sometimes loved. (The author's Web site is www.pinkwater.com.)

Themes: family relationships; humorous fiction; linked stories

Rosner, Elizabeth

The Speed of Light. Ballantine Books, 2001. 241p. `YA` 📖

In three typographically distinct voices, Julian and Paula Perel, and their housekeeper Sola Ordonio, tell intertwined stories of how terrible secrets have shaped their lives. Julian lives a secluded life, scarred by the burden of sorrow and shame passed to him by his Holocaust-survivor father, while his sister takes care of him and pursues her singing career. Sola, the only survivor of the massacre of her village, starts the healing process for all of them. (The author's Web site is www.elizabethrosner.com.)

Themes: brothers and sisters; children of Holocaust survivors; housekeepers; men's lives; mental illness

Related Titles: The struggles of the second generation of Holocaust survivors, their silence, and the healing power of music is also the theme of Joyce Hackett's

Disturbance of the Inner Ear and Anne Raeff's *Clara Mondschein's Melancholia*. Raeff's book is annotated in the "Character" section of this chapter. Readers who enjoyed the rich poetic language and interesting use of "voice" in this novel may enjoy *Sister Crazy* by the Canadian author Emma Richler, also about a close sister–brother relationship.

Shteyngart, Gary

The Russian Debutante's Handbook. Riverhead Books, 2002. 452p.

A picaresque, satiric trip told by Russian immigrant Vladimir Girshkin, whose eye for the chance to get rich and become a real American leads him into adventures with an S/M girlfriend, artsy American graduate students, and con artists in Eastern Europe. (Winner of the National Jewish Book Award.)

Themes: fraud; immigrants; Russian Americans; satirical novels

Related Titles: Readers who enjoyed Shteyngart's satire may also like the novels of Tova Reich or Rhoda Lerman, annotated in the "Story" section of this chapter.

Stollman, Aryeh Lev

Stollman's novels reward the reader who appreciates language and character over plot. His luminous writing style lays bare the hearts and souls of his characters, as readers share their secret fears and sorrows. Love of Jewish learning permeates his books in a mystical way. (The author's Web site is www.aryehlevstollman.com.)

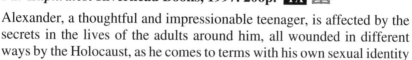

The Far Euphrates. Riverhead Books, 1997. 206p. **YA** 📖

Alexander, a thoughtful and impressionable teenager, is affected by the secrets in the lives of the adults around him, all wounded in different ways by the Holocaust, as he comes to terms with his own sexual identity in Windsor, Ontario, in the 1950s. (An ALA Notable Book.)

Themes: Canadian authors; coming-of-age stories; family secrets; gays/lesbians/bisexuals; Holocaust—survivors

The Illuminated Soul. Riverhead Books, 2002. 274p. **YA** 📖

Elegant Eva Laquedem Higashi, a World War II refugee, arrives in Windsor, Ontario, with her precious treasure, an illuminated Hebrew manuscript, and spends a few weeks with the Ivri family, changing their lives with her wisdom, compassion, and scholarship. Joseph, the older of two brothers, relates the story fifty years later, when he is a successful author, neuroanatomist, and companion for brother Asa.

Themes: Canadian authors; family relationships; Holocaust—refugees and displaced persons; Holocaust—survivors; illuminated books and manuscripts

Related Titles: Readers who enjoy Stollman's unusual linking of science, faith, and mysticism may also enjoy his collection of stories, *The Dialogues of Time and Entropy*.

Sukenick, Ronald
Mosaic Man. **FC2, 1999. 261p.**

Ron's very hip, postmodern, and dissolute journey through late twentieth-century America, Europe, and Israel, in search of his Jewish roots. Chapter titles are puns on books of the Bible: "Genes," "Ex/Ode," "Umbilicus," etc. (The author's Web site is www.mosaicman.com.)

Themes: Americans in Israel; anti-Semitism; experimental fiction; family relationships; Jewish identity

Wisenberg, S. L.
The Sweetheart Is In: Stories. **TriQuarterly Books, 2001. 137p.**

Linked stories, set in Texas and Chicago, about Ceci Rubin, from different points of view, and in several different styles, about the unknowableness of others and the meaning of belonging. Ceci is the daughter of a liberator of Mauthausen and the sister of the "sweetheart."

Themes: Jewish identity; linked stories; teenaged girls; women's lives

Zucker, Benjamin
Blue. **Overlook Press, 2000. 247p.**

The narrative of this experimental novel set is displayed Talmud-style, with the text in the center of each right-hand page surrounded by commentary. In the central text, jeweler Abraham Tal counsels the young Rachel on how to obtain a marriage proposal from her boyfriend while the outer commentaries provide embellishments from real and fictional characters.

Themes: experimental fiction; jewelers; love affairs

Related Titles: A second novel written in the same format, *Green* continues the story of the love affair between Dosha and Raphael. Readers who enjoyed the experimental style of *Blue* and *Green,* in which the author's voice mixes in with the narrative, may also like Jerzy Kosinski's *The Hermit of 69th Street.*

Setting

In these novels, character and plot are intertwined with time and place. The haunting—and haunted—landscape of Joseph Skibell's *A Blessing on the Moon*, the South Florida condo lifestyle of Paula Marantz Cohen's *Jane Austen in Boca*, and the tension-filled world of the Israeli Orthodox families in Risa Miller's *Welcome to Heavenly Heights* are all examples of novels in which setting is thoroughly a part of story and characters. Novels in this section display an extraordinary range of tone, from elegiac to satirical to magical realist and beyond. Readers who enjoy these novels are willing to accept fanciful or not-quite-real settings to enter a fully realized world.

Abraham, Pearl

Giving Up America. **Putnam, 1998. 320p.** 📖

Deena, a Hasidic Jew, marries Orthodox Daniel despite her father's misgivings; as they remodel their house, Daniel's betrayals cause Deena to question her religious commitment and her marriage.

Themes: Brooklyn, N.Y.; Hasidism; marriage; Orthodox Jews; women—religious life

The Romance Reader. **Riverhead Books, 1995. 296p.** **YA** 📖

Rachel Benjamin, teenaged daughter of a Hasidic rabbi in upstate New York, catches tantalizing glimpses of a freer, secular world by reading novels forbidden in her religious home while her parents try to keep her within the bounds of her community.

Themes: coming-of-age stories; Hasidism; marriage, New York State; teenaged girls

Related Titles: Abraham allows readers to enter the inner lives of Hasidic and Orthodox girls and women in her empathetic novels. Readers may also be interested in the nonfiction title *Around Sarah's Table: Ten Hasidic Women Share Their Stories of Life, Faith, and Tradition*.

Cohen, Paula Marantz

Jane Austen in Boca. **St. Martin's, 2002. 258p.** 📖

A witty and hilarious take-off on *Pride and Prejudice* set in the Boca Festa retirement community in Boca Raton, Florida, this comedy of manners examines the mating and courtship rituals of three women friends in the over-seventy set.

Themes: elderly women; Florida; marriage; satirical novels

Related Titles: Readers who enjoyed Cohen's humorous and clear-eyed look at older women may also like *Anna in Chains* and *Anna in the Afterlife* by Merrill Joan Gerber, two collections of stories annotated in the "Character" section of this chapter.

Lelchuk, Alan

Brooklyn Boy. **1990; reprint, University of Wisconsin Press, 2003. 304p.** **YA**

An autobiographical collection of linked stories following teenager Aaron Schlossberg in the 1950s, as he learns about the strange and sometimes terrifying adult world and sets his own course. Brooklyn, its history, and especially the Dodgers, its baseball team, are as much characters as Aaron's parents, friends, and teachers.

Themes: baseball and baseball players; Brooklyn, N.Y.; fathers and sons; teenaged boys

Related Titles: Another nostalgic Brooklyn novel is Steve Kluger's *Last Days of Summer*, annotated in the "Modern Period, United States and Canada" section of chapter 3.

Miller, Risa

Welcome to Heavenly Heights. **St. Martin's, 2003. 230p.** 📖

An intelligent portrait of four Orthodox American women who have made *aliyah* and are living with their families in an apartment condominium in Israel's West Bank. Against a background of political violence and small privations, the women struggle to make sense of their new lives.

Themes: Americans in Israel; immigrants; Orthodox Jews; women—religious life

Related Titles: Readers may also enjoy the novel *Quiet Street* by Zelda Popkin, set at the difficult time of the creation of the modern State of Israel, which follows a group of families living in a Jerusalem suburb. *Quiet Street* is annotated in the "Modern Period, Middle East" section of chapter 3.

Nahai, Gina Barkhordar

Moonlight on the Avenue of Faith. **Harcourt, Brace, 1999. 376p.**

Born in 1938 in the Jewish ghetto of Tehran, beautiful, unlucky Roxanna is given away by her parents at the age of eight. Gifted with mystical powers, she is still unable to save herself from a tragic, nomadic existence, and ultimately abandons her daughter Lili. A final reunion in Los Angeles after the Shah is overthrown completes this exotic tale of love and loss.

Themes: Iran; magical realism; mothers and daughters; women's lives

Related Titles: Nahai's first novel, *Cry of the Peacock*, also about Iranian Jews, is annotated in the "Modern Period" section of chapter 3. Readers who enjoyed the surreal quality of this novel with its exotic Iranian setting and tragic heroine may also enjoy *Foreign Brides* and *Strand of a Thousand Pearls* by the Israeli novelist Dorit Rabinyan. Readers who are intrigued by the Judeo–Persian literature and culture glimpsed in these novels may be interested in the collection *In Queen Esther's Garden: An Anthology of Judeo-Persian Literature,* edited by Vera Basch Moreen, or the autobiography *Wedding Song: Memoirs of an Iranian Jewish Woman* by Farideh Goldin.

Obejas, Achy

Days of Awe. **Ballantine Books, 2001. 371p.** 📖

Alejandra San José, born in Havana at the start of the Cuban revolution in 1959, leaves Cuba with her family two years later, settling in Chicago, where she struggles with her religious, ethnic, and sexual identities, as well as the condition of exile. Returning to Cuba years later as a translator, she begins to connect the pieces of her parents' hidden Jewish lives and understand the history that brought Spanish Jews to the New World centuries earlier.

Themes: *conversos*; Cuba; exile; gays/lesbians/bisexuals; Hispanic Americans; Jewish identity

Related Titles: Obejas won a Lambda Literary Award for this novel. Other accounts of the dislocation of exile for Latin American Jews can be found in Marjorie Agosín's biographical writings, annotated in the "Childhood and Family" section of chapter 8, and Ilan Stavans's autobiography *On Borrowed Words: A Memoir of Language,* annotated in the same section.

Papernick, Jon

The Ascent of Eli Israel, and Other Stories. **Arcade Publishing, 2002. 182p.**

A dark and sometimes surreal collection that explores the tangle of Arab–Jewish relations in Israel from the late 1940s to the present. In *An Unwelcome Guest*, Yossi confronts an Arab family's claims to his house in a ghostly visitation. In *The King of the King of Falafel* competition between *felafel* stands takes a biblical turn, and in the title story, a newly arrived immigrant is caught up in the violence of a border settlement.

Themes: Israel; Jewish–Arab relations; Palestinians; short stories

Prose, Francine

Guided Tours of Hell: Novellas. **Holt, 1997. 241p.**

In the title novella, filled with layers of irony, an American playwright and a celebrity Holocaust survivor tour Auschwitz during a literary conference on Kafka and almost come to blows in the former SS canteen.

Themes: dramatist; Holocaust—concentration camps; Holocaust—survivors

Related Titles: Prose's many novels range widely in theme and genre. Readers may also enjoy her *Hungry Hearts*, annotated in the "Modern Period" section of chapter 3. Another complex novel about Holocaust memory is W. G. Sebald's *Austerlitz*.

Reich, Tova

 Master of the Return. **Harcourt Brace Jovanovich, 1988. 240p.**

Samuel Himmelhoch gave up his sinful life on the road as lighting effects guru for rock groups to become the leader of a group of former hippie penitents in Israel following the teachings of Reb Nahman of Bratslav. The author's obvious affection for her characters tempers this hilarious satire of misguided faith. (Winner of the E. L. Wallant Award.)

Themes: Americans in Israel; Hasidism; Jerusalem; satirical novels

Related Titles: Readers who enjoy Reich's offbeat, satirical style may also like Rhoda Lerman's novel *God's Ear,* about a rabbi who believes God tells him to buy land from an Indian tribe. It is annotated in the "Story" section of this chapter.

Rudner, Lawrence

Memory's Tailor. **University Press of Mississippi, 1998. 295p.** 📖

Zelig-like, Alexandr Davidowich Berman's expert tailoring abilities bring him into contact with the rich and famous, but he finds his true calling as a collector of Russian Jewish memories, which he gathers as he mends clothing. A unique blend of fantasy, humor, and the tragic history of the Russian Jewish community in the twentieth century.

Themes: magical realism; Russia; tailors

Scliar, Moacyr

The Centaur in the Garden. **1985; reprint, University of Wisconsin Press, 2003. 224p.**

Guedali Tartakovsky is born a centaur and hidden by his frightened parents during his childhood. At eighteen he runs away, embarking on a series of comic adventures that bring him love and loss, and a chance for acceptance. A lively, literate fable about the Jewish condition in Latin America, this is on the National Yiddish Book Center's list of the *100 Greatest Works of Modern Jewish Literature.* Translated by Margaret Neves.

Themes: Brazil; centaurs; humorous fiction; Latin American authors; magical realism; picaresque novels

Related Titles: Readers can find short stories by Scliar in the collection *With Signs and Wonders: An International Anthology of Jewish Fabulist Fiction,* annotated in chapter 4.

The Strange Nation of Rafael Mendes. **Harmony Books, 1986. 309p.**

One morning in 1975, Brazilian businessman Rafael Mendes awakens to find his world turned upside down: His company is bankrupt, his daughter has joined a cult, and a strange package has been delivered to his door that unlocks the secret of his family's past. An inventive and irreverent family history starting with Jonah and the whale. Translated by Eloah F. Giacomelli.

Themes: Brazil; *conversos*; Inquisition; Latin American authors; magical realism; men's lives

Related Titles: Another Latin American novel in which reality and identity are not what they seem, is Alicia Steimberg's *Call Me Magdalena,* set in Argentina.

Setton, Ruth Knafo

The Road to Fez. **Counterpoint, 2001. 231p.**

Eighteen-year-old Brit Lek finds forbidden love when she returns to the land of her birth to fulfill a promise to her mother. Set against the exotic backdrop of the Moroccan Jewish community and intertwined with the story of the death of the mysterious young girl Suleika, whose grave is a pilgrimage site for Jews and Arabs. (The author's Web site is www.ruthknafosetton.com.)

Themes: love affairs; Morocco; Sephardim; uncles

Related Titles: An intense and unusual love story is the focus of Curt Leviant's novel *Diary of an Adulterous Woman*, annotated in the "Language" section of this chapter.

Skibell, Joseph

A Blessing on the Moon. **Algonquin Books of Chapel Hill, 1997. 256p.** 📖

Chaim Skibelski was killed when the Jews in his village were massacred; he returns to wander as a spirit through Poland at the end of the Holocaust. In this dangerous and nightmarish world, the moon has fallen out of the sky, the Rabbi has become a crow, and even the ghosts of murdered Jews are persecuted.

Themes: fantasy; Holocaust—survivors; magical realism; Poland

Related Titles: Skibell's latest novel, *The English Disease*, published in 2003, is about a contemporary American Jew struggling with questions of identity, and is written in a realistic style.

Tel, Jonathan

Arafat's Elephant. **Counterpoint, 2002. 186p.**

Haunting stories written by a physicist with an eye for the telling details of character that offer a glimpse into the complexities and ironies of contemporary Israeli life. In "The Red Button," we enter the mind of an Arab terrorist on a suicide mission only to find that the story is about something quite different. In "Beautiful, Strong, and Modest," a young Hasidic woman's life is turned upside down by the purchase of a scarf.

Themes: Israel; short stories

Related Titles: Another fine collection of stories, many of which are set in Israel about diaspora Jews, is Jonathan Wilson's *Schoom*.

Unger, David

Life in the Damn Tropics. **Syracuse University Press, 2002. 301p.**

A moderately suspenseful political novel about choices, deceit, and family loyalties set in 1980s Guatemala. Government corruption, terrorists, and family betrayals threaten the newfound happiness of Marcos Eltaleph, fiftyish playboy, and his lover, the sexy Esperanza, when their nightclub becomes an antigovernment hangout.

Themes: corruption (in politics); family relationships; Guatemala; Latin American fiction

Related Titles: Another political novel with an unusual setting, *One of Us*, by David Freeman, takes place in Egypt in the 1930s. Readers interested in nonfiction about the Jewish community in Latin America may enjoy Victor Perera's autobiography about his boyhood in Guatemala, *Rites: A Guatemalan Boyhood*.

Viertel, Joseph
Life Lines. Simon & Schuster, 1982. 526p.

Soviet physician Yuri Karpeyko believes that his family's patriotic record and ignorance of Judaism should insulate him from state-supported anti-Semitism, but when he is publicly branded a Zionist, he appeals to his Jewish relatives in the West for help. Set in the late 1970s and written with the ratcheting tension of a thriller, the appealing characters and setting make this a vivid picture of the dangers and choices faced by Soviet Jews in the 1970s.

Themes: anti-Semitism; doctors; family relationships; refuseniks; Soviet Union

Weiss, David
The Mensch. Mid-List Press, 1998. 177p.

Leon Roth's sensitivity and compassion make his job collecting rents and managing apartment houses in the decrepit South Bronx difficult. The pain of his tenants' lives and memories of his old girlfriend, now in a mental institution, build within him to a shattering climax.

Themes: Bronx, N.Y.; Hispanic Americans; landlord and tenant; slum life

Related Titles: Another novel of someone who tries to be a *mensch* in a difficult situation is Bernard Malamud's *The Assistant*, annotated in the "Classics and Major Authors" section of this chapter.

Zelitch, Simone
Louisa. Putnam, 2001. 377p.

Nora, a Hungarian Jew and Holocaust survivor, arrives in Israel with her gentile daughter-in-law Louisa to start a new life and find Nora's beloved cousin Bela. The Israelis Nora meets are uncomfortable with the German Louisa, but the two women will not be separated, in this modern retelling of the biblical story of Naomi and Ruth.

Themes: daughters-in-law; Holocaust—survivors; Israel; mothers-in-law; widows; Zionism

Related Titles: Zelitch's second novel, *Moses in Sinai*, is annotated in the "Biblical and Ancient Worlds" section of chapter 3.

Sources of Additional Information

In addition to the sources below, readers will find excellent discussions of literary fiction in the introductions to the anthologies annotated in this chapter. General readers' advisory sources for literary fiction, not specific to American Jewish literature, can be found in chapter 9. The sources described in chapter 1 for keeping up with the literature are also helpful for literary fiction.

Biro, Adam. *Two Jews on a Train: Stories from the Old Country and the New*. Chicago: University of Chicago Press, 2001.
A study of the sources of Jewish humor.

Diner, Hasia. *Lower East Side Memories: A Jewish Place in America.* Princeton, NJ: Princeton University Press, 2000.
An exploration of what the Lower East Side means in the collective Jewish memory, including a chapter on the Lower East Side in fiction.

Furman, Andrew. *Contemporary Jewish American Writers and the Multicultural Dilemma: The Return of the Exiled.* Syracuse, NY: Syracuse University Press, 2000.
An overview of late twentieth-century Jewish American literature and how it relates to American multiculturalism.

Halio, Jay, and Ben Siegel, eds. *Daughters of Valor: Contemporary American Jewish Women Writers.* Newark: University of Delaware Press, 1997.

Harap, Louis. *In the Mainstream: The Jewish Presence in Twentieth-Century American Literature, 1950s–1980s.* Westport, CT: Greenwood Press, 1987.

Holtz, Barry. *The Schocken Guide to Jewish Books: Where to Start Reading About Jewish History, Literature, Culture, and Religion.* New York: Schocken Books, 1992.

Keenoy, Ray, and Saskia Brown. *The Babel Guide to Jewish Fiction.* Boulevard in association with the European Jewish Publication Society, 1998.
An annotated listing of Jewish authors and their works, with worldwide scope.

Neugroschel, Joachim, ed. and trans. *No Star Too Beautiful: Yiddish Stories from 1382 to the Present.* New York: W.W. Norton, 2002.
An extensive collection of Yiddish literature that includes fables; tales from the mystical tradition; and modern writers like Isaac Bashevis Singer, Sholom Aleichem, S. Ansky, Der Nister, Sholem Avrom Reyzen, and many more.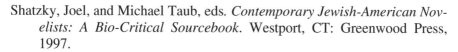

Shapiro, Ann, ed. *Jewish-American Women Writers: A Bio-bibliographical and Critical Sourcebook.* Westport, CT: Greenwood Press, 1994.

Shatzky, Joel, and Michael Taub, eds. *Contemporary Jewish-American Novelists: A Bio-Critical Sourcebook.* Westport, CT: Greenwood Press, 1997.

Syme, Daniel, and Cyndy Frenkel Kanter. *100 Essential Books for Jewish Readers.* Secaucus, NJ: Carol Publishing Group, 1998.
The authors recommend books on a variety of subjects, including Jewish thought and beliefs, history, the Holocaust, Israel, fiction, humor, and anti-Semitism.

Terry, Michael. *Reader's Guide to Judaism.* Chicago: Fitzroy Dearborn Publishers, 2000.
Contains signed bibliographic essays on 450 topics, including literature, the arts, history, famous individuals, and Jewish practice and thought.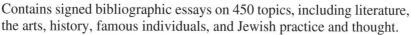

Wade, Stephen. *Jewish American Literature Since 1945: An Introduction.* Chicago: Fitzroy Dearborn Publishers, 1999.

Wisse, Ruth. *The Modern Jewish Canon: A Journey Through Language and Culture.* New York: The Free Press, 2000.
A survey of twentieth-century Jewish fiction written in English, Yiddish, Russian, and Hebrew.

Chapter 7

Holocaust Literature: Fiction and Memoirs

> *As I finish the last chapter of my book, I feel at peace, at last. I have discharged a burden, and paid a debt to many nameless heroes, resting in their unmarked graves. For I am haunted by the thought that I might be the only one left to tell their story.*—Gerda Weissman Klein
>
> *Frankly, in my opinion, Holocaust novels don't sell, even a book like this one, which is admittedly a clever, humorous, dark, and heartbreaking post-Holocaust tale.*—Thane Rosenbaum
>
> *. . . the past is a country from which one cannot emigrate.*—Michael Skakun
>
> *A novel about Treblinka is either not a novel or not about Treblinka.*—Elie Wiesel

Introduction

The popularity of Holocaust literature attests to the fact that not all of our reading is for entertainment and distraction. It is certainly difficult to think of Holocaust literature in those terms. We read it to honor those who died, endured, or resisted. We read it to remember that evil exists and must be fought. We read it to understand what people are capable of: endurance and dignity in the face of the unspeakable, and its opposite, unmitigated cruelty and the absence of humanity.

We also turn to Holocaust literature for absorbing personal stories that give us the opportunity to make the acquaintance of remarkable people and share with them a range of strong emotions, as much as that is possible through literature. The memoirs and stories penned by survivors make powerful literature because they are so personal and vivid. They force us to think about the responsibilities we have to one another and examine our own consciences.

Scope

The Holocaust, a European event, came to the United States with the survivors, who saw in the United States an opportunity to rebuild shattered lives. The survivors, and the GIs who liberated the concentration camps, brought inescapable knowledge of the dimensions of Hitler's Final Solution. Initially, the survivors were silent in print; it was only in the late 1960s that memoirs and fiction began to appear. In the last thirty-five years, many survivors have been moved to write about their experiences. In the quote above, Gerda Weissman Klein expressed the strong emotions many survivors feel about recounting their experiences. It would be impossible to do justice to the literature of the Holocaust by limiting this chapter to fiction. Holocaust fiction is so autobiographical and Holocaust memoir so unimaginable, that the line separating the two is hard to discern.

As much as it has been possible to ascertain, the memoirs in this chapter were written by survivors or by those close to them on their behalf. The memoirs in the "Next Generation" section were written by the children of survivors trying to understand their parents' experiences. Since Holocaust literature is written in many languages and in many countries, this chapter contains only memoirs written in English by survivors who have made their homes in America. This approach excludes some of the most well-known Holocaust memoirs, like *The Diary of Anne Frank* and Primo Levi's *The Periodic Table*. A few are translations of books by writers living in the United States who prefer to write in another language, like Elie Wiesel. The titles in the "Fiction" section were written primarily by survivors. Novels by writers like William Styron (*Sophie's Choice*) and Thomas Keneally (*Schindler's List*), who have no direct connection to the Holocaust, are not included.

The chapter is not a comprehensive bibliography of Holocaust literature, but a selected list of titles that appear frequently on recommended lists. It offers the reader a range of accounts of the experiences of survivors and victims in memoir and fiction. Extensive bibliographies, histories, and collections of survivor literature can be found in some of the "Sources for Additional Information" at the end of the chapter, along with analyses of America's response to the presence of Holocaust survivors in our midst.

Some of the titles in this chapter were written for young adults and are often found in both adult and young adult sections of libraries. Suggestions for young adult titles, as in other chapters, have been taken from bibliographies of recommended books and award titles.

There has been some discussion about whether fiction written by the children of Holocaust survivors is Holocaust literature. Thane Rosenbaum, Melvin Jules Bukiet, and Sonia Pilcer, for example, are often referred to as writers who belong to "2G," the generation that grew up with the Holocaust as their legacy. As a rule, they do not write directly about the Holocaust. Some of those authors claim that what they write should not be called Holocaust fiction. Following their lead, their books are annotated in chapter 6. By searching the index under the subject heading "children of Holocaust survivors," readers will be able to find these authors and titles.

Organization of the Chapter

The chapter is divided as follows:

Fiction

Memoirs

Children's Experiences

Resistance and Rescue

Personal Narratives

The Next Generation

Appeal of the Genre/Advising the Reader

It is difficult to think about Holocaust literature as a genre like any other. As Ruth Angress writes, "But if the Holocaust was a significant event of our century and not a gruesome fluke, then thoughtful books about it are not a literary subgenre, not a kind of historical Gothic."[1]

"Appeal" may not be the appropriate word to use when thinking about readers' advisory work in this area, but it is important nonetheless to understand what the reader is looking for. Though often terrifying, the stories draw us in for many reasons. Some readers want to understand survival under unspeakable conditions. They may feel a need to be witnesses to the experiences of the survivors. Some readers are interested in learning about a certain aspect of the Holocaust, for example, resistance movements, the Holocaust in a particular country, or righteous Gentiles. Other readers may want to educate themselves about one of the most horrific events in human history. Holocaust stories are generally filled with drama, heart-wrenching emotion, and unforgettable character. They demonstrate the extremes of good and evil that reside within humanity. Readers experience strong emotions but also find opportunities for reflection, discussion, and enlightenment. Some stories are filled with action and suspense; others may offer intriguing character studies; still others illuminate a dark era with historical background and detail. This is the stuff of great literature.

7

Readers' advisors need to remember that readers have varying tolerances for graphic depiction of Holocaust experiences. The annotations in this chapter give some indication of the level of graphic violence depicted. It is important to keep in mind that fiction can be more intense and disturbing than nonfiction.

Fiction

Many of the novels in this section are based on personal experiences and are very close to memoir. Some authors, like Arnost Luštig and Ilona Karmel, write about the experiences of the camps using the devices of fiction to dramatize the bleakest, most difficult circumstances imaginable. Some writers, like Elie Wiesel, set their novels after the Holocaust, examining the lives of the survivors who carry the burden of their terrible experiences. Elly Welt, in *Berlin Wild*, and Harold Nebenzal, in *Café Berlin,* use the threat of exposure and deportation in their novels. Although the main character may be alive at the end of these novels—and grateful to have survived—the endings are bittersweet at best.

> ### *Art From the Ashes: A Holocaust Anthology*. Edited by Lawrence L. Langer. Oxford University Press, 1995. 689p. **YA** 📖
>
> An extensive and well-chosen anthology of fiction, drama, poetry, and memoir from well-known and unknown authors that illuminates the darkest corners of the Holocaust. Most selections are complete works, including the play *Ghetto* by Joshua Sobol and Appelfeld's novel *Tzili*. Poetry by Nelly Sachs and reproductions of paintings from Terezin concentration camp are included.
>
> **Themes:** art; essays; poetry; short stories
>
> **Related Titles:** An anthology of short fiction and nonfiction by Canadian survivors and historians is *Beyond Imagination: Canadians Write About the Holocaust*, published by McClelland and Stewart.

Begley, Louis

> ### *Wartime Lies*. Alfred A. Knopf, 1991. 197p. 📖
>
> At a distance of some forty years, the narrator tells of Maciek, the child he once was, and the disintegration of his privileged childhood, as the Nazis consolidated control over his Polish town. In an unadorned style, the more poignant for its simplicity, he describes how he and his aunt Tania spent the war years moving from place to place, constructing and rehearsing lies, surviving the war physically, but entirely changed.
>
> **Themes:** aunts; Holocaust—children; Poland
>
> **Related Titles:** Since *Wartime Lies*, Begley has written several critically acclaimed novels, elegiac in tone, usually character studies of unsympathetic, alienated men who suffer from an inability to form stable relationships, including *The Man Who Was Late*, *About Schmidt*, and *Mistler's Exit*.

Demetz, Hanna

> ### *The House on Prague Street*. St. Martin's, 1980. 186p. **YA**
>
> For Helenka, the daughter of a Jewish mother and non-Jewish German father, the Prague Street house of her maternal grandparents symbolized the privilege and luxury that were gradually withdrawn as the Nazi noose tightened around the Czechoslovakian Jewish community. In this quietly absorbing tale, Helenka spends her teenaged years trying to find some normalcy in increasingly desperate situations, while the postcards from deported Jewish relatives become more ominous. Translated by the author. (Winner of the National Jewish Book Award.)
>
> **Themes:** Czechoslovakia; teenaged girls; World War II
>
> **Related Titles:** Helenka survived while her mother's family did not, because her father was not Jewish. To the Nazis, because of her mixed parentage, she was a *mischling*. A young adult novel about someone caught in the same circumstances is *Mischling, Second Degree: My Childhood in Nazi Germany* by Ilse Koehn.

Elberg, Yehuda

The Ship of the Hunted. **Syracuse University Press, 1997. 299p.**

In the Warsaw Ghetto, Golda Heshl tries desperately to stay a step ahead of Nazi roundups and save her children Yosef and Hannele, but they are ultimately separated, with Yosef and Hannele hiding in the countryside, while Golda is taken to Treblinka. Elberg vividly captures the tense and fevered lives of those trying to escape certain death. Translated from Yiddish by the author.

Themes: brothers and sisters; Canadian authors; Holocaust—ghettos

Related Titles: Elberg, an ordained rabbi, born in Poland in 1912, now lives in Montreal. Another of his novels, *The Empire of Kalman the Cripple*, is set in rural Poland and ends as Hitler assumes power in Germany.

Epstein, Leslie

King of the Jews. **Coward, McCann & Geoghegan, 1979. 350p.** 📖

When Isaiah Trumpelman becomes the leader of the *Judenrat*, the council that does the selection for the Nazi transports, he hopes to save lives. A combination of realistic and fantastic elements enlivens this fable about the morality and delusions of Jews who worked with the Nazis, based on the life of Mordecai Chaim Rumkowski, head of the Lodz Ghetto. (An ALA Notable Book.)

Themes: Holocaust—ghettos; Nazis; Poland

Helmreich, Helaine G.

The Chimney Tree. **University Press of Colorado, 2000. 279p.**

Red-haired Breindel, independent but naïve, runs away from her new husband when he turns out to be delusional. Her comfortable life in Warsaw is shattered by the arrival of the Russians and Nazis; she is forced to learn new ways to survive in a nightmarish world.

Themes: Hasidism; Holocaust—survivors; marriage; shtetl life

Hershman, Marcie

Tales of the Master Race. **HarperCollins, 1991. 223p.** 📖

A collection of linked stories that examine the effects of Nazi persecution on ordinary Aryan citizens in the fictional German town of Kreiswald in the 1930s and 1940s; their feelings of guilt, responsibility, and the menacing fear that comes from knowing too much. Written in an unadorned style, with excerpts from historical documents, these are stories that will trouble the reader.

Themes: Germany; guilt; Nazis; small town life

Karmel, Ilona

An Estate of Memory. **1969; reprint, The Feminist Press, 1986. 457p.**

In a brutal Nazi work camp in Poland, four women conspire to save the life of a baby in a true test of friendship and sacrifice under unspeakable conditions. Unusual for its realistic detail and emphasis on women's experience in the camps.

Themes: friendship; Holocaust—labor camps; pregnancy

Related Titles: The Feminist Press edition has an excellent afterword by Ruth K. Angress. Readers may also be interested in Nechama Tec's book on the differing experiences of men and women in the Holocaust, *Resilience and Courage: Women, Men and the Holocaust.*

Kosinski, Jerzy N.

The Painted Bird. **2nd ed. Houghton Mifflin, 1976. 234p.**

The unnamed narrator, a small boy, is sent away by his parents for safekeeping, but he is abandoned and lives by his wits in rural Poland as an outcast, trying to make sense of the world around him. The graphic first person narrative records the boy's isolation and degradation at the hands of the cruel and superstitious peasants for whom he works in exchange for food and shelter.

Themes: abandoned children; anti-Semitism; Poland

Luštig, Arnost

A Prayer for Katerina Horovitzova. **Harper & Row, 1973. 164p.**

Katerina Horovitzova becomes part of a group of nineteen wealthy American men held in a concentration camp who are to be part of a prisoner exchange with the Allies for Nazi officers. As the Nazi officers toy with their American prisoners, extorting huge sums of money from them, Katerina realizes their true predicament. Translated from the Czech by Jeanne Němcová.

Themes: Holocaust—concentration camps; hostages; Nazis

Related Titles: Luštig often writes about women's experiences in the Holocaust. *Dita Saxova*, set after the war, is about a young girl who survived but finds the memory of her experiences unbearable.

Darkness Casts No Shadow. **Inscape, 1976. 144p.** `YA`

Two teenaged boys manage to escape from a train that is taking them to another concentration camp. Hungry, filthy, and sick, they make their way through the forest sorting through the horrific events they've already lived through, uncertain of what's to come. Translated by Jeanne Němcová.

Themes: Holocaust—concentration camps; Poland; teenaged boys

Related Titles: This is the first novel in Luštig's *Children of the Holocaust* series, based on personal experience. The other two are *Street of Lost Brothers* and *Cowards and Heroes.*

Lovely Green Eyes. **Arcade Publishing, 2002. 248p.**

Hanka Kaudersová sees a chance to escape certain death at the next Auschwitz "selection" by pretending to be Aryan and becoming a prostitute in a field brothel servicing German officers. In doing so, she enters a world filled with loneliness and degradation. Translated by Ewald Osers.

Themes: Holocaust—survivors; prostitution

Related Titles: Leo Litwak, in his memoir *The Medic: Life and Death in the Last Days of WWII,* writes movingly of how he took part in a Passover seder that was arranged for a group of Jewish women who had served as prostitutes for German officers during the war.

The House of Returned Echoes. **Northwestern University Press, 2001. 311p.**

An autobiographical novel about the author's father, who perished in Auschwitz in 1944. Emil Ludvig struggled to keep his family afloat in Prague. Translated by Josef Luštig.

Themes: Czechoslovakia; Holocaust

The Unloved: from the Diary of Perla S. **1985. Reprint. Northwestern University Press, 1996. 172p.**

In laconic diary entries Perla records the daily visits of camp inmates and German officers, as she sells her body to survive and avoid the transports to the east and certain death. After two years in Theresienstadt, she has no illusions; living in each moment, she cherishes the time spent with friends who gradually disappear and the memories of her prewar life.

Themes: diaries; friendship; Holocaust—concentration camps; prostitution

Michaels, Anne

Fugitive Pieces. **Alfred A. Knopf, 1997. 294p.** **YA** 📖

After young Jakob Beer's parents are murdered in his Polish village, he is rescued by Athos, a compassionate Greek geologist who hides him for the duration of the war, helping him to heal, and eventually they move to Toronto. In the second part, Jakob's poetry helps Ben, the child of survivors, come to terms with his own pain.

Themes: Canadian authors; children of Holocaust survivors; Holocaust—survivors; poets

 7

Nebenzal, Harold

Café Berlin. **The Overlook Press, 1992. 281p.**

Daniel Saporta, hiding in a Berlin attic during World War II, recounts his experiences, from childhood in a wealthy Jewish family in Damascus to owner of the Klub Kaukasus, a popular Berlin nightclub that featured exotic dancers and attracted Nazi officers. A novel rich with historical detail and atmosphere and empathetic characters

Themes: espionage; 1930s; Sephardim; World War II

Related Titles: The author was one of the producers of the movie *Cabaret*, and readers will find some similarities in the setting, although this novel is broader in scope, involving Nazi activities in Muslim countries.

Readers who enjoyed the dark tone and moral ambiguity of this novel may also enjoy Joseph Kanon's *The Good German*, set in Berlin, but after World War II.

Samuels, Gertrude

Mottele: A Partisan Odyssey. **Harper & Row, 1976. 179p.** **YA**

Mottele is twelve, but old beyond his years, when he appears at Diadia's partisan camp with his violin, becoming a member of the group and taking part in dangerous missions. The author calls this a "documentary novel," as it is based on the stories told to her by partisans who fought in the forests of Poland and the Soviet Union.

Themes: Holocaust—children; Holocaust—resistance and rescue; partisans

Schaeffer, Susan Fromberg

 Anya. **Macmillan, 1974. 489p.** **YA**

In a detailed, visual style, Anya recounts how her fairy tale childhood in Vilno, Poland, was cut short by the Holocaust, and how she fought to save her life and her daughter's. Filled with sensual descriptions that absorb the reader into Anya's perception of the world. (Winner of the E. L. Wallant Award.)

Themes: doctors; family relationships; immigrants; mothers and daughters

Related Titles: Readers who appreciate Schaeffer's strong narratives and vivid characters set in richly developed settings may enjoy her novels *Falling* and *Love*.

Stark, Marisa Kantor

Bring Us the Old People. **Coffee House Press, 1998. 218p.**

In her distinctive, artless, Yiddish-inflected voice, Maime Lieber Schatz recounts how she and her husband survived the Holocaust by hiding in a root cellar. Now in her nineties and in a nursing home, Maime is haunted by the memories of terrible decisions made in those days.

Themes: elderly women; Holocaust—survivors; Poland

Szeman, Sherri

The Kommandant's Mistress. **HarperCollins, 1993. 273p.**

When she becomes the mistress of the Kommandant Maximilian von Walther in a concentration camp, Rachel Sarah Levi escapes immediate death but enters a relationship fraught with humiliation and depravity. Von Walther and Rachel each tell their version of the relationship.

Themes: adultery; Holocaust—concentration camps; Nazis; sexual abuse

Taylor, Katherine Kressman

Address Unknown. **Story Press, 1995. unpaged** **YA**

Two business partners and friends, one in San Francisco and one in Munich, correspond in the years 1932 to 1934 regarding the changing German political climate for Jews and the power of the Nazi ideology. Their differences of opinion have a chilling result.

Themes: friendship; Germany; Nazism; novellas

Related Titles: This novella was originally published, to popular acclaim, in 1938 in *Story Magazine*.

Uris, Leon

Mila 18. Doubleday, 1961. 539p. **YA**

A thoroughly researched re-creation of the heroic, doomed Warsaw Ghetto resistance movement, told with emotion, energy, and dramatic intensity.

Themes: Holocaust—resistance and rescue; Warsaw Ghetto

Related Titles: John Hersey's earlier novel about this epic battle, *The Wall*, won the National Jewish Book Award.

Welt, Elly

Berlin Wild. Viking, 1986. 368p. 📖

Josef Bernhardt, seventeen years old, son of a mixed marriage, is lucky to be taken in by a group of scientists in a research institute near Berlin and protected from the brutality of the war years, but later, in the United States he is assailed by feelings of guilt. A very literate coming-of-age story with an interesting scientific backdrop.

Themes: doctors; Holocaust—survivors; scientists; teenaged boys

Wiesel, Elie

Elie Wiesel's novels, nonfiction, and memoirs based on his Holocaust experiences have made him a well-known figure around the world. His admonitions against forgetting have become powerful watchwords for people everywhere. Issues of faith, guilt, and survival recur in his novels; madness and sanity often change places. Wiesel was born in Sighet, Transylvania, in 1928, where the isolated villagers lived in relative peace until 1944, when Hitler, in an effort to complete the Final Solution, hastily deported Hungary's Jews to the camps. The teenaged Wiesel was separated from his mother and sisters; he and his father stayed together until almost the end of the war, when his father died of the effects of the brutal treatment they suffered. Wiesel spent the postwar years in France but became an American citizen in 1963. His books are generally written first in French and then translated into English, often by his wife, Marion. He has also published poetry, drama, and studies of the lives of biblical, Hasidic, and Talmudic teachers. In 1986 he was awarded the Nobel Peace Prize for his humanitarian work around the world.

Night. Hill and Wang, 1960. 116p. **YA**

Deported from his home town of Sighet in Transylvania when he was fifteen, Wiesel and his father entered the hellish concentration camps of Auschwitz, Buna, and Buchenwald, supporting and caring for each other as best they could until his father died at the end of the war shortly before liberation. This poignant account of how Jews were stripped of everything they owned, including their faith, and often their humanity, was one of the first and is still one of the most powerful Holocaust novels. Translated by Stella Rodway.

Themes: fathers and sons; Holocaust—concentration camps

Related Titles: In recent editions, *Night* has been published as a trilogy with *Dawn* and *Day*.

Dawn. **Hill and Wang, 1961. 89p.** `YA`

A Holocaust survivor, now in Israel fighting in the underground movement against the British, Elisha has been assigned the task of executing a British officer in reprisal for the execution of a Jewish resistance fighter. In the light of his camp experiences he contemplates the deed he must do at dawn. Translated by Frances Frenaye.

Themes: murder and murderers; Palestine; soldiers

The Accident. **Hill and Wang, 1962. 120p.** `YA`

A taxi in New York hits the unnamed protagonist, a Holocaust survivor. While recuperating in the hospital, his conversations with his girlfriend and doctor, and his memories of the past, bring into sharp relief his continuing spiritual torment and inability to find meaning in life. Translated by Anne Borchardt.

Themes: accidents; Holocaust—survivors; love affairs

Related Titles: In later editions, this title is known as *Day*, and is often published as a trilogy with *Night* and *Dawn*.

A Beggar in Jerusalem. **Random House, 1970. 211p.**

After the Israelis recapture Jerusalem in the Six-Day War, a group of beggars gather at the Western Wall to share Hasidic and Talmudic tales and to importune God on His silence during the Holocaust. Translated by Lily Edelman. (An ALA Notable Book.)

Themes: Holocaust; immigrants; Israel–Arab War, 1967; Jerusalem

The Oath. **Random House, 1973. 283p.**

The sole Jewish survivor of the village of Kolvillag, Azriel, now an old man, breaks an oath of silence to tell the story of the 1920 pogrom to a young man, and in so doing, saves the young man's life and transmits the burden of carrying the story to him.

Themes: Holocaust—survivors; Jews—persecutions; memory

The Testament. **Summit Books, 1981. 346p.**

While in a Soviet prison awaiting execution, poet Paltiel Kossover writes about his transformation from devout student of the Talmud to Communist. The manuscript gives his grieving son Grisha a chance to understand the father he never knew. Translated from the French by Marion Wiesel.

Themes: Communism; fathers and sons; poets; prisoners and prisons

❀ *The Town Beyond the Wall.* 1964; reprint, Schocken Books, 1982. 179p.

Michael returns to his hometown after the war with his friend Pedro, where he is betrayed and arrested by the Communists and tortured to reveal political secrets. In his efforts to survive the torture, he recalls the people and events of his childhood, particularly the face of the man who stood by as the Jews were deported years earlier. Translated by Stephen Becker. (Winner of the National Jewish Book Award.)

Themes: betrayal; guilt; Holocaust—survivors; prisoners and prisons

***The Fifth Son.* 1985; reprint, Schocken Books, 1998. 220p.**

The narrator, son of a Holocaust survivor and inheritor of his father's demons, is driven to seek revenge against the Nazi officer who killed his brother.

Themes: children of Holocaust survivors; fathers and sons; Holocaust—survivors; Nazis; revenge

***Twilight.* 1988; reprint, Schocken Books, 1998. 289p.**

Raphael Lipkin, a survivor tormented to the edge of insanity by the loss of his family and the fate of his friend Pedro, visits a mental clinic in upstate New York. Part patient, part researcher, he finds much in common with the inmates who see themselves as biblical characters, arguing with God.

Themes: family relationships; guilt; insanity

***The Forgotten.* 1992; reprint, Schocken Books, 1995. 316p.**

Elhanan Rosenbaum, aging Holocaust survivor, is horrified to find his memory fading; he encourages his son Malkiel to travel back to his Romanian village to become the repository of his father's complex memories. Translated by Stephen Becker.

Themes: fathers and sons; Holocaust—survivors; memory

Related Titles: Another Wiesel title about a survivor trying to come to terms with his wartime experiences is *Gates of the Forest.*

Wiesenthal, Simon

***The Sunflower; On the Possibilities and Limits of Forgiveness.* 2nd ed. Schocken Books, 1998. 289p.** **YA** 📖

Wiesenthal is called from a work detail in the camps to the hospital, where a dying Nazi asks him to hear his confession and forgive him for his crimes against the Jews, but Wiesenthal refuses to speak. In this edition (the first edition was published in 1970), fifty-three men and women comment on the questions Wiesenthal poses about his actions, including the Dalai Lama, Primo Levi, Abraham Joshua Heschel, Cynthia Ozick, Martin Marty, Nechama Tec, and others.

Themes: ethics; guilt; Holocaust—concentration camps; Nazis; philosophical novels

Memoirs

Many survivors' memoirs open with descriptions of the tranquil, warm, and loving homes they remember, sharing the rituals of the Jewish year in close-knit families. Assimilated families felt comfortable that they were part of the larger community. Often there was a sense of family continuity stretching back for several generations and expectations that life would continue in the same pattern.

The vicious state-sponsored anti-Semitism and ever-increasing restrictions on Jewish life in the 1930s shocked some families into escape, but numbed others. Too many believed that the madness would pass and did nothing; to their horror, it spread and they were caught in the relentless machine of the Final Solution. In so many of these accounts, there are instances where people felt that their rural village would be spared, or that by traveling east or west for a distance they would be out of range. We read these memoirs in a state of shock and disbelief, hoping each time that history can be rewritten.

The events of history may present similar general outlines for survivor stories, but every story is unique. Many of the memoirs in his chapter are by people who were herded into ghettos and then transported to concentration camps. In *The Seamstress*, Sara Tuvel Bernstein writes about how she was the one who set the rules for her sister and friends that kept them alive in the women's camp of Ravensbruck. *Himmler's Jewish Tailor: The Story of Holocaust Survivor Jacob Frank,* is a remarkable account of a man who survived four camps by running a uniform factory for the Nazis. Other survivors, by various subterfuges, managed to live in the midst of the enemy. In *The Nazi Officer's Wife*, Edith Hahn-Beer describes the daily terror of passing as a Gentile, especially after her marriage to a volatile Nazi officer who was aware that she was Jewish. Martin Goldsmith writes about his parents' romance while they were members of the Kulturbund, the Jewish orchestra maintained by the Nazis, in *The Inextinguishable Symphony*. Some people were hidden by friends or neighbors, often in the most unimaginable conditions. Children were taken in by Gentile families or hidden in convents. Irene Gut Opdyke, a young Polish Christian, writes in her memoir *In My Hands* how she simply felt it was her duty to save Jewish lives. A few of the accounts here are by people who managed to escape to the woods and join partisan fighters. And there are accounts of resisters who fought back in the ghettos or were able to maintain businesses supplying the armies and employing Jews during the war. The diversity of the stories is as great as the diversity of the individuals who lived them. Individually, they are shocking; collectively they provide an unparalleled historical testament.

Children's Experiences

Bernstein, Sara Tuvel, and with Louise Loots Thornton and Marlene B. Samuels

The Seamstress: A Memoir of Survival. Putnam, 1997. 353p. YA

As a child in Romania, Seren Tuvel had a strong, independent spirit that helped her face down the anti-Semitism in her school. With that same determination and courage she was able to set rules that kept her sister and several friends alive in the all-women's concentration camp, Ravensbruck. Tuvel's intense desire to live pervades this memoir.

Themes: Holocaust—concentration camps; sisters; teenaged girls

Bitton-Jackson, Livia

Elli: Coming of Age in the Holocaust. Times Books, 1980. 212p. YA

Elli, thirteen when the Germans invaded Hungary in 1944, was first sent with her family to a ghetto, then deported to a camp where she and her mother were chosen for a labor detail, while her younger siblings perished. Elli's courage and religious convictions inspired others and helped keep her mother alive during the horrors they suffered. In the aftermath of the war, they realized that Hungary was no longer their home and left for New York.

Themes: Holocaust—concentration camps; Holocaust—slave labor; Hungary; teenaged girls

Related Titles: Bitton-Jackson has adapted this memoir for the middle grades as *I Have Lived a Thousand Years: Growing Up in the Holocaust* and *My Bridges of Hope: Searching for Life and Love After Auschwitz*, adding more material about her life after the Holocaust. Readers may be interested in Arnost Luštig's searing portrayals of children's experiences in his novels in the *Children of the Holocaust* series: *Diamonds of the Night*, *Darkness Casts No Shadow*, and *Night and Hope*. *Darkness Casts No Shadow* is annotated in the "Fiction" section of this chapter.

Children in the Holocaust and World War II: Their Secret Diaries. Edited by Laurel Holliday. Pocket Books, 1995. 409p. YA

These excerpts are extraordinary for the way they illustrate the courage of their authors, many of them young children who wrote under difficult conditions. Ephraim Shtenkler survived the war in a cupboard in a Polish farmhouse from ages two to seven and wrote his account at age eleven in Israel. Ina Konstantinova, a Russian teenager, joined the partisans to fight the Nazis, giving her life in this cause. Eva Heyman, in Hungary, records the privations that her family endured as the Germans constricted the lives of the Jewish community, ending with her deportation to a concentration camp.

Themes: diaries; Holocaust—personal narratives; Holocaust—resistance and rescue; teenagers

Related Titles: Another collection of children's Holocaust diaries is *Salvaged Pages: Young Writers' Diaries of the Holocaust*, collected and edited by Alexandra Zapruder. A history of children's experiences in the Holocaust can be found in Deborah Dwork's book *Children with a Star: Jewish Youth in Nazi Europe*. Readers may also sppreciate Miriam Darvas's memoir *Farewell to Prague*, about the experiences of a young girl who was half-Jewish.

Clary, Robert

From the Holocaust to Hogan's Heroes: The Autobiography of Robert Clary. Madison Books, 2001. 209p.

As the adored youngest child of a large family, Robert Clary had a charmed life in a close-knit Jewish community in Paris in the 1930s, where he developed a love of singing, dancing, and acting. In 1942, when he was sixteen, he and his family were deported to the French transit camp, Drancy, and from there he spent time as a slave laborer and inmate in several camps, including Buchenwald, sometimes gaining extra rations or special treatment by entertaining camp brass. One of the few members of his family to survive, Clary went on to a successful acting career in the United States; he is most well-known here for his role in the television program *Hogan's Heroes*.

Themes: actors and acting; France; Holocaust—concentration camps; Holocaust—survivors; teenaged boys

Cretzmeyer, Stacy

Your Name Is Renée: Ruth Kapp Hartz's Story as a Hidden Child in Occupied France. **Oxford University Press, 1999. 208p.** YA

Ruth Kapp's family moved to France from Germany when she was an infant, hoping to escape round-up by the Germans, but once France was occupied they were again at risk, dependent for survival on non-Jews and the French Resistance. As a kindergartner, Ruth was taught to call herself Renée and spent the last part of the war hidden in a convent.

Themes: convents; France; Holocaust—hidden children

Related Titles: Young Simon Jeruchim also spent the war pretending to be a Catholic, separated from his parents and siblings, as he recounts in *Hidden in France: A Boy's Journey Under the Nazi Occupation*. In her novel for young adults, *Touch Wood: A Girlhood in Occupied France*, Renée Roth-Hano writes about her own years hidden in a convent. Frida Scheps Weinstein was also hidden in a convent, among other places; she describes her experiences in *A Hidden Childhood: A Jewish Girl's Sanctuary in a French Convent, 1942–1945*.

Denes, Magda

Castles Burning: A Child's Life in War. **W. W. Norton, 1997. 384p.**

When Magda was five, her wealthy, spoiled father fled to the United States, taking all their money and leaving the family behind to endure the horrors of the Holocaust. With her mother and beloved brother Ivan, she endured unspeakable conditions, vividly described; as a psychoanalyst, she records the permanent emotional damage to family relationships.

Themes: brothers and sisters; Holocaust—survivors; Hungary

Flares of Memory: Stories of Childhood During the Holocaust. **Edited by Anita Brostoff and Sheila Chamovitz. Oxford University Press, 2001. 344p.** YA

These short memoirs were gathered as a result of a project at the Holocaust Center of Pittsburgh to encourage survivors and liberators to write about their experiences. Most were children and teenagers during the Holocaust; their unedited writings are vivid testaments to the desperate situations they endured.

Themes: children; Holocaust—personal narratives; teenagers

Related Titles: Readers may also be interested in another very personal collection of Holocaust memoirs, *When They Came to Take My Father: Voices of the*

Holocaust, edited by Leora Kahn and Rachel Hager, with photographs by Mark Seliger.

Fluek, Toby Knobel

Memories of My Life in a Polish Village, 1930–1949. **Alfred A. Knopf, 1990. 110p.** `YA`

Artist Toby Knobel Fluek hid on her own in the Polish countryside, depending on the kindness of strangers for food and shelter. Her account of life in her little Polish village before the Holocaust and the subsequent loss of family members is made all the more poignant by the inclusion of many of her own paintings.

Themes: children; Holocaust—survivors; Poland; shtetl life

Related Titles: Artist Nelly Toll's memoir *Behind the Secret Window: A Memoir of a Hidden Childhood During World War II* contains her watercolor paintings, made during the time she and her mother were hidden in Poland by a Christian family. Readers may also appreciate Ida Fink's hauntingly written short stories about the Holocaust, collected in *A Scrap of Time* and *The Journey.*

Gelissen, Rena Kornreich, and Heather D. Macadam

Rena's Promise: A Story of Sisters in Auschwitz. **Beacon Press, 1995. 274p.** `YA`

Rena's promise to her mother to care for her younger sister Danka sustained her through the years they spent as teenagers in Auschwitz, where they arrived on one of the first transports.

Themes: Holocaust—concentration camps; Poland; sisters

Related Titles: The support of family and friends in the camps was often crucial for survival. Shoshana Rabinovits writes about how her mother's devotion to her safety saved her life as an eight-year-old in the camps, in *Thanks To My Mother.*

Grove, Andrew S.

Swimming Across. **Warner, 2001. 290p.**

7

The Grove family's secular orientation was no protection from persecution by the Nazis and the Communists in Hungary in the 1940s and 1950s. They came to the United States after the 1956 uprising, where Andrew quickly took advantage of the schooling available to him. This memoir stops when Andrew (formerly Andris) is admitted to college, leaving the story of his remarkable success as CEO of Intel perhaps to another time.

Themes: Holocaust—survivors; Hungary; immigrants

Related Titles: Grove's other titles are in the field of business management; this is his only memoir. Another Jewish Hungarian immigrant who achieved unusual business success in the United States is George Soros.

His story is told by Michael Kaufman in *Soros: The Life and Times of a Messianic Billionaire.*

Harris, Mark Jonathan, and Deborah Oppenheimer
Into the Arms of Strangers: Stories of the Kindertransport. **Bloomsbury, 2000. 292p.**

Beginning in 1938, 10,000 children from Germany, Austria, Czechoslovakia, and Poland were sent to foster homes, camps, and hostels in England, the only country with the generosity and foresight to accept them. Although they were saved from almost certain death, the trauma of separation from family in a wartime situation left lifelong scars. This poignant collection of first person accounts follows the children from their prewar homes, leave-taking, experiences in England, and life following the war.

Themes: children; England; Kindertransport; parents and children

Related Titles: Oppenheimer was only dimly aware of her own mother's Kindertransport experience; it was not until after her death that she began the research that led to this book and a film. The first book about this rescue operation, Olga Levy Drucker's *Kindertransport*, was written for children.

Hautzig, Esther
Remember Who You Are: Stories About Being Jewish. **Crown, 1990. 220p.** `YA`

Hautzig spent the first ten years of her childhood in Vilna; in 1940 she and her immediate family were deported to Siberia, where they spent the war years, while the relatives who remained in Vilna perished in concentration camps. These gemlike vignettes lovingly recall family and friends, their lives and deaths.

Themes: children; family relationships; Holocaust—survivors; Poland; Russia

Related Titles: Hautzig also wrote an account of this period for younger readers, *The Endless Steppe: Growing Up in Siberia.*

Klein, Gerda Weissman
All But My Life. **1957; revised ed., Hill and Wang, 1995. 263p.** `YA`

Gerda recounts her comfortable childhood in Bielitz, Poland, where she attended Catholic school until the age of fifteen to obtain an academic education. When the Nazis occupied Poland, she was separated from her family and endured a harrowing existence in labor and concentration camps, culminating in a thousand-mile march, before liberation by the American army. This was one of the earliest Holocaust memoirs published in the United States.

Themes: Holocaust—concentration camps; Holocaust—labor camps; teenaged girls

Related Titles: Kurt Klein, an American Jew who had left Germany in 1937, liberated Gerda. The two fell in love while Gerda was recuperating in a Czech hospital. *The Hours After: Letters of Love and Longing in the War's Aftermath* contains the couple's letters during the year they were separated before they were able to marry.

Kluger, Ruth

Still Alive: A Holocaust Girlhood Remembered. **The Feminist Press, 2001. 214p.**

Thrust into the maelstrom of the Final Solution when she was eleven, Kluger and her mother somehow survived Theresienstadt, Auschwitz-Birkenau, and Christianstadt, continuing their edgy relationship into a new life in the United States. Kluger raises important questions about survival and Holocaust remembrance in this complex and literate memoir.

Themes: children; Holocaust—concentration camps; mothers and daughters

Related Titles: Readers may also be interested in Nechama Tec's book *Resilience and Courage: Women, Men and the Holocaust.* Tec writes about the characteristics of the people who were caught up in the Holocaust and how those characteristics affected their survival, particularly the ways that gender affected experience.

Kuper, Jack

Child of the Holocaust. **1967; reissue, Berkley, 272p. 1993.** **YA**

Jacob Kuperblum lost his entire family at the age of eight and was left to survive on his own, confronted daily by life-threatening situations. Throughout the war he moved around the countryside, from one family to another, trying to pass as a gentile and find a safe haven. The reader shares the boy's thoughts as he contrasts his dangerous and lonely existence with the happiness of his early childhood.

Themes: Canadian authors; Holocaust—hidden children; Holocaust—survivors; Poland

Lobel, Anita

No Pretty Pictures: A Child of War. **Greenwillow Books, 1998. 193p.** **YA**

Lobel, the well-known children's book illustrator, was five years old at the start of World War II, and her brother only three. Separated from their parents, they endured a harrowing existence hiding in the country with their nanny and then in a convent, before they were captured by the Germans and taken to Ravensbruck concentration camp. A haunting memoir told from a child's point of view. (The author's Web site is www. anitalobel.com.)

Themes: brothers and sisters; convents; Holocaust—hidden children; Holocaust—survivors; Poland

7

Related Titles: Other well-written, thought-provoking accounts of children's experiences that can be recommended to young adults are Ruth Minsky Sender's memoir *The Cage* and the sequel *To Life* and Aranka Siegal's memoirs *Upon the Head of a Goat* and *Grace in the Wilderness.*

Nir, Yehuda

The Lost Childhood: A World War II Memoir. Scholastic, 2002. 284p. `YA`

When the Germans took nine-year-old Yehuda Nir's father in 1941, it signaled to the remaining family members that they had entered a period of increasing danger and brutality. Relying on forged documents and alliances with Jews and Christians, Nir, his sister, and his mother spent the war years posing as Catholics, hiding under the noses of the Nazis.

Themes: Catholic faith; Holocaust—survivors; Poland

Related Titles: Nir's story was published first in 1989 as an adult title; the Scholastic edition is marketed for young adults.

Tec, Nechama

Dry Tears: The Story of a Lost Childhood. 1982; reprint, Oxford University Press, 1984. 242p. `YA`

Nechama Bawnik's parents were under no illusions about the Nazis' intentions when the German army occupied Lublin, Poland, in 1939. The family immediately set about trying to secure their safety with money, jobs, and connections. Ultimately they obtained papers to pass as Poles and were hidden by Catholic families.

Themes: Holocaust—hidden children; Holocaust—survivors; Poland

Related Titles: Tec's clear-eyed account of the privations and terrors of wartime life is compelling for its psychological insights. She has written several other nonfiction works on the Holocaust, most notably *Resilience and Courage: Women, Men and the Holocaust*, about the effects of gender on Holocaust survival, and *Defiance: The Bielski Partisans*, about an extraordinary group of Jewish resistance fighters in Belorussia and their charismatic leader, Tuvia Bielski. Her own experiences as a hidden child motivated her to explore the reasons why some people survived.

Velmans, Edith

Edith's Story: The True Story of a Young Girl's Courage and Survival During World War II. Soho Press, 1999. 239p. `YA`

When it was clear that Dutch Jews would no longer be safe, Edith's parents arranged for her to live as a Christian with a Protestant family, where part of her cover was to care for a German officer billeted in their house. Diary notes and letters contribute immediacy to this account.

Themes: Holland; Holocaust—hidden children; righteous gentiles in the Holocaust

Zandman, Felix, with David Chanoff

Never the Last Journey. Schocken Books, 1995. 428p.

Zandman's gratitude for his good luck in escaping death repeatedly as a teenager in the Holocaust and his subsequent successful career in business in America motivated him to recount his experiences. When the Nazis liquidated the ghetto of Grodno, Poland, he hid with three others in a five-foot-long trench under the floorboards of a peasant's house for a year and a half. Devastated by the loss of his family, he rebuilt his life in France and America, becoming CEO of his own Fortune 500 company.

Themes: businessmen; Holocaust—ghettos; Holocaust—hidden children; Poland

Resistance and Rescue

Appleman-Jurman, Alicia
Alicia: My Story. **Bantam, 1988. 356p.** YA

Nine years old when World War II began, Alicia managed to elude death at the hands of Communists and Nazis but lost her entire family. With incredible courage and nerve, she not only survived but ran a Jewish orphanage, later becoming a leader of the secret transports to Palestine and running the British blockade.

Themes: Holocaust—survivors; Palestine—Immigration; Poland

Isenberg, Sheila
A Hero of Our Own: The Story of Varian Fry. **Random House, 2001. 349p.** YA

Fry, the only American honored at *Ya*d Vashem as one of the "Righteous Among the Nations," spent 1940–1941 in France helping Jews escape by legal and illegal means, saving more than a thousand, including Marc Chagall and Hannah Arendt. His private rescue mission was undertaken at great risk and in opposition to the U.S. government, which ultimately forced him to leave France.

Themes: France; refugees; righteous gentiles in the Holocaust

Related Titles: Fry's own memoir, *Assignment: Rescue,* was published by Scholastic, and is suitable for middle and high school readers.

Jagendorf, Siegfried
Jagendorf's Foundry: Memoir of the Romanian Holocaust, 1941–1944. **HarperCollins, 1991. 209p.** YA

One of the Romanian Jews deported to Moghilev in 1941 was the engineer Siegfried Jagendorf, who convinced the local authorities to allow him to rebuild the city's electrical system and repair the iron works using Jewish labor. Aron Hirt-Manheimer provides commentary on Jagendorf's memoir, shedding light on this complex man who was brought up in an Orthodox home but became an assimilated, imperious dandy, able to negotiate productive and life-saving work for thousands of Jews.

Themes: engineers; Holocaust—survivors; Romania

Related Titles: Jagendorf was able to rescue Jews while remaining openly a Jew himself. Information about non-Jewish rescuers can be found in *Conscience and Courage: Rescuers of Jews During the Holocaust* by Eva Fogelman and *Rescuers: Portraits of Moral Courage in the*

Holocaust, a book of short biographies and photographs by Gay Block and Malka Drucker. The remarkable story of Oskar Schindler, a non-Jew who saved over a thousand Jews by providing factory work, is familiar to many from the novel and movie *Schindler's List* by the Australian author Thomas Keneally.

Meed, Vladka

On Both Sides of the Wall: Memoirs from the Warsaw Ghetto. **Holocaust Library, 1979. 276p.** `YA`

Vladka was the only member of her family who escaped deportation from the Warsaw Ghetto. Aided by her Aryan looks and fluent Polish, she was smuggled out of the Ghetto by the Jewish resistance, where she became a courier, helping others escape and find refuge, eventually taking part in the Warsaw Ghetto uprising. A compelling narrative that captures the terror, hysteria, and heroism of the period. Photos included. Translated by Dr. Steven Meed.

Themes: Poland; smuggling; Warsaw Ghetto

Oliner, Samuel P., and Kathleen Lee

Who Shall Live: The Wilhelm Bachner Story. **Academy Chicago Publishers, 1996. 277p.**

Although Bachner was Polish, he spoke impeccable German and was able to talk his way out of the Warsaw Ghetto and into a job with a German engineering firm, allowing him to hire Jews for his staff and provide them with false papers. A page-turning account of heroism under extreme conditions.

Themes: engineers; Poland; Warsaw Ghetto

Opdyke, Irene Gut, with Jennifer Armstrong

In My Hands: Memories of a Holocaust Rescuer. **Alfred A. Knopf, 1999. 276p.** `YA`

Irene, teenaged daughter of a Polish Catholic family, was forced to serve German officers in a hotel near the Jewish ghetto, where she saw how Jews were treated. She began to slip food into the ghetto, then smuggled out a group of Jews and hid them in the home of a German officer, risking her life to save them when they were discovered. (Opdyke was awarded the Israel Medal of Honor and named one of the "Righteous Among the Nations" by the Israeli Holocaust Commission.)

Themes: righteous gentiles in the Holocaust; teenaged girls

Related Titles: Readers, including young adults, may be interested in Corrie ten Boom's story of how her family of devout Dutch Christians hid Jews in their home during the Holocaust, titled *The Hiding Place,* or in Nechama Tec's book *When Light Pierced the Darkness: Christian Rescue of Jews in Nazi-Occupied Poland.*

Sutin, Jack, and Rochelle Sutin

Jack and Rochelle: A Holocaust Story of Love and Resistance. **Edited by Lawrence Sutin. Graywolf Press, 1995. 225p.**

In alternating accounts, edited by their son, Jack and Rochelle Sutin narrate how they escaped from Nazi ghetto labor camps and fled separately to a partisan group in the Polish forest, lived and fought back in unspeakable conditions, and fell in love.

Themes: Holocaust—labor camps; love stories; partisans

Related Titles: Two other books by Jews who fought against the Nazis, albeit in different circumstances, are *The Brigade: An Epic Story of Vengeance, Salvation, and World War II* by Howard Blum, and *Fighting Back: A Jewish Commando's War Against the Nazis* by Peter Masters. Readers may also enjoy two books about a very successful group of partisans, *Defiance: The Bielski Partisans* by Nechama Tec and *The Bielski Brothers* by Peter Duffy.

Werner, Harold

Fighting Back: A Memoir of Jewish Resistance in World War II. **Edited by Mark Werner. Columbia University Press, 1992. 253p.**

A stirring account of how Harold Werner spent two years in the woods in Poland with a large group of Jewish partisan fighters who dynamited bridges and trains, attacked convoys, destroyed food supplies, and sheltered Jews who managed to escape from ghettos and concentration camps.

Themes: partisans; Poland

Personal Narratives

Alexy, Trudi

The Mezuzah in the Madonna's Foot: Marranos and Other Secret Jews. **Simon & Schuster, 1993. 306p.**

Alexy and her family were living in France when World War II began; they were baptized as Catholics and moved to Spain. Even after coming to America they lived as Catholics, and it was not until she began to suffer from depression in adulthood that Alexy investigated her Jewish heritage, interviewing other survivors who had taken refuge in Spain and the historical communities of *conversos* in the American Southwest.

Themes: conversion to Christianity; *conversos*; Holocaust—survivors; Spain

7

Related Titles: Although Alexy started out to investigate her family's experiences during World War II, she includes information about hidden Jews living in the Southwestern United States who trace their ancestry back to Inquisition-era Spain. Readers who would like to learn more about these modern-day crypto-Jews may enjoy *Suddenly Jewish: Jews Raised as Gentiles Discover Their Jewish Roots* by Barbara Kessel, annotated in the "Collected Biography" section of chapter 8.

Filar, Marion, and Charles Patterson

From Buchenwald to Carnegie Hall. **University Press of Mississippi, 2002. 231p.**

Filar was a musical prodigy, a soloist with the Warsaw Philharmonic at the age of twelve. When the war began, his musical studies were cut short, and he was transported out of the Warsaw Ghetto to the first of a series of concentration camps. He endured slave labor and a serious injury to his hand, but his self-described "luck" helped him survive, recover his pianistic skills, and make a triumphant 1952 Carnegie Hall debut.

Themes: Holocaust—concentration camps; Holocaust—slave labor; musicians

Related Titles: Readers may be interested in the experiences of another musician, Fania Fenelon, who survived by playing in an orchestra organized by the Nazis in the camps. She describes her experiences in *Playing for Time*, subsequently made into a movie with a screenplay written by Arthur Miller.

Goldsmith, Martin

The Inextinguishable Symphony: A True Story of Music and Love in Nazi Germany. **John Wiley & Sons, 2000. 346p.**

Music literally saved the lives of Goldsmith's parents, Gunther and Rosalie, who played flute and viola in the Kulturbund, the Jewish orchestra supported by the Nazis in the 1930s for propaganda purposes. Martin, unaware of their story until late in his father's life, recounts the history of this orchestra alongside his parents' romance and escape.

Themes: Germany; Holocaust—survivors; love stories; musicians

Related Titles: In a contrasting memoir, cellist Anita Lasker-Wallfisch recounts her experiences playing in the Auschwitz camp orchestra, in *Inherit the Truth: A Memoir of Survival and the Holocaust.*

Hahn-Beer, Edith, and Susan Dworkin

The Nazi Officer's Wife: How One Jewish Woman Survived the Holocaust. **Rob Weisbach Books/ Morrow, 1999. 305p.** **YA** 📖

After deportation to the Viennese ghetto and several stints in labor camps, Edith Hahn became a "U-boat," passing as a non-Jew in wartime Germany, trying to find work and stay alive, until marriage to a willing but volatile Nazi officer provided her with precarious protection.

Themes: Holocaust—slave labor; marriage; Nazis

Related Titles: Another young woman who lived a harrowing existence in Germany as a Christian with false papers was Rose Zar, who describes her experiences in *In the Mouth of the Wolf.*

Helmreich, William B.

🏵 *Against All Odds: Holocaust Survivors and the Successful Lives They Made in America.* **Simon & Schuster, 1992. 348p.**

Over 140,000 Holocaust survivors came to the United States, rebuilding their lives in very different ways. For this study, Helmreich interviewed 170 survivors to provide a picture of those whose lives were uprooted and how they chose to go on, from the famous to the unknown. (Winner of the National Jewish Book Award.)

Themes: Holocaust—survivors; immigrants

Large, David Clay

And the World Closed Its Doors: The Story of One Family Abandoned to the Holocaust. **Basic Books, 2003. 278p.**

Max Schohl was a loyal German citizen, an officer decorated in World War I, but on Kristallnacht his house was ransacked by neighbors and employees. Max tried to obtain passage out of Germany through contacts with relatives and friends in the United States and elsewhere but no country would give him a visa. He died in Auschwitz; his wife and daughters, who were not Jewish, were sent to labor camps. Author Large based this account on records provided by Schohl's daughter, now living in the United States.

Themes: Germany; Holocaust—concentration camps

Related Titles: To learn more about the American policy toward the Jews in that era, readers may be interested in David S. Wyman's book *The Abandonment of the Jews: America and the Holocaust, 1941–1945*. Max Schohl's experience was not unique. In the 1930s, few countries were willing to accept Jews. Some did manage to escape to Latin America, although there were stringent quotas in most countries. Bolivia, an exception, took in 20,000 Jews, as recounted in Leo Spitzer's *Hotel Bolivia: The Culture of Memory in a Refuge of Nazism.*

Leitner, Isabella, and Irving A. Leitner

Isabella: From Auschwitz to Freedom. **Anchor Books, 1994. 233p.**

One of the earliest published accounts, stunning in its simplicity, of the experiences of a young Hungarian woman in Auschwitz and after, trying to pick up the pieces of her life. This edition combines two accounts: *Fragments of Isabella*, first published in 1978, and *Saving the Fragments*, published in 1985.

Themes: Holocaust—concentration camps; Holocaust—survivors

Related Titles: The author published a version of her experiences for middle and high school readers titled *The Big Lie: A True Story.*

Lewis, Mark, and Jacob Frank

Himmler's Jewish Tailor: The Story of Holocaust Survivor Jacob Frank. **Syracuse University Press, 2000. 299p**

This careful memoir, based on interviews with Jacob Frank, and preserving his "voice," tells the remarkable story of a young man who was put in charge of a tailoring operation that made Nazi uniforms, and was a survivor of four concentration camps, the sole member of his family alive at the end of the War.

Themes: Holocaust—concentration camps; Holocaust—slave labor; Poland

Orbach, Larry, and Vivian Orbach-Smith

Soaring Underground: A Young Fugitive's Life in Nazi Berlin. **Compass Press, 1996. 343p.**

Larry (then Lothar) Orbach came of age during the Holocaust, disguised as a Christian and living in Berlin after it was considered *Judenrein*, free of Jews. Such Jews were known as "divers" or "U-boats." In this perilous existence, Orbach was still able to find a ray of light in a moment of friendship, romance, or adventure until betrayal sent him to a concentration camp.

Themes: Germany; Holocaust—survivors

Pogany, Eugene L.

In My Brother's Image: Twin Brothers Separated by Faith After the Holocaust. **Viking, 2000. 327p.**

An unusual story of twins who were born Jewish but brought up Catholic; separated in the Holocaust, one became a priest and the other reclaimed his Jewish identity. Written by the psychologist son of the Jewish twin.

Themes: conversion to Christianity; conversion to Judaism; Holocaust—survivors; Jewish identity; Jewish–Christian relations; twins

Popescu, Petra

The Oasis: A Memoir of Love and Survival in a Concentration Camp. **St. Martin's, 2001. 355p.**

Blanka Dawidovich arranged to transfer illegally from Auschwitz to Dachau, where she believed she would have a better chance of surviving, but a slip of the tongue put her in danger. Another prisoner, Mirek, a Czech resistance fighter, saved her, and in this unlikely setting, a romance began.

Themes: Holocaust—concentration camps; Holocaust—resistance and rescue; love stories

Related Titles: Based on taped recollections and written by their novelist son-in-law, who himself defected from Ceausescu's Romania, this is a riveting story of love under the most harrowing conditions. Another memoir recording the horrific conditions at the camps is *Surviving Treblinka* by Samuel Willenberg, one of Treblinka's handful of survivors.

Rosenberg, Blanca

To Tell At Last: Survival Under False Identity: 1941–45. **University of Illinois Press, 1993. 178p.** **YA**

After the loss of her baby son and protective brother in the town of Kolomyja, Blanca Rosenberg was helped by generous non-Jewish friends to obtain papers that identified her as an Aryan and helped her survive the war. A gripping, detailed account of the Nazi stranglehold on the Jewish population of Poland and the remarkable courage required to survive.

Themes: Holocaust—ghettos; Poland

Rosenblum, Joe, with David Kohn

Defy the Darkness: A Tale of Courage in the Shadow of Mengele. **Praeger, 2001. 300p.**

Joe Rosenblum was fourteen when the Nazis invaded his hometown in eastern Poland, shattering his family's well-ordered and comfortable existence forever. Initially Joe was sheltered by a gentile farmer, then he joined the Russian partisans, but eventually he spent time in three of the most infamous concentration camps—Maidanek, Auschwitz-Birkenau, and Dachau—where his contacts with the notorious Dr. Mengele may have actually saved his life.

Themes: Holocaust—concentration camps; Mengele, Josef; partisans

Related Titles: Another memoir by a camp survivor is *The Dentist of Auschwitz* by Benjamin Jacobs. Jacobs's medical skills contributed to his survival in horrifying conditions.

Rosner, Bernat, and Frederic Tubach, with Sally Patterson Tubach

An Uncommon Friendship: From Opposite Sides of the Holocaust. **University of California Press, 2001. 271p.** 🔲 📖

The story of an unusual and healing friendship between Bernat Rosner, survivor of Auschwitz, and Frederic Tubach (who joined the Hitler Youth in 1944), when their paths crossed in California years later.

Themes: friendship; Germany; Holocaust—survivors; Hungary; Nazism

Schimmel, Betty, and Joyce Gabriel

To See You Again: A True Story of Love in a Time of War. **Dutton, 1999. 279p.**

Betty Markowitz and Richie Kovacs were lovestruck teenagers in Budapest when the Nazis separated them. Betty survived the horrors of Mauthausen and a death march; she found Richie's name on a list of the dead. She accepted an offer of marriage and moved to America, still mourning Richie's loss, only to find him alive years later.

Themes: Holocaust—survivors; Hungary; love stories; marriage

7

Skakun, Michael

On Burning Ground: A Son's Memoir. **St. Martin's, 1999. 235p.**

Skakun's father Joseph, a Talmud student before the war, took the terrifying route of hiding in plain sight as a Christian, a Muslim, and finally as a member of the Nazi SS. Skakun examines the extraordinary efforts at deception that kept his father alive, and the costs of such a solitary, intense existence.

Themes: fathers and sons; Holocaust—survivors; Nazis; Poland

Related Titles: A memoir of a Jewish teenager who survived the war through membership in the Hitler Youth is Solomon Perel's *Europa, Europa: A Memoir of World War II.*

Spiegelman, Art

 Maus: A Survivor's Tale, I: My Father Bleeds History. **Pantheon Books, 1986. 159p.**
Maus: A Survivor's Tale, II: And Here My Troubles Began. **Pantheon Books, 1991. 135p.**

Art Spiegelman, comic book artist and son of Holocaust survivors, records his father Vladek's story of how he and his wife were swept up into the Holocaust, while Art navigates a trying relationship with his father in the present, shadowed by the horror of Vladek's past. The visual representation of Vladek's plight, with the Jews as mice and the Nazis as cats, adds a unique intensity. (Winner of the Pulitzer Prize.)

Themes: children of Holocaust survivors; fathers and sons; graphic novels; Holocaust—concentration camps; Poland

Szpilman, Wladyslaw

The Pianist: The Extraordinary True Story of One Man's Survival in Warsaw, 1939–1945, with Extracts from the Diary of Wilm Hosenfeld. **Picador USA, 1999. 221p.**

Wladyslaw Szpilman was a well-known pianist for Polish Radio when he and his family were forced out of their home into the Warsaw Ghetto. Given a chance to avoid transport to a camp, he barely survived the war by hiding out in empty apartments, helped by a few Poles and Germans, and wracked by fear and guilt. Written just after the war, this is a harrowing tale of desperation and the sustaining power of music. Translated by Anthea Bell. (The book was made into a film of the same name, directed by Roman Polanski.)

Themes: Holocaust—survivors; pianists; Poland; Warsaw Ghetto

Wiesel, Elie

All Rivers Run to the Sea. **Alfred A. Knopf, 1995. 432p.**

Wiesel describes his boyhood in the mountain town of Sighet, Hungary, where he was a serious student of Talmud and Kabbalah; the upheaval of World War II when he was transported to Auschwitz; and the years after the war when he studied in France and became a journalist. He concludes with his experiences as a journalist in Israel and the importance of writing about events that are essentially impossible to explain.

Themes: Holocaust—concentration camps; Holocaust—survivors; Hungary; journalists

Related Titles: The second volume of Wiesel's autobiography is *And the Sea Is Never Full.*

Witness: Voices from the Holocaust. **Edited by Joshua M. Green and Shiva Kumar. The Free Press, 2000. 270p.** `YA`

Powerful first person accounts, taken from the Yale University Fortunoff Archive for Holocaust Testimonies, that put a very human face on the terrifying and dehumanizing experiences of camp survivors, resistance fighters, non-Jews, and

American POWs. (The Web site of the Yale Fortunoff Archive is www.library.yale.edu/testimonies.)

Themes: Holocaust—concentration camps; Holocaust—resistance and rescue; Holocaust—survivors

Related Titles: This anthology served as the companion to a PBS documentary of the same name that aired in 2001. An anthology of survivors' memoirs suitable for young adults is *Bearing Witness: Stories of the Holocaust,* selected by Hazel Rochman and Darlene Z. McCampbell.

The Next Generation

Many survivors came to this country desperate to start over, but they were haunted by profound feelings of loss, guilt, responsibility, and sadness. Psychologically changed by their experiences, they had difficulties living normal lives. Their children's lives couldn't help but be affected. As Melvin Jules Bukiet puts it,

> Of course, some survivors spoke incessantly of the Holocaust while others never mentioned it. Of those who didn't speak, some were traumatized while others hoped to protect their offspring from knowledge of the tree of evil . . . Other kids' parents didn't have numbers on their arms. Other kids' parents didn't talk about massacres as easily as baseball. Other kids' parents had parents.[2]

The memoirs in this section reveal how survivors coped with their past experiences and memories, and how the children and grandchildren understood their parents' and grandparents' lives. In several emotional accounts, survivors return with their descendants to the places where they lived before the war. The first writer to seek out the stories of survivors' children was Helen Epstein, who writes about the people she interviewed in *Children of the Holocaust: Conversations with Sons and Daughters of Survivors.* Fern Shumer Chapman writes in *Motherland: Beyond the Holocaust: A Daughter's Journey to Reclaim the Past* about traveling to Germany with her mother, who left home as a twelve-year-old, never to see her family again. For some people, the memories were so terrible that a new life in America meant abandoning everything about their prior lives, even Judaism. *After Long Silence* by Helen Fremont records how Helen and her sister, brought up as Catholics in the Midwest, unearthed and reclaimed their Judaism, coming to terms with their parents' decisions.

Berger, Joseph
Displaced Persons: Growing Up American After the Holocaust. Scribner, 2001. 347p. YA

Berger takes as his theme the experience of surviving the Holocaust and making a new life in America. His parents lived with memories of terror while they navigated the difficult journey of immigrants. For Berger and his brother, as they worked to become assimilated into American culture, there was always the pull of their parents' painful memories making their lives bittersweet.

Themes: 1950s; 1940s; parents and children; refugees

Chapman, Fern Shumer

Motherland: Beyond the Holocaust: A Daughter's Journey to Reclaim the Past. Viking, 2000. 190p. YA 📖

In 1938, Edith Westerfeld's parents sent her away from her home in a small German town to relatives in Chicago; she never saw her family again. After fifty-two years, she agreed to go back to Stockstadt with her pregnant daughter Fern, to unearth and confront the past that was taken from them both.

Themes: Germany; Holocaust—survivors; Jewish identity; mothers and daughters

Related Titles: In the same vein, readers may be interested in *Bashert: A Granddaughter's Holocaust Quest* by Andrea Simon.

Epstein, Helen

🏵 *Children of the Holocaust: Conversations with Sons and Daughters of Survivors.* 1979; reprint, Penguin Books, 1988. 355p.

Epstein was the first to write about the inner lives, childhoods, and family relationships of the children of survivors. The child of survivors herself, she understood full well the irrational fears and demons experienced by her generation, "possessed by a history they had never lived." (An ALA Notable Book.)

Themes: family relationships; Holocaust—survivors

Where She Came From: A Daughter's Search for Her Mother's History. Little, Brown, 1997. 322p.

Epstein combines family and social history in this chronicle of her Czech mother, grandmother, and great-grandmother, all assimilated Jews who endured persecution from the mid-nineteenth century though the Holocaust, sparked by her need to understand her mother's history. A well-researched memoir with the appeal of historical fiction.

Themes: businesswomen; grandmothers; Holocaust—survivors; mothers and daughters

Fremont, Helen

After Long Silence. Delacorte, 1999. 319p. YA 📖

Helen Fremont's parents were Polish Jews who survived the horrors of the war, but in the process obliterated their memories and their Judaism, raising their children as Catholics in a small Midwestern city. It was not until adulthood that Helen uncovered the truth of her family's heritage and, with her sister, researched and finally understood "the hole that lay like an enormous crater" at the center of her family's life. Gracefully and compellingly written, this memoir combines past and present in a beautiful and often terrifying narrative.

Themes: conversion to Christianity; family relationships; Holocaust—survivors; Poland

Rose, Daniel Asa

Hiding Places: A Father and Son Retrace Their Family's Escape from the Holocaust. **Simon & Schuster, 2000. 380p.** 📖

Journalist Rose takes his two young sons to Europe to retrace the route taken by his family as they fled the Nazis through France and Belgium. The trip is a chance for father and sons to understand the past for the sake of future generations.

Themes: children of Holocaust survivors; fathers and sons; Jewish identity

Related Titles: Rose's relationship with his young sons is an important part of this story. Another account of a close father–son relationship is *The Way Home: Scenes from a Season, Lessons from a Lifetime* by Henry Dunow, annotated in the "Childhood and Family" section of chapter 8.

Salamon, Julie

The Net of Dreams: A Family's Search for a Rightful Place. **Random House, 1996. 336p.** **YA**

Julie Salamon returned to Czechoslovakia and Poland with her mother in an effort to understand how her parents' personalities and particular experiences during the Holocaust affected their lives as refugees in the United States and shaped her own childhood in a small Ohio town.

Themes: doctors; Holocaust—concentration camps; Holocaust—survivors; parents and children

Second Generation Voices: Reflections by Children of Holocaust Survivors and Perpetrators. **Edited by Alan L. Berger and Naomi Berger. Syracuse University Press, 2001. 378p.** 📖

An unusual collection that juxtaposes the stories of children of Holocaust survivors with accounts contributed by Germans who grew up after World War II. Among the contributors, Melvin Jules Bukiet writes about a trip to Auschwitz with his father, in "Memory Macht Frei"; Anna Rosmus, whose story is told in the film *The Nasty Girl*, writes about the repercussions of her search for Nazis in her hometown of Passau.

Themes: children of Holocaust survivors; children of Nazis

Related Titles: Young adults may be interested in Sabine Reichel's *What Did You Do in the War Daddy?* written by a German woman now living in the United States, trying to come to terms with her family's Nazi past.

Sources for Additional Information About the Holocaust

Popular and scholarly titles on the Holocaust continue to appear every publishing season. This list is a sample of book and online sources in a range of subject areas: general Holocaust history, Eastern European history, bibliographies of literature, survivor testimonies, and political and social analyses.

Print Resources

Abella, Irving, and Harold Troper. *None Is Too Many: Canada and the Jews of Europe, 1933–1948*. Toronto: Key Porter, 2000.

Bauer, Yehuda. *A History of the Holocaust*. Rev. ed. Danbury, CT: Franklin Watts, 2001.

Dawidowicz, Lucy S. *The War Against the Jews 1933–1945*. New York: Holt, Rinehart & Winston, 1975.

Dwórk, Deborah, and Robert Jan van Pelt. *Holocaust: A History*. New York: W. W. Norton, 2002.

Eliach, Yaffa. *There Once Was a World: A Nine-hundred-year Chronicle of the Shtetl of Eishyshok*. Boston: Little, Brown, 1998.

Fernekes, William R. *The Oryx Holocaust Sourcebook*. Westport, CT: Oryx Press, 2002.

Flanzbaum, Hilene, ed. *The Americanization of the Holocaust*. Baltimore: Johns Hopkins University Press, 1999.

Gilbert, Martin. *The Holocaust: A History of the Jews of Europe During the Second World War*. New York: Holt, Rinehart & Winston, 1985.

Goldhagen, Daniel Jonah. *Hitler's Willing Executioners: Ordinary Germans and the Holocaust*. New York: Alfred A. Knopf, 1996.

Gross, Jan. *Neighbors: The Destruction of the Jewish Community in Jedwabne, Poland*. Princeton, NJ: Princeton University Press, 2001.

Hilberg, Raoul. *Perpetrators, Victims, Bystanders: The Jewish Catastrophe, 1933–1945*. New York: Aaron Asher Books, 1992.

Hoffman, Eva. *Shtetl: The Life and Death of a Small Town and the World of Polish Jews*. Boston: Houghton Mifflin, 1997.

Kremer, S. Lillian. *Holocaust Literature: An Encyclopedia of Writers and Their Work*. 2v. New York: Routledge, 2002.

Langer, Lawrence. *Holocaust Testimonies: The Ruins of Memory*. New Haven, CT: Yale University Press, 1991.

Mintz, Alan. *Popular Culture and the Shaping of Holocaust Memory in America*. Seattle: University of Washington Press, 2001.

Niewyk, Donald, and Francis Nicosia, eds. *The Columbia Guide to the Holocaust*. New York: Columbia University Press, 2000.

Patterson, David, and others, eds. *Encyclopedia of Holocaust Literature*. Westport, CT: Oryx Press, 2002.

Rogasky, Barbara. *Smoke and Ashes: The Story of the Holocaust*. Rev. and expanded ed. New York: Holiday House, 2002.
A history of the Holocaust that is suitable for young adults.

Rosen, Philip, and Nina Apfelbaum. *Bearing Witness: A Resource Guide to Literature, Poetry, Art, Music, and Videos by Holocaust Victims and Survivors*. Westport, CT: Greenwood Press, 2002.
Provides information about authors and their works and recommends age appropriateness.

Sullivan, Edward T. *The Holocaust in Literature for Youth: A Guide and Reference Book*. Lanham, MD: Scarecrow Press, 1999.
Lists fiction, nonfiction, poetry, and plays suitable for elementary through high school students and includes information for teachers.

Vishniac, Roman. *A Vanished World*. New York: Farrar, Straus & Giroux. 1991.
These photographs, taken during the 1930s in Eastern Europe and smuggled out of Europe, preserve a record of the cities and towns destroyed by the Holocaust.

Online Resources

Fortunoff Video Archive for Holocaust Testimonies: library.yale.edu/testimonies
Provides information about this collection of over 3,700 videotaped interviews with witnesses and survivors.

Survivors of the Shoah Visual History Foundation: vhf.org
Founded by Steven Spielberg after the filming of *Schindler's List*. The site provides information about the organization's efforts to create an archive of videotaped interviews with Holocaust survivors around the world.

U.S. Holocaust Memorial Museum: www.ushmm.org
The official site of the Washington, D.C., museum.

Yad Vashem: ad-vashem.org.il
The museum in Israel devoted to Holocaust memory.

Notes

1. Ruth Angress, "Afterword," in Ilona Karmel, *An Estate of Memory* (New York: The Feminist Press, 1986), 445.

2. Melvin Jules Bukiet, ed. *Nothing Makes You Free: Writings by Descendants of Jewish Holocaust Survivors*, (New York: W. W. Norton, 2002), 13–14.

Chapter 8

Biography and Autobiography

Actually, the true story of a person's life can never be written. It is beyond the power of literature. The full tale of any life would be both utterly boring and utterly unbelievable.—Isaac Bashevis Singer

Since the best way to tell why something happened is to tell what happened, I have concentrated here on the 'what.' In doing so, I have been mindful of the speed with which facts, even those closely and directly observed, change under the pressures of self-interest and uncertain memory, turning first into a mixture of fact and fiction, then into myth, and finally—if we're lucky—into a residual truth that may say something more than what originally passed for reality.—Leonard Garment

Why is autobiography the most popular form of fiction for modern readers?—Jill Ker Conway

Introduction

Published Jewish American autobiography begins with the great wave of immigration in the late 1800s. Although there were Sephardic and German Jews in the United States before that time, their lives are recorded primarily through letters and public documents. The Eastern European Jews who flooded into the United States between 1880 and 1924 are the ones who set down their experiences in autobiographies and novels. These are the stories that have by and large come to stand for the Jewish immigrant experience. Sophie Trupin, in her autobiography *Dakota Diaspora,* wrote that "each was a Moses in his own right, leading his people out of the land of bondage—out of Czarist Russia, out of anti-Semitic Poland, out of Roumania and Galicia."[1] Many of the children of these immigrants grew up hearing stories about the persecutions their parents suffered or escaped; the difficult voyage across the Atlantic; the confusing experience of being a greenhorn; and how relatives, luck, and ambition helped them get started. The importance of hard work and the value of education were impressed upon the next generation. Leonard Garment, who grew up in Brownsville,

Brooklyn, a neighborhood that was primarily Jewish for many years, describes going off to a high school

> filled with hundreds of first-generation Jews, bright, ambitious, intensely competitive kids who were reminded each morning over breakfast of their obligation to justify the sacrifices of their parents. Along with the cornflakes came the constant assurance that the world was ours to conquer; wide-eyed with excitement, we set out to do just that.[2]

Children who accepted the challenge found that the price of success, American style, often required abandoning religious traditions their parents had left the Old World hoping to preserve. Many authors in this chapter write about conflict with their parents as teenagers, particularly about difficult relationships with fathers, in the section called "Childhood and Family." The section called "Spiritual Autobiographies" chronicles the return of second- and third-generation children to the religion of their parents and grandparents, sometimes in its most devout form.

Although this guide is primarily concerned with fiction, biography and autobiography are included because they provide an important window into the experiences of Jewish Americans from another point of view. Biographical works are often the raw material of fiction. And reading stories about people's lives—whether fiction or nonfiction—is very satisfying for many readers. Some portion of the nonfiction checked out of libraries and purchased from bookstores is read for informational purposes. But a great deal of nonfiction is read for the same reasons and pleasures that we read fiction—entertainment, enlightenment, insight and understanding, or to experience drama, comedy and tragedy. The biographies and autobiographies here are filled with those qualities; all readers will enjoy them.

Scope

All the annotated autobiographies and biographies in this chapter are about people whose lives show evidence of Jewish values, observance, or concern for the Jewish community. Calvin Trillin, in his autobiography *Messages from My Father*, writes about how his father always encouraged him to be a *mensch*, a long-cherished concept of good behavior in the Jewish community.[3] Several authors cite their Jewish education as the source of their commitment to social activism. Late in life Kirk Douglas found meaning in study, ritual, and support of Israel; he writes about his experiences in *Climbing the Mountain*. Vanessa Ochs, in her autobiography *Words on Fire*, writes about feeling compelled to leave her home in New York and study Torah in Jerusalem. Some people grew up in assimilated homes, with only a cultural attachment to Judaism, but turned back to Judaism later in life. Leonard Garment writes of how his Jewish identity "adhered to me like a faded but indelible birthmark that would later become more visible."[4]

For many, that search for reconnection became urgent, a path to healing and inner peace. Emily Benedek's *Through the Unknown, Remembered Gate* and David Klinghoffer's *The Lord Will Gather Me In* are examples of this kind of spiritual autobiography. There are also examples of people whose families hid or repudiated their Jewishness: Stephen Dubner's *Turbulent Souls,* for example. Books that are gossipy or whose purpose is to diminish their subject are not included.

The "Related Titles" in this chapter include many references to other nonfiction titles. Some authors have written biographies of other Jewish figures, or relevant historical works. Other titles expand the scope of the chapter by providing another point of view about the same era. In the entry for André Aciman's *Out of Egypt*, there is a recommendation to Claudia Roden's Middle Eastern cookbook, which includes wonderful vignettes from her own Egyptian Jewish childhood. Some recommended titles are more history than biography. The entry for Harriet Lane Levy's book *920 O'Farrell Street*, about Jewish life in San Francisco in the early twentieth century, includes a reference to the book *How We Lived* by Kenneth Libo, which documents the lives of the pioneer Jews who settled in the West.

Organization of the Chapter

Titles have been grouped into four broad categories to facilitate readers' advisory work. Introductory text defines the scope of the category. Themes listed with each entry, and additional subject headings that appear only in the index, will help readers find books about particular places, times, occupations, and themes.

Collected Biography: books that contain biographical information about several people.

Childhood and Family: primarily autobiographies covering one person's life through childhood, adolescence and into early adulthood.

Public Lives: biographies and autobiographies of well-known people that focus on their adult lives.

Spiritual Autobiographies: books with a focus on the role of religion in the subject's life.

Appeal of the Genre/Advising the Reader

Biography and autobiography fashion lives into stories, conferring the organizing power of hindsight on events that seemed random when they occurred, or occurred at a time, like childhood, when perspective was not possible. Often, when we revisit memories we become aware of motives and consequences, causes and connections that were missed. We hope to be able to look back at the narrative of our own lives and see purpose, structure, and meaning. Reading biographies provides us with the reassurance that our lives have a narrative thread.

The appeal of autobiography and biography is similar to the appeal of fiction because of this narrative thread. Autobiography in particular lends itself to comparison with fiction. Autobiography can be consciously shaped like a novel, with a beginning, full of exposition and character development; a middle, often with climactic events; and an ending that ties up what came before and provides some resolution or closure. In fiction, the writer has used memory, experience, imagination, and all the tools of creative writing. The same elements can be found in autobiographies.

Biography is one of the most popular nonfiction genres in libraries. Readers often specifically comment that they love reading biographies. Most nonfiction read for enjoyment emphasizes personal experiences. Cookbooks are filled with anecdotes about the cook, popular histories focus on the role of the individual, self-help books reveal the struggles of the author, and true crime is perennially popular.

An interesting recent trend is the blurring of the lines between fiction and autobiography. A number of recent books marketed as novels have subtitles that sound like nonfiction, like Nora Eisenberg's *The War at Home: A Memoir-Novel*. Revelations of writers who admit to changing some facts of their autobiographies, for example, making up conversations or combining characters for effect, have left readers with an unsettled feeling, and some critics angry. The popularity of "reality" shows on television, in which viewers are purportedly watching people's lives in real time, further complicates the traditional separation between fiction and nonfiction. These developments require the readers' advisor to understand the close relationship between autobiography and fiction.

Even though Library of Congress practice is to catalog most biographies in a subject area, many libraries continue to maintain a separate biography section, since librarians know that readers want to browse for "a good biography." Students often ask for biographies or autobiographies for school reports. What is the appeal of this genre? It may be helpful to think about the relationship between biography, autobiography, and fiction by using Joyce Saricks's appeal characteristics as a guide. General readers' advisory information is provided in chapter 9; some information specifically for advising readers on this genre focusing on the appeal characteristics is provided below.

If readers enjoy an author's novels, they may enjoy the author's autobiography. Max Apple, Dani Shapiro, Isaac Bashevis Singer, Joseph Heller, and Philip Roth have all written autobiographies that are annotated in this chapter. If readers enjoy novels with memorable characters, biographical works can introduce them to people they would adore having lunch with, or would be reluctant to meet even in an elevator. Readers who enjoy compelling plots can find accounts in this chapter filled with adventure and heartbreak. Those who relish interesting settings will find stories that take them far from their known world or on a nostalgic trip to the old neighborhood. And when it comes to language, there are autobiographies and biographies that are written so that the writer's voice is unforgettable.

Character

Some readers want to identify with, or simply explore, the subject of a biography or autobiography. Reading about someone else's life may encourage, inspire, or give us confidence to embark on some course of action, or reinforce life decisions already made. Many of the autobiographies in this chapter offer a chance to identify and relate to the author's experiences. Kate Simon, in *Bronx Primitive*, writes about the childhood experiences that prepared her to strike out on her own. Sherwin Nuland examines the aftereffects of a difficult relationship with his father in *Lost in America*. Max Apple's loving relationship with his grandfather Rocky, described in *Roommates*, was an anchor for him as a boy and young adult. Readers of these memoirs recognize themselves in the writers' struggles to achieve independence and self-knowledge.

Novels in which character is paramount, like *Swimming toward the Ocean* by Carole L. Glickfeld, *Paradise Park* by Allegra Goodman, or *Consent* by Ben Schrank, may interest these readers. Coming-of-age novels would also be appropriate suggestions.

Story

Some readers are looking for a good story when they read biographical works. They enjoy escaping into another time period, part of the world, or style of life. Stella Suberman's *The Jew Store*, about her family's experiences in a small town in Tennessee in the 1930s, is a good story well told and a fascinating look at one family's history. The story that Stephen Dubner tells in *Turbulent Souls* is a page-turner that examines religious choices his parents made and the consequences that rippled through their lives. Anne Roiphe's autobiography about her childhood, *1185 Park Avenue,* is as riveting as any novel about a dysfunctional family.

These readers may also be interested in autobiographies and memoirs of well-known people that describe how they achieved success. Stories like this can be found in Burton Bernstein's *Family Matters: Sam, Jenny and the Kids*, *Rewrites* by Neil Simon, or *Life So Far* by Betty Friedan. Novels with a strong narrative drive, tied to actual events, like Philip Roth's novels about American society in the last half of the twentieth century, *I Married a Communist*, *American Pastoral*, and *The Human Stain,* may be appropriate recommendations. Other choices might be Myla Goldberg's *The Bee Season* or Jay Neugeboren's *The Stolen Jew*. Realistic fiction with a historical setting may appeal to these readers, like Zelda Popkin's *Quiet Street*, Joanne Greenberg's *The King's Persons,* or Edna Ferber's *Fanny Herself.*

Language

Readers to whom language is important may be interested in books with varying subjects and settings. It is not the content or subject of the book that is important, but the way the language is used. Readers may describe the language they enjoy as experimental, haunting, lyrical, colloquial, poetic, evocative, etc. Although fiction is usually where we look for interesting use of language, there are many autobiographies that can be suggested for this characteristic. Calvin Trillin's distinctive wry tone, so hilarious in his food essays, is moderated only slightly in his memoir *Messages from My Father*. Unadorned, direct language in the telling of the remarkable story of survival on the plains of North Dakota as a mail-order bride distinguishes *Rachel Calof's Story*. Marjorie Agosín uses a very literary and haunting style in her biography of her father, *Always from Somewhere Else*. Readers who enjoyed these books may be referred to novels like Elizabeth Rosner's *The Speed of Light*, Jonathan Safran Foer's *Everything Is Illuminated,* or Arthur Miller's *Focus*.

Setting

Biographies and autobiographies may be read by history buffs or armchair travelers to expand their knowledge about a particular era or geographic locale. History is populated by great personalities, but reading about ordinary lives can enrich our understanding of a time. Readers may enjoy the perspective of a person involved in events that they too shared, or an analysis that puts those events in perspective.

Reading about a particular person in another era allows us to think about a life we might have lived. By examining the choices other people made, the relationships, experiences, and social forces that shaped and formed them, biography and autobiography give us perspective on our own lives. They may also help us understand our parents' or grandparents' lives: how their point of view was shaped by their times, the reasons why they lived out their lives in certain ways. Ilan Stavans's memoir *On Borrowed Words: A Memoir of Language* describes the close-knit Mexican Jewish community of Stavans's childhood and the effect it had on his sense of identity. In *Out of Egypt*, Andre Aciman describes his unusual upbringing in Cairo during a time of political upheaval for the Jewish community there. Joseph Heller's detailed and loving description of his childhood in the Coney Island neighborhood of Brooklyn in the 1930s, in his memoir *Now and Then*, transports the reader back to that place and time. Fiction with a strong sense of place and time, like Gloria Goldreich's *West to Eden, Brooklyn Boy* by Alan Lelchuk, *Welcome to Heavenly Heights* by Risa Miller, or *Moonlight on the Avenue of Faith* by Gina Nahai, would be appropriate for these readers.

Biographies and Autobiographies

Collected Biography

The books in this section combine biography with social history. There is often a fine line between collected biography and history of an era; these titles were chosen because they focus on personalities rather than events. Some histories have been listed in the "Sources of Further Information" section for those readers who want to go further.

Daughters of Kings: Growing Up as a Jewish Woman in America. **Edited by Leslie Brody. Faber & Faber, 1997. 230p.** YA 📖

> In thirteen personal essays about being Jewish today, women discuss anti-Semitism, the legacy of the Holocaust, and assimilation. Authors include Rachel Kadish, Barbara Grossman, and Paula Gutlove.
>
> **Themes:** Jewish identity; women—literary collections; women's lives
>
> **Related Titles:** Readers may also enjoy *The Journey Home: Jewish Women and the American Century* by Joyce Antler, which combines social history with profiles of prominent Jewish women. *Her Face in the Mirror*, edited by Faye Moskowitz, collects essays, stories, and poems about the relationship between mothers and daughters. An excellent recent history of Jewish women in America can be found in *Her Works Praise Her—A History of Jewish Women in America from Colonial Times to the Present* by Hasia Diner and Beryl Lieff Benderly.

Found Tribe: Jewish Coming Out Stories. **Edited by Lawrence Schimel. Sherman Asher Publishing, 2002. 212p.**

> A collection of very personal essays by Jewish men about their experiences of coming out as gays in the Jewish community. Authors include David Bergman, Daniel M. Jaffe, Julian Padilla, Lev Raphael, and Rabbi Steve Greenfield.
>
> **Themes:** gays/lesbians/bisexuals; Jewish identity; men's lives
>
> **Related Titles:** Schimel edited an earlier collection of fiction and nonfiction by Jewish gays, *Kosher Meat*. Readers should be aware that these collections include

explicit sexual scenes. Readers may also be interested in *Queer Jews*, a collection of essays edited by David Schneer and Caryn Aviv.

Growing up Jewish: An Anthology. **Edited by Jay David. Morrow, 1996. 249p.**

A varied collection of short stories, essays, and autobiographical excerpts from well-known and not-so-well-known writers and public figures, exploring the universal themes of childhood and adolescence as well as issues particular to the Jewish community, in late nineteenth- and early twentieth-century America. Authors include Edna Ferber, Gertrude Berg, Philip Roth, Paul Cowan, Chaim Potok, and Michael Chabon.

Themes: childhood; Jewish identity; teenagers

Related Titles: Another oral history readers may enjoy is *Growing Up Jewish in America* by Myrna Katz Frommer and Harvey Frommer. Faye Moskowitz edited a collection of essays, stories, and poems on the mother–daughter relationship, *Her Face in the Mirror: Jewish Women on Mothers and Daughters.*

Nice Jewish Girls: A Lesbian Anthology. **Rev. ed. Edited by Evelyn Torton Beck. Beacon Press, 1989. 333p.**

This pioneering fiction and nonfiction anthology, now in its third edition, spans a range of emotions and subjects: invisibility in the Jewish and lesbian communities, establishing a Jewish identity, anti-Semitism, relationships between mothers and daughters, and the lesbian community in Israel.

Themes: essays; feminists; gays/lesbians/bisexuals; short stories; women's lives

Nice Jewish Girls: Growing Up in America. **Edited by Marlene Adler Marks. Plume, 1996. 292p.**

A collection of fiction, essays, and poetry on growing up Jewish in America from the feminine point of view by forty well-known authors, including Allegra Goodman, Erica Jong, Letty Cottin Pogrebin, and Vivian Gornick.

Themes: essays; poetry; short stories; women's lives

Related Titles: Readers may also enjoy *A Spiritual Life: A Jewish Feminist Journey*, a collection of poetry, prose, and meditations from playwright and poet Merle Feld.

Twice Blessed: On Being Lesbian, Gay, and Jewish, Edited by Christie Balka and Andy Rose. **Beacon Press, 1989. 305p.**

A groundbreaking anthology when it was issued, this collection reflects a range of life stories of gay and lesbian Jews trying to establish their identity within the Jewish community, struggling to live openly and with the acceptance of their families and communities. It includes information for Jewish educators about homosexuality and homophobia.

Themes: gays/lesbians/bisexuals; Jewish identity

Writing Our Lives: Autobiographies of American Jews, 1890–1990. **Edited by Steven J. Rubin. Jewish Publication Society, 1991. 347p.**

The twenty-eight autobiographies excerpted in this collection allow the reader a glimpse of the major themes and issues of Jewish American life. In the first section, "Views of the Promised Land: The Early Years," the writers are mainly immigrants. In their memoirs we see the tensions over the loss of one culture and the struggles to adjust to a new one. In the second section, "The Ghetto and Beyond: The First Generation," writers like Meyer Levin and Faye Moskowitz, who were born in the United States, explore the problems that come with assimilation and loss of connection to their parents' culture. The final section, "Contemporary Writers," is more diverse, consisting of writers who were born here or came following the Holocaust, like Norman Podhoretz, Vivian Gornick, and Eva Hoffman. The acceptance of Jews into mainstream American society allows these writers to maintain and even strengthen their ties to the Jewish community.

Themes: assimilation; immigrants; Jewish identity

Related Titles: For another collection of first person accounts, readers may enjoy *How We Lived: A Documentary History of Immigrant Jews in America, 1880–1930* by Kenneth Libo and Irving Howe. They have put together photographs and primary source material for a picture of early immigrant life, mainly from New York's Lower East Side.

Birmingham, Stephen

The three books annotated below are popular accounts of Jewish immigrant life in the United States, filled with personalities and details of social history.

"Our Crowd": The Great Jewish Families of New York. **Harper & Row, 1967. 404p.** `YA`

An entertaining history of the families that became the German-Jewish aristocracy of New York in the nineteenth century and into the twentieth. The Seligmans, Belmonts, Loebs, Lewisohns, and others came from Germany to make their fortunes in business.

Themes: bankers; businessmen; immigrants

Related Titles: Birmingham's novel set within the wealthy German-Jewish social world, *The Auerbach Will*, is annotated in the "Modern Period, United States and Canada" section of chapter 3. For a more in-depth treatment of some of the families profiled in this book, see *The Warburgs: The Twentieth-Century Odyssey of a Remarkable Jewish Family* by Ron Chernow or *The Guggenheims (1848–1988); an American Epic* by John H. Davis.

"The Rest of Us": The Rise of America's Eastern European Jews. **Little, Brown, 1984. 392p.**

Between 1881 and 1915, thousands of Eastern European Jews sailed into New York harbor yearly in an effort to escape poverty and persecution in czarist Russia. Most came only with what they could carry, and with little or no knowledge of English. This is a portrait of the successes they had, focusing on some of the best known: Louis B. Mayer, Helena Rubinstein, David Sarnoff, Irving Berlin, and others.

Themes: assimilation; Eastern European Jews; immigrants

Related Titles: For more information on Jews who were successful in the motion picture industry, try Neal Gabler's *An Empire of Their Own: How the Jews Invented Hollywood*, annotated in this chapter. *A Summer World: The Attempt to Build a Jewish Eden in the Catskills from the Days of the Ghetto to the Rise and Decline of the Borscht Belt* by Stefan Kanfer describes the vacation world built by Eastern European Jews in New York State. Readers may enjoy some of the novels about the experiences of immigrants in the business world: *Max* by Howard Fast and *West to Eden* by Gloria Goldreich, both annotated in the "Modern Period, United States and Canada" section of chapter 3.

The Grandees: America's Sephardic Elite. **Harper & Row, 1971. 318p.**

An informal history of the Sephardic families who came to the United States, starting in 1654 with the boatload of twenty-three who wrested permission from the Dutch West India Company to settle in New Amsterdam. The ancestors of the Nathans, de Solas, Peixottos, and Mendeses, among others, began a long and illustrious history intertwined with the colony and new republic. Birmingham describes the nature of the Sephardic community, concentrating on their successes, personalities, modesty, and contributions.

Themes: immigrants; New York City; Sephardim

Related Titles: Another group of Sephardim arrived during the mass migrations of Jews in the late nineteenth and early twentieth centuries, although in much smaller numbers than Ashkenazi Jews. Readers who are interested in learning more about the Sephardic community in America may enjoy Marc Angel's *La America: The Sephardic Experience in the United States.*

Cohen, Rich

Tough Jews: Fathers, Sons, and Gangster Dreams. **Simon & Schuster, 1998. 271p.**

Rich Cohen learned about Jewish gangsters in Brooklyn in the 1920s and 1930s from his father. Some were well known, like "Bugsy" Siegel, Meyer Lansky, Louis Lepke, and some were the lower level thugs who worked for them. Cohen concentrates on these street toughs and their exploits, and the way they broke out of the Jewish stereotypes of their era.

Themes: Brooklyn, N.Y.; crime and criminals; gangsters

Related Titles: Cohen has also written *The Avengers: A Jewish War Story*, about a group of survivors of the Vilna Ghetto who became resistance fighters during the Holocaust. Other books about Jewish gangsters are *But—He Was Good to His Mother* by Robert Rockaway, *Little Man: Meyer Lansky and the Gangster Life* by Robert Lacey, and *The Big Bankroll: The Life and Times of Arnold Rothstein* by Leo Katcher. Readers may also enjoy the autobiographical novel *An Impossible Life: A Bobeh*

Myseh by David Black, for its look at a shady family history. It is annotated in the "Story" section of chapter 6.

Epstein, Lawrence J.

The Haunted Smile: The Story of Jewish Comedians in America. **Public Affairs, 2001. 384p.**

A history of Jewish comedy, from vaudeville to Seinfeld, and how it has affected and interacted with American popular culture. Sid Caesar, Soupy Sales, Buddy Hackett, and Al Franken are some of the more than seventy comedians included. (More information can be found at the Web site www.hauntedsmile.com.)

Themes: actors and acting; comedians; Hollywood

Gabler, Neal

An Empire of Their Own: How the Jews Invented Hollywood. **Crown, 1988. 502p.** `YA`

Many of the early Hollywood studio heads, producers, writers, talent agents, and lawyers were Jewish, among them Fox, Mayer, Goldwyn, and the Warners. Their films shaped the motion picture industry and our views of ourselves.

Themes: motion picture industry

Related Titles: For another side to the Hollywood success story, the biography *A Very Dangerous Citizen: Abraham Lincoln Polonsky and the Hollywood Left* by Paul Buhle and Dave Wagner tells the story of one of the Jewish screenwriters blacklisted in the 1950s when he refused to give names to the House Un-American Activities Committee. Readers may enjoy Budd Schulberg's classic Hollywood novel *What Makes Sammy Run?* annotated in the "Character" section of chapter 6.

Harris, Leon A.

Merchant Princes: An Intimate History of Jewish Families Who Built Great Department Stores. **Harper & Row, 1982. 411p.** `YA`

Not a business history, but a glimpse of the personal lives of the Gimbels, Filenes, Magnins, Strauses, and others who built retail empires. Many started as peddlers, but with success came power and influence in their communities and the ability to shape cultural institutions with their philanthropy.

Themes: department stores; family relationships; immigrants; merchants

Related Titles: For another look into the life of a Jewish merchant family, readers may enjoy *The Jew Store* by Stella Suberman, about a family-owned dry goods store in a small town in Tennessee, annotated in this chapter in the "Childhood and Family" section. A fictional version of a department store success story can be found in Gloria Goldreich's *West to Eden*, annotated in the "Modern Period, United States and Canada" section of chapter 3.

Kessel, Barbara

Suddenly Jewish: Jews Raised as Gentiles Discover Their Jewish Roots. **Brandeis University Press, 2000. 130p.** `YA`

> Kessel interviewed people who grew up unaware of their Jewish heritage. Some were hidden with Gentile families during the Holocaust; others were descendants of those who were secret Jews during the Spanish Inquisition.
>
> **Themes:** adopted children; children of ex-Jews; children of Holocaust survivors; *conversos*; Jewish identity

Childhood and Family

The titles in this section are primarily autobiographies. Some of the authors, like Anne Roiphe or Calvin Trillin, became well known in adulthood, but chose to write about childhood influences and experiences. Other authors may not be well known, but their autobiographies give us a glimpse into an era or illuminate unusual situations. Several are vivid accounts of the immigrant experience.

Mary Antin's *The Promised Land* has long been a classic account of the enthusiasm with which many immigrants embraced the opportunities available here. But Antin's story does not speak for everyone. Rachel Calof's encounter with primitive conditions in North Dakota at the end of the nineteenth century, Harriet Lane Levy's perceptive dissection of Jewish upper-class distinctions in San Francisco in the same period, and Marjorie Agosín's books about her family's experiences in Chile help round out the picture. Some autobiographies, like Deborah Weisgall's *A Joyful Noise*, focus on the struggle to separate from family. Others, notably André Aciman's *Out of Egypt* and Burton Bernstein's *Family Matters*, paint nostalgic pictures of contentious, individualistic, but ultimately nurturing families. All of these titles offer insight into a particular time and place.

Aciman, André

Out of Egypt: A Memoir. **Farrar, Straus & Giroux, 1994. 339p.** `YA`

> Aciman grew up in Alexandria, Egypt, part of a large, close-knit, contentious Sephardic clan that settled there in 1905. Stories of fortunes made and lost, long-running feuds, fabulous parties, and summerhouses on the beach provide the background to Aciman's nostalgic look at his childhood in the 1950s and 1960s.
>
> **Themes:** exile; family relationships; Jews in Arab countries

> **Related Titles:** A sequel, *False Papers*, follows Aciman's life after leaving Alexandria, in a collection of linked essays. In *Letters of Transit*, edited by Aciman, five authors, (Aciman, Eva Hoffman, Bharati Mukherjee, Edward Said, and Charles Simic) write on the theme of exile. Readers may also enjoy Gini Alhadeff's *The Sun at Midday: Tales of a Mediterranean Family*. For another glimpse of Jewish life in Egypt and the Middle East, Claudia Roden, in her cookbook *The Book of Jewish Food: An Odyssey from Samarkand to New York*, recalls episodes from her childhood in Egypt along with mouth-watering recipes. Ilan Stavans,

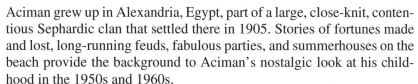

who grew up in Mexico, writes about dislocation in his autobiography, *On Borrowed Words: A Memoir of Language*, annotated in this section.

Agosín, Marjorie

Agosín writes about the dislocation of the divided self: as a Jew in Chile and as a Latina in the United States. In addition to writing fiction, nonfiction, and poetry, her own experiences have made her a spokesperson against human rights abuses.

A Cross and a Star: Memoirs of a Jewish Girl in Chile. **University of New Mexico Press, 1995. 179p.** YA 📖

Told mostly in her mother Frida's voice, Agosín's vividly imagined re-creation of her mother's life is filled with sensual detail about life in Chile in an extended family with eccentric relatives, shadowed by Chilean anti-Semitism and pro-German sentiment during World War II. Translated by Celeste Kostopulos-Cooperman.

Themes: anti-Semitism; Chile; exile; immigrants; mothers and daughters

Related Titles: Agosín has collected the life stories of Jewish Latin American women in *Taking Root: Narratives of Jewish Women in Latin America*. She also wrote *Uncertain Travelers: Conversations with Jewish Women Immigrants to America*, about nine women who came to the United States from various other countries.

Always from Somewhere Else: A Memoir of My Chilean Jewish Father. **The Feminist Press, 1998. 260p.** YA 📖

Traces the life and family of Agosín's father Moises, who grew up in Quillota, Chile, in the 1930s and 1940s, experiencing the anti-Semitism of the pro-German population. Although he had a successful career as a doctor and later moved to the United States, his life was pervaded by feelings of dislocation and loss, which he shared with his daughter. Translated by Celeste Kostopulos-Cooperman.

Themes: anti-Semitism; Chile; exile; fathers and daughters; immigrants

Related Titles: Although she has lived in the United States for many years, Agosín always writes in Spanish. In addition to memoir, she has written about human rights abuses, and edited a collection of stories, *The House of Memory: Stories by Jewish Women Writers of Latin America*, annotated in the "Anthologies" section of chapter 6.

The Alphabet in My Hands: A Writing Life. **Rutgers University Press, 2000. 187p.** YA

In brief entries, Agosín conveys what it was like to grow up a Jew, always an outsider, in Chile, but among extended family in a warm, embracing culture. After Allende was assassinated, her family came to the United States, and she spent her teenaged years in Georgia, where to be a foreigner and a Jew were considered disgraceful. Writing in Spanish gave her a way to express her authentic self. Translated by Nancy Abraham Hall.

Themes: anti-Semitism; Chile; exile; Jewish identity; language and languages

Related Titles: Another autobiographical work by Agosín is *Invisible Dreamer: Memory, Judaism, and Human Rights*. Eva Hoffman, in her memoir *Lost in*

Translation: A Life in a New Language, annotated in this chapter, writes about how the loss of her native language and country left her feeling bereft of her identity. A haunting autobiographical coming-of-age novel about growing up as a Latina in the United States and Cuba is *Days of Awe* by Achy Obejas, annotated in the "Setting" section of chapter 6.

Antin, Mary

The Promised Land. **1912; reprint, Modern Library, 2001. 400p.**

A lyrical, idealistic memoir, written when Mary Antin was thirty years old, describing the tumultuous first nineteen years of her life, first in the shtetl of Polotzk, Russia, then from age fourteen in Boston, Massachusetts. Although living in the poorest of slums, education and ambition enabled her to transcend her surroundings and meet and correspond with well-known intellectuals of her day. (This memoir was a best seller when it was published in 1912, and it has been in print ever since.)

Themes: immigrants; slum life; women's lives

Related Titles: Readers may also enjoy the following historical novels, which give a vivid picture of the experience of women immigrants—Gay Courter's *The Midwife* and *The Midwife's Advice*, and Meredith Tax's *Rivington Street* and *Union Square*—all annotated in the "Modern Period, United States and Canada" section of chapter 3.

Apple, Max

Roommates: My Grandfather's Story. **Morrow, 1994. 240p.**

The close and loving relationship between Max Apple and his grandfather Rocky survived the changing world of the 1960s, girlfriends, marriage, illness, and death.

Themes: aging; family relationships; grandfathers

Related Titles: Apple's *I Love Gootie: My Grandmother's Story*, is a nostalgic account of his grandmother, Rocky's wife. He has also written fiction, including the short story collection *Free Agents* and the novel *The Propheteers*. Readers who enjoy cross-generational memoirs may also like Joy Horowitz's *Tessie and Pearlie: A Granddaughter's Story*, or Mitch Albom's *Tuesdays with Morrie*. Readers may also enjoy these autobiographical novels about intergenerational relationships: *My Suburban Shtetl* by Robert Rand or Faye Moskowitz's *Peace in the House*.

Apte, Helen Jacobus

Heart of a Wife: The Diary of a Southern Jewish Woman. **Edited by Marcus D. Rosenbaum. SR Books, 1998. 222p.**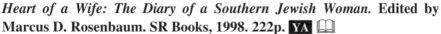

A frank and revealing look at the life of a Jewish woman (1886–1946) living in the South, through a diary never intended for publication. Apte was born in the United States and was more assimilated than her first-generation counterparts on the Lower East Side.

Themes: diaries; marriage; women's lives

Related Titles: Another early history of a Southern Jewish family can be found in *Mordecai: An Early American Family* by Emily Bingham. Apte's diary is one of four titles recommended by the Jewish Women's Archive (www.jwa.org). The other titles, all annotated in this chapter, are *Rachel Calof's Story: Jewish Home-steader on the Northern Plains* by Rachel Calof; *Out of the Shadow: A Russian Jewish Girlhood on the Lower East Side* by Rose Cohen; and *A Joyful Noise: Claiming the Songs of My Fathers* by Deborah Weisgall.

Bernstein, Burton

Family Matters: Sam, Jennie, and the Kids. **Summit Books, 1982. 200p.** `YA`

"The Kids" are Leonard Bernstein, his sister Shirley, and brother Burton, the author of this insightful memoir. The elder Bernsteins followed the traditional immigrant path: Escaping from persecution in the shtetls of Russia, they settled in Boston, worked hard to raise a family, and moved to the suburbs. But Leonard's musical career turned what would ordinarily be a private story into a very public one.

Themes: family relationships; immigrants; musicians

Related Titles: Bernstein's other books are well worth reading for his graceful writing style. In *Sinai, the Great and Terrible Wilderness*, he explores that part of the desert once thought to be the location of the giving of the Ten Commandments. For biographies of Leonard Bernstein, try Meryle Secrest's *Leonard Bernstein: A Life* or Humphrey Burton's *Leonard Bernstein*.

Calof, Rachel

Rachel Calof's Story: Jewish Homesteader on the Northern Plains. **Edited by Sanford J. Rikoon. Indiana University Press, 1995. 157p.** `YA` 📖

In 1894, Rachel Bella Kahn left Russia to come to America and marry Abraham Calof, a man she had never met. She moved with him to North Dakota, where they worked to carve out a life as homesteaders in a harsh and inhospitable climate, raising nine children, farming the land, and remaining observant Jews. Additional essays provide historical context about the Calofs and other Jewish settlers on the Great Plains.

Themes: frontier and pioneer life; immigrants; marriage

Related Titles: Calof's book is one of four titles recommended by the Jewish Women's Archive (www.jwa.org). The other titles, all annotated in this chapter, are *Heart of a Wife: The Diary of a Southern Jewish Woman* by Helen Jacobus Apte; *Out of the Shadow: A Russian Jewish Girlhood on the Lower East Side* by Rose Cohen; and *A Joyful Noise: Claiming the Songs of My Fathers* by Deborah Weisgall. For another point of view about what life was like for the early Jewish settlers on the Great Plains, readers may enjoy Sophie Trupin's *Dakota Diaspora*.

Charyn, Jerome

Bronx Boy: A Memoir. **St. Martin's, 2002. 184p.**

An account of Charyn's twelfth year in a rough-and-tumble Bronx neighborhood in the late 1940s, energetically told. Still known as "Baby," although he is no longer the youngest, Charyn wins a soda-making contest, serves as the bodyguard for a beautiful prostitute, and becomes a gang member.

Themes: authors; gangsters; teenaged boys

Related Titles: The third in an autobiographical trilogy that began with *The Dark Lady of Belorusse* and *The Black Swan*, Charyn's distinctive hard-boiled style of description gives an edgy quality to these memoirs that read like crime novels.

Cohen, Rose

Out of the Shadow: A Russian Jewish Girlhood on the Lower East Side. **1918; reprint, Cornell University Press, 1995. 313p.** **YA** 📖

In 1892, at the age of twelve, Rose Cohen left Russia and boarded a steamship to join her father on the Lower East Side of New York City, working in the garment trade, helping to save money to bring over the rest of the family. Cohen's account of life in the tenements and sweatshops vividly illuminates the religious, economic, and family conflicts so common among immigrant families.

Themes: 1890s; garment industry; immigrants; Lower East Side, N.Y.; 1900s

Related Titles: Cohen's book is one of four titles recommended by the Jewish Women's Archive (www.jwa.org). The other titles, all annotated in this chapter, are *Rachel Calof's Story: Jewish Homesteader on the Northern Plains* by Rachel Calof; *Heart of a Wife: The Diary of a Southern Jewish Woman* by Helen Jacobus Apte; and *A Joyful Noise: Claiming the Songs of My Fathers* by Deborah Weisgall. A fascinating follow-up to Cohen's memoir is *A Bintel Brief: Sixty Years of Letters from the Lower East Side to the Jewish Daily Forward.* (The Yiddish title means "a bundle of letters.") Readers may also enjoy the novel *Red Ribbon on a White Horse* by Anzia Yezierska, a fictionalized autobiography from a slightly later period, annotated in the "Classics and Major Authors" section of chapter 6.

Delman, Carmit

Burnt Bread and Chutney: A Memoir of an Indian Jewish Girl. **Ballantine/ One World, 2002. 261p.** **YA** 📖

An affectionate memoir of growing up at the intersection of two Jewish traditions: Delman's father was an Ashkenazi Jew and her mother came from the ancient Bene Israel community in India. As a multicultural family in the 1950s and 1960s, they were treated as outsiders in the United States and Israel; it was not until Delman discovered her Indian grandmother's diary that she was able to balance her unique heritage.

Themes: Ashkenazim; Bene Israel; family relationships; grandmothers; Jewish identity

Related Titles: Three very different Jewish communities exist in India: the Bene Israel, the Jews of Cochin, and the Baghdadi Jews. A history of

these communities can be found in *Who Are the Jews of India?* by Nathan Katz. Readers may also enjoy Gay Courter's novel *Flowers in the Blood*, for its colorful depiction of the Baghdadi Jewish community. It is annotated in chapter 5.

Dunow, Henry

***The Way Home: Scenes from a Season, Lessons from a Lifetime*. Broadway Books, 2001. 256p.**

Coaching his seven-year-old son Max's Little League team gives Henry Dunow a chance to build a stronger relationship with his son and reflect on his relationship with his own father, a Yiddish writer.

Themes: baseball and baseball players; fathers and sons; Jewish identity

Related Titles: Novels about sports, especially baseball, are often nostalgic and deal with relationships between men and boys. Readers may enjoy the following novels with this theme: *The Last Days of Summer* by Steve Kluger, annotated in the "Modern Period, United States and Canada" section of chapter 3, or Alan Lelchuk's *Brooklyn Boy*, annotated in the "Setting" section of chapter 6.

Felman, Jyl Lynn

***Cravings: A Sensual Memoir*. Beacon Press, 1997. 195p.**

Growing up in Dayton, Ohio, the youngest of three girls who wore the same clothes, and whose names all began with J, Jyl Felman's mother had rules to explain how Jewish girls should look, behave, and dress in every situation. In this episodic, impressionistic autobiography, Felman writes of painful and fractured relationships with her sisters and parents.

Themes: gays/lesbians/bisexuals; mothers and daughters; sisters

Related Titles: Another memoir by a Jewish lesbian who had very difficult family relationships is Lillian Faderman's *Naked in the Promised Land*.

Fries, Kenny

***Body, Remember: A Memoir*. Dutton, 1997. 224p.**

A frank and affecting memoir of Fries's efforts to understand himself as a physically handicapped, gay, Jewish male, and find peace with his multiple identities.

Themes: authors; gays/lesbians/bisexuals; Jewish identity; physically handicapped

Related Titles: Fries is also a poet and playwright. Readers may enjoy Lev Raphael's collection of stories, *Dancing on Tisha B'Av*, which deals with issues of being Jewish and gay, annotated in the "Character" section of chapter 6.

Gallagher, Dorothy

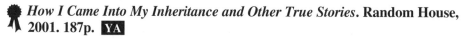 ***How I Came Into My Inheritance and Other True Stories*. Random House, 2001. 187p. YA**

Gallagher's eccentric and cantankerous family members come alive in these hilarious and loving vignettes of life in New York City in the 1940s and 1950s in an extended family of Communist sympathizers, who battled with the world and each other. (Winner of the Koret Jewish Book Award.)

Themes: authors; Communism; parents and children

Related Titles: Readers may also enjoy *The War at Home: A Memoir-Novel* by Nora Eisenberg, about her desperate childhood in the Bronx experiencing her mother's descent into madness and her father's desertion.

Gornick, Vivian

 *Fierce Attachments: A Memoir.* **1987; reprint, Beacon Press, 1997. 203p.** **YA**

The author's close but often difficult relationship with her mother underlies this vivid memoir of growing up in a socialist apartment complex in the Bronx in the 1940s and 1950s. Gornick's mother and neighbors provided some unusual life lessons in love, sex, and politics that served as a counterpoint to Gornick's own efforts to find her way in life. (An ALA Notable Book.)

Themes: authors; Bronx, N.Y.; mothers and daughters; 1950s; 1940s

Related Titles: Gornick's two other autobiographical titles are *In Search of Ali Mahmoud: An American Woman in Egypt* and the essay collection *Approaching Eye Level. In My Mother's House* by Kim Chernin is another autobiography about a stormy mother–daughter relationship. Readers may also enjoy *Sleeping Arrangements* by Laura Cunningham, another account of an unusual family situation.

Hoffman, Eva

Lost in Translation: A Life in a New Language. **Dutton, 1989. 280p.** **YA**

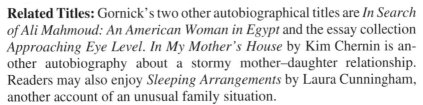

After World War II, Hoffman's survivor parents remained in Poland, but continuing anti-Semitism made life difficult. In 1959, when she was thirteen years old, the family immigrated to Vancouver, Canada. This is the story of Hoffman's efforts to make a place for herself in America as the daughter of survivors, and as an exile from her beloved Cracow. She writes movingly of the difficulties of learning to express herself in a new language.

Themes: children of Holocaust survivors; immigrants; language and languages

Related Titles: Hoffman also wrote *Exit into History*, about Eastern Europe following the break-up of the Soviet Union, and *Shtetl: The Life and Death of a Small Town and the World of Polish Jewry*, concerning the town of Bransk and the history of Jewish life there from the 1500s through the Holocaust. Another insightful memoir by a child of Holocaust survivors that talks about the pain of being an outsider in a new country is *Last Dance in the Hotel Kempinski* by Robin Hirsch.

Kaufman, Alan

Jew Boy. Fromm International, 2000. 400p.

Kaufman grew up in the Bronx, where his traumatized Holocaust-survivor mother beat him regularly with a coat hanger. Emotionally scarred, he left home, vowing not to become a victimized Jew; his wandering included time spent on an Israeli kibbutz and alcoholism in San Francisco before he was able to accept his Jewishness.

Themes: children of Holocaust survivors; Jewish identity; poets

LaZebnik, Edith

Such a Life. Morrow, 1978. 287p. **YA**

LaZebnik's memoir is a humorous and loving portrait of the Russian shtetl, with emphasis on her father David's romances and marriages. Written in a colloquial style, in English with Yiddish syntax, *Such a Life* starts with her father's childhood, and ends with her own arrival in Chicago as an adolescent.

Themes: immigrants; Russia; shtetl life

Related Titles: Readers may enjoy Sholom Aleichem's autobiographical *From the Fair*, about growing up in a Russian village, in a slightly earlier period of time. The novels of Isaac Bashevis Singer, set in Poland and annotated in the "Classics and Major Authors" section of chapter 6, are an incomparable source for understanding that long-lost era. Readers may enjoy some of the novels that evoke that time and place: *Bociany* by Chana Rosenfarb and *Your Mouth Is Lovely* by Nancy Richler, both annotated in the "Modern Period, Eastern Europe and Russia" section of chapter 3, or *The River Midnight* by Lillian Nattel, annotated in the "Language" section of chapter 6.

Levy, Harriet Lane

920 O'Farrell Street. 1947; reprint, Heyday Books, 1996. 196p. **YA**

Growing up in San Francisco at the end of the nineteenth century, Levy writes about the lives of her parents and their wealthy Jewish neighbors. Alice B. Toklas lived next door to the Levys; she and Harriet became friends and traveled to Europe together on the trip on which Alice met Gertrude Stein.

Themes: family relationships; San Francisco, California

Related Titles: *We Lived There Too* by Kenneth Libo and Irving Howe and *Pioneer Jews: A New Life in the Far West* by Harriet and Fred Rochlin provide excellent histories of the pioneering generation of Jews who went West with so many others to make their fortunes. For another look at the Old West, readers may enjoy the autobiography of Wyatt Earp's Jewish wife, *I Married Wyatt Earp* by Josephine Marcus Earp. Gloria Goldreich's *West to Eden*, annotated in the "Modern Period, United States and Canada" section of chapter 3, is a fictional treatment of life in the far West in this period, partly set in San Francisco. *The Reformer's Apprentice*, the first volume of Harriet Rochlin's <u>Desert Dwellers Trilogy</u>, annotated in the same section, is set in San Francisco at the end of the nineteenth century. Readers looking for primary source materials may enjoy *Jewish Voices* *of the California Gold Rush: A Documentary History, 1849–1880,* edited by Ava Fran Kahn.

Nuland, Sherwin

Lost in America. **Alfred A. Knopf, 2003. 212p.**

A well-known surgeon and author, Nuland's childhood was dominated by his father Meyer Nudelman, a bitter, ailing man with an explosive temper, whose forceful personality shadowed his son's life and caused him episodes of crippling depression as an adult.

Themes: doctors; fathers and sons; immigrants

Related Titles: Nuland received the National Book Award in 1994 for a nonfiction work, *How We Die.*

Raphael, Lev

Journeys and Arrivals: On Being Gay and Jewish. **Faber & Faber, 1996. 166p.**

A coming-of-age memoir about the author's struggle with his sexual and religious identities. This collection of thirteen essays, some of which have been published elsewhere, covers both personal history and issues relating to the wider gay community. Raphael also writes about his relationship with his Holocaust-survivor parents. (The author's Web site is www.levraphael.com.)

Themes: children of Holocaust survivors; gays/lesbians/bisexuals

Related Titles: Raphael's short story collection *Dancing on Tisha B'Av* and a coming-of-age novel, *Winter Eyes,* are both annotated in the "Character" section of chapter 6. His Nick Hoffman mystery series, set in academia, is annotated in the "Amateur Detectives" section of chapter 2.

Rich, Frank

Ghost Light: A Memoir. **Random House, 2000. 315p.** YA

The difficulties of being a child of divorced parents in the 1950s and 1960s, with a generous but sometimes abusive stepfather, were mitigated for Frank by his love of the theater and determination to make a career there.

Themes: divorce; stepfathers; theater life

Related Titles: A novel about a boy for whom divorce was a mixed blessing is *The Lost Legends of New Jersey* by Frederick Reiken.

Roiphe, Anne Richardson

1185 Park Avenue. **The Free Press, 1999. 257p.**

The Upper East Side of Manhattan is the setting for this autobiography of growing up in the 1940s and 1950s in a wealthy but spiritually impoverished and dysfunctional family. Roiphe, her younger brother, and their parents lived in separate worlds, each trying to construct a life that would quiet their inner demons.

Themes: family relationships; fathers and daughters; mothers and daughters; women—social conditions

Related Titles: Roiphe also wrote the historical novel *The Pursuit of Happiness*, annotated in the "Modern Period, United States and Canada" section of chapter 3, and *Lovingkindness,* annotated in the "Character" section of chapter 6. In another autobiographical work, *Generation without Memory: A Jewish Journey in Christian America*, Roiphe writes about the lack of authentic Judaism in her childhood. Another account of a wealthy dysfunctional family is *Mommy Dressing*, Lois Gould's autobiography of growing up as the daughter of fashion designer Jo Coupland. A novel about a dysfunctional New York City family that readers may enjoy is *Sleepless Nights* by Andrew Bergman, annotated in the "Character" section of chapter 6.

Rothstein, Natalie

An American Family. Fithian Press, 1999. 190p. [YA] 📖

When her granddaughter asked the question "where do I come from?" Rothstein wanted to give more than a cursory answer. In telling the story of one immigrant family's journey from the shtetls of Russia to a comfortable life in Boston, she also provides the wider picture that links her family's history to the great migration of the late nineteenth and early twentieth centuries.

Themes: family relationships; genealogy; immigrants

Related Titles: *An American Family* would be of interest to anyone considering writing a family history; it is especially rich in detail about the Boston area. Readers may also enjoy the novel *The Reason for Wings* by Joyce Reiser Kornblatt, in which a woman looks back on her family history to set it down in writing for her grandchildren. It is annotated in the "Modern Period, Eastern Europe and Russia" section of chapter 3.

Rubin, Louis Decimus

My Father's People: A Family of Southern Jews. Louisiana State University Press, 2002. 139p.

A graceful memoir of the author's paternal relatives, the seven children of Hyman and Fannie Rubin, who grew up in early twentieth-century Charleston, South Carolina. They were unusual, creative individuals, shaped by dire poverty and the experience of being Jewish in that place and time. (Rubin is a scholar of Southern literature and founder of Algonquin Books of Chapel Hill.)

Themes: Charleston, S.C.; family relationships; immigrants

Related Titles: A novel by Rubin, *The Golden Weather*, follows a thirteen-year-old boy through the summer of 1936 in Charleston. Another memoir of a Southern Jewish family with a compelling story of involvement in Southern politics is *Time's Tapestry: Four Generations of a New Orleans Family* by Leta Weiss Marks.

Shapiro, Dani

Slow Motion: A True Story. **Random House, 1998. 245p.**

A story of self-destructive behavior that started in college when Dani had an affair with the wealthy, egocentric father of a friend and dropped out of school to become his mistress. It was only when her parents were injured in a car accident that she was able to reclaim her life from this dependent relationship of sex, alcohol, and drugs. (The author's Web site is www.danishapiro.com.)

Themes: accidents; fathers and daughters; love affairs; mothers and daughters; 1980s

Simon, Kate

Bronx Primitive: Portraits in a Childhood. **1982; reprint, Penguin USA, 1997. 179p.** **YA** 📖

Simon's perceptive eye for nuance and detail illuminates this classic autobiography of growing up in an immigrant neighborhood in the Bronx in the 1930s, separating from her parents, and striking out on her own path.

Themes: Bronx, N.Y.; family relationships; immigrants; neighbors; 1930s

Related Titles: Simon's autobiography is completed by the two volumes *A Wider World: Portraits in an Adolescence* and *Etchings in an Hourglass*. Readers who found Simon's autobiography compelling for the description of how she went her own way may enjoy Rebecca Goldstein's novel *Mazel*, about three very different generations of women, annotated in the "Character" section of chapter 6.

Singer, Isaac Bashevis

In My Father's Court. **Farrar, Straus & Giroux, 1966. 307p.**

Singer's father was a rabbi in Warsaw; in his house he held a *bet din* (rabbinical court), ruling on points of Jewish law. The cases that came before him were of many kinds, often touching on issues of deep significance in people's lives. Singer overheard these cases as a young boy, absorbing the scholarly wisdom and psychological insights his parents provided to their troubled neighbors, and evokes for the reader a picture of religious practice and Yiddish culture from a vanished era. Translated by Channah Kleinerman-Goldstein and Elaine Gottlieb.

Themes: fathers and sons; Hasidism; mothers and sons; rabbis

Related Titles: Twenty-seven additional stories that first appeared in Yiddish in the newspaper *The Forward* are collected in *More Stories from My Father's Court.* Singer also wrote three autobiographical works: *A Little Boy in Search of God, A Young Man in Search of Love,* and *Lost in America,* which bring him from childhood in Poland to his mid-thirties in New York City. Attentive readers will find much here that appears in his fiction. Readers interested in learning more about his life can read Paul Kresh's biography *Isaac Bashevis Singer: The Magician of West 86th Street*, *Isaac Bashevis Singer: A Life* by Janet Hadda, or Dvorah Telushkin's *Master of Dreams; A Memoir of Isaac Bashevis Singer*. His son, Israel Zamir, has written *Journey to My Father, Isaac Bashevis Singer*. Singer's older brother, Israel Joshua Singer, wrote his own recollection of life in Poland, *Of a World That Is No More*. Singer's many wonderful novels and short story collections are described in the "Classics and Major Authors" section of chapter 6. He received the Nobel Prize in 1978.

Solotaroff, Ted

Truth Comes in Blows. W. W. Norton, 1998. 285p. **YA**

Growing up in New Jersey in the 1930s and 1940s, Solotaroff fought against seeing himself as the failure his bullying father told him he would be. It was only through a growing love of literature and relationships with encouraging friends and relatives that he was able to free himself from the abusive relationship and find his own path.

Themes: authors; fathers and sons; mothers and sons

Related Titles: Solotaroff continues his very personal and pain-filled memoir in *First Loves*, which focuses on marriage and career. Readers may also enjoy *The Last Marlin: The Story of a Family at Sea* by Fred Waitzkin, another account of divisive family relationships.

Stavans, Ilan

On Borrowed Words: A Memoir of Language. Viking, 2001. 263p.

Stavans's unusual upbringing, in a close-knit, Yiddish-speaking Jewish community in Mexico City, failed to provide him with a sense of identity as a citizen of any country. It took several years of traveling, to the United States, Spain, Israel, and back again to Mexico, for him to find a home in the United States. Each chapter in this perceptive memoir focuses on his relationship with a different family member.

Themes: authors; language and languages; Mexico; Yiddish language

Related Titles: Readers may also enjoy *King David's Harp*, a collection of autobiographical essays by Latin American Jewish authors, edited by Stephen A. Sadow.

Suberman, Stella

The Jew Store. Algonquin Books of Chapel Hill, 1998. 298p. **YA** 📖

In 1920, the Subermans arrived by horse and wagon in a small town in northwestern Tennessee to open a dry goods store. Local prejudices, Klan activity, and the absence of any other Jewish families made their adjustment difficult. Although bacon fat would never replace chicken fat in Reba Suberman's pantry, by the time the family reluctantly left, thirteen years later, the children had Southern accents and Southern friends, and the family and store had become part of the fabric of Concordia.

Themes: Jews—relations with African Americans; merchants; small-town life; Southern states

Related Titles: Suberman has written a second memoir, *When It Was Our War: A Soldier's Wife in World War II*. Other books about Jews in the South include *The Peddler's Grandson: Growing up Jewish in Mississippi* by Edward Cohen and *The Temple Bombing* by Melissa Fay Greene. Readers may also enjoy *Postville* by Stephen G. Bloom, about the cultural conflict in a small town in Iowa when a group of Hasidim move in to open a slaughterhouse.

Trillin, Calvin

Messages from My Father. **Farrar, Straus & Giroux, 1996. 117p.** YA

Trillin's father Abe, who came to the United States from Russia as a baby, was a small businessman in Kansas City. His son says, "My father, I think, did not make a strong first impression." Despite this, Abe's values, his messages, were deeply felt and communicated to his son: the importance of being a *mensch*, of going to Yale, of behaving modestly, of not complaining, and of being an American.

Themes: authors; fathers and sons; Midwest

Related Titles: Trillin's humorous and perceptive essays on food, many of which appeared in the *New Yorker* magazine, can be found in several collections, among them *American Fried* and *The Tummy Trilogy*. Faye Moskowitz's two memoirs *A Leak in the Heart: Tales from a Woman's Life* and *And the Bridge Is Love: Life Stories* also describe the life lessons learned in close family relationships.

Weisgall, Deborah

A Joyful Noise: Claiming the Songs of My Fathers. **Atlantic Monthly Press, 1999. 262p.** YA

The author grew up surrounded by a rich tradition of Jewish music. Her grandfather was a cantor in a large Conservative Baltimore congregation, and her father, a composer of opera, led the choir. It was a tradition that nurtured her, but as a woman, excluded her participation, requiring her to search for her own voice.

Themes: cantors; fathers and daughters; women—religious life

Related Titles: Weisgall's book is one of four titles recommended by the Jewish Women's Archive (www.jwa.org). The other titles, all annotated in this chapter, are *Rachel Calof's Story: Jewish Homesteader on the Northern Plains* by Rachel Calof; *Out of the Shadows: A Russian Jewish Girlhood on the Lower East Side* by Rose Cohen; and *Heart of a Wife: The Diary of a Southern Jewish Woman* by Helen Jacobus Apte.

Public Lives

The titles in this section were selectively chosen for variety. They range from people who made history, like Golda Meir and Judah P. Benjamin; to those who witnessed history, like Ruth Gruber and Daniel Schorr; to those who were caught up in history, like Jacobo Timerman and Leonard Garment; to those who entertained and enlightened us, like Irving Berlin and Cyrus Gordon; to those who made headlines, like Bess Myerson and the Rosenbergs; to those who spearheaded social change, like Betty Friedan and Rose Schneiderman. Some are more widely known than others, but all their life stories enrich our understanding of the Jewish American experience.

Adler, Jacob

A Life on the Stage. **1977, reprint, Applause Theatre Book Publishing, 2001. 403p.**

A legendary actor, Jacob Adler was synonymous with Yiddish theater on New York's Lower East Side for many years. He was famous for his portrayals of King Lear and Shylock (in Yiddish), and for his flamboyant style on and off the stage. The Yiddish theater in Adler's day was wildly popular. Translated, edited, and with commentary by Lulla Rosenfeld.

Themes: actors and acting; theater life; Yiddish culture

Related Titles: A biography of Adler, *Bright Star of Exile*, was written by his granddaughter Lulla Rosenfeld. *Funny Woman: The Life and Times of Fanny Brice* is a biography of another very popular Jewish stage star. There is extensive material on the Yiddish theater and Yiddish culture on the Lower East Side in *World of Our Fathers: The Journey of the East European Jews to America and the Life They Found and Made* by Irving Howe and Kenneth Libo. Readers may enjoy Francine Prose's well-researched historical novel *Hungry Hearts*, about a Yiddish theater troupe, annotated in the "Modern Period, Latin America" section of chapter 3.

Lax, Eric

Woody Allen: A Biography. **Alfred A. Knopf, 1991. 385p.** **YA**

Lax had close access to Allen for four years; he writes about his childhood; his career as a gag writer and stand-up comic; and his success in acting, writing, and directing films. Lots of quotes from the comedy routines and insight into Allen's creative process.

Themes: actors and acting; comedians; motion picture directors

Related Titles: Marion Meade's *The Unruly Life of Woody Allen: A Biography* covers the scandal surrounding Allen's relationship with Mia Farrow's adopted daughter Soon-Yi.

Barr, Roseanne

Roseanne: My Life as a Woman. **Harper & Row, 1989. 202p.** **YA**

Roseanne grew up in Salt Lake City, often singled out, patronized, or discriminated against for being Jewish. The feminist movement helped her give voice and purpose to the anger that had raged inside her for years. Performing in local comedy clubs followed, then national success and her own television program. Part comedy routine, part memoir, this is a glimpse into what it's like to be Roseanne Barr. (The author's Web site is www.roseanneworld.com.)

Themes: comedians; television actors and actresses; women's lives

Related Titles: Readers looking for other books about celebrities may enjoy Gilda Radner's *It's Always Something*, written during the author's battle with cancer. Readers may enjoy *The Jews of Prime Time* by David Zurawnik, a social history of Jews in the television industry.

Evans, Eli N.

Judah P. Benjamin, The Jewish Confederate. **The Free Press, 1988. 469p.**

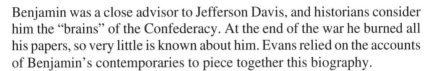

Benjamin was a close advisor to Jefferson Davis, and historians consider him the "brains" of the Confederacy. At the end of the war he burned all his papers, so very little is known about him. Evans relied on the accounts of Benjamin's contemporaries to piece together this biography.

Themes: politicians; U.S.—History—Civil War

Related Titles: A vivid picture of the Union point of view about the Civil War is found in *Your True Marcus: The Civil War Letters of a Jewish Colonel*, edited by Frank Byrne and Jean Soman. Evans also wrote about the experiences of Southern Jews in his book of essays *The Lonely Days Were Sundays: Reflections of a Jewish Southerner*. In an earlier book, *The Provincials: A Personal History of Jews in the South*, his own family's experiences serve to illuminate the larger story of Southern Jews.

Dawidoff, Nicholas

The Catcher Was a Spy: The Mysterious Life of Moe Berg. **Pantheon Books, 1994. 453p.** `YA`

Berg was unique: a lawyer who played baseball, an athlete who became a spy, a secretive man of many acquaintances but no friends. He played shortstop and catcher in professional baseball in the 1920s and 1930s, and during World War II was recruited by the OSS, the forerunner of the CIA.

Themes: baseball and baseball players; spies; World War II

Related Titles: Readers may enjoy Jay Neugeboren's novel *Before My Life Began,* which follows a boy who grows up to play several very different roles in his life. It is annotated in the "Story" section of chapter 6.

Bergreen, Laurence

As Thousands Cheer: The Life of Irving Berlin. **Viking, 1990. 658p.** `YA`

Berlin was unable to read music and could only play in one key; nevertheless, he was a musical genius whose many songs, like *God Bless America*, remain standards of the musical repertoire. The youngest of eight children, he came to America in 1893 from Russia. Like so many other immigrant families, poverty forced him out on his own at the age of thirteen, to make his way by singing in bars and music halls. Bergreen covers not only Berlin's life but the times he lived in and the Tin Pan Alley milieu.

Themes: composers; musicians

Related Titles: Another biography of Irving Berlin is Philip Furia's *Irving Berlin: A Life in Song.* George Gershwin, whose popular and serious music played a major role in the twentieth century, is profiled in Edward Jablonski's *Gershwin, a Biography. Fascinating Rhythm* by Deena Rosenberg examines George's collaboration with his brother Ira, a great lyricist. Two other Jewish brothers who influenced American popular music are found in *Spinning Blues into Gold: The Chess Brothers and the Legendary Chess Records* by Nadine Cohodas.

Grossman, Barbara W.
Funny Woman: The Life and Times of Fanny Brice. **Indiana University Press, 1991. 287p.** YA

Brice was a star in vaudeville, musical comedy, film, and radio from 1916 until her death in 1951. Her comical songs and the characters she created, most notably Baby Snooks, were wildly popular. Barbra Streisand starred in the musical based on her life, *Funny Girl.*

Themes: actors and acting; comedians; singers

Dershowitz, Alan M.
Chutzpah. **Simon & Schuster, 1992. 378p.** YA

The prominent, outspoken lawyer describes his Orthodox upbringing in a Jewish neighborhood in Brooklyn, N.Y., encountering discrimination in the legal profession, and defending high-profile clients like Claus Von Bulow and Leona Helmsley. He reflects on the current generation of Jews in America and analyzes the issues facing them: assimilation, the Holocaust, Zionism, and civil rights, among others.

Themes: civil rights movement; Jewish identity; lawyers

Related Titles: Dershowitz's two legal thrillers, annotated in the "Legal Thrillers" section of chapter 2, explore issues of ethics and justice. His *Letters to a Young Lawyer,* while not autobiographical, does convey a strong sense of his personal code of ethics. Other biographies of social activists are *My Life as a Radical Lawyer* by William Kunstler with Sheila Isenberg, *For the Hell of It: The Life and Times of Abbie Hoffman* by Jonah Raskin, and *Joe Rapoport: The Life of a Jewish Radical* by Kenneth Kann. Readers may enjoy the series of legal thriller by Ronald Levitsky about a civil rights lawyer who travels around the United States defending the rights of minorities, annotated in chapter 2.

Douglas, Kirk
The Ragman's Son: An Autobiography. **Simon & Schuster, 1988. 510p.**

Literally a rags to riches story by the boy who helped his father stuff bags with the rags he collected and ultimately became one of Hollywood's most famous leading men. Douglas grew up as Issur Danielovitch, dirt poor, in upstate New York, the only boy in a family of six girls. The anger stored up during a childhood of trying to please a distant and domineering father fueled his acting career.

Themes: actors and acting; Hollywood; motion picture industry

Related Titles: Douglas reconnected with the Judaism that was part of his childhood after a brush with death, and he writes about that experience in *Climbing the Mountain: My Search for Meaning.* For insight into the Jewish influence on the motion picture industry, readers may enjoy Neal Gabler's *An Empire of Their Own: How the Jews Invented Hollywood.*

Frankel, Max

The Times of My Life and My Life with **The Times. Random House, 1999. 526p.**

Frankel's nearly fifty-year career at *The New York Times*, from foreign correspondent to Washington bureau chief to executive editor in 1986, placed him at the center of many of the pivotal events of our time and gave him access to major political figures. His interest in politics dated from his escape from Nazi Germany just before Kristallnacht. Frankel was often accused by Jewish readers of being anti-Israel, particularly during the Begin era, and he takes this opportunity to explain his views as well as the history of *The Times's* ambivalence toward reporting on Jewish issues.

Themes: journalists; *The New York Times;* U.S.—Politics and government

Friedan, Betty

Life So Far: A Memoir. **Simon & Schuster, 2000. 399p.** 🟥**YA** 📖

From the woman who jumpstarted the feminist revolution, a history of how it all came to be. Friedan's memoir starts with her lonely childhood in Peoria, early literary triumphs at Smith College, stints as a labor reporter, and life as a suburban housewife in the 1950s. Her insights into the frustrations and inequities in women's lives led her to write *The Feminine Mystique* (1963), and later to the founding of NOW and leadership in the fight for women's equality.

Themes: feminists; National Organization for Women (NOW); women—social conditions; women's lives

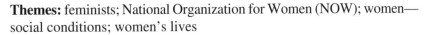

Related Titles: For another perspective on Friedan's life, try the biography by Judith Hennessee, *Betty Friedan: Her Life.* Readers who enjoyed *Life So Far* may also be interested in Letty Cottin Pogrebin's memoir *Deborah, Golda and Me: Being Jewish and Female in America.* Another title readers may enjoy, from a different era, is the autobiography of Emma Goldman, *Living My Life.* Goldman (1869–1940) was an anarchist and freethinker. In the early years of the twentieth century she was an advocate for social and economic equality for women. So radical and threatening were her ideas that she was deported from the United States to the Soviet Union in 1919. Rose Schneiderman was involved in the development of the labor movement and became an advisor to President Franklin Delano Roosevelt. She writes about her experiences in *All for One*. Readers may also enjoy *Going South: Jewish Women in the Civil Rights Movement* by Debra L. Schultz.

Garment, Leonard

Crazy Rhythm: My Journey from Brooklyn, Jazz, and Wall Street to Nixon's White House, Watergate, and Beyond. **Times Books, 1997. 418p.**

Growing up in Brownsville, Brooklyn, the son of a clothing manufacturer who expected his son to follow him into the business, Garment detoured into jazz and the army before finding his way to law school. A close adviser to Nixon during his White House years, he was involved in the aftermath of Watergate and the turmoil of domestic and international politics in the 1960s and early 1970s.

Themes: Brooklyn, N.Y.; Nixon, Richard; politicians; U.S.—Politics and government

Related Titles: Nat Hentoff, who was also involved in jazz and politics, wrote about his life in *Boston Boy* and *Speaking Freely*. Solotaroff's autobiography *Truth Comes in Blows*, annotated in the "Childhood and Family" section of this chapter, also deals with a difficult father. Henry Kissinger's memoir *The White House Years* offers another insider's view of the difficult Vietnam War period.

Ginsberg, Allen, and Louis Ginsberg

Family Business: Selected Letters Between a Father and Son. **Edited by Michael Schumacher. Bloomsbury, 2001. 412p.**

Correspondence between two poets, so very different in their life experiences, reveals their close relationship and the influence they exerted on each other. These letters were written from the time Allen was eighteen until Louis's death in 1944.

Themes: correspondence; fathers and sons; poets

Related Titles: Readers unfamiliar with Allen Ginsberg's poetry may enjoy the first two of his many published collections: *Howl, and Other Poems* and *Kaddish, and Other Poems*. *Howl* is one of the most well-known poems of the twentieth century.

Glickman, Marty, and Stan Isaacs

The Fastest Kid on the Block: The Marty Glickman Story. **Syracuse University Press, 1996. 201p.** YA

Glickman's talent as a runner earned him a spot on the U.S. Olympic team at the infamous Nazi Olympics in 1936, but due to anti-Semitic pressure he and another Jewish teammate were not allowed to participate. Glickman went on to a career in sports broadcasting.

Themes: anti-Semitism; athletes; Olympic Games

Related Titles: Other biographies of Jewish sports stars are *Hank Greenberg: The Story of My Life* written with Ira Berkow and *Koufax* by Ed Gruver. A collection of profiles of Jewish sports figures, including Moe Berg, Mark Spitz, and

Kerri Strug, can be found in *Great Jews in Sports* by Robert Slater. Readers may also enjoy the sports novels *The Last Days of Summer* by Steve Kluger and *In Days of Awe* by Eric Rolfe Greenberg, both annotated in the "Modern Period, United States and Canada" section of chapter 3.

Gordon, Cyrus H.

 A Scholar's Odyssey. **Society of Biblical Literature, 2000. 149p.**

One of the great biblical scholars of the twentieth century, Gordon discovered connections among the ancient civilizations of the Middle and Near East, enriching our knowledge of those cultures. In this modest and inspiring memoir, he recounts his classical education, his major accomplishments, and his encounters with other well-known figures in archaeology, with the grace of a scholar and a gentleman. (Winner of the National Jewish Book Award.)

Themes: archaeologists; linguists; scholars

Gruber, Ruth

Ahead of Time: My Early Years as a Foreign Correspondent. **Wynwood Press, 1991. 319p.**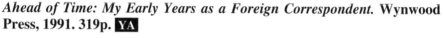

Gruber knew from an early age that she needed to escape the limiting expectations of her family and pursue her need to study, write, and travel. At twenty-three, as a foreign correspondent for the *Herald Tribune*, she began a lifetime of travel to distant places, often finding herself literally on the frontier of the news.

Themes: journalists; women's lives

Related Titles: Gruber continues her memoirs in *Inside of Time: My Journey from Alaska to Israel*. She was involved in several Jewish rescue operations, which she writes about in *Rescue: The Exodus of the Ethiopian Jews*, *Haven: The Unknown Story of 1,000 World War II Refugees*, and *Exodus 1947: The Ship That Launched a Nation*. Two other women who lived unconventional lives write about their friendship and career in the rare book business in *Bookends: Two Women, One Enduring Friendship* by Leona Rostenberg and Madeline Stern.

Heller, Joseph

Now and Then: From Coney Island to Here. **Alfred A. Knopf, 1998. 259p.**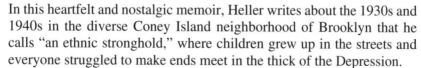

In this heartfelt and nostalgic memoir, Heller writes about the 1930s and 1940s in the diverse Coney Island neighborhood of Brooklyn that he calls "an ethnic stronghold," where children grew up in the streets and everyone struggled to make ends meet in the thick of the Depression.

Themes: Brooklyn, N.Y.; family relationships; 1940s; 1930s

Related Titles: In a semiautobiographical novel, *Portrait of an Artist, as an Old Man*, completed before his death, Heller writes about the problems of celebrity and the writing life. Another memoir, *No Laughing*

Matter, written by Heller and his friend Speed Vogel, recounts his experience with Guillain-Barre syndrome. Heller is most well-known for his first novel, *Catch-22*, a comic novel about the absurdities of war. A later novel, *God Knows*, about the life of King David, is annotated in the "Biblical and Ancient Worlds" section of chapter 3. A novel that does a good job of capturing the rhythms of life in Brooklyn in that same era is Wallace Markfield's *Teitlebaum's Window*.

Hertzberg, Arthur

A Jew in America: My Life and a People's Struggle for Identity. **HarperSanFrancisco, 2002. 468p.**

An activist on many Jewish fronts, confidant of politicians in the United States and Israel, congregational rabbi, and scholar, Hertzberg has always championed the role of traditional Judaism—the importance of living in America without loss of religious identity. He credits his parents with passing on a legacy of love for Jewish ritual and learning, which he embraced despite his feelings of "otherness" growing up in Youngstown, Ohio. (Winner of the National Jewish Book Award.)

Themes: civil rights movement; immigrants; Jewish identity; men—religious life; Orthodox Jews; Zionists

Howe, Irving

A Margin of Hope: An Intellectual Autobiography. **Harcourt, Brace, 1982. 352p.**

Howe was introduced to socialism as a teenager in the Bronx during the Depression, and it influenced his view of the world for the rest of his life. One of a group of intellectuals who shaped discourse about political and social issues, he also helped to bring the great Yiddish writers to the attention of the English-speaking world.

Themes: authors; intellectuals; literary life; radicals and radicalism

Related Titles: A recent biography of Howe, *Irving Howe: A Life of Passionate Dissent* by Gerald Sorin, received a National Jewish Book Award.

Kroeger, Brooke

Fannie: The Talent for Success of Writer Fannie Hurst. **Times Books, 1999. 478p.**

Fanny Hurst enjoyed enormous popularity as a writer from the 1920s through the 1940s. Her numerous short stories appeared in popular magazines, and her best-selling novels were made into successful movies. Women were especially drawn to her stories, which illuminated the lives of working-class women and Jewish immigrant girls and women. Ambivalent about Judaism for many years, Hurst only came to terms with her Jewishness toward the end of her life.

Themes: authors; 1940s; 1930s; 1920s

Related Titles: Hurst's autobiography, *Anatomy of Me*, was published in 1958.

Gottfried, Martin

Nobody's Fool: The Lives of Danny Kaye. **Simon & Schuster, 1994. 352p.**

Danny Kaye was an inspired comic, talented in song, dance, and mimicry. The youngest son of an immigrant Brooklyn family, he dropped out of high school and found a foothold as an entertainer in the Catskill Mountains resorts in the 1930s. With the astute help of his wife Sylvia, a talented musician, he built a career on the Broadway stage and in movies that captivated audiences for decades. Gottfried's biography relates the highlights of his career and provides some insight into the psychological underpinnings of Kaye's personality.

Themes: actors and acting; comedians

Related Titles: For an overview of the Jewish presence in comedy, readers may enjoy *The Haunted Smile*, annotated in the "Collected Biography" section of this chapter. Kaye starred in some of the Jewish writer Moss Hart's Broadway shows. Readers may enjoy Hart's memoir *Act One*.

Kazin, Alfred

Kazin is most well-known as a literary critic, particularly for his groundbreaking study of American literature, *On Native Grounds* (1942). He was part of the group known as the New York Intellectuals. This autobiographical trilogy traces his development as a writer.

Themes: Jewish identity; literary life; 1930s; 1920s

A Walker in the City. 1946; reprint, Harvest Books, 1969. 176p.

Kazin captures the sights, sounds, and smells of life in the Brooklyn neighborhood of Brownsville as a young boy and adolescent. We see the beginnings of his interest in literature and politics and the start of the conflict between his provincial family life and the more sophisticated world outside of Brownsville.

Starting Out in the Thirties. 1965; reprint, Cornell University Press, 1989. 166p.
New York Jew. 1978; reprint, Syracuse University Press, 1996. 307p.

Related Titles: In 1995, Kazin published another memoir, *Writing Was Everything,* a compilation of lectures covering the same time period as his autobiographical trilogy, but from a later perspective. Another member of the New York Intellectuals, Norman Podhoretz, writes of growing up in Brownsville and making his way into the wider literary world in his memoir *Making It*. The autobiography of Irving Howe, *A Margin of Hope*, another member of the group, is annotated in this chapter. An inside look at the relationships among the New York Intellectuals is found in Diana Trilling's *The Beginning of the Journey: The Marriage of Diana and Lionel Trilling*.

Leavy, Jane

Sandy Koufax: A Lefty's Legacy. HarperCollins, 2002. 282p. YA

Koufax was a modest, principled, and incredibly talented pitcher for the Dodgers in the late 1950s and 1960s, well-known for pitching a perfect game in 1965 and refusing to pitch the starting game of the 1965 World Series, which fell on Yom Kippur. His life and accomplishments are seen in the context of baseball and social history, enriched with descriptions of crucial games and anecdotes from those who knew and appreciated him.

Themes: baseball and baseball players; Brooklyn Dodgers (baseball team)

Related Titles: An earlier biography, *Koufax*, was written by Ed Gruver. *Hank Greenberg: The Story of My Life* is a biography of another Jewish baseball player. Readers may also enjoy *The Big Book of Jewish Baseball* by Peter S. Horvitz and Joachim Horvitz for biographical, statistical, and anecdotal information on many who played in the major and minor leagues.

Lacey, Robert
Little Man: Meyer Lansky and the Gangster Life. Little, Brown. 1991. 547p. YA

A legendary underworld figure, Lansky was involved in bootlegging and gambling with Lucky Luciano and "Bugsy" Siegel in the 1920s and 1930s.

Themes: gambling; gangsters; Mafia

Related Titles: For another biography of a well-known Jewish gangster, try *The Big Bankroll: The Life and Times of Arnold Rothman* by Leo Katcher. Overviews of Jewish organized crime can be found in *Tough Jews: Fathers, Sons, and Gangster Dreams* by Rich Cohen, annotated in the "Collected Biography" section of this chapter, and *But He Was Good to His Mother* by Robert Rockaway. Readers may also enjoy *Bronx Boy*, the third volume of Jerome Charyn's autobiography, in which he writes about how he became involved with gangsters and prostitutes as a twelve-year-old. It is annotated in the "Childhood and Family" section of this chapter.

Louvish, Simon
Monkey Business; The Lives and Legends of the Marx Brothers: Groucho, Chico, Harpo, Zeppo with Added Gummo. St. Martin's, 2000. 471p.

The Marx brothers started their careers on the vaudeville circuit in 1908 to bolster the family income. Louvish's detailed biography follows them from the early years to their successes on Broadway, in the movies, and on television, and includes many excerpts from their well-known routines.

Themes: comedians; motion pictures

Related Titles: Groucho published several autobiographies. Readers may enjoy *Groucho and Me* or *Memoirs of a Mangy Lover*. Stefan Kanfer has written the biography *Groucho: The Life and Times of Julius Henry Marx*. Harpo, the silent brother, reveals his thoughts in *Harpo Speaks*. George Burns, another well-loved Jewish comedian, recounts his life in show business in *All My Best Friends*, coauthored by David Fisher. *The Haunted Smile: The Story of Jewish Comedians in America* by Lawrence J. Epstein provides biographies and context for some of the many popular Jewish comedians, from vaudeville to Seinfeld. It is annotated in the "Collected Biography" section of this chapter.

Meir, Golda

My Life. **Putnam, 1975. 480p.**

Meir is so closely associated with Israel that it is often forgotten that she spent her childhood and adolescence in the United States. From an early age, she fought her parents to obtain an education and live her life according to her own desires. After her marriage in 1917 she and her husband immigrated to Palestine, joining the early Zionist pioneers. Her very straightforward memoir traces the hardships they endured, her own growing role in politics culminating with her election as prime minister in 1969, and her inner conflicts in balancing her personal and political roles.

Themes: Israel—Politics and government; politicians; Zionism

Related Titles: Henrietta Szold is another well-known figure in the development of the Jewish community in Palestine. Joan Dash writes about her in *Summoned to Jerusalem: The Life of Henrietta Szold.*

Dworkin, Susan

Miss America, 1945: Bess Myerson and the Year That Changed Our Lives. **Newmarket Press, 1987. 229p.** YA

Myerson grew up in the Bronx during the Depression, one of three sisters in a close-knit family. Despite her parents' misgivings, she entered the Miss America contest in 1945 and became the first Jewish woman to claim the title. Myerson's experiences with anti-Semitism during and after the pageant, and the revelations of the extent of the Holocaust, led her to political activism on behalf of the Jewish community.

Themes: anti-Semitism; 1940s; 1930s; women—social conditions

Related Titles: Dworkin coauthored *The Nazi Officer's Wife: How One Jewish Woman Survived the Holocaust* with Edith Hahn-Beer, an unusual Holocaust survival story annotated in the "Memoirs" section of the Holocaust chapter.. Her novel *The Book of Candy* is annotated in the "Character" section of chapter 6. Readers who enjoyed the mix of biography and social history in this book may enjoy the novels *The Activist's Daughter* by Ellen Bache, annotated in the "Setting" section of chapter 6, or Jo Sinclair's *The Changelings*, annotated in the "Story" section of chapter 6.

Miller, Arthur

 *Timebends: A Life.* **Grove Press, 1987. 614p.**

Miller has penned some of the most enduring plays of the twentieth century: *Death of a Salesman*, *The Crucible*, and *All My Sons*. His own life has been full of drama. This graceful, insightful memoir reveals the sources of his plays, his relationship with Marilyn Monroe and other well-known figures in the performing arts, and the significant events of his early Jewish upbringing in Harlem. (An ALA Notable Book.)

Themes: literary life; Monroe, Marilyn

Related Titles: Miller has also published a collection of autobiographical and literary essays entitled *Echoes Down the Corridor*. Readers may also be interested in *An Unfinished Woman*, the autobiography of playwright Lillian Hellman, who came from a Southern Jewish family.

Morgenthau, Henry

 Mostly Morgenthaus: A Family History. **Ticknor & Fields, 1991. 501p.**

A thoughtful, reflective memoir about a remarkable family, starting with the humble beginnings of the author's great-grandfather, Lazarus, in mid-eighteenth-century Germany. In America, the Morgenthaus were members of that special world of the wealthiest New York German Jews, but their contributions in public life and government give this memoir its fascination. The author also writes movingly about his family's commitment to Jewish causes and his own return, as an adult, to a deeper Jewish commitment. (Winner of the National Jewish Book Award.)

Themes: businessmen; immigrants; U.S.—Politics and government

Piercy, Marge

Sleeping with Cats: A Memoir. **HarperCollins, 2002. 345p.** 📖

Piercy grew up in a working-class family in Detroit, in the 1930s and 1940s, with a Jewish mother and a non-Jewish father. Her turbulent childhood included membership in a gang and struggles with her volatile father. Smart in an era that devalued women's intelligence, politically and sexually active when women were expected to be neither, she was always at odds with traditional women's roles. The strength of this memoir lies in its evocation of Piercy's emotional life, with special note of her many beloved cats. (The author's Web site is archer-books.com/Piercy/.)

Themes: cats; literary life; women—social conditions

Related Titles: Piercy has often written novels and poetry with Jewish themes and characters. Her novel *He, She and It*, annotated in chapter 4, alternates chapters of the *golem* story with a science fiction novel in the cyberpunk genre. *Gone to Soldiers*, annotated in chapter 3, includes material on Jewish resistance fighters in World War II. A book of poems, *The Art of Blessing the Day*, uses Jewish thematic material. Piercy was a feminist before there was a movement to support her; readers who enjoy learning about how she struggled to free herself from the expectations of her parents and lovers may also enjoy the novel *Funny Accent* by Barbara Shulgasser-Parker, annotated in the "Character" section of chapter 6.

Bianco, Anthony

The Reichmanns: Family, Faith, Fortune, and the Empire of Olympia & York. **Times Business, 1997. 810p.**

The Reichmann brothers were at one time the world's most successful real estate developers, balancing their Orthodox Judaism with the demands of international business. Bianco traces the family back to humble origins in Hungary in the 1600s.

Themes: immigrants; Orthodox Jews; real estate developers

Related Titles: Other books about successful business families are *The Warburgs: The Twentieth-Century Odyssey of a Remarkable Jewish Family* by Ron Chernow (an ALA Notable Book), *The Making of a Jew* by Samuel Bronfman, and *The Guggenheims (1848–1988); an American Epic* by John H. Davis.

Radosh, Robert, and Joyce Milton

The Rosenberg File: A Search for the Truth. **2nd ed. Yale University Press, 1997. 616p.**

During the hysteria over Communism in the 1950s, Julius and Ethel Rosenberg were convicted of passing atomic secrets to the Soviet Union and sentenced to death. It was a case that divided the country then and continues to be debated. The second edition contains new information from the National Security Agency and Soviet sources. (An ALA Notable Book.)

Themes: Communists; Rosenberg, Julius and Ethel; spies; trials

Related Titles: Another perspective on the Rosenberg case can be found in *The Brother* by Sam Roberts, about Ethel Rosenberg's brother David Greenglass and his damaging testimony in the Rosenberg trial. In *We Are Your Sons: The Legacy of Ethel and Julius Rosenberg*, Robert and Michael Meeropol, the Rosenbergs' children, write about their lives after their parents' execution. In 2003, Robert Meeropol wrote an autobiography called *An Execution in the Family*, about how he came to terms with his family history and began a life of political activism. A novel loosely based on the Rosenberg case, written from the point of view of one of their imagined children, is E. L. Doctorow's *The Book of Daniel*, annotated in the "Classics and Major Authors" section of chapter 6. In an interesting sidelight, Abel Meeropol, the adopted father of the Rosenbergs' sons, wrote the lyrics to Billie Holiday's controversial signature song "Strange Fruit," about Southern lynchings. Readers who want to follow this thread may enjoy David Margolick's book *Strange Fruit: Billie Holiday, Café Society, and an Early Cry for Civil Rights.*

Roth, Philip

The Facts; A Novelist's Autobiography. **Farrar, Straus & Giroux. 1988. 195p.**

Episodes from five periods of Roth's life, including childhood in Newark, New Jersey; college years at Bucknell; and the angry reaction of the critics to his first novel. Nathan Zuckerman, one of his fictional creations, adds comments.

Themes: fathers and sons; 1950s; 1940s; 1930s

Related Titles: Another autobiography, *Patrimony: A True Story,* is about Roth's relationship with his aging father (an ALA Notable Book and winner of the National Book Critics Circle Award). Roth's novels and short stories are listed in the "Classics and Major Authors" section of chapter 6.

Schneiderman, Rose, and Lucy Goldman
All for One. Paul S. Eriksson, 1967. 265p.

Tiny, red-haired Rose was a force to be reckoned with in the women's labor movement. Beginning in 1895 when she was thirteen, she worked in the New York garment industry sweatshops and was active in the trade union movement. A charismatic speaker and tireless organizer for women's rights, she advised Franklin and Eleanor Roosevelt on labor issues.

Themes: labor unions; Lower East Side, N.Y.

Related Titles: Many girls and women who lived on the Lower East Side at the turn of the twentieth century worked in the garment industry sweatshops. Rose Cohen describes what that work was like in her autobiography *Out of the Shadow: A Russian Jewish Girlhood on the Lower East Side.* Anzia Yezierska's short stories in the collection *Hungry Hearts,* and her autobiographical novel *Red Ribbon on a White Horse,* give a vivid picture of the backbreaking work. Yezierska's novels are annotated in the "Classics and Major Authors" section of chapter 6. Other autobiographies by women active in social causes are Lillian Wald's *The House on Henry Street* and Gerda Lerner's *Fireweed.* A biography of a man involved in organizing the labor movement in the garment industry is *Joe Rapoport: The Life of a Jewish Radical* by Kenneth Kann. Readers may enjoy Julie Ellis's novels about strong, independent women. They are annotated in chapter 5.

Schorr, Daniel
Staying Tuned: A Life in Journalism. Pocket Books, 2001. 368p.

From the vantage point of his mid-eighties, Schorr looks back on a career in journalism that took him to the hottest spots. He grew up fluent in Yiddish, Hebrew, and English, was recruited by Edward R. Murrow to work at CBS, and began a distinguished career in radio, newspapers, and television that included interviewing Khrushchev and being threatened with imprisonment by the House Ethics Committee.

Themes: journalists; radio; U.S.—Politics and government

Greenfield, Howard
Ben Shahn: An Artist's Life. Random House, 1998. 366p.

From childhood, Ben Shahn had a strong sense of justice and fair play, attributes that led him to involvement in social causes. As an artist, he was famous for his portraits of Sacco and Vanzetti, his murals of the working class, and World War II propaganda posters. A complex man with extraordinary talent as a painter and photographer, his personal life was far from serene, involving stormy marriages, difficult personal relationships, and estrangement from his children.

Themes: artists; family relationships; social problems

Simon, Neil

Rewrites; A Memoir. Simon & Schuster, 1996. 397p. **YA**

The author of some our most beloved comedies (*The Odd Couple, Come Blow Your Horn*, and *Plaza Suite*) turns to his own life and the sources of his inspiration. With warmth and humor, Simon reveals more than the details of his journey to success; he provides insight into the craft of playwriting and the nurturing relationships with family and friends that helped him survive.

Themes: dramatists; literary life

Related Titles: Several of Simon's plays, notably *Brighton Beach Memoirs* and *Biloxi Blues*, are autobiographical. Readers who enjoy theater history may also enjoy *Act One* by the playwright Moss Hart (an ALA Notable book) or Wendy Wasserstein's collection of personal essays, *Shiksa Goddess*.

Stern, Isaac, and Chaim Potok

My First 79 Years. Alfred A. Knopf, 1999. 317p.

A chatty and anecdotal memoir from the violinist who saved Carnegie Hall. Stern grew up in San Francisco and began performing at an early age. By the mid-1940s he was touring the world and playing with the great orchestras. His credo: "Two things are necessary for a life in music: a clear idea of what you want to be, and the arrogance to pursue it."

Themes: musicians

Related Titles: A biography of another famous classical Jewish musician is *Horowitz: His Life and Music* by Harold C. Schonberg.

Timerman, Jacobo

Prisoner Without a Name, Cell Without a Number. 1981; reprint, University Wisconsin Press, 2002. 176p.

In the 1970s, Argentina went through a period of extreme social turmoil and terrorism; thousands of people were murdered and thousands more disappeared. Timerman was arrested for his advocacy of human rights and was tortured and interrogated for thirty months before being expelled from the country in 1979. He describes the harrowing experience, the anti-Semitism of his captors, and the climate of repression in Argentina. Translated from the Spanish by Toby Talbot. (An ALA Notable Book.)

Themes: anti-Semitism; Latin America; political prisoners

Related Titles: The University of Wisconsin reprint has a new introduction by Ilan Stavans and a foreword by Arthur Miller.

Weintraub, William

Getting Started: A Memoir of the 1950s: With Letters from Mordecai Richler, Mavis Gallant and Brian Moore. McClelland & Stewart, 2001. 286p.

> When Weintraub traveled to Europe as an aspiring writer in the 1950s, he was sustained and encouraged by the friendship of other Canadian expatriate writers, whose correspondence he includes. (Winner of the Canadian Jewish Book Award for biography.)
>
> **Themes:** Canadian authors; correspondence; France; Spain

Spiritual Autobiographies

This genre may have started with Paul Cowan's *An Orphan in History*, originally published in 1982 and annotated below. Some of the writers in this section were brought up in observant families but turned away, only to find later in life that a spiritual dimension was missing from their lives. Many looked for spiritual guidance at difficult times. The feminist movement inspired some women to look for ways that they could participate in the study and ritual traditionally restricted to men. There are also examples of "hidden Jews," families who concealed or repudiated Judaism. In *Turbulent Souls,* Stephen Dubner tries to understand why his parents converted to Catholicism, and in the process returns to their childhood faith.

Benedek, Emily

Through the Unknown, Remembered Gate. Schocken Books, 2001. 335p. **YA** 📖

> In the midst of studying the Navajo people, and while working as a television reporter, Benedek felt a spiritual hunger to reconnect with Judaism. Her search led her to Orthodox and Conservative rabbis, synagogues in Texas and New York, and a struggle to reconcile feminism with Orthodox tradition.
>
> **Themes:** return to Orthodox Judaism; women—religious life
>
> **Related Titles:** Readers may be interested in journalist Lis Harris's *Holy Days: The World of a Hasidic Family*. Harris reveals how the time she spent in the Hasidic community led her to examine her own religious commitment. Readers may enjoy Pearl Abraham's two novels *The Romance Reader* and *Giving up America*, annotated in the "Setting" section of chapter 6, for their insight into observant lifestyles.

Cowan, Paul

An Orphan in History: One Man's Triumphant Search for His Roots. 1982; reprint, Jewish Lights, 2002. 288p. **YA** 📖

> Cowan's upbringing as, in his words, "a Jewish WASP," left him feeling rootless. He embarked on a personal journey to discover the religious, intellectual, and cultural heritage lost in his assimilated childhood, and to find a way to live as an American and a Jew. In retrieving his lost family history and religion, his life was changed and enriched.
>
> **Themes:** assimilation; Jewish identity; men—religious life

Related Titles: Cowan's story is the classic that inspired others to record their spiritual journeys. Another account readers may enjoy is *The Year Mom Got Religion: One Woman's Midlife Journey into Judaism* by Lee Meyerhoff Hendler. Readers may also enjoy Joshua Henkin's novel *Swimming across the Hudson*, a coming-of-age novel about the role religion plays in one young man's search for identity. It is annotated in the "Character" section of chapter 6.

Douglas, Kirk

Climbing the Mountain: My Search for Meaning. Simon & Schuster, 1997. 269p. **YA**

A stroke and a brush with death in a helicopter accident led Douglas to reorder his priorities and reconnect with Judaism.

Themes: accidents; actors and acting; motion picture industry

Related Titles: Douglas's autobiography, *The Ragman's Son*, follows his life from childhood up to a point about ten years before the accident. It is annotated in the "Public Lives" section of this chapter. In *My Stroke of Luck* he writes about how he battled the depression that followed his stroke. For those who enjoy reading about the insights that come with age or adversity, *Tuesdays with Morrie* by Mitch Applebom may be of interest.

Dubner, Stephen J.

Turbulent Souls: A Catholic Son's Return to His Jewish Family. Morrow, 1998. 320p. **YA**

Dubner's parents, raised in observant Jewish families, found their separate ways to Catholicism, then found each other. Disowned by most of their relatives, they raised eight children and remained devout Catholics. Their youngest son, Steven, curious about the religion his parents rejected and the relatives he never knew, discovered his own spiritual path in Judaism. (The author's Web site is www.stephenjdubner.com.)

Themes: children of ex-Jews; conversion to Christianity; conversion to Judaism; Jewish identity

Related Titles: There have been several recent autobiographies and biographies about "hidden" Jews, including Susan Jacoby's *Half-Jew: A Daughter's Search for Her Family's Buried Past*, Michael Dobbs's *Madeline Albright: A Twentieth-Century Odyssey*, Mary Gordon's *The Shadow Man*, James McBride's *The Color of Water*, and Yvette Melanson's *Looking for Lost Bird: A Jewish Woman's Discovery of Her Navajo Roots*.

8

Ehrlich, Elizabeth

Miriam's Kitchen: A Memoir. Viking, 1997. 370p. **YA**

Her mother-in-law's loving attention to Jewish observance and preparation of traditional foods helped Ehrlich understand the value of ritual and

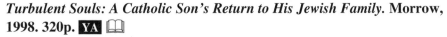
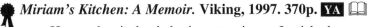

tradition. She includes many of Miriam's recipes. (Winner of the National Jewish Book Award.)

Themes: cookery; Holocaust—survivors; recipes; women—religious life

Related Titles: Other autobiographies in which traditional Jewish foods play an important role are *Walking on Walnuts* by Nancy Ring, *The Soup Has Many Eyes: From Shtetl to Chicago: A Memoir of One Family's Journey* by Joann Rose Leonard, and *Stuffed* by Patricia Volk. A collection of autobiographical stories in which a woman grows and changes as she comes to terms with her Jewishness is Faye Moskowitz's *Peace in the House: Tales from a Yiddish Kitchen*.

Fink, Nan

Stranger in the Midst: A Memoir of Spiritual Discovery. BasicBooks, 1997. 250p. 📖

In her search for a spiritual home, Fink converted to Judaism, but found acceptance within the Jewish community difficult, and ended up creating her own path.

Themes: conversion to Judaism; *Tikkun Magazine;* women—religious life

Goldman, Ari L.

The Search for God at Harvard. Random House, 1991. 283p.

Goldman, a *New York Times* reporter and an Orthodox Jew, spent a year as a Harvard Divinity School student, observing his fellow students and learning more about his own faith in the process. (The author's Web site is www.arigoldman.com.)

Themes: Christianity; Harvard Divinity School; men—religious life; Orthodox Judaism

Related Titles: Goldman went to Harvard with an unshakable faith in his own Orthodox Judaism, but others found a need to test their faith. In *God at the Edge: Searching for the Divine in Uncomfortable and Unexpected Places*, Niles Elliot Goldstein visited Jewish communities in Alaska and Central Asia, among others, before understanding his own Jewish path. Roger Kamenetz, in *The Jew in the Lotus: A Poet's Rediscovery of Jewish Identity in Buddhist India,* writes of his experience of traveling with a group of Jewish rabbis and scholars to meet with the Dalai Lama.

Hammer, Joshua

Chosen By God: A Brother's Journey. Hyperion, 1999. 241p. 📖

Two brothers, Joshua and Tony Hammer, growing up in the same assimilated Jewish household in New York, chose very different paths. Joshua, a journalist, traveled overseas covering major news stories; Tony, now Tuvia, joined an Orthodox community. After decades of estrangement, Joshua contacted Tuvia to try to understand the life choices they made.

Themes: brothers; Hasidism; men—religious life

Related Titles: Another autobiography that focuses on the relationship between brothers is *The End of the Twins: A Memoir of Losing a Brother* by Saul Diskin. Returning to a more Orthodox form of Judaism is the central theme in Roy Neuberger's *From Central Park to Sinai: How I Found My Jewish Soul*. Another account of brothers separated in the Holocaust who chose very different paths is *In My Brother's Image* by Eugene L. Pogany, annotated in the "Memoirs" section of chapter 7.

Hays, David

Today I Am a Boy. **Simon & Schuster, 2000. 255p.**

At the age of sixty-six, David Hays decided to study for the bar mitzvah he never had as a thirteen-year-old. He describes his preparation, in the company of twelve- and thirteen-year-olds, to become a bar mitzvah, and the development alongside it of a rich spiritual life.

Themes: bar mitzvah and bat mitzvah; faith; Jewish identity; men—religious life

Related Titles: *The Year Mom Got Religion: One Woman's Midlife Journey into Judaism* by Lee Meyerhoff Hendler tells a similar story from a woman's point of view.

Katch, Elise Edelson

The Get: A Spiritual Memoir of Divorce. **Simcha Press, 2001. 284p.**

Katch records her spiritual journey through the dissolution of her marriage, leading to the traditional ceremony for obtaining a Jewish divorce, or *get*.

Themes: divorce; Orthodox Judaism; women—religious life

Related Titles: Another woman's encounter with male-centered Jewish ritual can be found in *Mornings and Mourning: A Kaddish Journal* by E. M. Broner. Readers may also enjoy Broner's novel about women in Israel facing down stereotypes, *A Weave of Women*.

Klinghoffer, David

The Lord Will Gather Me in: My Journey to Jewish Orthodoxy. **The Free Press, 1999. 262p.**

Klinghoffer is a *baal teshuvah*, one who returns to the practice of Judaism. He describes the path he followed, from an assimilated upbringing in Southern California to his current life as an Orthodox Jew, and how that transformation intersected with his search for the birth mother who gave him up for adoption.

Themes: adopted children; Reform Judaism; return to Orthodox Judaism

Related Titles: In *From Central Park to Sinai: How I Found My Jewish Soul* Roy Neuberger writes about how he found his way to Orthodox Judaism after exploring Hinduism, Buddhism, Protestantism, and Catholicism. In *Kaddish* by Leon Weseltier, we see how the traditional recitation of the prayer for the dead helped Weseltier through a year of mourning for his father. (Winner of the National Jewish Book Award.) Another autobiography in which adoption plays a pivotal role is Michael Blumenthal's *All My Mothers and Fathers.* A memoir about a Jew who was attracted to Buddhism is Rosie Rosenzweig's *A Jewish Mother in Shangri-La.*

Lester, Julius

 Lovesong: Becoming a Jew. **Holt, 1988. 248p.** **YA** 📖

A very personal memoir, beginning with the author's childhood in the pre-civil rights era South. Lester's father was a Methodist minister; religion was a constant in his life from an early age. He writes of his long search for a spiritual home, how he explored and rejected several faiths along the way, and how his public comments have often involved him in controversy in the Jewish and African American communities. (An ALA Notable Book.)

Themes: African Americans; conversion to Judaism

Related Titles: Readers may also be interested in Rebecca Walker's *Black, White and Jewish: Autobiography of a Shifting Self*, a poignant account of the multiple problems of growing up the daughter of an African American mother and a white Jewish father. Readers may also enjoy *How I Became Hettie Jones* by Hettie Jones, about her unconventional life and relationship with the African American poet LeRoi Jones.

Morinis, Alan

Climbing Jacob's Ladder: One Man's Journey to Rediscover a Jewish Spiritual Tradition. **Broadway Books, 2002. 256p.** 📖

Morinis was always a spiritual seeker; he studied Eastern religions as a young man in India but became involved in the film industry and ignored the spiritual side of his life while chasing material success. When he fell into a depression following a business failure, he discovered Musar, a little-known Jewish movement that emphasizes the practice of ethics and morality.

Themes: men—religious life; Orthodox Judaism; rabbis

Ochs, Vanessa L.

Words on Fire: One Woman's Journey Into the Sacred. **Rev. ed. Westview Press, 1999. 358p.** 📖

While living in a small college town in rural New York, one of only a handful of Jewish families, Ochs felt drawn to study Torah. During a sabbatical year in Jerusalem, she found schools where women could study Torah, and where many of the teachers were learned and inspiring women.

Themes: Americans in Israel; Orthodox Judaism; women—religious life

Related Titles: Readers may be interested in Judith Rotem's book that describes the life of ultra-Orthodox women in Israel, *Distant Sisters: The Women I Left Behind.*

Orsborn, Carol Matzkin

Return from Exile: One Woman's Journey Back to Judaism. **Continuum, 1998. 215p.** **YA**

Orsborn turned away from the Reform Judaism of her youth and found an active spiritual life studying and practicing a mix of religions in the liberal atmosphere of California. Moving to Nashville gave her the opportunity to continue her spiritual quest as a student in the Divinity School at Vanderbilt University. She writes about how the students and professors challenged her to redefine her long dormant relationship to Judaism in ways she never imagined.

Themes: Jewish–Christian relations; spiritual life; women—religious life

Related Titles: Another memoir by a religious seeker is Lauren Winner's *Girl Meets God: On the Path to a Spiritual Life*, in which she writes about her conversion to Orthodox Judaism as a teenager followed by her growing interest in, and conversion to, Christianity.

Rosen, Jonathan

The Talmud and the Internet. **Farrar, Straus & Giroux. 2000. 144p.**

In mourning the death of his grandmother, Rosen considers the death of another grandmother during the Holocaust, and the connections between ancient and modern traditions, embodied in the Talmud and modern technology.

Themes: grandmothers; Internet; men—religious life; Talmud

Related Titles: Rosen also wrote the novel *Eve's Apple*, annotated in the "Character" section of chapter 6.

Sources of Further Information

The titles below are a small selection of books on the history of the American Jewish community that focus on lives rather than events. The "Collected Biography" portion of this chapter also contains some excellent titles and should be checked for further reading. Readers wishing to pursue the subject beyond this chapter should look at the bibliography on The American Jewish Historical Society's Web site, www.ajhs.org/reference/essential_readings.cfm.

American Jewish Historical Society. *American Jewish Desk Reference: The Ultimate One-volume Reference to the Jewish Experience in America.* New York: Random House, 1999.
An extensive compilation about every aspect of the Jewish community in America, both past and present, including timelines, biographies, and essays, divided into chapters by subject.

Antler, Joyce. *The Journey Home: Jewish Women and the American Century.* New York: The Free Press, 1997.
A history of women's contributions to the Jewish community through profiles of fifty women from a variety of backgrounds.

Cowan, Neil M., and Ruth Schwartz Cowan. *Our Parents' Lives: The Americanization of Eastern European Jews.* New York: Basic Books, 1989.

Frommer, Myrna Katz, and Harvey Frommer. *Growing Up Jewish in America: An Oral History.* New York: Harcourt, Brace, 1995.

Howe, Irving, with the assistance of Kenneth Libo. *World of Our Fathers: The Journey of the East European Jews to America and the Life They Found and Made.* New York: Harcourt Brace Jovanovich, 1976.
An extensive and illuminating account of the wave of immigration that brought two million Eastern European Jews to the United States, how it transformed the immigrants, and how the immigrants transformed the United States. Full of information about people, social and political issues, culture, mores, and *Yiddishkeit.*

Hyman, Paula E., and Deborah Dash Moore, eds. *Jewish Women in America: An Historical Encyclopedia.* 2 vols. New York: Routledge Press for the American Jewish Historical Society, 1997.
Contains biographical essays on 800 women in all fields of endeavor, from the 1600s to the present, and 110 topical essays.

Meltzer, Milton, ed. *The Jewish Americans: A History in Their Own Words, 1650-1950.* New York: Crowell, 1982.
In a varied collection of excerpts, primarily from diaries, autobiographies, speeches, and novels, we hear the voices of the Jewish men and women who struggled with issues of survival, freedom, and equality as immigrants to America. Excerpts include Haym Solomon's letter to a poor relative refusing to send more money, Morris Schloss's description of the ups and down of a businessman's life in the California Gold Rush years, a letter from Lillian Wald describing conditions on the Lower East Side, and other vivid evocations of social and economic conditions.

Sharp, Rosalie, Irving Abella, and Edwin Goodman, eds. *Growing Up Jewish: Canadians Tell Their Own Stories.* Toronto: McClelland & Stewart, 1997.

Weinberg, Sydney Stahl. *The World of Our Mothers: The Lives of Jewish Immigrant Women.* Chapel Hill: University of North Carolina Press, 1988.
Weinberg weaves together the oral histories of ordinary Jewish women who were too busy living their lives to write autobiographies. These women all came to America before 1925.

Notes

1. Sophie Trupin, *Dakota Diaspora* (Lincoln: University of Nebraska Press, 1988.), 1

2. Leonard Garment, *Crazy Rhythm: My Journey from Brooklyn, Jazz, and Wall Street to Nixon's White House, Watergate, and Beyond* (New York: Times Books, 1997), 19.

3. Calvin Trillin, *Messages from My Father* (New York: Farrar, Straus & Giroux, 1996), 25.

4. Garment, *Crazy Rhythm,* 19.

Chapter 9

Readers' Advisory Resources

One of the great joys of reading is following a trail of recommendations to other related books and writers, followed closely by sharing and discussing favorite books with others. Readers do this informally; librarians have developed resources for assistance. For those who are interested in understanding the philosophy and techniques of readers' advisory service, the titles in the first section below are the best place to start. The genre resources that follow are of a general nature. For information on specifically Jewish resources, check the last section of each genre chapter.

More and more, readers are getting together to talk about the books they read. Book discussion groups are organized by friends, libraries, or organizations and often bring together people of diverse ages and backgrounds. Some discussion groups have a theme, for example, classics, nonfiction, or women's fiction, while other groups just look for that elusive next good book. Publishers have responded to the growth of discussion groups by making discussion guides available on their Web sites and even binding discussion guides into the trade paperback editions of popular novels. Resources for organizing and leading book discussion groups are included at the end of this chapter, along with sources for discussion guides.

Selected Sources for Learning About Judaism

Readers' advisors and readers who wish to learn more about modern-day Judaism will find the sources below a good place to start. They explain the distinguishing characteristics of the various branches of Judaism in the United States and describe Jewish beliefs, holidays, and customs, as well as the basic religious texts. (The Web addresses are for the official sites of the four major religious movements.) Follow the links in the Web sites; look into the bibliographies in the printed texts. Judaism is rich in commentary and discussion; many more sources await the curious learner.

Einstein, Stephen J., and Lydia Kukoff. *Every Person's Guide to Judaism*. New York: UAHC Press, 1989.

Goldman, Ari L. *Being Jewish: The Spiritual and Cultural Practice of Being Jewish Today*. New York: Simon & Schuster, 2000.

Hertzberg, Arthur, and Aron Hirt-Manheimer. *Jews: The Essence and Character of a People*. San Francisco: HarperCollins, 1998.

Holtz, Barry W., ed. *Back to the Sources: Reading the Classic Jewish Texts*. New York: Simon & Schuster, 1986.

Jewish Reconstructionist Federation (Reconstructionist Judaism): www.jrf.org

Kertzer, Morris N. *What Is a Jew?* Revised by Lawrence A. Hoffman. New York: Collier Books, 1993.

Kolatch, Alfred J. *The Jewish Book of Why*. Rev. ed. New York: Penguin, 2003.

Kushner, Harold. *To Life! A Celebration of Jewish Being and Thinking*. Boston: Little, Brown, 1993.

Orthodox Union (Orthodox Judaism): www.ou.org

Robinson, George. *Essential Judaism: A Complete Guide to Beliefs, Customs, and Rituals*. New York: Pocket Books, 2000.

Rosenthal, Gilbert S. *The Many Faces of Judaism: Orthodox, Conservative, Reconstructionist & Reform*. New York: Behrman House, 1978.

Shenker, Lois Sussman. *Welcome to the Family! Opening Doors to the Jewish Experience*. Ashland, OR: White Cloud Press, 2001.

Telushkin, Joseph. *Jewish Literacy: The Most Important Things to Know About the Jewish Religion, Its People and Its History*. New York: Morrow, 1991.

Union of Reform Judaism: www.urj.org

United Synagogue of Conservative Judaism (Conservative Judaism): www.uscj.org

The following novels and autobiographies offer another approach to learning about Judaism: combining information with a good story. (Page numbers refer to the location of annotations in this book.)

Abraham, Pearl. *The Romance Reader*, p. 177.

Chefitz, Mitchell. *The Thirty-Third Hour of Moshe Katan*, p. 159.

Ehrlich, Elizabeth. *Miriam's Kitchen*, pp. 255–56.

Goodman, Allegra. *Kaaterskill Falls*, p. 141.

Kemelman, Harry. *The Rabbi David Small Mysteries*, pp. 23–24.

Klinghoffer, David. *The Lord Will Gather Me In: My Journey to Jewish Orthodoxy*, pp. 257–58.

Krich, Rochelle. *The Molly Blume Mysteries*, p. 25.

Miller, Risa. *Welcome to Heavenly Heights*, p. 178.

Mirvis, Tova. *The Ladies' Auxiliary*, p. 164.

Ochs, Vanessa. *Words on Fire: One Woman's Journey into the Sacred*, p. 258.

Potok, Chaim. *The Chosen*, p. 123.

Rosen, Jonathan. *The Talmud the Internet*, p. 259.

Singer, Isaac Bashevis. *In My Father's Court*, pp. 237–38.

General Sources on Readers' Advisory Service

Print Resources

Herald, Diana Tixier. *Genreflecting: A Guide to Reading Interests in Genre Fiction.* 5th ed. Englewood, CO: Libraries Unlimited, 2000.
This is the latest edition of the popular readers' advisory guide that discusses multiple genres, providing definitions of subgenres and lists of popular authors and titles.

Herald, Diana Tixier. *Teen Genreflecting*. Englewood, CO: Libraries Unlimited, 2003.
A guide to over 1,500 popular genre fiction titles for middle and high school readers.

McCook, Kathleen de la Pena, and Gary O. Rolstad, eds. *Developing Readers' Advisory Services: Concepts and Commitments.* New York: Neal-Schuman, 1993.
A compilation of articles on the history, theory, and practice of readers' advisory work. In addition to the expected articles on genre fiction, there are articles on readers' advisory work for children, young adults, the disabled, and different ethnic groups.

Ross, Catherine Sheldrick, and Mary K. Chelton. "Reader's Advisory: Matching Mood and Material." *Library Journal* 126 (2001): 52–55.

Saricks, Joyce. *The Readers' Advisory Guide to Genre Fiction.* Chicago: American Library Association, 2001.
Individual genres are discussed in separate chapters: the appeal characteristics of each genre, its subgenres, and popular authors in each genre.

Saricks, Joyce G., and Nancy Brown. *Readers' Advisory Service in the Public Library.* 2nd ed. Chicago: American Library Association, 1997.
A clear and insightful description of the readers' advisory process. It includes techniques for thinking about genres, analyzing genres, interacting with library patrons, and promoting readers' advisory services.

Shearer, Kenneth D., ed. *Guiding the Reader to the Next Book.* New York: Neal-Schuman, 1996.
The articles in this collection cover some specifics of providing readers' advisory services in public libraries. Especially interesting is the article

by Sharon Baker, "A Decade's Worth of Research on Browsing Fiction Collections," which covers practices that promote fiction use.

Shearer, Kenneth D., and Robert Burgin, eds. *The Readers' Advisor's Companion.* Englewood, CO: Libraries Unlimited, 2001.
Essays on various aspects of readers' advisory work: the state of readers' advisory education, current practices in readers' advisory work, and how current services can be expanded.

Online Resources

This list includes several public libraries whose Web sites have resources for readers' advisory service.

AllReaders.com: www.allreaders.com
A search engine—the "Gordonator"—allows readers to search for books by plot, character, adversary, setting, and style.

Genreflecting.com: www.genreflecting.com
The home page of the <u>Genreflecting Readers' Advisory Series</u>. It features definitions of genres and suggests titles.

Genrefluent.com www.genrefluent.com
The personal Web site of Diana Tixier Herald, author of *Genreflecting: A Guide to Reading Interests in Genre Fiction.* The site contains hundreds of brief reviews of genre fiction and links to additional resources.

"If you like" database at Hennepin County Library: www.hclib.org/pub/books/iyl
Allows readers to search by keyword for subjects or genres.

Morton Grove Public Library Webrary Reader Services: www.webrary.org/rs/rsmenu.html
Has genre resources for readers on the Web and available through the library.

NoveList: Your Guide to Fiction
A commercial database marketed by EBSCO and available through libraries. It contains over 100,000 titles searchable by author, title, genre, or subject. A "read-alikes" feature allows users to search for novels by entering plot descriptors. Book discussion guides; sample book talks; and feature articles on genres, topics, and authors provide additional resources.

Mysteries and Thrillers

Print Resources

Bleiler, Richard J. *Reference and Research Guide to Mystery and Detective Fiction.* 2nd ed. Englewood, CO: Libraries Unlimited, 2004.
Part of the series *Reference Sources in the Humanities,* this is a good source for information on the world of the mystery in print and on the Internet. It includes

lists of mysteries by genre, mystery magazines, awards, bibliographies, and critical works. All entries are annotated.

Charles, John, and others. *The Mystery Readers' Advisory: The Librarian's Clues to Murder and Mayhem.* Chicago: American Library Association, 2002.
An overall approach to readers' advisory work with mystery fans. This volume defines the mystery and its subgenres, provides information on the readers' advisory interview, collection development, marketing of mysteries in the library, and lists of mysteries by subgenre and theme.

Gannon, Michael. B. *Blood, Bedlam, Bullets, and Bad Guys: A Reader's Guide to Adventure/Suspense Fiction.* Englewood, CO: Libraries Unlimited, 2004.

Gorman, Ed, and others. *The Fine Art of Murder: The Mystery Reader's Indispensable Companion.* New York: Carroll & Graf, 1993.
A collection of essays on every aspect of the literature by practitioners and critics of the genre.

Herbert, Rosemary, ed. *The Oxford Companion to Crime and Mystery Writing.* New York: Oxford University Press, 1999.

Niebuhr, Gary Warren. *Make Mine a Mystery: A Reader's Guide to Mystery and Detective Fiction.* Englewood, CO: Libraries Unlimited. 2003.
This title in the *Genreflecting* series contains annotations of over 2,000 mysteries as well as information about mystery genres, readers' advisory work, and collection development.

Smith, Myron J., and Terry White. *Cloak and Dagger Fiction: An Annotated Guide to Spy Thrillers*, 3rd ed. New York: Greenwood Press, 1995.
Lists more than 5,000 spy thrillers written between 1940 and 1995.

Stilwell, Steven A. *What Mystery Do I Read Next? A Reader's Guide to Recent Mystery Fiction.* Chicago: Gale Press, 1997.

Swanson, Jean, and Dean James. *Killer Books: A Reader's Guide to Exploring the Popular World of Mystery and Suspense.* New York: Berkeley Prime Crime, 1998.
Discusses the primary genres of mystery and suspense and describes the work of the major authors in those genres.

Winks, Robin, ed. *Mystery and Suspense Writers: The Literature of Crime, Detection, and Espionage.* 2 vols. New York: Scribner, 1998.
Essays on individual writers and genres.

Online Resources

Searching the Internet on almost any author's name will yield either the author's own Web site or Web sites sponsored by publishers and fans. The addresses below are a selected list of general sites for mystery fans.

Cluelass: www.cluelass.com
> Consists of the Bloodstained Bookshelf (listings of new mysteries), Deadly Directory Online (a database of information about authors and mystery publishing), and the Mysterious Home Page (a collection of links to online mystery sources).

Mystery Guide: www.mysteryguide.com

The Mystery Reader: www.themysteryreader.com
> Lists and rates mysteries and provides reviews, interviews with authors, and articles about the genre.

Palm Beach County Library: www.pbclibrary.com/read-mysteries.htm
> The mystery section of Palm Beach County Library's Web site is a good pointer to online resources for information about the genre, organizations, reviews, and general mystery sites.

The Poisoned Pen: www.poisonedpen.com
> The site of one of the largest mystery bookstores in the United States, stocking over 15,000 titles and a good source for lists of books by subgenre.

Stop You're Killing Me: www.Stopyourekillingme.com
> Lists more than 15,000 mysteries, indexed by author and series character, with brief information on titles.

Historical Fiction

Print Resources

The subject indexes in the general sources below can help readers find additional historical fiction with Jewish themes and settings.

Adamson, Lynda G. *American Historical Fiction: An Annotated Guide to Novels for Adults and Young Adults.* Westport, CT: Oryx Press, 1999.
> Includes annotations of over 3,000 titles, with indexes by author, title, genre, subject, and geographic setting.

Adamson, Lynda G. *World Historical Fiction: An Annotated Guide to Novels for Adults and Young Adults.* Westport, CT: Oryx Press, 1998.
> Includes annotations for more than 6,000 titles and multiple indexes that include geographic setting and time period.

Burt, Daniel. S. *What Historical Novel Do I Read Next?* Detroit: Gale Research, 1997.

Simone, Roberta. *The Immigrant Experience in American Fiction: An Annotated Bibliography.* Lanham, MD: Scarecrow Press, 1995.
> An annotated listing of fiction dealing with the immigrant experience among all ethnic groups. The section on Jewish immigrant fiction covers some lesser-known titles.

Online Resources

Historical Novel Society: www.historicalnovelsociety.com

Soon's Historical Fiction Site: uts.cc.utexas.edu/~soon/histfiction

Science Fiction and Fantasy

Print Resources

Barron, Neil, ed. *Anatomy of Wonder 4: A Critical Guide to Science Fiction.* New York: R. R. Bowker, 1995.
  A comprehensive guide with annotations grouped by period or type, with introductory signed essays. It includes chapters on history and criticism, film and television, magazines, library collections, and core collections.

Barron, Neil. *What Fantastic Fiction Do I Read Next?: A Reader's Guide to Recent Fantasy, Horror and Science Fiction.* Detroit: Gale Press, 1998.
  Provides information on titles published from 1989 to 1997.

Buker, Derek M. *The Science Fiction and Fantasy Readers' Advisory: The Librarians' Guide to Cyborgs, Aliens, and Sorcerers.* Chicago: American Library Association, 2002.
  Provides readers' advisory information and annotations and listings of titles by subgenre of science fiction and fantasy.

Clute, John, and John Grant, eds. *The Encyclopedia of Fantasy.* New York: St. Martin's, 1997.

Clute, John, and Peter Nicholls, eds. *The Encyclopedia of Science Fiction.* New York: St. Martin's, 1993.

Herald, Diana. *Fluent in Fantasy: A Guide to Reading Interests.* Englewood, CO: Libraries Unlimited, 1999.

Herald, Diana Tixier, and Bonnie Kunzel. *Strictly Science Fiction: A Guide to Reading Interests.* Englewood, CO: Libraries Unlimited, 2002.
  Annotations and lists of titles by multiple subgenres, with lists of award winners and titles suitable for children and young adults.

Magill's Guide to Science Fiction and Fantasy Literature. 4 vols. Pasadena, CA: Salem Press, 1996.

Pederson, Jay, ed. *St. James Guide to Science Fiction Writers.* Detroit: St. James, 1996.

Winston, Kimberly. "Other Worlds, Suffused With Religion: A Hybrid with a Long History Seems to Be Gaining in Popularity." *Publishers Weekly* (April 16, 2001): 35–39.

Online Resources

Science Fiction Resource Guide: sflovers.rutgers.edu/SFRG

The SF Site, sfsite.com, provides reviews and information about authors and conventions.

Stories of Love and Romance

Print Resources

Bouricius, Ann. *The Romance Reader's Advisory: The Librarians' Guide to Love in the Stacks*. Chicago: American Library Association, 2000.

Krentz, Jayne Ann, ed. *Dangerous Men and Adventurous Women: Romance Writers on the Appeal of the Romance*. Philadelphia: University of Pennsylvania Press, 1992.
Essays by writers about the genre.

Ramsdell, Kristin. *Romance Fiction: A Guide to the Genre*. Englewood, CO: Libraries Unlimited, 1999.
An extensive guide to the genre, with annotations and lists of authors, and guides to the literature.

Online Resources

Affaire de Coeur: www.affairedecoeur.com

Romance Writers of America: www.rwanational.org
A popular association for romance writers, RWA bestows the RITA award to the best in romantic fiction in multiple categories. Their Web site defines the genre and lists member authors.

Literary Fiction

Print Resources

Hooper, Brad. *The Short Story Readers' Advisory: A Guide to the Genre*. Chicago: American Library Association, 2000.

Lesher, Linda Parent. *The Best Novels of the Nineties: A Readers' Guide*. Jefferson, NC: McFarland, 2000.

Miller, Laura, ed. *The Salon.com Reader's Guide to Contemporary Authors*. New York: Penguin USA, 2000.
A collection of short essays on literary authors.

Pearl, Nancy. *Now Read This: A Guide to Mainstream Fiction*. Englewood, CO: Libraries Unlimited, 1999.

Pearl, Nancy. *Now Read This II: A Guide to Mainstream Fiction, 1990–2001.* Englewood, CO: Libraries Unlimited, 2002.
Although these two titles are primarily annotated listings of recent fiction rather than manuals for readers' advisory work, the idea of "appeal characteristics" on which they are based is simply explained and wonderfully helpful to the librarian and the general reader in thinking about and recommending books.

Biography and Autobiography

Conway, Jill Ker. *When Memory Speaks: Reflections on Autobiography.* New York: Alfred A. Knopf, 1988.

Heilbrun, Carolyn G. *Writing a Woman's Life.* New York: Ballantine Books, 1988.

Miller, Nancy K. *But Enough About Me: Why We Read Other People's Lives.* New York: Columbia University Press, 2002.

Smith, Sidonie, and Julia Watson. *Reading Autobiography: A Guide for Interpreting Life Narratives.* Minneapolis: University of Minnesota Press, 2001.

Reading Group Resources

Sharing and discussing favorite authors and books with an empathetic and sociable group of readers is a memorable experience. In the last decade book clubs have flowered in libraries, in synagogues, and even on the Internet. The titles below provide guidance on how to organize a book discussion group or club, choose books, lead discussions, and find discussion guides.

Print Resources

Dodson, Shireen, and Teresa Barker. *The Mother-Daughter Book Club: How Ten Busy Mothers and Daughters Came Together to Talk, Laugh and Learn Through Their Love of Reading.* New York: HarperPerennial, 1997.

Jacobson, Rachel W. *The Reading Group Handbook: Everything You Need to Know From Choosing Members to Leading Discussions.* Rev. ed. New York: Hyperion, 1998.

Laskin, David, and Holly Hughes. *The Reading Group Book: The Complete Guide to Starting and Sustaining a Reading Group, With Annotated Lists of 250 Titles for Provocative Discussion.* New York: Plume, 1995.

Moore, Ellen, and Kira Stevens. *Good Books Lately: The One-Stop Resource for Book Groups and Other Greedy Readers*. New York: St. Martin's Griffin, 2004.

Pearlman, Mickey. *What to Read: The Essential Guide for Reading Group Members and Other Book Lovers*. Rev. and updated. New York: HarperPerennial, 1999.

Slezak, Ellen. *The Book Group Book: A Thoughtful Guide to Forming and Enjoying a Stimulating Book Discussion Group*. 3rd ed. Chicago: Chicago Review Press, 2000.

Online Resources

For additional discussion guides, check publishers' Web sites. Internet searches by title or author will yield leads to discussion guides and author information.

Amazon.com: www.amazon.com
> The vast online bookstore prints reading group guides on its Web site for many titles.

Book Spot: www.bookspot.com
> Provides discussion guides, information for book group leaders, and information about the book business.

BookBrowse.com: www.bookbrowse.com
> Offers reviews, excerpts, author information, and discussion guides.

Reading Group Choices: www.readinggroupchoices.com
> Provides information on starting and running a discussion group, as well as discussion guides.

ReadingGroupGuides.com: www.readinggroupguides.com
> Highlights books appropriate for discussion groups with reviews, interviews with authors, and discussion guides.

Author/Title Index

Numbers in boldface indicate the page where a title is annotated or the location of the main entry for an author.

Subject Index

Series titles (underscored) are indexed rather than individual titles in series, e.g., <u>The Mommy Track Mysteries</u> rather than the individual titles.

About the Author

ROSALIND REISNER has worked in public, academic, special, and school libraries for over 25 years. She is currently the Program Coordinator at Central Jersey Regional Library Cooperative in Freehold, New Jersey, and serves on the Editorial Board of Judaica Librarianship, published by the Association of Jewish Libraries. She writes and speaks about synagogue library management, collection development, and readers' advisory services.